Foundation HTML5
with CSS3

Craig Cook

Jason Garber

friendsof

DESIGNER TO DESIGNER™

an Apress® company

Foundation HTML5 with CSS3

ISBN-13 (pbk): 978-1-4302-3876-8

ISBN-13 (electronic): 978-1-4302-3877-5

Distributed to the book trade worldwide by Springer Science+Business Media New York, 233 Spring Street, 6th Floor, New York, NY 10013. Phone 1-800-SPRINGER, fax (201) 348-4505, e-mail orders-ny@springer-sbm.com, or visit www.springeronline.com.

For information on translations, please e-mail rights@apress.com or visit www.apress.com.

Apress and friends of ED books may be purchased in bulk for academic, corporate, or promotional use. eBook versions and licenses are also available for most titles. For more information, reference our Special Bulk Sales—eBook Licensing web page at www.apress.com/bulk-sales.

Any source code or other supplementary materials referenced by the author in this text is available to readers at www.apress.com. For detailed information about how to locate your book's source code, go to www.apress.com/source-code.

Credits

President and Publisher: Paul Manning	**Coordinating Editor:** Jennifer Blackwell
Lead Editor: Ben Renow-Clarke	**Copy Editor:** Lori Cavanaugh
Technical Reviewer: Karen Tegtmeyer	**Compositor:** Bytheway Publishing Services
Editorial Board: Steve Anglin, Ewan Buckingham, Gary Cornell, Louise Corrigan, Morgan Ertel, Jonathan Gennick, Jonathan Hassell, Robert Hutchinson, Michelle Lowman, James Markham, Matthew Moodie, Jeff Olson, Jeffrey Pepper, Douglas Pundick, Ben Renow-Clarke, Dominic Shakeshaft, Gwenan Spearing, Matt Wade, Tom Welsh	**Indexer:** SPi Global **Artist:** SPi Global **Cover Designer:** Anna Ishchenko

Contents at a Glance

Contents

Contents

Contents

About the Authors

Craig Cook has been designing and building websites since 1998, though he still silently harbors the aspiration to draw comic books. His background is in traditional graphic design, and although he spent years learning how to make ink stick to paper, he fell in love with the Web and the affair continues to this day. In addition to his passions for design and technology, Craig has an affinity for science-fiction novels, zombie movies, and black T-shirts. He occasionally muses on these subjects and others at his personal website, focalcurve.com. Craig lives and works near San Francisco.

Jason Garber is a web developer living and working near Washington, DC. He got his start building websites in 1996, long before turning a hobby into a career in 2003. Jason founded Refresh DC, a community of web designers, developers, and other new media professionals. He remains active in the community and continues to help organize monthly Refresh DC meetings. Jason also plays guitar in a DC post-rock band, The Orchid, and obsessively collects vinyl records. He sometimes writes on his personal site, sixtwothree.org.

About the Technical Reviewer

 **Karen Tegtmeyer** is an independent consultant and software developer with more than 10 years of experience. She has worked in a variety of roles, including design, development, training, and architecture. She also is an Adjunct Computer Science Instructor at Des Moines Area Community College. Her website is www.KarenTegtmeyer.com

Acknowledgments

I must first thank all of the authors, artists, designers, coders, bloggers, evangelists, and gurus on whose shoulders I stand. I've been inspired and guided by the work and teachings of Dan Cederholm, Tantek Çelik, Joe Clark, Chris Coyier, Derek Featherstone, Mark Norman Francis, Aaron Gustafson, Christian Heilmann, Molly Holzschlag, Jeremy Keith, Bruce Lawson, Ethan Marcotte, Scott McCloud, Eric Meyer, Chris Mills, Dave Shea, Greg Storey, Jeffrey Zeldman... and many others equally deserving of a name-drop but I'm trying to keep this short.

I should also extend gratitude to all the daily-grinders, cubicle-dwellers, and impassioned community members who strive to build a better Web—not for riches and adoration but simply because they love what they do and care about doing it right. You're making the Web a better place to live. Take a bow.

Many kind thanks to my co-author, Jason, for jumping in feet first. What with the glacial pace of my writing, your two chapters easily shaved months off the schedule. Thanks also to everyone at Apress/Friends of ED for your patience with my aforementioned glacial pace throughout this entire process. It's done now.

Thank you Bill, Jannyce, and Jolene for your continued friendship and support, and big thanks to Stephanie Hobson, Cindy Li, and Matt Harris for being my super heroes.

I'm endlessly grateful for my parents, R.L. and Beverly, who instilled me with a desire to learn, a passion to create, and a compulsion to instruct.

Craig Cook

First and foremost, thanks to Craig for asking me to pitch in on the book and for your willingness to help a novice writer. Your guidance and feedback were incredibly helpful. Thank you as well to everyone at Apress for answering my many, many questions about the whole book-writing process.

Special thanks to Cindy Li and Kevin Lawver for your support and mentorship through the years. You've both opened so many doors for me and I don't think I could ever fully repay either of you.

Since 2006, the Refresh DC community has been a constant source of inspiration and knowledge. I absolutely believe that Washington, DC has the best web design and development community out there. Thank you to everyone who has presented, helped organize, and attended one of our meetings. You keep me professionally energized year-round.

Mom, Dad, Kim, Bayleigh, Heather, Phillip, Logan, Grandma, and Granny: You're the best family I've ever had. I love you all and promise to call and write more!

And lastly, thank you to Lauren for your patience and love.

Jason Garber

Introduction

The World Wide Web has come a long way in a relatively short time. Since its debut in the early 1990s, the Web has quickly developed from an esoteric collection of academic papers into a full-fledged and pervasive medium, an equal to print, radio, and television. It's a vast repository of information on every subject imaginable, from astrophysics and ancient history to the care and feeding of hermit crabs. The Web has become an integral part of many people's daily lives and is the platform for many aspects of modern business and commerce. But at its heart, the Web is still just a way to share documents.

This book will show you how to create your own documents so you can share them on the Web. You'll become intimately familiar with the rules and constructs of HyperText Markup Language (HTML), the computer language on which the Web is built. It's a simple language, and the basic rules are easy to pick up and put to use. HTML is a tool, and once you know how to use it, you're limited only by your imagination.

Like any other language, HTML has changed and evolved over time. New features are added, existing features are redefined, and outdated features are removed. The latest iteration of HTML is HTML5—ostensibly the fifth version of the language—and it's quite an evolutionary leap indeed. HTML5 incorporates a wide range of new features and introduces new types of functionality far beyond the humble text document.

We won't be going quite that far in this book. Instead of diving into all the shiny new advancements in Web technology, this book offers the true foundation of HTML5, the supporting structure beneath all that innovation. You'll learn how to use HTML effectively and responsibly, to build web pages with clean, meaningful code, and to make them accessible to as many people and devices as possible. In the chapters that follow we'll show you the heart of HTML5 and set the stage for your next leap into the Web's frontier. This book is a starting point, and there's no limit to where you can go from here.

Along the way, we'll also introduce Cascading Style Sheets (CSS). CSS is a language that describes the presentation of web documents, declaring what colors and fonts to use, and the size, shape, and placement of elements on the page. It's very powerful and flexible, and is also really cool. But CSS is a fairly complex language in its own right, and we can't possibly cover every facet of it in a single book.

However, as you'll soon see, CSS relates directly to HTML, and you'll first need to understand HTML before you can put CSS to good use. This book will show you the basics of CSS and offer practical examples of how you can use it. We'll give you the solid grounding in HTML you'll need as a platform to delve deeper into the art and craft of designing web pages with CSS.

The CSS language also continues to evolve. CSS3 is the next generation of CSS, bringing with it exciting new features and effects, offering new ways to design web pages that weren't possible before. We'll introduce just a few of the new advancements in CSS3 and show you how to apply them to your content.

Who This Book Is For

This book is for anyone interested in learning how to build web pages from the ground up using modern best practices. We assume you're familiar with the Internet and the World Wide Web, and you probably wouldn't pick up a book with "HTML" in the title unless you'd at least heard of it. Beyond that, we don't assume any prior knowledge of web design or computer programming. As you advance through this book, the topics get a little more advanced as well. But fear not: this is a book for beginners, and we'll walk you through the tough parts.

Even if you're not a beginner, this book may still be well worth your time. Quite a bit has changed in HTML5, so if you're a more experienced web developer looking to get back to basics and see what all these new-fangled elements are about, this is the book for you. Although we've put the book together following a general narrative from beginning to end, it's also pretty handy as a reference book so you can turn to any section and find the information you need.

Technical books can be intimidating and hard to read, with a lot of prickly jargon to slog through. We've done our best to keep this book simple and easy to follow, and we define the technical terms as they appear. If you make it through this introduction and find yourself excited rather than bored, you should definitely keep reading.

How This Book Is Structured

The first two chapters lead you through the bare essentials you'll need to start making web pages. Throughout the bulk of this book, Chapters 3 through 8, you'll dig into different subject areas within HTML, becoming familiar with all of the different elements and attributes at your disposal. Along the way, you'll see examples of some of the many ways you can use CSS to style your content, and we've dedicated Chapter 9 to showing you just a few techniques to lay out pages with CSS. We finish up with Chapter 10, where you'll see a case study that takes much of what you've learned throughout the previous chapters and puts it together into a functional website, built from scratch with HTML and CSS.

Here's a brief road map of where this book is going to take you:

- Chapter 1, "Getting Started," takes a high-level view of how the Web works and what you'll need in order to create your own websites.

- Chapter 2, "HTML and CSS Basics," presents the fundamental rules to follow when you assemble web documents and style sheets, laying the groundwork for the rest of the book.

- Chapter 3, "The Document," explains the structure of an HTML document, establishing a framework that you can fill with content.

- Chapter 4, "Structuring Content," explores how you'll add content to your documents and support your text with a stable, meaningful structure.

- Chapter 5, "Embedding Media," describes how you can add pictures, audio, and video to your web pages for meaningful communication as well as decoration and entertainment.

- Chapter 6, "Linking the Web," looks at the all-important hyperlink, the very cornerstone of the Web. Hyperlinks are the vital connections between web pages.

- Chapter 7, "Constructing Tables," shows you how to structure complex data in tables, organizing related information in sets of connected rows and columns.

- Chapter 8, "Building Forms and Applications," will show you how to create forms that allow your visitors to input their own information and interact with your website.

- Chapter 9, "Page Layout with CSS," dives deeper into the craft of using CSS to arrange content on the page, covering a few of the simple techniques you'll use to design for the Web.

- Chapter 10, "Putting It All Together," puts the topics discussed throughout the book to practical use, taking you step-by-step through the process of building a website from top to bottom.

Conventions

Throughout this book we'll show you many examples of HTML and CSS coding. Most of these examples appear in numbered listings, separated from the regular text, like you see in Listing 1. In most cases we'll only show you a short snippet of code that you can assume resides alongside other code in a complete document or style sheet.

Listing 1. An example of a code listing

```
<!DOCTYPE html>
<html>
  <head>
    <meta charset="utf-8">
    <title>Document Title</title>
  </head>
  <body>
    <p>Hello, world!</p>
  </body>
</html>
```

Sometimes a line of code is too long to fit within the limited width of a printed page and we're forced to wrap it to a second line. When that happens, we'll use the symbol ↪ to let you know a line is wrapped only to fit the page layout; the real code would appear on a single line.

We'll occasionally add notes, tips, and cautions that relate to the section you've just read. They appear distinct from the main text, like so:

> *Don't overlook these extra tidbits. They're relevant to the current topic and deserve some attention.*

We may also sometimes wander off on a slight tangent that isn't really part of the topic at hand but is still important information you should know. To keep things flowing smoothly, we'll place such supplemental information in sidebars, which look like this:

SIDEBARS

Sidebars offer extra information, exploring a related topic in more depth without derailing the main topic. The term *sidebar* comes from magazine and newspaper publishing, where these sorts of accompanying stories are often printed in another column alongside the main article.

Downloading the code

All of the HTML and CSS examples you'll see in this book are available for download from the Apress website (apress.com). Once you've downloaded and unzipped the file, you'll find each chapter's source code in a separate folder; you can pick it apart and refer to it at your leisure. You can also find the source code and other information at this book's companion website, foundationhtml.com.

Chapter 1

Getting Started

We're sure you're champing at the bit to start building web pages, but we'd like to set the stage first and cover some general information about the Internet and World Wide Web, as well as some background on HTML and CSS. This chapter isn't a comprehensive overview by any means, but it will get you up to speed on some of the terminology and concepts you'll need to be familiar with throughout the rest of this book. If you're already pretty web-savvy, and if you've used and worked with websites for some time, feel free to skip ahead to Chapter 2 and start getting your hands dirty.

Introducing the Internet and the World Wide Web

"The Internet" is simply a catchall name for the vast, globe-spanning network of computers that are connected to each other and can transmit and receive data, shuttling information back and forth around the world at nearly the speed of light. It's been around in some form for nearly half a century now, ever since a few smart people figured out how to make one computer talk to another computer. The Internet has since become so ubiquitous and pervasive, impacting so many aspects of modern life, that it's hard to imagine a world without it.

The World Wide Web is one facet of the Internet, like a bustling neighborhood in a much larger city (other Internet "neighborhoods" include e-mail, news groups, and chat rooms). The Web is made up of millions of files and documents residing on different computers across the Internet, all interconnected to weave a web of information around the world, which is how it gets its name. In its relatively short history, the Web has grown and evolved far beyond the simple text documents it began with, carrying other types of information through the same channels: images, video, audio, and fully immersive interactive experiences. But at its core, the Web is fundamentally a text-based medium, and that text is usually encoded in HTML (more on that in a minute).

Many different devices can access the Web: desktop and laptop computers, tablets and PDAs, mobile phones, game consoles, and even some household appliances. Whatever the device, it in turn operates software that interprets HTML. These programs are technically known as *user-agents*, but the more familiar term is *web browsers*. A web browser is specifically a program intended to visually render web documents, whereas some user-agents interpret HTML but don't display it.

In this book we'll generally use the word *browser* to mean any user-agent capable of handling and rendering HTML documents, and we may use the term *graphical browser* when we're specifically referring to one that renders the document in a visually enhanced format, in full color, and with styled text and images. It's important to make this distinction because some web browsers are *not* graphical and only render plain, unstyled text without any images.

A browser or user-agent is also known as a *client*, because it is the thing requesting and receiving service. The computer that serves data to the client is called, not surprisingly, a *server*. The Internet is riddled with servers, all storing and processing data and delivering it in response to client requests. The client and the server are two ends of the chain, connected to each other through the Internet.

What Is HTML?

The World Wide Web originated as a purely textual medium, built upon the written word. Pictures were soon added to the mix, and eventually sound, animation, and video made the Web the rich multimedia tapestry it is today. But the overwhelming bulk of Web content still takes the form of written text, and that's not likely to change any time soon. Most of the time you spend surfing the Web is probably spent reading.

The Web, for all its multimedia richness, is still essentially a textual medium. It's a weave of documents, cross-referenced and interconnected by the humble *hyperlink*, wherein a bit of text in one document is linked directly to another document somewhere else on the Web. And just like that, what would otherwise be ordinary text becomes the much more exciting and dynamic *hypertext*, and hypertext needs to be encoded in a whole new language: HyperText Markup Language (HTML).

HTML is the computer coding language that describes the structure of a web page. It converts ordinary text into active text for display and use on the Web, and also gives plain, unstructured text the sort of structure human beings rely on to read it. As you read this book, you're looking for visual cues to help you organize the words into smaller portions that you can process and comprehend. You recognize the significance of things like punctuation, capitalization, spacing, and font sizes. You know just by looking at it that this paragraph ends after this sentence.

Computers don't read text the same way humans do—they can't interpret a string of words and grasp the concept behind them, they don't see the visual cues we use to separate one group of words from another, and they can't automatically group related sentences into meaningful paragraphs. Instead of visual cues, a computer requires a structure composed of clear markers that designate the nature of each portion of text. That's the essence of a markup language: embedded instructions that a computer can follow in order to make content readable and usable by humans.

HTML consists of encoded markers called *tags* that surround and differentiate portions of text, indicating the function and purpose of the content those tags "mark up." Tags are embedded directly in a plain-text document where they can be interpreted by a browser. They're called *tags* because, well, that's what they are. Just as a price tag displays the cost of an item and a toe tag identifies a cadaver, so too does an HTML tag indicate the nature of a portion of content and provide vital information about it. Listing 1-1 is a very simple bit of HTML, just a heading and a paragraph.

Listing 1-1. An example of text marked up with HTML. The tags are highlighted in bold.

```
<h1>This is a Level One Heading</h1>
<p>This is a paragraph.</p>
```

A browser doesn't display the tags themselves; tags only tell the browser how to treat the content between them. A matched pair of start and end tags (the end tag has a slash) forms an *element*, comprising the tags and everything in between them. You'll learn a lot more about tags and elements in Chapter 2, and you'll learn about the full range of HTML elements throughout the rest of this book.

From its inception, HTML has been carefully designed to be a simple and flexible language. It's a free, open standard, not owned or controlled by any company or individual. There is no license to purchase or specialized software required to author your own HTML documents. Anyone can create and publish web pages, and it's that very openness that makes the Web the powerful, far-reaching medium it is. HTML exists so that we can all share information freely and easily.

However, you do need to follow certain rules when you author documents in HTML—there are certain ways they should be assembled to make certain they'll work properly. The Web runs on agreement, with all the different authors and programmers and clients and servers agreeing to abide by the same basic rules, collectively referred to as *web standards*. Standardizing web languages ensures that the Web can work consistently and reliably for everyone—users and authors alike. Sticking to the agreed-upon rules makes communication possible, like the rules of grammar and punctuation that help you understand this sentence.

Of course, it follows that someone needs to write down the rules to which we should agree. The technical specifications for many of the core languages (including HTML) that make up the Web are overseen and maintained by the World Wide Web Consortium (W3C), an international, non-profit organization founded in 1994 for just this purpose—to standardize the languages and map a clear path for the Web of the future.

You can learn more about the W3C and read all of their public specifications, past and present, at their website, `w3.org`. The specifications can be difficult to read because they're extremely technical in nature, written primarily for computer scientists and software vendors who program web user-agents. But this kind of standardization is essential for the widespread adoption of the Web, ensuring that websites function properly across different browsers and operating systems. The Web is meant to be "platform independent" and "device independent," and adherence to web standards makes that possible.

The Evolution of HTML

HTML first appeared in 1990—built upon the pre-existing Standard Generalized Markup Language (SGML)—as the foundational language for the newborn World Wide Web, but it wasn't formally defined until 1993. It was further refined and extended with HTML 2.0, the first official HTML standard, in 1995. Version 3.2 arrived in early 1997 with a slew of new features, and HTML 4.0 came shortly thereafter near the end of the same year.

In those early years of the Web, the language specifications weren't always followed as closely as they should have been. Different browsers supported different features of HTML, and introduced their own nonstandard features just to get a leg up on the competition. Given the unruly landscape of the time, authors didn't follow the standards any better than the browsers did. The early web was a tangle of bloated, convoluted markup and proprietary, browser-specific functionality. Developers often resorted to making multiple versions of their sites targeted to different browsers, or even worse, they built websites that worked properly in only one browser and failed utterly in others. Ask an old timer about the Browser Wars of the mid-90s and they'll regale you with frightening tales of forked scripts, nested tables, and pixel shims. Those were dark days indeed.

Thankfully, this is no longer the case. The web browsers of today follow the standardized specs much more consistently than in previous generations, encouraging authors to do the same, and thus advancing the Web toward the ultimate goal of a truly universal medium.

As the Web really took off in the late 1990s, a few minor (but significant) changes to HTML 4.0 were released in 1999 as HTML 4.01. After a decade of rapid innovation, HTML 4.01 was expected to be the last complete specification of the HTML language. A new kid called XHTML had joined the class, and it was praised as the wave of the future.

The Age of X

Around the turn of the century (way back in the year 2000), the W3C was convinced that the future of the Web lay in eXtensible Markup Language (XML), a powerful language that allows authors to create customized elements rather than relying only on the elements predefined by the language itself. Extensible HTML (XHTML) is a reformulation of HTML following the more stringent syntax of XML. It was meant to bridge the gap between HTML and XML, preparing web authors for this bright XML future everyone expected to arrive any day now.

Whereas XML is extensible, XHTML offers a finite set of predefined elements to choose from—all the same elements that were available in HTML 4.01, in fact. The only real differences between HTML 4.01 and XHTML 1.0 are stylistic, with just a few more rules dictating how XHTML must be written. HTML is a lax language designed to be tolerant of minor transgressions in syntax, whereas XML is fussy and demands strict adherence to its rules. XHTML simply applies the strictness of XML to HTML, resulting in a hardened set of rules for authoring a document. An XHTML document is essentially just an HTML document written to a more exacting standard.

It was also right around the time XHTML came on the scene that web designers and developers began a serious campaign to improve the state of the Web, encouraging their clients and colleagues to develop in accordance with web standards, and pressuring browser makers to correctly support those same standards in their products. XHTML, with its stricter rules of conformance, was the darling of the web standards movement because it encouraged authors to pay closer attention to how they constructed their documents.

> *The Web Standards Project (WaSP) was founded in 1998 in reaction to the inconsistent browser behaviors and unsustainable development practices of the era. This group led the charge in what became "the web standards movement," promoting a new set of best practices for web designers and developers, ultimately changing the way web sites are made and improving the state of the web, for authors and users alike. WaSP continues to work with web authors, educators, browser vendors, and standards bodies to advance and promote web standards. Their website is* `webstandards.org`*.*

Meanwhile, the W3C immediately began work on XHTML 2.0. No simple reformulation of existing standards, this was going to be a radical overhaul of the language from the ground up, a whole new approach to authoring documents for the Web. That was over a decade ago. The XHTML 2.0 specification stagnated and eventually stalled, while the Web continued to move inexorably forward, innovating on top of a foundation that was beginning to show its age. By the mid-2000s it became clear to some that XHTML 2.0 was perhaps not the best way forward after all, and it was time to re-examine and refresh good old HTML.

Out with the X, in with the 5

A splinter group formed within the W3C in 2004 and began to craft new addendums to HTML. They called themselves the Web Hypertext Application Technology Working Group (WHATWG, `whatwg.org`) and their side projects were dubbed Web Apps 1.0 and Web Forms 2.0, both meant to be extensions of the stale HTML 4.01 spec. Eventually these two projects were united in a new fledgling specification: HTML5.

In due time the W3C also came to accept that XHTML 2.0 wasn't working out as planned, and recognized that this new HTML5 business was something worth paying attention to. The W3C started the process of adopting and formalizing the work produced by WHATWG. And so HTML5 gained official status as the next HTML standard.

As all versions of HTML have done, HTML5 builds on what came before, always refining and extending and improving. In fact, HTML5 is still taking shape as we write this in the summer of 2011, though they're aiming for the spec to be completed in 2012. But, although the specification is incomplete at the moment, it's relatively stable at the time of this writing (knock on wood) and there's nothing preventing you from using the fundamentals of HTML5 on the Web today.

> *Two groups—WHATWG and the W3C—are working on HTML5 in tandem. Although the specification is still taking shape, you can read the work in progress at their respective websites: WHATWG's version is at* `whatwg.org/html` *and the W3C's is at* `w3.org/TR/html5/`*. Depending on when each was last updated, there may be some differences between the two versions of the spec, and both are works in progress and subject to change. Generally speaking, the WHATWG version includes the very latest changes, and the W3C version is a bit more refined and finalized.*

One of the tenets of HTML5 is to maintain backward compatibility (something XHTML 2 would have broken); existing content must continue to function under HTML5. In that sense, any document marked up in any version or variant of HTML is already an HTML5 document, and any browser that interprets HTML already supports most of HTML5. What really matters is browser support for the few specific features that are brand new.

HTML5 introduces a number of new tags and attributes that didn't exist in any prior HTML version. Current versions of most popular browsers already support many of these new features, whereas some other advanced features aren't fully developed and aren't yet supported by browsers, but that tide is changing at a breakneck pace. All the major browser makers—Mozilla, Microsoft, Apple, Google, and Opera—are releasing frequent updates to their browsers, improving support for the finer points of HTML5 with each new version.

What's in HTML5?

As often happens with any advance in technology, "HTML5" was quickly seized upon as a buzzword to make things sound bleeding edge and cool, even if what was being discussed wasn't part of HTML5 at all. A broad range of technologies and techniques were soon lumped together under the banner of "HTML5," leading to a great deal of confusion about just what was and wasn't, in actuality, HTML5.

HTML5 is simply the next iteration of HTML, the language that gives web content its necessary structure. As you read earlier in this chapter, HTML tags form structural elements in a document, allowing readers (and programs) to differentiate a headline from a paragraph, or a paragraph from a list, or a list from a quotation, and so on. Content without structure is content without meaning. This latest version of HTML introduces a number of new, meaningful elements that were lacking in HTML 4 and XHTML. In addition to the usual headings, paragraphs, tables, and lists, there are new elements for things like navigation, menus, articles, summaries, dates and times, figures with captions, and a heap of new interactive form elements. All the useful elements from previous versions of HTML have been kept, but HTML5 eliminates some legacy elements that have outlived their usefulness. You'll learn all about the elements of HTML5, both old and new, in detail throughout the rest of this book.

Also new in HTML5 are elements for embedding rich media in documents. Images have been on the Web almost from the beginning, but for years authors had to rely on third-party plug-in applications—such as Adobe's Flash or Apple's QuickTime—to play sound and video over the Web. HTML5 makes it possible to play sound and video natively in the browser, without plug-ins. HTML5 also brings the canvas element, an area in a document where scripts and programs can draw live graphics. You'll learn more about embedding media in Chapter 5.

After all our "the Web is made of documents" talk, we shouldn't gloss over the prevalence of *web applications*. A web application might be similar to other computer applications you're familiar with—like an email program, a word processor, or the spreadsheet shown in Figure 1-1—but it works directly in a web browser. Under the surface, a great many web apps are actually nothing more than enhanced documents, using sophisticated code to manipulate HTML right before your eyes, yet still built on that same HTML foundation. HTML5 is being written with web apps in mind, offering new abilities and frameworks to enhance the applications built on top of it.

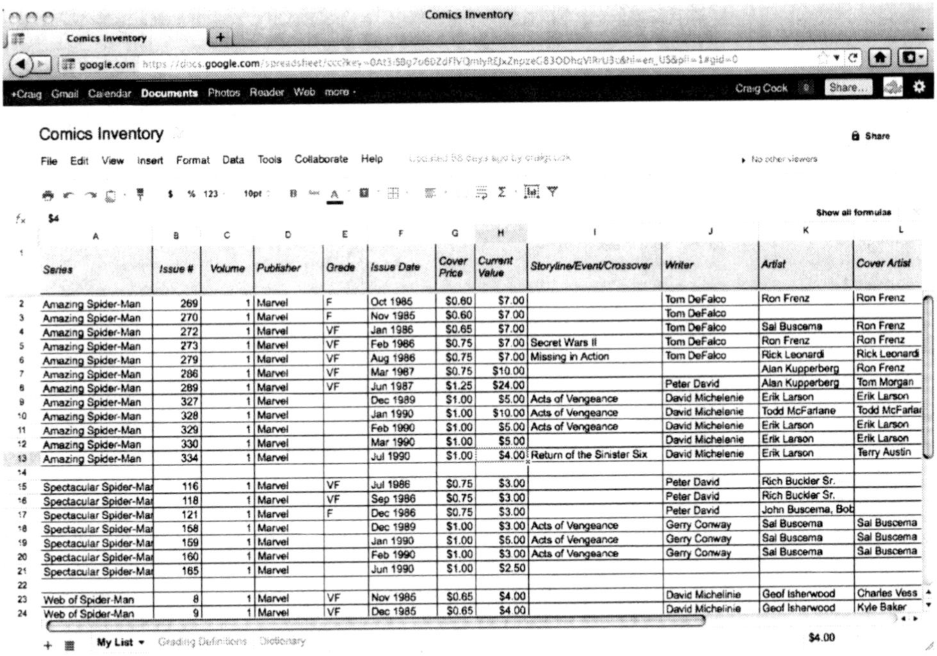

Figure 1-1. A Google Docs spreadsheet offers most of the features of a desktop spreadsheet application like Microsoft Excel, but runs within a web browser and stores its data online. This web app is built entirely with HTML, CSS, and JavaScript.

Alongside HTML5 and its regular content-structuring markup duties, a number of related scripting APIs (Application Programming Interfaces) are being developed and standardized to help web apps work with HTML5 content. For example, with HTML5-empowered web apps, you'll be able to store application data offline, edit web documents directly in the browser, use a web app to work with files stored on your computer, send messages between web documents, share your location, and more. But don't get too excited just yet; we won't be covering these scripting APIs in any detail in this book. They're related to HTML5, and are often grouped under the HTML5 umbrella, but they are not necessarily HTML5. As far as we're concerned right now—and for the rest of this book—HTML5 is still just a language to mark up documents for the Web.

Separating Content from Presentation

HTML is intended to bestow a meaningful structure upon unstructured text, showing that different blocks of words are in fact different types of content. A headline is not the same as a paragraph; those two types of content should be marked up with different tags, making their innate difference absolutely clear to another computer. But human beings don't want to read encoded tags. We're used to reading text that looks a certain way—we expect headlines to appear in a large, boldfaced font to let us know that it's a headline and not something else. Early browser developers knew this, and they programmed their software to display different types of content in different styles.

From its humble roots, the Web quickly blossomed and soon was no longer the exclusive domain of academics and computer scientists. Graphic designers discovered this exciting new medium and sought ways to make it more aesthetically appealing than ordinary, unadorned text. However, HTML lacked a proper means of influencing the display of content; it was strictly intended to provide structure, with only a few conceits to graphic design. Designers were forced to repurpose existing features of HTML, taking advantage of the way browsers displayed content in an effort to create something more visually compelling. Unfortunately, this resulted in many websites of the day being built with *presentational markup* that was messy, overcomplicated, hard to maintain, and had nothing to do with what the content *meant* but only how it should *look*.

In 1996, when the Web was still in its infancy, the W3C introduced Cascading Style Sheets (CSS). It was an entirely different language, one specifically created to describe how HTML documents should be visually presented while leaving the structural markup clean and meaningful. A style sheet written in CSS can be applied to an HTML document, adding an attractive layer of design without negatively impacting the markup that serves as its foundation. The code that gives the content its structure is kept separate from the code describing its presentation.

Separating content from presentation allows both aspects to become stronger and more adaptable. An HTML document can be changed without completely reconstructing it to correct the design. An entire website can be redesigned by changing a single style sheet without rewriting one line of structural markup.

It took some time for the major browsers to catch up and fully support the early versions of CSS as they were intended, but today's browsers (a few lingering bugs notwithstanding) support CSS levels 1 and 2 well enough that presentational markup should be a thing of the past. In the chapters to come you'll learn to write meaningful, structural markup to support your content according to its inherent meaning and purpose. Along the way, you'll see many examples of how you can visually style your content with CSS, avoiding the trap of presentational markup.

The Next Level of CSS

Like HTML, CSS is an open standard developed and maintained by the W3C (`w3.org/Style/CSS/`). And like HTML, CSS has changed and adapted over the years, adding new features at each step along the way. CSS level 1 debuted in 1996, with CSS level 2 expanding on it in 1998. The browser uptake was slow for these first iterations of the CSS spec. In fact, as of this writing, there still isn't a browser in the land that has fully implemented every last part of CSS 2.1. But that hasn't slowed down development of CSS level 3. No, what has slowed down CSS3 is the fact that CSS3 is vastly more complicated than CSS1 or CSS2.

The first two versions of CSS were focused on relatively basic aspects of presentation: font sizes, spacing, drawing boxes, defining colors, positioning elements on the page, and so on. Once those fundamentals were pretty well hammered out, the next generation of CSS was going to reach toward much broader horizons. CSS3 promises multi-column layouts, color gradients, embedded typefaces, rounded corners, border images, shadows, transitions, animations, and much more. It's been a long process, and it's still ongoing.

Given the breadth and depth of CSS3, as well as the programmatic complexity of producing some of the intended effects, the specification was split apart into a number of *modules*, each focusing on one particular area. Modules like Fonts, Animations, Backgrounds and Borders, Color, Grid Layout, Speech—over 40 modules in all—can each be drafted and rolled out independently. As such, there isn't really single specification called "CSS level 3," and there may never be a time when the whole thing could be considered "completed." But its modular nature means a number of CSS3 features are already stable and well supported in modern web browsers, and you'll learn how to use some of them later in this book.

Progressive Enhancement

HTML5 and CSS3 are still taking shape as we're writing this book and they'll continue to evolve for the foreseeable future. Although the W3C is nearing completion of the HTML5 specification, this iteration will only be a snapshot of the ever-advancing, living HTML standard. The modular nature of CSS3 means some parts of it are already complete, other parts still need more work, and some modules have barely started. Furthermore, there's already some very early planning for future iterations of these languages, vaguely referred to as HTML6 and CSS4 for the time being.

You don't have to wait for all of HTML5 and CSS3 to be "finished" before you can use them. When you can use these emerging standards isn't really a question of how complete the standards are; it's more a question of browser support for the newly introduced features. Web browsers are evolving rapidly alongside the web standards, and the browser makers are directly involved in defining the very standards they follow. Quite simply, as soon as a browser—or a few browsers, hopefully—supports a given feature, that's when you can use it.

> You can get up-to-date information on which browsers support which new features in HTML5 and CSS3 as well as some of the new JavaScript APIs at Can I Use (`caniuse.com`) and at HTML5 Please (`html5please.com`).

It probably goes without saying that only newer web browsers support the newer features of HTML and CSS; older browsers couldn't support what didn't exist. However, not every web surfer out there is using the very latest browser, and even among the latest versions, not every current browser supports every new feature equally. Even so, you can still employ some of the more advanced features of HTML5 and CSS3 without shutting out less capable browsers and devices by following *progressive enhancement*.

Progressive enhancement isn't a specific technique; it's a general methodology, a particular approach to making websites that applies more advanced web technologies in a layered fashion. You'll begin with pure content and basic structure, then enhance that with additional layers of meaning, presentation, and behavior in such a way that browsers and devices that support those enhancements can benefit from them, but those that don't support the enhancements can still access the original content.

Web browsers are pretty easy-going when it comes to parsing HTML and CSS. When a browser encounters some piece of markup or styling it doesn't support, rather than lock up and refuse to proceed, the browser will simply ignore that unsupported code and continue on its merry way. The directive to ignore unsupported code is baked right into the web standards. The browsers' built-in fault tolerance is what makes progressive enhancement possible; they'll just skip over any code they don't understand and get on with rendering the code they already know.

With progressive enhancement, you can add bells and whistles from HTML5 and CSS3 without destroying the nutritious kernel of content underneath. The real key to a progressive enhancement methodology is to avoid making your websites completely dependent on a specific bell or whistle. Start simple and add layers of complexity in such a way that each subsequent layer is an optional enhancement on top of the layer that supports it.

First give your content a solid and stable structure with simple HTML that every web-capable device will have no trouble processing. Enhance that basic structure with some of the more cutting edge parts of HTML5 and browsers that don't support the newer features will still have the basic structure to fall back on. Use simple, well-supported CSS to further enhance your content and make it more presentable. Add in some of the newer techniques from CSS3—the ones that only the latest browsers support—and older browsers will still render the simpler, time-tested styling (and any devices that don't even support the simple styling will still fall back to the unadorned HTML). Enhance that styled content even further with layers of behavior and interaction using JavaScript, and devices that don't support the scripting will still render readable, accessible, styled content.

> Unlike HTML and CSS, JavaScript is not a fault tolerant language. Any unsupported methods or functions that appear in your JavaScript—even a simple syntax mistake—will generate an error and bring the script to a screeching halt. Every part of a script needs to be in working order or else the entire thing can fall apart. However, you can incorporate checks and failsafes into your JavaScript to detect whether the browser supports a given feature, and to fail gracefully if it doesn't. JavaScript is another important layer in the progressive enhancement stack, but that's a subject for another book.

At every stage and with every new layer of enhancement you add, think about how the content will degrade if and when that layer is stripped away. If removing a layer would make the content nonfunctional or unusable, then perhaps you need to revise your strategy.

Working with HTML and CSS

Though HTML and CSS can seem overwhelming when you first dive in, creating your own web pages is actually quite easy once you get the hang of it. All you really need is a way to edit text files, a browser to view them in, and a place to store the files you create.

Choosing an Editor

HTML documents are plain text, devoid of any special formatting or style—all of the visual formatting happens when a graphical web browser renders the document. To create and edit plain-text electronic documents, you'll need to use software that can do so without automatically imposing any formatting of its own. Fortunately, every operating system comes with some kind of simple text-editing program:

- Windows users can use Notepad, which you will find under Start ↗ All Programs ↗ Accessories ↗ Notepad. WordPad is another Windows alternative, but it will format documents by default. If you use WordPad, be sure to edit and save your documents as plain text, not "rich text."

- Linux users can choose from several text editors, such as vi, vim, or emacs.

- Mac users can use TextEdit, which ships natively with OS X in the Applications folder. Like WordPad for Windows, TextEdit defaults to a rich-text format. You can change this by selecting Format ↗ Make Plain Text.

In addition to these basic text editors, more advanced, specialized text editors are available for Windows, Linux, and Macintosh systems, many specially designed for editing web documents. Some of them are even available free of charge. There are also so-called *What You See Is What You Get* (WYSIWYG, pronounced as "wizzy wig") editors on the market that offer a graphical interface wherein you can edit documents in their formatted, rendered state while the software automatically produces the markup behind it. However, this is no substitute for understanding how HTML and CSS really work, and some WYSIWYG editors can generate convoluted, presentational markup. Handcrafting your documents in plain text is really the best way to maintain control over every aspect of your markup, and many professionals swear by it.

Choosing a Web Browser

As we mentioned earlier, a web browser is the software you use to view websites, and you almost certainly have one already. Every modern computer operating system comes with some sort of web browser installed, or you can choose one of the many others on the market:

- Microsoft Internet Explorer is the default browser on Windows operating systems.

- Apple Safari is the default browser for Mac OS X, and is also available for Windows.

- Mozilla Firefox is a free browser available for Windows, Mac OS X, and Linux (`mozilla.org/firefox`).

- Opera is another free browser available for a wide range of operating systems (`opera.com`).

- Google Chrome is a free browser for Windows, Mac OS X, and Linux (`google.com/chrome`).

- Konqueror is a free browser and file manager for Linux (`konqueror.org`).

Ordinary HTML documents don't require any other software to operate. All of your files can be stored locally on your computer's hard drive, and you can view pages in their rendered state by simply launching your browser of choice and opening the document you want to view (you can find the command to open a local file under the File menu in most browsers).

Validating Your Documents

Having a standardized set of rules is all well and good, but how can you be sure you've followed them correctly, crossing all the *t*s and dotting all the *i*s? You should *validate* your HTML documents, checking them against the standard rule set to ensure that they're put together properly. It's like a spell-checker for markup. The W3C has created an online validation tool (available at `http://validator.w3.org/`, shown in Figure 1-2) for just this purpose. This web-based service allows you to validate your documents by either entering the location of a page on the Web, uploading a file from your computer, or simply pasting your markup directly into a form on the website.

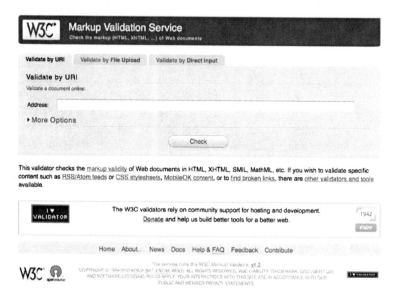

Figure 1-2. The W3C Markup Validation Service

The W3C validator can automatically analyze your markup and display any errors it encounters so you can correct them. It will also display validation *warnings*, which are simply cautions about issues you might want to address but are not quite as severe as errors; warnings can be ignored if you have good reason to do so, but *errors* are flaws that really must be fixed. When no errors are found, you'll see a joyful banner declaring that your document is valid. A document that is valid and correctly assembled according to the rules of the language is said to be *well-formed*. Other validation tools are also available—both online and offline—that can help you check your documents.

CSS also needs to be authored in accordance with the specifications, and the W3C offers a similar CSS validation service (`http://jigsaw.w3.org/css-validator/`) to check your CSS files for problems.

Most web browsers are still able to interpret and render invalid documents, but only because they've been designed to compensate for minor errors. Valid, well-formed documents are much more stable, and you won't have to depend on a browser's built-in error handling to display them correctly.

Hosting Your Web Site

You can save all of your work locally on your own computer, but when it's time to make it available to the World Wide Web, you need to move those files to a web server. You have a few hosting options if you're building your own website:

- Using web space provided by your ISP: An Internet service provider (ISP) is the company that connects you to the Internet. Many service providers offer a limited amount of web space where you can host your own site. Ask your ISP whether web space is included with your service contract and how you can use it.

- Using free web space: Many companies provide free web hosting, though "free" is a relative term because free web hosts are usually supplemented by advertising. If you're not bothered by such ads appearing on your website, free hosting may be a quick solution to getting your files online.

- Paying for web hosting: Perhaps the best option is to purchase service from a company that specializes in hosting websites. Many offer hosting packages for as little as $10 (US) per month and include more robust features than free hosting or ISP hosting provides (such as e-mail service, server-side scripting, and databases). Research your options, and choose a host that can meet your needs.

If you opt for paid web hosting, you'll also need to purchase and register a unique *domain name* to be your site's address on the Web. Some hosting companies offer domain registration as an included service (and some domain registrars also offer hosting services), but securing a domain and securing a host are usually two separate processes.

We won't go into all the particulars of registering a domain and getting your site online with a web host. After all, this is still the first chapter, and numerous resources online can provide more information. To learn more about hosting your websites when the time comes, just visit your favorite search engine and have a look around for information about "web hosting basics" or some similar phrase. One good place to start is the Wikipedia entry about web hosting service (`http://en.wikipedia.org/wiki/Web_hosting`), which offers a fairly detailed introduction to set you on your way.

Introducing the URL

Every file or document available on the Web resides at a unique address called a Uniform Resource Locator (URL). The term Uniform Resource Identifier (URI) is sometimes used interchangeably with URL, though URI is a more general term; a URL is a type of URI. We'll be using the term URL in this book to discuss addressed file locations. It's this address that allows a web-connected device to locate a specific file on a specific server in order to download and display it to the user (or employ it for some other purpose; not all files on the Web are meant to be displayed).

The Components of a URL

A web URL follows a standard form that can be broken down into a few key parts, diagrammed in Figure 1-3. Each segment of the URL communicates specific information to both the client and the server.

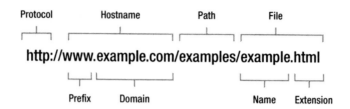

Figure 1-3. The components of a URL

The *protocol* indicates one of a few different sets of rules that dictate the movement of data over the Internet. The Web uses HyperText Transfer Protocol (HTTP), the standard protocol used for transmitting hypertext-encoded data from one computer to another. The protocol is separated from the rest of the URL by a colon and two forward slashes (`://`).

A *hostname* is the name of the site from which the browser will retrieve the file. The web server's true address is a unique numeric Internet Protocol (IP) address, and every computer connected to the Internet has one. IP addresses look something like "66.211.109.45," which isn't very easy on the eyes and is certainly a challenge to remember. A *domain name* is a more memorable alias that directs Internet traffic to an IP address. Many web hostnames feature a *domain prefix*, further naming the particular server being accessed (especially when there are multiple servers within a single domain), though that prefix is frequently optional. A prefix can be almost any short text label, but "www" is traditional. It's possible for another entire website to exist separately within a domain under a different prefix, known as a *subdomain*. A hostname will also feature a *domain suffix* (sometimes called an *extension*) to indicate the domain's category, such as ".com" for a U.S. commercial domain, ".edu" for a U.S. educational institution, or ".co.uk" for a commercial website in the United Kingdom. Every country also has its own domain extension, and you'll often see URLs that indicate a country of origin but not any particular category.

The *path* specifies the directory on the web server that holds the requested document, just as you save files in different virtual folders on your own computer. Files on a web server may be stored in subdirectories—folders within folders—and each directory in the path is separated by a forward slash (/). This path is the route a client will follow to reach the ultimate destination file. The top-level directory of a website (the one that contains all other files and directories) is called the *site root* directory and doesn't appear in the URL.

The specific file to retrieve is identified by its file name and *extension*. You can give your files just about any name you want, and a file extension indicates what type of file it is. An HTML (or XHTML) document will have an extension of .html or .htm (the shorter version is used on some servers that support only three-letter file extensions). CSS files use the .css extension, JavaScript files use .js, and so forth. Web servers are configured to recognize these extensions and handle the files appropriately, processing different types of files in different ways.

You won't see a file name and extension in every URL you encounter. Most web servers are configured to automatically locate a specially named file when a directory is requested without a specified file name. This could be the file called `index.html`, `default.html`, or some other name, depending on the way the server has been set up. Indeed, most of the various parts of the URL may be optional depending on the particular server configuration.

The URL is the instrument that allows you to build links to other parts of the Web, including other parts of your own site. You'll use URLs extensively in the HTML and CSS you author, which is why we've spent so much time exploring them in this first chapter.

Absolute and Relative URLs

A URL can take either of two forms when it points to a resource elsewhere within the same site. An *absolute URL* is one that includes the full string, including the protocol and hostname, leaving no question as to where that resource is found on the Web. You'll use an absolute URL when you link to a site or file outside your own site's domain, though internal URLs can also be absolute.

A *relative URL* is one that points to a resource within the same site by referencing only the path and/or file, omitting the protocol and hostname because those can be safely assumed. It might look something like this:

examples/chapter1/example.html

If the destination file is kept within the same directory as the file where the URL occurs, the path can be assumed as well so only the file name and extension are required, like so:

example.html

If the destination is in a directory above the source file, you can indicate that relative path with two dots and a slash (../), instructing the browser to go up one level to find the resource. Each occurrence of ../ indicates one up-level directive, so a URL pointing two directories upwards might look like this:

../../example.html

Almost all web servers are configured to interpret a leading slash in a relative URL as the site root directory, so URLs can be "site root relative," showing the full path from the site root down:

/examples/chapter1/example.html

Lastly, if the destination is a directory rather than a specific file, only the path is needed:

/examples/chapter1/

Relative URLs are a useful way to keep file references short and portable; an entire site can be moved to another domain and all of its relative URLs will remain intact and functional.

Summary

This chapter has provided a high-level overview of what the Internet and World Wide Web are and how they work. You've been introduced to HTML and CSS and are beginning to understand how you can make these languages work together to produce a rendered web page. You got a short history lesson on how HTML and CSS have changed over time, and some inkling of what the future holds for these fundamental web languages. We mentioned a few different text editors you can use to create your documents and some popular web browsers with which to view them. You've also learned a little about web hosting and a lot about the components of a URL, information you'll find essential as you begin assembling your own websites. We haven't gone into all the gory details in this introduction—after all, we've got the rest of the book to cover them. In Chapter 2 you'll finally get to sink your teeth into some real HTML and CSS. Buckle up; this should be a fun ride!

Chapter 2

HTML and CSS Basics

HTML5 is the latest and greatest, and is still taking shape as we write. But it's flexible and forward-looking by design, and most of HTML5 is ready to use right now. This book will show you how. Chapter 1 briefly introduced you to HTML and CSS, and in this chapter we'll go a bit deeper and show you how you can write markup and style sheets to create your own web pages. You'll become familiar with the fundamental components of HTML and how to use them. As you know by now, you must adhere to some standards when constructing a document for the Web, and we're going to be writing lean, valid, semantically rich HTML5 throughout the chapters to come.

Later in the chapter, we'll walk you through the essentials of CSS so you can use it to visually style your web pages. HTML provides the structure that supports the content of your web pages, whereas CSS adds some polish to make your content more attractive and memorable. Designing websites with CSS isn't possible without some solid bedrock of markup underneath, so let's begin at the beginning.

The Parts of Markup: Tags, Elements, and Attributes

The linchpin of HTML is the *tag*. Tags are the coded symbols that separate and distinguish one portion of content from another while also informing the browser about what type of content it's dealing with. A web browser (or any user-agent) can interpret the tags embedded in an HTML document and treat different types of content appropriately. Most of the tags available in HTML have names that describe exactly what they do and what sort of content they designate, such as headings, paragraphs, lists, images, quotations, and so on.

Tags in HTML are surrounded by angle brackets (< and >) to clearly distinguish them from ordinary text. The first angle bracket (<) marks the beginning of the tag, immediately followed by the specific tag name, and the tag ends with an opposing angle bracket (>). For example, this is the HTML tag that begins a paragraph:

`<p>`

We've written the tag name in lowercase, but you can use uppercase (`<P>`) if you prefer. Tag names are not case-sensitive in HTML, but they must be lowercase in XHTML (that's one of those more stringent rules that separates XHTML from HTML). Whereas XHTML demands lowercase for all tags and attributes, HTML5 isn't so picky, and doesn't draw any distinction between a `<p>` and a `<P>` so it's entirely up to you whether your tags are uppercase or lowercase.

Most tags come in matched pairs: one *start tag* (also called an *opening tag*) to mark the beginning of a portion of content and one *end tag* (also called a *closing tag*) to mark its end. For example, the beginning of a paragraph is marked by the start tag, `<p>`, and the paragraph ends with a `</p>` end tag; the slash after the opening bracket is what distinguishes it as an end tag. A complete (if short) paragraph would be marked up like this:

`<p>Hello, world!</p>`

These twin tags and everything between them form a complete *element*, and elements are the basic building blocks of an HTML document.

A few elements don't require an end tag in select circumstances. For example, if certain elements are immediately followed by certain other elements, the start tag for the following element implies the end of the previous element, so that previous element's end tag may be optional, depending on the elements in play. This is true in HTML5, as it was in HTML 4 and earlier, but not in XHTML: XHTML requires an end tag for *all* elements. Even in HTML5, it's not a bad idea to include end tags, if only because it can be hard to remember which elements allow tag omission in which cases. When in doubt, close your elements. We'll include end tags on all the elements in markup examples you see in this book... almost all, that is.

Some tags indicate *void elements* (also called *empty elements*), which are elements that do not, and in fact cannot, hold any contents. Void elements don't require a closing tag because there's nothing to enclose; a single tag represents the complete element. In XHTML, which strictly requires end tags for all elements, these void elements are "self-closed" with a trailing slash at the end of the tag. For example, the `br` element represents a line break that forces the text that follows it to wrap to a new line on the rendered page. It's a void element that can't hold any content, so in XHTML it would be self-closed like so:

`<br/>`

Trailing slashes to end void elements are valid in HTML5, but they're not required. The choice is yours.

Some void elements are also known as *replaced elements*; the element itself isn't actually rendered by a graphical browser but is instead replaced by some other content. The most common example is the `img` element, which occurs in the document to mark where an image should appear on the rendered page. When the browser renders the document, the image file replaces the `img` element. You'll learn all about using images and other media in Chapter 5.

There are a very few special circumstances where even an element's start tag can be omitted and the entire element is merely implied. In the case of these *implied elements*, the element still "exists" within the rendered page because browsers will generate it automatically, but its start and end tags are optional in the markup. For instance, the tbody element defines the body of a table in HTML, and its start tag is often optional because the beginning and ending of the table body is implied by the other elements around it. You'll learn about HTML tables in Chapter 7.

Attributes

An element's start tag can carry *attributes* to provide more information about the element—specific traits or properties that element should possess. An attribute consists of an *attribute name* followed by an *attribute value*, like so:

<p **class="greeting"**>Hello, world!</p>

This paragraph includes a class attribute with a value of "greeting," making it distinct from other paragraphs that don't include that attribute (you'll learn more about the class attribute later). An attribute's name and its value are connected by an equal sign (=) with no spaces allowed between; class = "greeting" isn't valid.

The quotation marks enclosing the value are optional in HTML5, but are required in XHTML. In HTML5, the attributes class=greeting and class="greeting" are equally valid so the choice is yours. When you do choose to quote attribute values, you can use either single quotes ('...') or double quotes ("...") so long as both of them match; quoting a value like "...' wouldn't be valid. Some attributes may possess multiple values separated by spaces, or a value composed of several words with spaces between, and in those cases the entire value or set of values must be enclosed in quotation marks.

Some attributes don't require a value at all and the very presence of the attribute provides all the information a user-agent needs. An attribute without a value is called a *minimized attribute*. For example, here's the markup for a pre-checked checkbox, with the checked attribute in its minimized form (highlighted in bold):

<input type="checkbox" **checked**>

This is also called a *Boolean attribute*, named after the 19th Century mathematician George Boole, who devised a system of logic based on true and false values represented by the digits 1 (true) and 0 (false). Boolean logic is the foundation for much of computer science; a bit in binary is either 1 or 0, a switch is either on or it's off. There's no need for any other value for the checked attribute because a checkbox is either checked or not checked; the attribute's mere presence indicates "true." XHTML's strictness requires values for *all* attributes and doesn't allow minimizing attributes, not even Boolean ones. Thus, the same checkbox would appear in XHTML with a non-minimized checked attribute:

<input type="checkbox" **checked="checked"** />

It seems redundant, and it is, but it's just part of XHTML's strictness. XML requires values for *all* attributes, so XHTML requires them too. HTML5 doesn't require values for Boolean attributes, but nor does it forbid them. Some newer Boolean attributes introduced in HTML5 accept true and false values rather than repeating the attribute name XHTML-style. Also note the trailing slash in the example above, because `input` is a void element that must be closed in XHTML (see Chapter 8 for more about forms and checkboxes). The above example of XHTML is perfectly valid in HTML5 as well, so once again the choice of minimizing Boolean attributes is yours.

Like tag names, attribute names aren't case-sensitive in HTML but must be lowercase in XHTML. Attribute values are never case-sensitive; a good thing because some values might need to use capital letters.

An element's start tag can include several attributes, separated by spaces, and attributes must appear only in a start tag (or a void element's lone tag). Some elements require specific attributes whereas others are optional—it all depends on the individual element, and you'll be learning about all of them throughout the rest of this book, including which attributes each element may or must possess.

Figure 2-1 illustrates the components of an element.

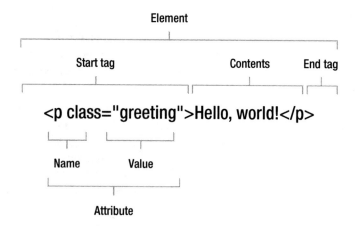

Figure 2-1. The basic components of an HTML element

Content Models

HTML5 has a variety of rules and requirements about where and when certain elements can appear in a document, and what types of content each element can and can't contain. To simplify these often-confusing rules, elements in HTML5 are divided into a few broad categories, or *content models*, classifying elements by their expected contents. For example, some elements are intended to contain lengthy passages of text, whereas other elements typically contain only a few words. It's important to be aware of this as you construct your documents, ensuring that you use the right element for the right content. The basic content models in HTML5 are:

- **Flow content**: This umbrella category actually includes almost every element. The model is called "flow content" because these elements influence the flow of other content on the page, like a stone influences the flow of a stream.

- **Phrasing content**: This category is for elements that contain a few words, distinct from the other words around them, such as a link or an emphasized word within a sentence. We'll cover most of the phrase elements in Chapter 4.

- **Heading content**: These elements are headings or titles, introducing the text that follows them. Headings are covered in Chapter 4.

- **Sectioning content**: These elements wrap around groups of elements to form larger, distinctive blocks of content, such as an article or a sidebar. These are covered in Chapter 4 as well.

- **Embedded content**: Elements that embed content into the page, like images, videos, audio, or dynamic graphics. You'll learn about most of these in Chapter 5.

- **Interactive content**: Interactive elements are typically found in forms that let web users send data directly to the web server, like text fields, checkboxes, and buttons. Forms and their interactive elements are covered in Chapter 8.

- **Metadata content**: These elements supply information about the document itself, or connect the document to additional resources like scripts and style sheets. You'll learn about these in Chapter 3.

Some elements may have more than one content model. For instance, a link (the a element, covered in depth in Chapter 6) is both a phrasing element and an interactive element. Although there are occasional exceptions and oddities, these content models are generally intuitive and easy to keep straight. As we introduce the individual elements in detail throughout this book we'll include their relevant content model(s) and any special rules about what they can or can't contain.

Block-level vs. Inline

In previous versions of HTML (including XHTML), most elements were divided into two broad categories: *block-level* and *inline*. A block-level element is one that contains a significant block of content that should be displayed on its own line, to break apart long passages of text into manageable portions such as paragraphs, headings, and lists. An inline element usually contains a shorter string of text and is displayed adjacent to other text on the same line, like a few emphasized words within a sentence. Inline elements could only contain text and other inline elements.

The block and inline classifications were always essentially presentational, and HTML5 has moved to the more nuanced and meaningful system of content models. If you're familiar with HTML 4.01 or XHTML 1.0, the flow and sectioning content models are roughly analogous to block-level, and phrasing elements are roughly analogous to inline.

Even though these classifications are gone from HTML5, their legacy remains in the form of the display property in CSS, which determines an element's formatting on the rendered page. If an element's display property is declared with the value block, the rendered element forms a "block box" and rests on its own line, occupying the full available width unless some other width is specified. The value inline indicates that the element appears on the same line as adjacent text or elements, and its width collapses to the width of its contents.

Graphical web browsers have their own built-in style sheets that dictate how various HTML elements display by default, including whether they should be treated as block-level or inline. You can override these browser defaults with your own CSS, as you'll soon see, but it's important to know which elements are styled as block-level or inline by default.

> You can learn more about the CSS display property from the Mozilla Developer Network (https://developer.mozilla.org/docs/CSS/display), or from the CSS 2.1 specification (w3.org/TR/CSS21/visuren.html#display-prop).

Nesting Elements

Elements can be *nested* like Russian matryoshka dolls, each one residing within its containing element. They must be nested correctly, with each end tag appearing in the correct order to close an inner element before you close its container. Here's an example of some improperly nested elements:

```
<p><em>Hello, world!</p></em>
```

The <em> start tag occurs after the <p> start tag, but the </p> end tag occurs *before* the </em> end tag— the em element here should be completely inside the p element. To ensure correct nesting of elements, always close them in the reverse order in which you opened them:

```
<p><em>Hello, world!</em></p>
```

A browser may still be able to render improperly nested elements so you can't always count on the mistake being obvious at a glance. A validator will catch these errors and keep you on the straight and narrow. It can be a bit more challenging to track when nested elements begin and end if you choose to omit end tags for those elements that allow it, so bear that in mind.

Global Attributes

We'll be listing each element's required and optional attributes as we introduce them individually throughout this book. However, some common attributes can be assigned to practically any element and are almost always optional. To spare you the repetition, we'll cover these *global attributes* here, divided into a few categories (they're also called *core attributes*). When we mention "global attributes" in later chapters you can just refer back to this list—it's not going anywhere.

General Purpose Attributes

These attributes include general information about the element, and you can validly include them in the start tag of almost any element:

- class: Indicates the class or classes to which a particular element belongs. Elements that belong to the same class may share aspects of their presentation, and classifying elements can also be useful in client-side scripting. Any number of elements may belong to the same class. Furthermore, a single element may belong to more than one class, with multiple class names separated by spaces in the attribute value (also note that a single class name can't contain spaces).

- id: Specifies a unique identifier for an element. An ID can be almost any short label without spaces, but it must be unique within a single document; more than one element cannot share the same identifier.

- `style`: Specifies CSS style properties for the element. This is known as *inline styling*, which you'll learn more about in the next chapter. Although the `style` attribute is valid for most elements, it mixes presentation with your content so you should avoid using it whenever possible.

- `title`: Supplies a text title for the element. This might be a note, a label, a warning, or indeed a title—the attribute accepts any short bit of text. Many graphical browsers display the value of a `title` attribute in a "tooltip," a small, floating window displayed when the user's cursor lingers over the rendered element.

- `hidden`: Indicates that the element is not relevant and that the browser shouldn't render it. This Boolean attribute is somewhat controversial—arguably, irrelevant and invisible elements shouldn't be in the document in the first place. The attribute was introduced because there may be some unusual situations when an element is irrelevant in one context but relevant in another. For example, a page might have special navigation that should be visible on a mobile device but should never be seen on a desktop computer, or a log in form that isn't relevant to users who are already logged in. The intent is that dynamic scripts could toggle the attribute to hide or show elements as needed, but there's a lot of potential for careless authors to misuse the `hidden` attribute, hence the debate on whether it should be allowed in HTML5 at all. This attribute should **not** be used to arbitrarily hide any old content you might want to hide. We've included the `hidden` attribute in this list because you might encounter it in the wild, and you might even come up with a legitimate use for it—but do so with care.

> Previous versions of HTML and XHTML imposed much stricter limitations on `class` and `id` values. No punctuation or symbols were allowed other than hyphens and underscores, and an ID had to begin with a letter of the alphabet, not a numeral or symbol. HTML5 has loosened these restrictions but they still apply if you're working with an HTML 4.01 or XHTML 1.0 document.

Internationalization Attributes

Internationalization attributes contain information about the natural language in which an element's contents are written such as English, French, Tamil, Latin, Klingon, and so forth. They can be included in almost any element, especially those that contain text in a language different from the rest of the document's content.

- `dir`: Sets the direction in which the text should be read, as specified by a value of `ltr` (left to right) or `rtl` (right to left). This attribute usually isn't necessary because a language's direction should be inferred from the `lang` attribute. It's a good idea to include it just the same. Most Earth languages are read left to right, with Arabic, Persian, and Hebrew being the most common right to left alphabets.

- `lang`: Specifies the natural language of the enclosed content, indicated by an abbreviated language code such as `en` for English, `es` for Spanish (Español), `ja` for Japanese, `ar` for Arabic, `rn` for Kirundi, and so on. You can find a listing of the most common language codes at `webpageworkshop.co.uk/main/language_codes`.

> An *xml:lang* attribute can also specify the content's language. This is the XML format for the *lang* attribute, as it should occur in XML documents. XHTML documents are both XML and HTML (depending on how the server delivers them), so both the *lang* and *xml:lang* attributes may be applied to an element in XHTML, both with the same value. The *xml:lang* attribute isn't needed (or valid) in an HTML5 document.

Focus Attributes

When some elements—especially links and form controls—are in a pre-active state, they are said to have *focus* because the browser's "attention" is concentrated on that element, ready to activate it. You can apply these focus attributes to some elements to enhance accessibility for people using a keyboard to navigate your web pages by cycling the browser's focus through the document:

- `accesskey`: Assigns a keyboard shortcut to an element for easier and quicker access through keyboard navigation. The value of this attribute is the character corresponding to the access key. The exact keystroke combination needed to activate an access key varies between browsers and operating systems.

- `tabindex`: Specifies the element's position in the tabbing order when the Tab key is used to cycle through links and form controls.

Interactive Attributes

HTML5 introduces a number of new attributes to indicate that elements can be manipulated by users and applications. You won't find these attributes in HTML 4.01 or XHTML 1.0, and even in HTML5 they're not all supported by every current browser. Some of these relate to those scripting APIs we mentioned in the last chapter, and they're very cool, but well beyond the scope of this book. We're briefly listing these attributes here so you'll recognize them when you come across them in the wild, but they're fairly advanced and you won't see them again in these pages. We're sorry to get your hopes up only to dash them.

- `contenteditable`: Indicates that users can edit the element's content. This attribute only accepts the values `true`, `false`, or `inherit`, and it can also be minimized. The minimized form with no value is equivalent to `contenteditable="true"`.

- `contextmenu`: Associates the element with a contextual menu elsewhere in the document. This attribute's value is the ID of a `menu` element within the same document (`menu` will be introduced in Chapter 8).

- `draggable`: Indicates that the element can be dragged by the user to another area of the rendered page (this is used by the Drag and Drop API). This attribute only accepts the values `true`, `false`, or `auto`, and is minimizable. The minimized form with no value is equivalent to `draggable="auto"`.

- dropzone: Indicates the element is an area where draggable elements can be dropped. This attribute only accepts the values copy (the dropped data is duplicated), move (the dropped data is moved to the new location), or link (creates a link to the original item, which returns to its previous location).

- spellcheck: Related to forms and contenteditable, this attribute indicates the element's content is available for automatic spelling and grammar checking. It only accepts the values true or false, and is minimizable, with the minimized attribute equivalent to true.

> Numerous **event attributes** are available for client-side scripting, including onclick, ondblclick, onkeydown, onkeyup, onmousedown, onmouseover, onmouseup, onscroll, onfocus, and many more. Each of these events occurs when the user performs the indicated action upon the element. However, you should try to avoid using such inline event handlers, so we won't be covering these optional attributes in any detail. Scripted behavioral enhancements are best separated from the document's content and structure, just as you should separate presentation. You won't really need to know about these event handlers until you dip your toe into JavaScript, and that's a subject for another book.

Custom Data Attributes

New in HTML5, *data attributes* allow web developers to create custom, descriptive attributes with the prefix data- followed by whatever attribute name you like (which you can hyphenate further if necessary), though it shouldn't include any uppercase letters. The attribute's value can be whatever text or data you might need. This is useful for scripts and web applications as it offers a place to store arbitrary meta-information about the element in a valid, unobtrusive way in the absence of any more suitable attributes. It's much better to use a custom data attribute rather than shoehorning machine-readable data into an inappropriate attribute, or exposing it as raw text when it's not meant to be read by your users. For example:

```
<p class="product" data-price="$9,799" data-product-id="V900-shrink-ray">
  V900 Portable Shrink Ray
</p>
```

Browsers don't display custom data attributes—they completely ignore them, in fact. Data attributes shouldn't be used for any CSS styling and shouldn't contain any information you intend to be usable by your visitors. These attributes only exist as hooks for scripts to latch onto and storage vessels for data that scripts can use. Hence, you won't see them again for most of this book. As with the standard interactive attributes, we've introduced data attributes here so you'll recognize them when you encounter them elsewhere.

White Space

When you create your HTML documents as plain text, you're free to format them however you want. Line breaks and indentations can help to make your markup more readable as you work, as you'll see in most of the markup examples in this book. Indenting nested elements can make it easier to see where a particular element begins and ends, and thus you're less likely to run into nesting problems or forget to close an element with the correct end tag.

Web browsers ignore any extra line breaks and carriage returns, collapsing multiple spaces into a single space. To illustrate, here's a bit of markup with a lot of extra space:

```
<p>

                Wide
                                open
                                        spaces!
                                                        </p>
```

This is a rather extreme example—one you'd probably never perpetrate yourself—but it serves to demonstrate how all of those spaces are collapsed when a browser renders the document. Although the spaces and returns are intact in the markup, your visitors would just see:

```
Wide open spaces!
```

Sometimes you may want to preserve extra spaces, tabs, and line breaks in your content—when you're formatting poetry or displaying computer code, for instance. The pre element can delineate passages of preformatted text in just such cases, and you'll learn more about that element in Chapter 4.

Adding Comments

It's often useful to embed comments in your documents. They're notes that aren't displayed in a browser but that you (or someone else) can read when viewing the source markup. Comments can include background on why a document is structured a particular way, instruction on how to update a document, or a recorded history of changes. Comments in HTML use a specialized tag-like structure:

```
<!-- Use an h2 for subheadings -->
<h2>Adding Comments</h2>
```

A comment starts with <!--, a set of characters the browser recognizes as the opening of a comment, and ends with -->. Web browsers won't render any content or elements that occur between those markers, even if the comment spans multiple lines. Comments can also be useful to temporarily "hide" portions of markup when you're testing your web pages.

```
<!-- Hiding this for testing
<h2>Adding Comments</h2>
End hiding -->
```

Although a browser doesn't visibly render comments, the comments are still delivered along with the rest of the markup and can be seen in the page's source code if a visitor views it. Don't expect comments to remain completely secret, and don't rely on them to permanently remove or suppress any important content or markup.

CSS Fundamentals

CSS can add style to your pages, enhancing and improving the presentation of your content. HTML supplies the structure—each element designates a different portion of content, and attributes pass along more information about those elements. CSS acts as another layer to influence the presentation of those HTML elements. Colors, fonts, text sizes, borders, backgrounds, and the arrangement of elements on the page are all presentational aspects of your content, and you can control them all through artful application of CSS.

Anatomy of a CSS Rule

If elements are the building blocks of markup, the building block of CSS is the *rule*. It's a set of instructions that a browser can follow to alter the appearance of HTML elements based on the presentational values you supply. A *style sheet* is a collection of rules gathered together in a particular order, telling the browser to "find this element and make it look like this, then find this other element and make it look like this" and so on, until you've described every element you want to style.

A CSS rule consists of a few component parts, diagrammed in Figure 2-2.

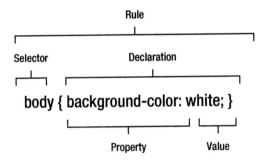

Figure 2-2. The components of a rule in CSS

The *selector* is the part of the rule that targets an element for styling. Its scope can be very broad, affecting every instance of a particular element, or very narrow and specific, affecting only a few elements or even just one. We'll cover some of the different kinds of selectors in the next section of this chapter.

A *declaration* comprises two more parts: a *property* and a *value*. The property is that aspect of an element's presentation that is changing, such as its color, its width, or its placement on the page. Dozens of properties are available in the CSS language, and you'll become familiar with many of them in the following chapters. The property's value delivers the specific style that should be applied to the selected element. The accepted values depend on the particular property, and some properties accept multiple values.

Declarations reside in a set of curly braces ({ and }), and multiple declarations can apply to the same selector, modifying several aspects of an element's presentation in the course of a single rule. A property and its value are separated by a colon (:) and the declaration ends with a semicolon (;). That semicolon is important to separate multiple declarations, but if there's only one declaration in the rule or if it's the last declaration in a series, the terminating semicolon is optional. It's not a bad idea to get in the habit of including a semicolon at the end of every declaration, even when there's only one, just to play it safe.

If your CSS doesn't conform to this basic structure and syntax—if you forget the closing brace or the colon separating a property from its value, for example—the entire rule or even the entire style sheet might fail. Just like HTML, a style sheet should be well formed and properly constructed. The W3C hosts a CSS validation service (`http://jigsaw.w3.org/css-validator/`, shown in Figure 2-3) that can help you catch goofs and glitches in your style sheets.

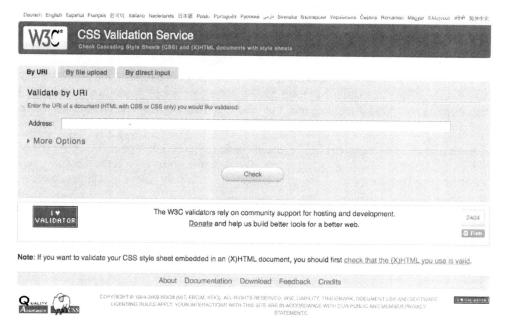

Figure 2-3. The W3C CSS Validation Service

CSS Selectors

A selector, as its name implies, selects an element in your HTML document. A number of different types of selectors are available, with varying levels of specificity to target a large number of elements or just a few. *Specificity* is a means of measuring a given selector's scope; in other words, how many or few elements it selects. CSS is designed so that more specific selectors override and supersede less specific selectors. Specificity is one of the more nebulous and hard-to-grasp concepts in CSS but it's also one of the most powerful features of the language. We'll cover the rules of specificity in more detail later, but first allow us to introduce some selectors.

Universal Selector

The *universal selector* is merely an asterisk (*) acting as a "wild card" to select any and all elements in the document. For example, this rule:

```
* { color: blue; }
```

would apply a blue foreground (text) color to all elements. Headings, paragraphs, lists, cells in tables, and even links—all would turn blue because the universal selector selects the entire universe. This is the least specific selector available, because it's not specific at all.

Element Selector

An *element selector* selects all instances of an element, specified by its tag name. This selector is more specific than the universal selector, but it's still not very specific because it targets every occurrence of an element, no matter how many of them there may be. For example, the rule:

```
em { color: red; }
```

gives every em element the same red foreground color, even if there are thousands of them in a document. Element selectors are also known as *type selectors*.

Class Selector

A *class selector* targets any element that bears the given class name in its class attribute. Because a class attribute can be assigned to practically any element in HTML, and any number of elements can belong to the same class, this selector is not terribly specific but is still more specific than an element selector. In CSS, class selectors are preceded by a dot (.) to distinguish them. For example, this rule will style any elements belonging to the "info" class, whatever those elements happen to be:

```
.info { color: purple; }
```

ID Selector

An *ID selector* will select only the element carrying the specified identifier. Practically any element can have an id attribute, but that attribute's value may be used only once within a single document. The ID selector targets just one element per page, making it much more specific than a class selector that might target many. ID selectors are preceded by an octothorpe (#). (This is often called a hash, number sign, or pound, but *octothorpe* is the character's proper name. It also sounds cool and will impress people at dinner parties.) The following rule would give the element with the ID "introduction" a green foreground color:

```
#introduction { color: green; }
```

Pseudo-class Selector

A *pseudo-class* is preceded by a colon (:) and is somewhat akin to a class selector (and is equal to classes in specificity), but it selects an element in a particular state. Some of the most common pseudo-classes relate to links:

```
:link { color: blue; }
:visited { color: purple; }
:hover { color: green; }
:focus { color: orange; }
:active { color: red; }
```

The :link pseudo-class selects all elements that are hyperlinks (which you'll learn much more about in Chapter 6). The :visited pseudo-class selects hyperlinks whose destination has been previously visited (recorded in a web browser's built-in history). The :hover pseudo-class selects any element that is being "hovered" over by a user's pointing device. Although any element can be in a hover state, this most commonly applies to links (and some older browsers supported this pseudo-class only for links and no other elements). The :focus pseudo-class selects any element in a focused state (including links), and the :active pseudo-class selects links in an active state, that interval when the link is being activated (while clicking a mouse or pressing the Enter or Return key).

Descendant Selector

One of the most useful and powerful selectors in the CSS arsenal, a *descendant selector* is assembled from two or more other selector types, separated by spaces, to select elements matching that particular context in the document (these are also called *contextual selectors*). An element nested within another element is called a *descendant*, and its containing element is its *ancestor*. We'll explain these terms in more depth in Chapter 3. But first, here's a style rule with a simple descendant selector:

```
.introduction em { color: yellow; }
```

That rule will select any em element that is itself within (descended from) any element with the class value "introduction" and apply a yellow text color. Descendant selectors allow for very precise selection of just the elements you want to target, based on the structure of your HTML document.

For a more elaborate example, the portion of HTML in Listing 2-1 shows an article element containing a section element that in turn contains a paragraph (the p element) that contains a link (the a element; you'll learn more about all of these elements in coming chapters).

Listing 2-1. Nested descendant elements

```
<article id="main">
  <section class="introduction">
    <p>Power Outfitters Superhero Costume and Supply Company is
    located in a nondescript building on Kirby Ave, a site that
    once housed a <a href="http://example.com/Sinnott_Inkworks">
    large printing plant</a>. Behind their modest storefront
    is an expansive warehouse positively packed to the portholes
    with paraphernalia.</p>
  </section>
</article>
```

A more complex descendant selector can target links in that very specific context:

```
#main .introduction p a { font-weight: bold; }
```

This would select all a elements that are descendants of a p element that is a descendant of any element with the class "introduction" that is a descendant of the element with the ID "main", and only those elements. Any links that don't exactly match this context wouldn't be affected by this CSS rule. You can see how the scope of a descendent selector can be very narrow indeed, targeting only a few elements that meet the selector's criteria.

Combining Selectors

You can combine two or more selector types, such as an element and an ID or an ID and a class. These combinations can also narrow down the specificity of your selectors, seeking out only the elements you want to style and leaving others alone. This rule:

```
p.info { color: cyan; }
```

selects only paragraphs (p elements) belonging to the "info" class. Another element in that class would be overlooked, and other paragraphs not belonging to the "info" class are also left untouched.

Combining selectors within a descendant selector can target elements with surgical precision:

```
p#introduction a.more-info:hover { color: silver; }
```

This rule would apply only to hovered links (a elements) belonging to the "info" class that are descendants of the paragraph with the ID "introduction." You'll rarely have to get this precise with your selectors but it's good to know the power is there if you need it.

Grouping Selectors

You can group several selectors together as part of a single rule so the same set of declarations can apply to numerous elements without redundantly repeating them. A comma separates each selector in the rule:

```
p, h1, h2 { color: maroon; }
```

The previous rule applies the same color value to every instance of the p, h1, and h2 elements. The more complex set of selectors in this rule:

```
p#introduction em, a.info:hover, h2.info { color: gold; }
```

will target all em elements descended from the paragraph with the ID "introduction" and all hovered links with the class "info" as well as h2 elements (a second-level heading) in the "info" class (remember that different types of elements can belong to the same class). Grouping and combining selectors is a great way to keep your style sheets compact and manageable.

Advanced Selectors

The selectors you've seen so far are all part of CSS level 1, the first standardized version of CSS introduced way back in 1996. A few more selectors were introduced in CSS level 2.1:

- *Attribute selectors* target an element bearing a particular attribute and even an attribute with a specified value.

- *Pseudo-element selectors* target elements that don't specifically exist in the document but are implied by its structure, such as the first line of a paragraph or the element immediately before another element.

- *Child selectors* select an element that is an immediate child of another element and not its other descendants.

- *Adjacent sibling selectors* target elements that are immediate siblings of another element, sharing the same parent in the document.

These CSS 2.1 selectors are well supported by the current generation of graphical browsers, a few stragglers notwithstanding. CSS 3 brings even more exciting and elaborate selectors to the table, including a bundle of new pseudo-classes and structural pseudo-elements. Browser support for some of the latest, cutting-edge selectors from CSS 3 isn't quite as far along, so such advanced features should be used with care and extensive cross-browser testing.

You'll get to see a few advanced selectors in action later in this book, but the basic selectors (universal, element, class, pseudo-class, ID, and descendant) will serve you well.

Specificity and the Cascade

As we mentioned earlier, each type of selector is assigned a certain level of *specificity*, measuring how many possible HTML elements that selector might influence. Examine these two CSS rules, one with an element selector and the other with a class selector:

```
h2 { color: red; }
.title { color: blue; }
```

and this snippet of HTML, an h2 element classified as a title:

```
<h2 class="title">Specificity and the Cascade</h2>
```

The first rule selects all h2 elements, and the second rule selects all elements belonging to the "title" class. But the element shown fits both criteria, causing a conflict between the two CSS rules. A browser must choose one of the two rules to follow before it can determine the heading's final color. In CSS, a more specific selector trumps a less specific selector. Because a class selector is more specific than an element selector, the second rule has greater specificity, and the heading is rendered in blue.

Modern web browsers follow a complex formula to calculate a selector's specificity, which can be rather confusing to noncomputers like us. Thankfully, you'll rarely need to calculate a selector's numeric specificity value if you just remember these few rules:

- A universal selector isn't specific at all.

- An element selector is more specific than a universal selector.

- A class or pseudo-class selector is more specific than an element selector.

- An ID selector is more specific than a class or pseudo-class.

- Properties in an inline style attribute are most specific of all.

Specificity is also cumulative in combined and descendant selectors. Each of the base selector types carries a different weight in terms of specificity—a selector with two classes is more specific than a selector with one class, a selector with one ID is more specific than a selector with two classes, and so on. The specificity algorithm is carefully designed so that a large number of less specific selectors won't outweigh a more specific selector. Even if you assembled a complex selector made up of hundreds of element selectors, another rule with just one ID selector could still override it. Understanding specificity will allow you to construct CSS rules that target elements with pinpoint accuracy.

> For a more in-depth explanation of how specificity is calculated by web browsers, see the W3C specification for CSS 2.1 (w3.org/TR/CSS21/cascade.html#specificity) along with Molly Holzschlag's more approachable clarification at molly.com/2005/10/06/css2-and-css21-specificity-clarified.

At this point you might be wondering what happens when two selectors target the same element and also have the same specificity. For example:

```
.info h2 { color: purple; }
h2.title { color: orange; }
```

If an h2 element belonging to the "title" class is a descendant of another element in the "info" class, both of these rules should apply to that h2. How can the browser decide which rule to obey? Enter the *cascade*, the C in CSS.

Assuming selectors of equal specificity, style declarations are applied in the order in which they are received, so later declarations override prior ones. This is true whether the declarations occur within the same rule, in a separate rule later in the same style sheet, or in a separate style sheet that is downloaded after a prior one. It's this aspect of CSS that gives the language its name: multiple style rules that cascade over each other, adding up to the final presentation in the browser. In the earlier example, the rendered h2 element would be orange because the second rule overrides the first.

For another example, the following rule:

```
p {
    color: black;
    color: green;
}
```

contains two declarations, but rendered paragraphs will be green because that declaration comes later in the cascade.

The sometimes-complex interplay between specificity and the cascade can make CSS challenging to work with in the beginning, but once you understand the basic rules, it all becomes second nature. You'll learn more about the cascade order in Chapter 3.

!important

In some extremely rare cases where both specificity and the cascade may not be sufficient to apply your desired value, the special keyword !important (complete with preceding exclamation point) can force a browser to honor that value above all others. This is a powerful and dangerous tool, and should be used only as a last resort to resolve conflicting styles beyond your control (for example, if you're forced to work with third-party markup that uses inline styles that you can't modify directly).

The !important directive must appear at the end of the value, before the semicolon, like so:

```
h1 { color: navy !important; }
```

A value declared as !important is applied to the rendered content regardless of where that value occurs in the cascade or the specificity of its selector. That is unless another competing value is also declared !important; specificity and the cascade once again take over in those cases. There's one notable exception to be aware of: users can create their own custom style sheets in their browsers to style websites to their preference, and !important values in a user style sheet always take precedence, even overriding !important values in author style sheets. This gives the ultimate power to the user, which is only right; after all, it's their computer.

Formatting CSS

Like HTML, CSS is a plain text language. You're free to format your CSS however you like, just as long as you follow the basic syntax. Extra spaces and carriage returns are ignored in CSS; the browser doesn't care what the plain text looks like, just that it's technically well formed. When it comes to formatting CSS, the most important factors are your own preferences. Individual rules can be written in two general formats: extended or compacted.

Extended rules break the selector and declarations onto separate lines, which many authors find more readable and easier to work with. It allows you to see at a glance where each new property begins and ends, at the expense of a lot of scrolling when you're working with long and complex style sheets. Listing 2-2 shows a few simple rules in an extended format.

Listing 2-2. CSS rules in extended format

```
h1, h2, h3 {
  color: red;
  margin-bottom: .5em;
}

h1 {
  font-size: 150%;
}

h2 {
  font-size: 130%;
}

h3 {
  font-size: 120%;
  border-bottom: 1px solid gray;
}
```

Compact formatting condenses each rule to a single line, thus shortening the vertical scrolling, but it can demand horizontal scrolling in your text editor when a rule includes many declarations in a row. Listing 2-3 demonstrates the same set of rules compacted to single lines and with unnecessary spaces removed.

Listing 2-3. CSS rules in compacted format

```
h1,h2,h3{color:teal;margin-bottom:.5em;}
h1{font-size:150%;}
h2{font-size:130%;}
h3{font-size:120%;border-bottom:1px solid gray;}
```

Another advantage of compacted rules is a slight reduction in file size. Spaces, tabs, and carriage returns are stored as characters in the electronic file, and each additional character adds another byte to the overall file size that must be downloaded by a client. A long style sheet might be a considerably larger file in an extended format because of all the extra space characters. In fact, you could choose to remove *all* excess spaces and place your entire style sheet on a single line for optimal compression, but that might be overkill and make your CSS much harder to work with. To reconcile maximum readability with minimal file size, some authors work with style sheets in an extended format and then automatically compress the entire thing to a single line when moving it to a live web server.

A few extra spaces in a compacted rule can at least make it easier to scan, spreading a one-line rule out a bit by including spaces between declarations and values. For lack of a better term, we'll call this format *semi-compacted*, as shown in Listing 2-4.

Listing 2-4 CSS rules in semi-compacted format

```
h1, h2, h3 { color: teal; margin-bottom: .5em; }
h1 { font-size: 150%; }
h2 { font-size: 130%; }
h3 { font-size: 120%; border-bottom: 1px solid gray; }
```

In the end, it's entirely up to you. Write your style sheets in a way that makes sense to you. If you collaborate with other web developers—as you almost surely will if you build websites professionally—authoring readable CSS will be beneficial to the entire team.

CSS Comments

You can add comments to your style sheets for the same reasons you might use comments in HTML: to make notes, to pass along instructions to other web developers, or to temporarily hide or disable parts of the style sheet during testing. A comment in CSS begins with /* and ends with */, and anything between those markers won't be interpreted by the browser. Just like comments in HTML, CSS comments can span multiple lines.

```
/* These base styles apply to all heading levels. */
h1, h2, h3, h4, h5, h6 { color: teal; margin-bottom: .5em; }

/* Adjust the size of each. */
h1 { font-size: 150%; }
h2 { font-size: 130%; }
h3 { font-size: 120%; }
```

```
/* Temporarily hiding these rules
h4 { font-size: 100%; }
h5 { font-size: 90%; }
h6 { font-size: 80%; }
End hiding */
```

Comment liberally. Unless you're strictly building personal websites for yourself, you should always strive to make your code (HTML and CSS both) easy to understand for other people who may wind up working with it. Comments can also be handy notes to yourself so when your revisit a style sheet a few months or years down the road, you can remember why you did things the way you did them.

Summary

This chapter has covered a lot of ground to get you up to speed on the inner workings of HTML and CSS. You've learned the basics of authoring HTML, using tags to define elements and adding attributes to relay more information about them. Throughout the rest of this book, you'll become intimately familiar with most of the elements you'll use when you create your own web pages.

The second part of this chapter gave you a crash course in CSS, unveiling the mechanics of this rich and powerful language. You learned about CSS selectors and how specificity and the cascade work together to give you great control over how your content is presented. You'll use HTML to build the structure that supports your content, and then use CSS to apply a separate layer of polished presentation. In the following chapters, you'll see glimpses of how you can use CSS in different ways to create different visual effects. Chapter 9 will delve a bit deeper to show you a few ways to use CSS to lay out your pages by placing elements where you want them to appear on-screen, all without damaging their underlying structure. Then in Chapter 10 you'll get to see some more of the bells and whistles CSS3 puts at your fingertips.

From here on, we'll assume you've reached an understanding of the basic rules of syntax for authoring your own HTML and CSS, and the rest of this book will dig into the real meat of markup. To get things rolling, Chapter 3 examines the document itself and how different elements relate to each other.

Onward, true believer!

Chapter 3

The Document

The Web is made of documents. Well, mostly. There's an awful lot of non-text content on the Web: millions of hours of video and audio, billions of photos and drawings, thousands of embeddable games and widgets that require plug-ins, and a vast array of APIs and services working behind the scenes to move information around the Web when it isn't in document form. But most of the time what you see and interact with—what you probably call a *web page*—is a rendered HTML document. It might exist as a single self-contained file on a web server, or it might be assembled on the server from separate pieces of code before it's sent to your web browser, and some or all of it might be generated by dynamic scripts right before your eyes... but it's still a document. When we refer to an HTML document we mean the entire collection of text and markup that a browser renders into a web page.

You can view the source HTML document underlying any web page you visit, usually by selecting an option in a contextual menu that appears if you right-click on the page, or from a View menu. Different browsers put the option in different places and give it different names—usually "View Source" or something similar—but every desktop browser has such a command. Viewing and studying the source code of live websites is one of the best ways to learn how they're put together. Just remember: a great many web pages still aren't built according to web standards and best practices, so quite often viewing the markup of a live website will serve as a better example of what *not* to do.

In this chapter you'll learn about the parts of an HTML document and how it forms the surrounding framework for the content of your web pages. The basic framework of a document is composed of just a few essential parts, with a few other optional parts that are less essential but no less useful. We'll cover each element one by one, explaining what it does, how to use it, what attributes it offers, and where the element fits into the document.

We'll be honest: some parts of this chapter will be pretty dry and technical, and if you're just starting out with HTML you may want to skip over some of the denser bits and move on to Chapter 4. Don't worry too much about things like metadata, character sets, media types, and JavaScript just yet if you're not quite ready for them. But it's important to understand the fundamentals of the documents you'll be working with from here on, so this is an important chapter to have near the beginning. You can always come back to this chapter later for a refresher; that's why pages turn both ways, after all (unless you're reading a digital edition, but scrollbars scroll both ways too).

The Anatomy of an HTML Document

An HTML document is put together from a few vital components: a *document type declaration* (or *doctype*), a *root element* that wraps around the entire document, a head element featuring a title and other information about the document, and a body element that holds all of the content. Listing 3-1 shows a simple document with all the pieces in place. If you've downloaded the source code that accompanies this book (you can get it from apress.com or from foundationhtml.com) you'll find this example document in the Chapter 3 folder, and this can serve as a starting point for all your documents to come.

Listing 3-1. A basic HTML document

```
<!DOCTYPE html>
<html>
  <head>
    <meta charset="utf-8">
    <title>Document Title</title>
  </head>
  <body>
    <p>This is a very simple web page.</p>
  </body>
</html>
```

Believe it or not, this relatively short block of code is a complete, valid, well-formed HTML document, authored in strict adherence to the rules of the HTML5 specification. That's not so difficult, is it? In fact, as minimal as it is, this example is even more verbose than strictly required. You could choose to omit some of the tags we've included, making the document even smaller while still complete and valid. We've included those optional tags in our examples, and we recommend including them in your own documents as well, if only to help you read your own markup as you work with it.

Next we'll dig a bit deeper to tell you what each of these component parts is all about, and introduce a few more optional parts you'll need further down the road.

The Doctype

The first essential piece of an HTML document is a *document type declaration*, or just *doctype* for short. This bit of code informs the user-agent what type of document it's dealing with, so it knows what to expect and can process the rest of the document accordingly. Though the doctype is contained in angle brackets (< and >), it isn't really a tag, it's an *instruction*—something like a special comment—and the ! at the beginning distinguishes it from any other code in the document.

The word "doctype" often appears in all uppercase letters but it isn't actually case sensitive; `<!doctype` is just as valid as `<!DOCTYPE`. The keyword "html" appears after the doctype opening, and is also case-insensitive (HTML is the same as `html`), but its case should match the case of the root element, which we'll cover next. This essentially tells the browser that the document it's reading has been authored in HTML and not some other markup language.

In past versions of HTML and XHTML, the doctype included additional information telling the browser that not only was the document an HTML or XHTML document, but which specific set of rules the document conformed to, like this doctype for HTML 4.01 Strict:

```
<!DOCTYPE html PUBLIC "-//W3C//DTD HTML 4.01//EN" "http://www.w3.org/TR/html4/strict.dtd">
```

The doctype has been greatly simplified for HTML5 with an eye toward the future; now just declaring that a document is HTML is sufficient. Browsers don't necessarily need to worry about which particular version of HTML it is, as long as it's HTML. However, if you happen to be working with a document authored in a specific older version, you should still declare that older version in your doctype. If your document relies on features or elements specific to the HTML 4.01 Frameset version, for instance, you should declare an HTML 4.01 Frameset doctype. If you're working with an XHTML document you'll need to declare an XHTML doctype. All the markup examples you'll see in this book conform to the rules of the HTML5 specification, at least as it stands as we write this in 2012; remember that the spec is still subject to change.

The HTML5 doctype is quite modest indeed:

```
<!DOCTYPE html>
```

This must be the very first line of text in an HTML document for it to be considered valid and well formed according to the HTML5 specification (only white space can appear before the doctype). Web browsers will usually still render a document even if the doctype is missing, but they'll render it in a very different way.

Doctype Switching and Rendering Modes

Some of the earliest browsers that supported CSS did so largely according to their own rules, rather than following the standardized specifications (in their defense, some of the early CSS specs were pretty vague to begin with). This inconsistency between browsers was a major stumbling block in the adoption of CSS and web standards in general. A page might render perfectly in one browser and appear completely broken in another.

As browsers improved their support for CSS—that is, moved toward an agreed standard for rendering web pages—they were faced with a dilemma. Many websites had already been designed with built-in dependencies on the inconsistent, inaccurate renderings of older browsers. Suddenly opting to follow the rules could cause millions of web pages to seem "broken" in the latest version of a web browser when they looked just fine the day before. The site didn't change overnight; only the browser's method of rendering it did. An oft-repeated mantra among browser vendors is "don't break the Web." As they implement new features or improve support for emerging standards, they must still maintain backwards compatibility with the content that already exists on the Web—even sites that were built poorly.

This dilemma inspired the introduction of the *doctype switch*. When a document includes a correct doctype, a modern browser will assume the entire document is well formed and authored according to web standards. The browser can then render the page in a mode intended to comply with the established standards for markup and CSS, a mode known as *compliance mode* or *strict mode*. If the doctype is missing, incomplete, or malformed, the browser will assume it's dealing with an outdated or badly made website and revert to a looser and more tolerant rendering mode, known as *quirks mode* because it's intended to adjust to the various quirks of nonstandard and improperly constructed markup (it's also sometimes called *compatibility mode*). Very old browsers lack a doctype switching mechanism and are forever locked in their outdated quirks modes.

To invoke standards compliance mode in modern web browsers, a complete doctype must be the very first line of text in a document; only white space is allowed to appear before it. Any unexpected text or code appearing before the doctype declaration will throw most modern browsers into quirks mode, with often-unpredictable results. Designing websites with CSS is considerably easier and the results are more consistent when you invoke compliance mode. Hence, including a correct doctype is essential. And because a doctype is already a required part of a valid document, modern browsers will always render your pages in compliance mode if you build your documents correctly.

> Peter-Paul Koch offers additional information and opinions on quirks mode at his appropriately named website, Quirks Mode (quirksmode.org/css/quirksmode.html). For a breakdown of just how browsers render documents differently in their quirks modes, check out Jukka Korpela's article "What Happens in Quirks Mode?" (www.cs.tut.fi/~jkorpela/quirks-mode.html).

The Root Element: html

After the doctype, the rest of the document is entirely contained in a single `html` element. This is also called the *root element* because it's the starting point for the *document tree*, and all other elements in the document branch off from the `html` element that contains them. The root element can only have one `head` and one `body` element as its direct children (both covered in this chapter) and every other element descends from one of those two. You can choose to omit the `html` element's start and end tags and the browser will simply generate them itself when it renders the document; the `html` element is always there because the doctype implies its existence.

However, it's still generally a good idea to include the root element's start and end tags in your markup, especially because the start tag can carry attributes. The `lang` and `dir` internationalization attributes are optional, but you should usually include them with the `html` element. The Web is a globe-spanning, borderless nation that speaks many languages—all of them, in fact. Declaring the *natural language* of your content can assist browsers in parsing and rendering it, especially if the browser and operating system are localized for a different language.

Listing 3-2 shows an HTML document with an `html` element that includes the `lang` and `dir` attributes, indicating that this page is written in American English (`lang="en-US"`) and should be read (and rendered) from left to right (`dir="ltr"`). These are *global attributes*, as we mentioned in Chapter 2, so they can appear on any element in HTML. Including them on the root `html` element declares the language and directionality for the entire document.

Listing 3-2. Internationalization attributes in a document's root element

```
<!DOCTYPE html>
<html lang="en-US" dir="ltr">
  <head>
    <meta charset="utf-8">
    <title>Document Title</title>
  </head>
  <body>
    <p>This is a very simple web page.</p>
  </body>
</html>
```

The `html` element can also carry an optional `manifest` attribute, the value of which is the URL of an *application cache manifest*. This file informs the browser about data resources that it can cache locally on the user's computer for later use when it isn't connected to the Internet. Offline application caching is one of the great new APIs introduced with HTML5 that, alas, we won't be covering in any detail in this book. You can find a brief introduction to the ApplicationCache API at HTML5 Rocks (`html5rocks.com/en/tutorials/appcache/beginner/`) and you can read all the gritty details in the W3C specification (`w3.org/TR/html5/offline.html`).

Required Attributes

The `html` element doesn't require any attributes.

Optional Attributes

- `manifest`: the URL of an application cache manifest. This attribute's value must be a valid URL, either relative or absolute, though absolute URLs must be within the same domain as the current document.

head

The head element acts as a container for other elements that provide information about the document itself, collectively known as the document's *header*. This *metadata* informs the browser about where to find external scripts or style sheets, or embeds such scripts and style sheets directly in the document, establishes relationships between the current document and other resources, and can provide additional data that's useful for user-agents but isn't intended for human visitors. Apart from the required `title` element, covered next in this chapter, browsers don't display any of the metadata content within the head at all; the header isn't part of the rendered web page.

The head element must be the first child of the `html` element; no other content or elements can appear before it. However, like the `html` element, you can opt to omit the head element's start and end tags and the element is still implied to exist. If you do omit the head element, any of the metadata content that would ordinarily occur inside it must still come before any body content.

Some of the metadata elements we'll be covering in this chapter can't appear anywhere else in a document except within the head element. That's one more good reason to include the element: it makes it very clear where the header ends and your other content begins. You'll see a few more examples of the head element in this chapter as we detail the metadata elements it contains.

Required Attributes

The head element doesn't require any attributes.

Optional Attributes

The head element doesn't have any optional attributes.

> *Previous versions of HTML and XHTML had an optional profile attribute for the head element, and its value was one or more URLs pointing to additional metadata profile definitions that extend the metadata already inherent in HTML. The profile attribute is obsolete in HTML5, and metadata profiles can be extended by the meta and link elements instead (both covered in this chapter).*

title

The title element provides a text title for the document. It appears as a child of the head element, and there can be only one title per document. It's also a required element; every HTML document must have exactly one title element.

Browsers display the contents of the title element in the browser window's title bar, and the page's tab in browsers that offer tabbed browsing (like Safari does in Figure 3-1). The title also acts as the default page name when a visitor bookmarks the page or saves it as a favorite, so it should describe the page even when read out of context.

This is a very simple web page.

Figure 3-1. Browsers display the contents of a title element in tabs and title bars

Perhaps most significantly, the contents of a `title` element will appear in search engine results as the default title for the page. A title should stand on its own in a different context, where people will read the title before seeing the page it introduces. Good titles help people find the content they want. Think about your titles and write them for people, not for search engines.

A title should be short, simple, easily understood, and descriptive of the page it labels:

```
<title>About The Company</title>
```

To make it stand alone better in different contexts, you can include the website's name in addition to the title of the single page:

```
<title>Power Outfitters Superhero Costume and Supply Co. - About Us</title>
```

Or, to be a bit more readable and put the most relevant information up front, include the single page title before the site name:

```
<title>About Us - Power Outfitters Superhero Costume and Supply Co.</title>
```

If your website is organized in a multi-level hierarchy, as many sites are, the `title` element can reflect that structure to help orient your visitors:

```
<title>Model MDTS40 / Domino Masks / Masks and Cowls / Power Outfitters</title>
```

If the main feature of your particular web page is a self-contained article or a blog post, the `title` element should carry the title or headline of the article:

```
<title>Earth Nations Join Forces to Resist Invaders from Space! | Daily Globe</title>
```

The `title` element can only appear as a child of the `head` element and nowhere else, and it can only contain text; no other elements are allowed within a `title`. This element belongs to the metadata content model (as most of these header elements do) and always requires both a start tag and an end tag.

Required Attributes

There aren't any required attributes for the `title` element.

Optional Attributes

The `title` element doesn't offer any optional attributes.

meta

The term *metadata* is often defined as "data about data." The HTML `meta` element carries information about the document itself, such as who created it, when it was published, or what software generated it. A `meta` element can also give special instructions to user-agents and web servers for how to handle the document, such as what set of characters to use for rendering the text, or how long the page should be stored in a browser's cache. It's a void element that holds no contents and has no end tag, but you can close it with a trailing slash (`/>`) if you prefer XHTML syntax. This element isn't rendered on the page itself and isn't seen by users at all (unless they view the source HTML, of course).

The `meta` element is multipurpose and can carry several kinds of data, depending on which attributes are present:

- With a name attribute, the `meta` element represents *document-level metadata* that applies to the entire document.

- With an `http-equiv` attribute, the element represents a *pragma directive*, which is information sent to the web server about how the document should be served.

- With a `charset` attribute, the element declares the character set used for rendering the page.

> HTML5 also introduces the `itemprop` attribute that combines with other attributes to allow web authors to include user-defined metadata in their documents. This microdata is very bleeding edge at the time we write this, and hasn't yet been fully defined or implemented, so we won't be covering it in this book, but there's some great potential for microdata in the near future as the standard takes shape. If you're curious, you can read more at whatwg.org/specs/web-apps/current-work/multipage/microdata.html

The `charset` attribute is new in HTML5 and turns a `meta` element into a *character set declaration* for the document, instructing browsers about how the document is encoded and what characters it should use to render the text. A *character encoding system* is the code computers use to draw letters and symbols, so declaring your document's character set will inform the browser about what characters it should call upon to display your text accurately. Declaring the wrong character set might cause incorrect rendering or missing symbols if the text requires a character that isn't part of the declared set. The de-facto standard character set for web pages is UTF-8—short for *UCS Transformation Format, 8-bit*—and you'll rarely need to use anything else:

```
<meta charset="utf-8">
```

Technically, declaring your document's character set in the header is optional. Web servers usually send character encoding information when they send the document to the browser, so if you include your own `meta charset` declaration in your page's header, make sure the character set you declare is the same as the server's. You can override the character set declared in the header for individual elements on the page using the `lang` attribute, handy if you need to include special characters from other languages that might not be part of the UTF-8 standard set (though UTF-8 includes thousands of characters).

Apart from the `charset` attribute, `meta` elements usually provide their metadata in the form of a name-value pair where a name or `http-equiv` attribute provides the name or category of the data and the content attribute provides the value:

```
<meta name="author" content="Craig Cook">
<meta name="title" content="Foundation HTML5 with CSS3 - Chapter 3: The Document">
<meta http-equiv="date" content="Thu, 15 Dec 2011 09:19:41 UTC">
<meta http-equiv="last-modified" content="Tue, 17 Apr 2012 22:34:13 UTC">
```

The `http-equiv` attribute lets a `meta` element act as an equivalent to an *HTTP response header*, settings typically sent directly to the browser by the web server. You may not always have the option of modifying server-side configurations to change these, so a `meta` element with `http-equiv` can step in.

Older versions of HTML didn't offer the `charset` attribute, instead relying on the `http-equiv` attribute with a value of `content-type` to declare a document's character set along with the content type, like so:

```
<meta http-equiv="content-type" content="text/html;charset=UTF-8">
```

This has been supplanted by the `charset` attribute in HTML5 so it's no longer necessary to declare character sets using an `http-equiv` attribute. However, some older browsers don't recognize the shortened `charset` declaration from HTML5 and so may fall back to a default character encoding, ignoring the `meta` element entirely. If you need to cater to older browsers that may otherwise have trouble rendering special characters, you should still declare your character set with `http-equiv`. You can use both methods together—`charset` for modern browsers and `http-equiv` for older browsers—just be sure to declare the same character set both times.

The `http-equiv` attribute only accepts a handful of predefined values, whereas the name attribute is more extensible and can hold almost any value you like (whether any browsers will understand or use your made up name value is another matter). You can learn more about `http-equiv` and its accepted values from Sitepoint's HTML reference (`http://reference.sitepoint.com/html/meta/http-equiv`).

Metadata for Search Engines

Web search engines like Google, Yahoo!, and Bing employ programs that endlessly crawl the Web, reading documents and following links, cataloging the immense variety of web content in order to help people find what they're looking for amidst the vast sea of information. These programs—affectionately called "robots," "spiders," or "crawlers"—are simple user-agents that parse HTML, and `meta` elements can give the robots additional information or special instructions.

If, for some reason, you'd rather not have your web page indexed by search engine robots, you can ask them politely not to index it and not to follow any outbound links from your page:

```
<meta name="robots" content="noindex, nofollow">
```

Or, as you'll more likely desire, you can ask the robots to please index the page and follow all its links (they'll probably do so even without this `meta` element, but some added encouragement doesn't hurt):

```
<meta name="robots" content="index, follow">
```

You can also include other metadata useful to search engines, such as offering a set of related keywords and a descriptive summary of the page:

```
<meta name="keywords" content="capes, masks, tights, superhero, costumes, gadgets">
<meta name="description" content="Power Outfitters manufactures and sells costumes,↪
accessories, supplies, and equipment for the contemporary costumed crime-fighter">
```

But beware: you're now heading into the murky waters of Search Engine Optimization (SEO), and there's plenty of conflicting and downright harmful advice out there about best practices. Early search engines paid a lot of attention to keywords in a `meta` element, so some unscrupulous characters would "game the system" by loading their `meta` elements with dozens (or even hundreds) of keywords that weren't relevant to the page's content but would cause that page to appear in results for searches on unrelated topics, all in an effort to lure visitors under false pretenses. This practice of "keyword stuffing" soon became so widespread and destructive—a search engine isn't effective when the results aren't what people are actually searching for—that search engines now largely ignore keywords in meta elements, and keywords have no impact on where a page will rank in the search results for a given term.

Even so, meta keywords may still be marginally beneficial to search engines and searchers. If you're going to include keywords in a meta element, keep the list reasonably short and make sure the terms are actually relevant to the contents of the page. You can also get along just fine without meta keywords at all; the search engines will still find you.

Including a meta description is much more useful than keywords because it will often appear in search engine results alongside the page title and URL. The description should be a very brief summary of the page's contents, or the introduction to an article, if that's the main content of the page. A site's home page might bear a description of the entire website whereas individual pages within the site should have more specific descriptions for each individual page.

Search engines exist to help people find content, so the very best advice is simply to provide content people will want to find. Good metadata can help nudge the search engine robots in the right direction, but it's the readable content of your page that really matters. Build your web pages for humans, not for robots.

Attributes

The meta element typically requires a content attribute in combination with either a name or http-equiv attribute. An exception is the charset attribute, which doesn't require the presence of a content attribute.

- charset: The document's character encoding set, usually UTF-8 unless you specifically need an alternative encoding (which usually depends on your content's natural language).

- content: The metadata value, paired with either a name or http-equiv attribute.

- http-equiv: A pragma directive, equivalent to an HTTP header typically passed to the browser from the server. This attribute specifies the particular metadata declared while the content attribute specifies the value.

- name: Arbitrary document-level metadata applying to the entire document, or special instructions for user-agents. This attribute specifies the particular metadata declared while the content attribute specifies the value.

link

The link element associates the current document with an external resource. The required rel attribute indicates the relationship between the current document and the linked resource, and the required href attribute carries the linked resource's URL. This is a void element with no text content and no end tag, and it can only appear within the head element.

The link element's most common duty is to connect a web page to an external style sheet, but it can also connect the document to alternative versions, specify an alternate URL for the page, associate the page with an icon that browsers can display in bookmarks and the address field, and more.

This element requires a rel attribute, with its value being a space-separated list of predefined keywords that indicate the relationship between the current document and the linked resource, thus also indicating what type of link the element represents. Some of the most common values for the `rel` attribute are `stylesheet` (for cascading style sheets), `alternate` (for alternative formats/versions of the document), and `icon` (for a shortcut icon to associate with the web page). The `link` element also requires an `href` attribute (short for *hypertext reference*; you'll see much more of this one in Chapter 6) to carry the URL of the linked resource.

Listing 3-3 shows two different `link` elements: one linking to a style sheet and one linking to a shortcut icon (commonly known as a "favicon").

Listing 3-3. Two `link` elements relating the document to two different external resources

```
<!DOCTYPE html>
<html lang="en-US" dir="ltr">
  <head>
    <meta charset="utf-8">
    <title>Power Outfitters Superhero Costume and Supply Co.</title>
    <link rel="stylesheet" type="text/css" href="/css/styles.css">
    <link rel="icon" type="image/ico" href="/favicon.ico">
  </head>
  <body>
    <h1>Welcome, Heroes!</h1>
    <p>Power Outfitters offers top of the line merchandise at
    rock-bottom prices for the discerning costumed crime-fighter.</p>
  </body>
</html>
```

There's no limit to the number of `link` elements you can include in a document's header. You can, for example, link to different style sheets for different media or to offer alternate styles, or multiple icons in different sizes, or link to multiple versions of your page in different languages.

Media Type (The type Attribute)

The `link` element's optional `type` attribute indicates the *Internet media type* of the linked resource. This is also called the *content type* or *MIME type* (MIME stands for Multipurpose Internet Mail Extensions; these media types were originally defined for use in e-mail but were later adopted for other Internet applications, including the Web).

Different types of files are served and handled in different ways. Text files are very different from image files, and both are different from video files or application files. The Internet media type is a two-part identifier consisting of a type and a subtype, separated by a slash, that indicates what type of file the browser is dealing with so it can process the data accordingly.

The media type for CSS files is `text/css`, indicating that the style sheet is a text file written in the CSS language, and that's the `type` value you're most likely to encounter in a `link` element. Other media files have their own content types, such as `text/html` for HTML documents, `text/javascript` for JavaScript files, `image/jpeg` for JPEG graphics, and `audio/mpeg` for MP3 audio files. The `type` attribute can appear on other elements besides `link`, and you'll see content types again in Chapter 5 when we cover embedding audio and video, but all in due time.

> You can browse the complete list of current Internet media types at *iana.org/assignments/media-types/* or refer to a shorter list of some of the most common ones at *wikipedia.org/wiki/Internet_media_type*

You don't always need to declare the content type for every resource. That information is typically sent automatically by the web server, or may even be embedded in the file itself. However, some types of files may not be recognized automatically by every browser, and including the content type in a type attribute can let the browser know what kind of data it can expect.

Although the type attribute's value is an "Internet media type," you might prefer (as we do) to use the term *content type* to avoid confusion—the term *media type* refers to something else entirely in CSS.

The Other Media Type (The media Attribute)

When the link element links to a style sheet, the optional media attribute can indicate the medium for which that style sheet is intended. This means you can easily tailor your site's layout and design for different media. For example, you could provide two separate style sheets, one for display on computer screens and another for use when the page is printed:

```
<link rel="stylesheet" href="/css/screen-styles.css" media="screen">
<link rel="stylesheet" href="/css/print-styles.css" media="print">
```

You can also include multiple media types in a single media attribute, separated by commas:

```
<link rel="stylesheet" href="/css/screen-styles.css" media="screen,projection,tv">
```

There are only a handful of media types you can use as the value of a media attribute:

- all: suitable for all devices and media (this is the default, assumed if the media attribute is absent).

- braille: for Braille tactile feedback devices, such as refreshable Braille displays that output text by mechanically raising small dots through holes in a flat surface.

- embossed: for Braille printers that emboss Braille text into paper.

- handheld: for handheld devices, typically with small screens, low resolution, and limited bandwidth. The newer classes of smartphones and tablets still have small screens, but also feature full-color displays of a higher resolution than the mobile phones and PDAs from just a few years ago. Many modern mobile devices have much more sophisticated web browsers than their predecessors, and are perfectly capable of displaying style sheets otherwise intended for desktop screens, so they'll honor the screen media type and often ignore handheld style sheets.

- print: for paged, printed material as well as documents viewed on screen in "print preview" mode.

- projection: for projected presentations.

- screen: primarily for color computer screens, like you find with desktop and laptop computers.

- `speech`: for speech synthesizers such as those in screen reading software for the visually impaired.

- `tty`: for media using a fixed-pitch character grid that outputs text one character at a time, such as teletypes (especially teleprinters used by the deaf) or old-fashioned computer terminals.

- `tv`: for televisions or television-type devices such as some touch-screen kiosks (low resolution, color, limited-scrollability screens).

Past versions of HTML and XHTML only accepted these values in a `link` element's `media` attribute, but in HTML5 the value can also be a comma-separated list of *media queries*. A media query consists of a media type and one or more expressions about the media features, such as screen width, height, resolution, or aspect ratio. This lets you link to different style sheets not only for different types of media, but also for different characteristics of the browser or device. For example, you can offer different layouts optimized for different screen widths simply by linking two separate style sheets with different media queries:

```
<link rel="stylesheet" href="wide.css" media="screen and (min-device-width: 600px)">
<link rel="stylesheet" href="narrow.css" media="screen and (max-device-width: 600px)">
```

Older browsers don't recognize or support these media queries in a `media` attribute, so if you use them in your document you should also provide a separate `link` element with a simple media type keyword as a fallback.

> *Media queries are a concept introduced in CSS3. They extend the functionality of media types and allow web developers to programmatically check for certain device or media properties, delivering different content or style rules to meet different criteria. You'll learn a bit more about media queries later on in this book, and you can also read up on them in the CSS specification (w3.org/TR/css3-mediaqueries).*

Required Attributes

- `rel`: indicates the relationship between the current document and the linked resource. This attribute's value is a space-separated list of a few predefined keywords. You can find the full list of accepted link type values at w3.org/TR/html5/links.html#linkTypes.

- `href`: the URL of the linked resource, which may be either a relative or absolute URL.

Optional Attributes

- `title`: this attribute, when combined with `rel="stylesheet alternate"`, indicates that the linked style sheet is an alternative style, and may not apply to the document unless selected by the user. This differs slightly from the global `title` attribute, as `title` has special semantics when it appears with a `link` element and `rel="stylesheet alternate"`.

- `type`: the content type of the linked resource. This attribute's value must be a valid Internet media type (also known as the content type or MIME type).

- media: the media for which the linked resource is intended. This attribute's value must be a valid media type or media query.

- hreflang: the natural (human) language of the linked resource, such as English, German, or Hindi, indicated by an abbreviated language code. This is similar to the global lang attribute, and is most important when the link's destination is in a language different from that of the current document.

- sizes: gives the sizes of icons for visual media. The attribute's value is a set of space-separated sizes, each in the format [width]x[height], for example: sizes="16x16 32x32". See w3.org/TR/html5/links.html#attr-link-sizes for more information. This attribute should only appear when the rel attribute has a value of icon.

base

The base element allows you to specify the *base URL* to be used for resolving any relative URLs within a document, or to specify a default target window where links in the document will open. This is an empty element that can only appear in a document's head, and there can be only one base element in a single document. It requires either an href attribute or a target attribute, though it can have both.

Base URL

When the base element has an href attribute, that attribute's value acts as the base URL for the entire document. Any relative URLs in the document following the base element will have the base URL prepended to them.

The value of the href attribute must be a valid URL, but it can be either absolute or relative. For example, if your page has been moved into a different subdirectory on the server but all of its relative URLs should still point to the original parent directory, you could use a base element with a relative URL in its href:

```
<base href="/products/">
```

Any subsequent relative URLs that are *relative to the current document*—meaning they don't begin with a leading slash (/) or up-level directive (../)—will be prepended with the relative base URL. Thus a URL written in the document as utility-belts.html would behave in the browser as if it were /products/utility-belts.html. This can be useful if your page has been moved from its original location or if your server isn't properly configured to handle relative URLs.

A base element with an absolute URL might look like:

```
<base href="http://power-outfitters.com">
```

Any relative URLs throughout the document (still limited to those relative to the current document, not those relative to the site root or to a higher directory) would then use that URL as their base and would point to the power-outfitters.com domain, even if the document itself is hosted somewhere else.

But this doesn't apply only to hyperlinks; **all** locally relative URLs throughout the document will use this URL as their base. That includes any link or script elements in the header (if they appear after the base element), images and other embedded media, inline frames with src attributes, forms with action attributes, and so on. The base element effectively rewrites every document-relative URL that follows it.

Base target

If the base element has a target attribute, the attribute's value is a name or keyword indicating the default location (a window, tab, or inline frame) where results are displayed when hyperlinks or forms in the document cause navigation. If the target is the name of a window or frame, any links in the document will display their results within that named window or frame. If the target name doesn't match any existing browsing context—if no window or frame exists by that name—links and forms will load their results in a new window instead.

In place of a target name, some reserved keywords (complete with their leading underscores) have special meanings:

- self: Loads the result into the same browsing context as the current one. This is the default if the target attribute isn't specified, or if the base element is missing altogether. In other words, this is how links and forms behave normally.

- blank: Loads the result into a new, unnamed browsing context (a new browser window or tab).

- parent: Loads the result into the parent browsing context of the current one. If there is no parent, this option behaves in the same manner as _self.

- top: Loads the result into the top-level browsing context, which is the window or inline frame that is an ancestor of the current one but has no parent of its own. If there is no parent, this option behaves in the same manner as _self.

You could, for example, declare that every link in your document should open in a new, blank window (or tab, if the browser is set to open tabs instead of windows):

```
<base target="_blank">
```

But that could be downright abusive to your visitors and there aren't many cases where it would be useful or justified. A more practical use case might be in a page intended for display within an inline frame (the iframe element is covered in Chapter 4) where any links within that document should open in the parent window rather than inside the frame:

```
<base target="_top">
```

Optional Attributes

The base element doesn't offer any other optional attributes apart from the global attributes that apply to all elements.

style

The style element contains style information applicable to the current document. In HTML, this is almost always written in CSS. Other style languages could be used for other types of structured documents, but in HTML—and as far as we're concerned for this book—CSS is the only style language that matters.

The optional type attribute indicates the content type of the enclosed style data, which is text/css for CSS, and browsers will assume that content type if the type attribute is omitted. The entire contents of the style element are hence written in the CSS language; the style element can't contain any HTML, so no nested elements are allowed and comments inside a style element must be CSS comments, not HTML comments.

Listing 3-4 shows an example of a simple style sheet enclosed in a style element.

Listing 3-4. CSS rules embedded in a style element

```
<!DOCTYPE html>
<html>
  <head>
    <meta charset="utf-8">
    <title>Power Outfitters Superhero Costume and Supply Co.</title>
    <style type="text/css">
      body { background-color: ivory; color: navy; }
      h1 { font-size: 1.6em; color: crimson; }
    </style>
  </head>
  <body>
    <h1>Welcome, Heroes!</h1>
    <p>Power Outfitters offers top of the line merchandise at
    rock-bottom prices for the discerning costumed crime-fighter.</p>
  </body>
</html>
```

Because this style information is included as part of the HTML document, it's known as an *embedded style sheet*, or sometimes an *internal style sheet*. Style sheets embedded in style elements are most useful for one-off, standalone web pages where those style rules don't need to be shared by any other documents. Otherwise, for websites consisting of numerous pages that should share common styles, it's much more practical to link to a separate external style sheet by way of a link element.

A single document can have any number of style elements, and like the link element, an optional media attribute can indicate the specific media for which those styles are intended. Also like the link element, the style element's media attribute can carry a media query, though older browsers may not support it. When the media attribute is absent, the browser will use the enclosed styles for all media by default (the same as including media="all").

The scoped Attribute

Ordinarily, a style element can only appear within the head element, and placing a style element anywhere else in the document isn't valid. But that could change in HTML5 with the introduction of the scoped attribute. This Boolean attribute, when present, allows a style element to appear outside the head, anywhere in the document's body element, and the enclosed CSS rules will apply only to the style element's immediate parent element and its contents.

Limiting the scope of a style element allows you to embed a set of style rules for just one section of a page. Or that's how it may work soon, at least—no browsers have yet implemented support for the scoped attribute at the time we write this.

There are some major problems with the scoped attribute even beyond the current lack of browser support. For one thing, it mixes presentation with structure, injecting CSS rules into the markup of a page where they arguably don't belong. But moreover, most browsers currently tolerate style elements in the body (invalid though it is) and will try to apply those style rules to the entire document, just as if it were in the header. Browsers that don't understand the scoped attribute (which is to say every web browser ever made to date) won't narrow the scope of the embedded rules and will still apply those styles to every matching element on the page, defeating the purpose of using a scoped style element in the first place. If or when the next generation of web browsers support scoped style elements, the scoped attribute still breaks backward compatibility with current and older browsers.

The HTML5 specification is a work in progress, and there's a chance the scoped attribute will be removed by the time you read this. Even if it survives in the spec, and even if browsers begin to support it, you're probably better off finding another way to style your elements. Simply adding a class attribute to some container element and using that class as a "hook" for more specific style rules in your external or embedded style sheet is a tried and true, completely failsafe approach. Don't use scoped unless you know very well what you're in for.

Required Attributes

The style element doesn't require any attributes. The type attribute was required in some previous strict versions of HTML and XHTML, but that requirement is lifted in HTML5 (browsers assume the content type is text/css unless told otherwise).

Optional Attributes

- media: the media for which the embedded style information is intended. This attribute's value must be a valid media type or media query.

- scoped: a Boolean attribute that, when present, applies the embedded style rules only to the parent element and its other descendants, not to the rest of the document. This attribute is new in HTML5 and isn't currently implemented in any browsers as of this writing. Even if it's implemented in the future, older browsers won't support it and may still apply the embedded styles to the entire document. This lack of current support and lack of backwards compatibility makes the scoped attribute impractical for the moment, and probably for the foreseeable future.

- title: this attribute, when present, indicates that the embedded style information is an alternative style sheet, and may not apply to the document unless selected by the user. This differs slightly from the global title attribute, as title has special semantics when it appears with a style element.

- `type`: the content type of the embedded style information. This attribute's value must be a valid Internet media type (also known as the content type or MIME type). It will almost always be `text/css` in HTML and XHTML documents, and web browsers will assume that content type if the attribute is omitted.

script

The `script` element encloses a series of instructions written in a scripting language, or it may link to an external script file specified by a URL in a `src` attribute. These scripts—almost always written in the JavaScript language—are processed and executed by the browser to perform a wide range of tasks, from fairly simple calculations to extremely complicated interactions and animated effects. The `script` element requires an end tag and cannot contain any HTML; the entire contents of a `script` element should be written in the particular scripting language.

An optional `type` attribute indicates the content type of the enclosed script, which is `text/javascript` for scripts written in JavaScript. There may be other scripting languages, such as Microsoft's proprietary VBScript, but they're rather obscure and rarely seen (VBScript is only supported by Internet Explorer). JavaScript is far and away the most ubiquitous scripting language on the Web, and browsers will assume a content type of `text/javascript` if the `type` attribute is omitted from a `script` element.

JAVASCRIPT

JavaScript is a scripting language. Unlike a full-fledged programming language that can execute all of its own commands, a scripting language only passes instructions to another program to execute. In the case of JavaScript, the program that does the real work is the web browser.

With JavaScript, web developers can dynamically manipulate HTML documents, creating, destroying, moving, and modifying elements and content on the fly as it lives in the browser. JavaScript can also facilitate communication between the browser and server, setting and reading cookies, or fetching new data from the server without reloading the page. It's a powerful and complex language in its own right, and is a subject for other, more advanced books than this one. We won't be delving into JavaScript in any detail in these pages.

Even so, JavaScript rarely exists independent of HTML, and indeed a great deal of what JavaScript does is manipulate the same markup and CSS you'll be seeing throughout this book. Scripting adds a progressive layer of behavior and interactivity on top of the underlying layers of content, structure, and presentation.

JavaScript should not be confused with the Java programming language—though the names are similar, Java and JavaScript have almost nothing in common.

Listing 3-5 shows a short bit of JavaScript embedded in a document's header. This script simply generates an alert dialog as soon as the page loads; not very useful, but it serves as an adequate demonstration.

Listing 3-5. A simple script embedded in a `script` element

```
<!DOCTYPE html>
<html>
  <head>
    <meta charset="utf-8">
    <title>Power Outfitters Superhero Costume and Supply Co.</title>
    <script>
      window.onload = function() {
        alert("Excelsior!");
      }
    </script>
  </head>
  <body>
    <h1>Welcome, Heroes!</h1>
    <p>Power Outfitters offers top of the line merchandise at
    rock-bottom prices for the discerning costumed crime-fighter.</p>
  </body>
</html>
```

Somewhat akin to the `style` element, a `script` element can embed scripts directly into the document for use within that document alone. But the `script` element can also attach an external script by way of the optional `src` attribute (short for "source"), the value of which is the URL where the external script can be found, usually with a `.js` file extension for JavaScript files.

Listing 3-6 shows a `script` element with a `src` attribute pointing to an external file. This allows any number of pages to share the same resources without writing the same scripts over and over for each page. It can also help pages load faster because the external files are cached after the first time they're downloaded, held in the browser's temporary memory for use on subsequent pages.

Listing 3-6. Linking to an external script file

```
<!DOCTYPE html>
<html>
  <head>
    <meta charset="utf-8">
    <title>Power Outfitters Superhero Costume and Supply Co.</title>
    <script src="/scripts/excelsior.js"></script>
  </head>
  <body>
    <h1>Welcome, Heroes!</h1>
    <p>Power Outfitters offers top of the line merchandise at
    rock-bottom prices for the discerning costumed crime-fighter.</p>
  </body>
</html>
```

When the `src` attribute is present the `script` element must be empty (it can still contain whitespace or comments, but no script statements). This means you can't use the same script element to both embed a script in the document and link to an external file. If you do, most browsers will only run the external script and will ignore the embedded contents of the element. Also note that even when linking to an external script, the `script` element still requires a closing `</script>` tag; it's not a void element even when it's empty, so it always needs an end tag.

The `script` element often appears in a document's head element, but it can also appear within the document's body. It's not uncommon to find scripts embedded or attached at the very end of a document so they load and execute last, after the rest of the page has been parsed. Scripts that must execute before the page fully loads—especially those that generate HTML for parts of the page itself—should still appear in the header so browsers can execute them at the correct time.

There's no specified limit to the number of `script` elements that can appear within a single document, either in the head or the body. However, browsers may have their own internal limitations if you try to link to a huge number of external scripts, so it's best to keep the number of `script` elements to a sensible minimum. There can also be serious performance issues when scripts become too numerous or complex, and it's possible that commands and functions written into those separate scripts can conflict with each other if you're not careful.

Required Attributes

There are no required attributes for the `script` element.

Optional Attributes

- `async`: a Boolean attribute that, when present, suggests that browsers should execute the script asynchronously, as soon as it is available. Only valid in combination with a `src` attribute (embedded scripts are always processed as the browser reads them). The `async` attribute is new in HTML5 so older browsers—and some current browsers—don't support it.

- `charset`: defines the character encoding of an external script. This is only valid in combination with a `src` attribute (embedded scripts automatically inherit the character encoding of the HTML document).

- `defer`: a Boolean attribute that, when present, suggests that browsers should defer execution of the external script until the page has finished loading. This is only valid in combination with a `src` attribute (embedded scripts are processed as the browser reads them).

- `src`: specifies the URL (either relative or absolute) of an external script file.

- `type`: indicates the content type of the external or embedded script, almost always `text/javascript`.

> *Past versions of HTML included a `language` attribute for the `script` element, to indicate the scripting language within and even the specific version of that language. The `language` attribute has long been deprecated in favor of the `type` attribute and it's completely obsolete in HTML5.*

body

The body element acts as a container for all of the page's contents, and that's pretty much all it does. Everything that's displayed by the browser and seen by the user is wrapped in a single body element (and only one body element is allowed per document). Its primary purpose is to separate regular content from the metadata in the head element.

As with the head element, you can omit the start and end tags for the body element in some cases and the element is still implied to exist. The browser will generate a body element even if the tags are missing, but you can avoid potential problems by including the start and end tags yourself, just to be safe and keep things tidy. Any content that appears outside the body element—actual or implied—could make the document invalid, and that content might not be displayed.

There aren't any required attributes for the body element, nor any special optional attributes, but it can carry the usual global attributes that apply to almost every other element. It can be especially useful to add an id or class attribute to identify the specific page, or classify general types of pages. Listing 3-7 shows a body element with the ID "home" and the class "landing", indicating that this is a landing-type page and that it's the home page, specifically.

Listing 3-7. The body element, identified and classified

```
<!DOCTYPE html>
<html>
  <head>
    <meta charset="utf-8">
    <title>Power Outfitters Superhero Costume and Supply Co.</title>
  </head>
  <body id="home" class="landing">
    <h1>Welcome, Heroes!</h1>
    <p>Power Outfitters offers top of the line merchandise at
    rock-bottom prices for the discerning costumed crime-fighter.</p>
  </body>
</html>
```

With these attributes in place on the body element, they can act as handy "hooks" from which to hang CSS rules, differentiating common types of pages or specific, unique pages. Listing 3-8 shows a few style rules for level one headings, the h1 element. The first rule applies to all h1 elements, the second to h1 elements on landing pages (any pages with the "landing" class), and the third is specific to h1 elements on the home page (with the ID "home"). Because every element on the page descends from the body element, these rules with their descendant selectors will be in effect no matter where the h1 might occur in the document or what other elements might surround it—unless they're overridden by another style rule, of course.

Listing 3-8. Using body attributes as style hooks in descendant selectors

```
h1 {
  font-size: 20px;
}

.landing h1 {
  font-size: 26px;
```

```
}
#home h1 {
  font-size: 34px;
}
```

The Document Tree

You can visualize the structure of an HTML document as a tree with elements for branches. If it helps you picture it, invert the tree so it begins with the root element at the top and all other elements descending downward, making it more like a family tree than the leafy, wooden sort. Because of this similarity, developers use genealogy terms to refer to the relationships between elements. Figure 3-2 shows the family tree of a simple document.

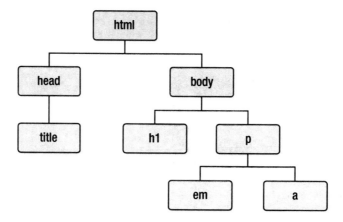

Figure 3-2. A simple document tree

In the diagram, the tree begins with the root html element, which has two *child* elements: the head and the body. That body element has two children of its own: a level-one heading (the h1 element, covered in Chapter 4) and a p element for a single paragraph (also covered in Chapter 4). Those two elements are *siblings* of each other, sharing the body element as their common *parent*. They're also *descendants* of the html element, which is their *ancestor*. The paragraph in turn contains an em element and an a element, sibling children of their parent paragraph, descended from the ancestral body and html elements.

We'll use these terms—parents, children, siblings, descendants, and ancestors—often in this book when we discuss the structure of an HTML document and the relationships between elements.

Connecting CSS

The HTML document contains all of the content that a browser will display. Every web browser in turn has its own built-in CSS rules for how the HTML elements should be rendered, including rules for which fonts to use and what sizes, what colors the page background, links, and regular text should be, and how much space should be between elements on the page. The ⟨...⟩ ·tyles aren't much to look at—really just the bare minimum to make a page readable, but no ⟨...⟩ attractive or memorable. If you want to improve on the default presentation you'll need to add ⟨...⟩ rules of your own.

CSS is a very different language from HTML, but is e⟨...⟩ ⟨...⟩dent on HTML to work. The HTML layer comes first and foremost, delivering content to the br⟨...⟩ ⟨...⟩rrounding it with a meaningful structure. CSS adds a separate layer of presentation on top of ⟨...⟩ ⟨...⟩ structure, further describing what those elements should look like. With CSS, the presentation ⟨...⟩ ⟨...⟩parated from the content layer, but the two are intimately related. The HTML layer must exist so ⟨...⟩ ⟨...⟩can enhance it; CSS can't survive on its own. There are a few methods you can use to apply this ⟨...⟩ ⟨...⟩SS styling to your HTML content, each with its own benefits and some drawbacks.

Inline Styling

You can include CSS declarations within the optional `style` attribute of each element in your markup, like you see in Listing 3-9. Chapter 2 showed you the anatomy of a CSS rule—with a selector and a declaration consisting of properties and values—but inline styles aren't constructed as rules. There's no selector because the properties and values are attached directly to the element at hand. In terms of specificity (also introduced in Chapter 2), an inline style is the most specific of all because it applies to exactly one element and no others.

Listing 3-9. An example of inline styling

```
<h1 style="color: blue;">Welcome, Heroes!</h1>
<p style="color: gray;">Power Outfitters offers top of the line merchandise
at rock-bottom prices for the discerning costumed crime-fighter.</p>
```

However, you should avoid using inline styles. They mix presentation with your structural markup, negating one of the main advantages of using CSS in the first place. Inline styling is also exceedingly redundant, forcing you to declare the same style properties again and again to maintain consistent presentation throughout a website. Should you ever want to update the site in the future—changing all your headings from blue to red, for example—you would need to track down every single heading on every single page to implement that change, a daunting task on a large and complex website.

Still, an inline style might be an efficient approach on some rare occasions, but those occasions are very few and far between indeed. Inline styling is most useful for temporary, from-the-hip testing and prototyping while you're working on a page, not as a permanent method of styling content. For anything meant to last, inline styles should be a last resort only when no other options are available.

Embedded Style Sheets

You can embed style rules within the head element of your document and those rules will be honored throughout the document in which they reside. An embedded style sheet (sometimes called an *internal* style sheet) is contained within a `style` element, shown in Listing 3-10 and covered in greater detail earlier in this chapter.

Listing 3-10. An example of an embedded style sheet

```html
<!DOCTYPE html>
<html>
  <head>
    <meta charset="utf-8">
    <title>Power Outfitters Superhero Costume and Supply Co.</title>
    <style>
      h1 { color: blue; }
      p { color: gray; }
    </style>
  </head>
  <body>
    <h1>Welcome, Heroes!</h1>
    <p>Power Outfitters offers top of the line merchandise at
    rock-bottom prices for the discerning costumed crime-fighter.</p>
  </body>
</html>
```

Embedding a style sheet in the header of your document does further separate presentation from your structured content, and those rules will be applied throughout that document, but it isn't an efficient approach if you're styling more than one page at a time. Other documents within the same website would require embedded style sheets of their own, so making any future modifications to your site's design would entail updating every single document in the site. That is unless your documents are assembled on the server-side, where you might be able to maintain a single file that gets included in the header of every page. In those cases, there can be some small performance advantages to using embedded styles over external style sheets (it's one less file to fetch from the server), but those advantages aren't always significant and might be negated by the additional code to download for each page.

> A `style` element can validly appear in the body of a document if it carries a `scoped` attribute, but that has yet to be implemented in any browsers at the time of this writing. Once browsers support `scoped`, such an embedded style sheet would apply only to the scoped element and not the entire document. See the section on the `style` element earlier in this chapter for more about scoped embedded styles.

External Style Sheets

The third and best option is to place all your CSS rules in a separate, external style sheet, directly connected to your document by way of a `link` element. An external style sheet is a plain-text file that you can edit using the same text editing software you use to create your HTML documents, saved with the file extension `.css`. This approach completely separates presentation from content and structure—they're not even stored in the same file. A single external style sheet can be linked from and associated with any number of HTML documents, allowing your entire website's design to be controlled from one central file. Changes to that file will propagate globally to every page that connects to it. It's by far the most flexible and maintainable way to design your sites, exercising the true power of CSS.

An HTML document links to an external style sheet via a link element in the document's head, as you learned earlier in this chapter. Listing 3-11 shows another example.

Listing 3-11. Linking to an external style sheet

```
<!DOCTYPE html>
<html>
  <head>
    <meta charset="utf-8">
    <title>Power Outfitters Superhero Costume and Supply Co.</title>
    <link rel="stylesheet" type="text/css" media="screen" href="styles.css">
  </head>
  <body>
    <h1>Welcome, Heroes!</h1>
    <p>Power Outfitters offers top of the line merchandise at
    rock-bottom prices for the discerning costumed crime-fighter.</p>
  </body>
</html>
```

When a browser downloads and begins processing the document, it will follow that link to retrieve the external style sheet and process it as well, automatically applying its rules to render the page. A browser downloads an external style sheet only once, then it's *cached* in the browser's memory for use on subsequent pages or even for future visits. This keeps your documents lighter and can improve the speed and performance of your entire website.

You're not limited to a single external style sheet; you can link to several different CSS files in one document, with each style sheet having its own link element in the document's head. Depending on the complexity of your site, you might have one style sheet containing general rules for the entire site while pages within a certain section can link to a second style sheet defining specific styles for that set of pages. You might also prefer to break your styles apart into separate files based on their purpose: for example, one style sheet defining colors and backgrounds and another style sheet defining your page layout.

You can also combine all three methods—inline, embedded, and external—to style your web pages, although it's rarely advisable. If just one page on your site needs some additional rules, you might choose to include an embedded style sheet for that page alone. You may even, very rarely, want to call out one element for special treatment and use an inline style for just that element. In almost every case, external style sheets are the best approach: they eliminate presentational markup, improve a site's performance, and are much easier to maintain.

With so many CSS rules being dictated from so many different sources, some overlap may be unavoidable. You already have specificity on your side, with more specific selectors overruling general selectors. But specificity alone isn't enough to resolve all the potential style conflicts a browser might run into when it's trying to render a web page. Where specificity fails, the *cascade order* steps in to sort things out.

The Cascade Order

Browsers apply CSS rules in the order in which they're received; later rules override previous rules. Browsers download separate style sheets in a particular order as well. In the case of external style sheets, their order is indicated by the order of the link elements in the document; rules in later linked style sheets override rules in previously linked style sheets (assuming equal specificity). If more than one style sheet is embedded in a document—each in its own style element—later embedded style sheets override previous ones. Inline declarations in an element's style attribute are applied last.

The style sheets web designers create are *author style sheets*, designing the web page as the author intends. Additionally, every graphical web browser has its own built-in style sheet to define the default presentation of various elements. When you view a web page without any of the author's CSS applied, you're simply seeing it rendered with the *browser style sheet*, which comes first in the cascade order, so all the author's styles override those defaults. To complicate matters just a bit further, most web browsers allow the end user to attach their own customized style sheets—known as a *user style sheet*—which comes second in the cascade order, thus overriding the browser's default styles but not the author's.

To break it down, the cascade order for multiple style sources is:

1. Browser style sheet

2. User style sheet

3. Author style sheets (in the order in which they're linked or embedded)

4. Inline author styles

And don't forget, the cascade works within each style sheet as well. To remember how the cascade works, follow this rule of thumb: *the declaration closest to the content wins*. Whichever value is declared last will be the one in effect when the content is finally rendered.

Style with Color

Color plays a pivotal role in everyday life, and is even integral to human survival. Our ability to recognize color allows us to coordinate our outfits, to safely cross busy streets, and to avoid eating poisonous mushrooms. Color, being so much a part of the visual sensory experience, is also a vital component in visual design. Artful application of color can draw the viewer's attention, clarify communication, and invoke powerful emotional responses.

CSS makes it easy to inject color into an otherwise drab web page. The color property declares a color for an element's text, and the background-color property declares a solid color that fills the entire element's area. Text and other content inside the element will overlap that background color. For example, the following rule sets the text (foreground) color to black and the background color to white for the entire body element, which covers the entire page and fills the browser window:

```
body {
  color: black;
  background-color: white;
}
```

The color property is *inherited*, passed down from a parent element to all its child elements. A child element that inherits its text color from its parent will pass that color down to its own children, and so on down the document tree until some other color is declared to override it. Because every other element on the rendered page descends from the body element, all regular text will be automatically displayed in black as inherited from the ancestral body.

For any element that requires a different text color, another style rule can easily override that base body color if the rule comes later in the cascade or if the style rule has a more specific selector, like this rule for the "hero" class:

```
.hero {
  color: blue;
}
```

The background-color property is **not** inherited by descendant elements; it applies only to the element (or elements) selected by the CSS rule. Any element without a declared background color will simply default to a transparent background (no color at all). If you need to, you can use the declaration background-color: transparent; to override and reset a background color declared elsewhere.

Specifying Colors in CSS

There are two general approaches to specifying a color in CSS: by name or by value. Specifying by name is very simple: blue is blue, red is red, and so on, but there aren't very many predefined color names from which to choose. Specifying a color value, on the other hand, offers a much broader palette. Furthermore, there are a few ways to specify a color value, the two most common being RGB or hexadecimal notation. These have been part of CSS from the beginning and every web browser supports them. CSS3 introduces a few new options—RGBA, HSL, and HSLA—and browser support for these newer color models is a bit less widespread so you'll need to use them wisely. We'll begin with the easy ones.

Color Name

The simplest and most self-explanatory way to indicate a color in CSS is by choosing from a set of predefined color name keywords. There are 147 named colors in all: 17 "standard" color names that date back to early versions of HTML (white, black, red, yellow, blue, green, orange, purple, gray, silver, aqua, fuchsia, lime, maroon, navy, olive, and teal) and an additional 130 that were added in CSS level 2. We won't list them all here but some of our favorites are Gainsboro, LemonChiffon, MintCream, PapayaWhip, and FireBrick. Color names aren't case sensitive, so "DarkSlateGray" is the same as "darkslategray." You can see the whole list in living color at html-color-names.com

RGB

Color televisions and computer screens create color by emitting different intensities of red, green, and blue light. These are the primary colors of light that are visible to the human eye, and various combinations of those same three colors produce every color you can see.

In CSS, you can represent the intensity of each of the three primary colors with a number ranging from 0 (no color) to 255 (full intensity). The rgb keyword indicates that this value is an RGB color with the individual color values contained in parentheses, separated by commas:

```
body {
  color: rgb(109,18,18); /* dark red */
  background-color: rgb(255,250,210); /* pale yellow */
}
```

The order is always red, green, blue; easy to remember because the keyword "rgb" is right there to remind you. You can also specify an RGB color as a set of three percentages from 0% to 100%, also using the rgb keyword with the values in parentheses, separated by commas:

```
body {
  color: rgb(43%,7%,7%); /* dark red */
  background-color: rgb(100%,98%,82%); /* pale yellow */
}
```

Hexadecimal Notation

Perhaps the most common method to express a color value in CSS is as a six-digit hexadecimal number—*hex*, for short—where each pair of digits represents a value of red, green, or blue (in that order). Hex color values are preceded by an octothorpe (#):

```
body {
  color: #6d1212; /* dark red */
  background-color: #fffad2; /* pale yellow */
}
```

Hexadecimal notation is simply a way of counting up to 16 in the space of one character, with letters representing numbers higher than 9. You can count from 0–9 normally, then use the letters A, B, C, D, E, and F to represent 10–15 (with 0, this brings it to 16 bits). Counting to 16 comes up a lot when you deal with computers because all digital data is based on multiples of 8; 1 byte comprises 8 bits.

With hexadecimal notation, it's possible to specify up to 16 values of a single color with one digit (a numeral or letter). Three hex digits—each representing a value of red, green, or blue—multiplies 16 by 16 by 16 to arrive at a palette of 256 possible colors. Using six hex digits cubes the number again (256 × 256 × 256) and the palette grows to over 16.7 million unique colors, approaching the limits of human vision. And a tiny, 6-digit number can represent any one of them.

As an example, the hex number #000000 represents black because it has no color value at all; it's nothing but zeros. At the other end of the scale (literally), the hex number #FFFFFF represents white; each color is turned up to full blast, saturating the pixels as well as your eyes. As you probably learned in science class, pure white light is made up of all three primary colors.

Specifying different intensities of the primary colors results in a mixed color. For example, #FF0000 represents the reddest red possible because that color is projected at full intensity, and isn't muddied by any blue or green wavelengths. For a more complex color, the hex number #2C498F is a nice, medium-dark, greenish-blue color made up of 17% red, 29% green, and 56% blue.

When a hexadecimal color value consists of three matched pairs of digits, you can abbreviate the value to only three digits in CSS. Thus #000000 becomes #000 and #ff88aa becomes #f8a. The letters in a hex number can be either upper- or lowercase in CSS; that's entirely a matter of personal preference.

But don't be afraid: you'll never have to memorize the hexadecimal encoded values of all 16,777,216 unique colors. There are abundant free utilities and online color-pickers (such as `colorpicker.com`) that allow you to visually mix or choose a color and find its RGB or hex value to use in your CSS. Any image editing software you might use to create graphics for the Web (such as Adobe Photoshop) will also provide both RGB and hex values in its built-in color-picker.

RGBA

RGBA color notation was introduced in CSS3 and is already widely supported in modern browsers. It's just like RGB, but adds a fourth value for an *alpha channel*, setting the color's opacity as a decimal between 0 (completely transparent) and 1 (completely opaque). For example, the following rule would fill an element belonging to the "hero" class with a light blue color at 0.75 opacity (the 0 is optional), allowing whatever color or content is behind the element to partially show through:

```
.hero { background-color: rgba(111,171,221,0.75); }
```

As with RGB, you can declare the color with either numeric values or percentages, but the alpha value must always be a decimal. You can simply translate the decimal to a percentage in your head, if it helps you to think of it that way—0.75 is 75% opaque:

```
.hero { background-color: rgba(44%,67%,87%,0.75); }
```

Older browsers don't support RGBA so you should use it carefully, with some consideration about how those browsers will render your page. If you declare a color in RGBA, a non-supporting browser will ignore the declaration entirely and render the element with no color at all, either defaulting to transparent (for backgrounds) or carrying over an inherited foreground color. You can accommodate old browsers by declaring colors twice; once with an opaque color using RGB or hex for older browsers, then again with RGBA for newer browsers:

```
.hero {
  background-color: #6fabdd;
  background-color: rgba(111,171,221,0.75);
}
```

A browser that understands RGBA will take the second `background-color` declaration in place of the first because it comes later in the cascade. A browser that only understands the hexadecimal value will ignore the second declaration.

You can create some very cool and sophisticated effects with translucent RGBA colors, especially if you layer them over other elements or textures. The annual web design advent calendar, 24 Ways to Impress Your Friends (`24ways.org`), makes striking use of RGBA in its design, as you can see in Figure 3-3. (It really looks much better in a browser; you should see it for yourself. Read it for the articles, too.)

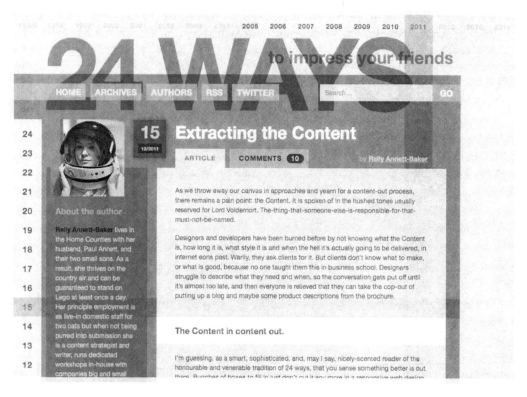

Figure 3-3. The 24 Ways website uses overlapping elements and translucent RGBA colors

HSL

The HSL color model expresses a color by three factors: hue, saturation, and lightness. A color's *hue* is represented by the color's angle on a color wheel, beginning and ending with red (so both 0 and 360 are red). The angle of a radius drawn on that color wheel represents a different color. Green has an angle of 120 degrees, blue is at 240 degrees, and every other color falls somewhere else around that spectrum wheel. Yellow is 60 degrees, cyan is 180 degrees, and 295 degrees is a sort of purplish pink, part way between blue and magenta.

The color's *saturation* is a measure of its intensity, expressed as a percentage between 0% (no color) to 100% (full intensity). The color's *lightness* is its value or brightness, also a percentage between 0% (completely dark) to 100% (full brightness). Once you form a mental picture of the color wheel, declaring colors in HSL is really very intuitive, and much more naturalistic than RGB or hexadecimal. You can just think of a color—a dark greenish-teal of medium brightness, perhaps—and even without using a color picker, you can write it out in HSL and probably get something pretty close to the color you want:

```
.villain { color: hsl(155,55%,40%); }
```

HSL color was introduced with CSS3 and is supported by most current browsers, but not by older browsers. To ensure your web page is suitably colorful in older browsers, you can declare the color twice; once in regular RGB or hexadecimal, and again in HSL:

```
.villain {
  color: #2e664f;
  color: hsl(155,55%,40%);
}
```

However, there isn't much benefit to declaring two equivalent opaque colors, which may be why HSL hasn't gained much popularity, despite its human friendliness. Alas, as long as there are still browsers that don't support HSL, you may be better off sticking with RGB and hex for opaque colors.

HSLA

Just like RGBA, HSLA specifies a color with hue, saturation, and lightness, plus an alpha value for its opacity, with the alpha channel expressed as a decimal between 0 and 1:

```
.sidekick { background-color: hsla(268,66%,79%,0.65); }
```

Also like RGBA and HSL, HSLA colors aren't supported by older browsers, so it's best to declare a simple opaque color first, followed by an HSLA color as a progressive enhancement for browsers that support it:

```
.sidekick {
  background-color: #a98dc9;
  background-color: hsla(268,66%,79%,0.65);
}
```

Summary

This chapter has given you a solid grounding in what HTML documents are and how they're assembled. You've learned about the all-important doctype, the root html element, and the head and body elements. We went into some depth on the various metadata elements you can find in a document's header, though some of them are more useful than others (you'll use the link and script elements a lot, but might live out the rest of your life without using the base element even once). You also started to get your feet wet with CSS, learning how style sheets can be attached to your HTML documents and a few ways to declare colors in CSS.

From here on, most of the markup examples we'll show you in this book won't include the complete HTML document around them, but you can assume they do indeed appear wrapped in a proper valid document. You can also assume the CSS examples we show you are appearing in an embedded or external style sheet associated with one of those complete, valid documents.

This has been a fairly intense chapter full of HTML elements you can't even see, but it's important to establish this foundation early on. Don't worry, Chapter 4 at last dives headlong into the real meat of HTML: adding readable, meaningful content to your web pages.

Now that you've got a handle ___ ___ ___ ___ shed a framework for your documents, the real fun can begin: it's time to start adding c... ...b pages. In this chapter, you'll learn about most of the HTML elements you'll need to give your content an organized, meaningful structure. We've divided the elements into general categories based on the purpose they serve, from dividing a document into logical sections to highlighting individual words. Along the way, you'll see examples of how web browsers render the different elements with their default styling. Then we'll show you just a few ways you can use CSS to enhance the presentation of your text.

Content and Structure

The content of your web page consists of everything your visitors will see, read, and use. However, content is more than simply words and images; it's also the message, the thing your words and images are actually *about*. Your content is the information that you're trying to communicate to your audience, and the Web is a conduit for moving that information from one place (you) to another (them).

In Figure 4-1, the "before" image shows a sample of text as it would appear in a web browser without any HTML structure. It's nothing but a large mass of words, all mashed together and hard to read (even if you're fluent in pseudo-Latin filler text). There's nothing to differentiate a headline from a list, nothing that clearly separates different blocks of text that represent different ideas. You can break that blob of words down into discernable, readable portions by adding a few bits of structural markup. The "after" image is much more readable (the words are still nonsense, but we're making a point here).

Figure 4-1. Some example text, with and without structure

Semantics is the study of meaning in language. Web developers have borrowed the term from the field of linguistics and use it to refer to the *inherent meaning* of an HTML element or attribute. Is this block of text a quotation? Mark it as a quotation. Is this string of words the title for an article? There's a tag for that. What about that list: do the items have to be in a particular sequence, or is the order unimportant? HTML has elements for both options. As you assemble your documents, consider the meaning and purpose of each bit of content and choose the most semantically appropriate HTML element to suit that purpose.

Providing a solid structure for your content will make it stronger and more flexible. By using semantic HTML to tell the browser that "this is a heading" and "this is a paragraph" and "this word is emphasized," you'll make your content work better, for both machines and people alike. In the course of organizing your content logically with the proper elements, you'll also build in the sturdy framework you'll need to style your pages with CSS.

Logical Sections

HTML elements describe the nature and purpose of their contents, with specific elements for headings, paragraphs, quotations, lists, and so on, and we'll cover most of those elements in this chapter. In addition to marking up these bite-sized portions of text, you can also use HTML to divide your document into larger blocks, collecting related content and elements together into logical sections. Your content might be an article comprising several paragraphs as well as a title and a few subheadings, with some footnotes and an author byline for good measure. You can gather all of that content together into one semantic unit with the article element, declaring that not only do your various bits of text serve different purposes, but also that all of them together form a cohesive whole.

If you like, you could further divide that article into distinct sections for each topic, and those sections would still be part of the larger article that contains them. Or perhaps your document features several separate articles—you could group all of them into one big section of the document, and still include lesser sections within each article.

HTML5 introduces a number of special *sectioning elements* to help you organize your content and collect elements together into unified, semantic chunks. These elements—section, article, aside, and nav—

belong to the *sectioning content* model. HTML5 also introduces new elements for marking a header or footer within one of these sections, or for the entire document.

Before the advent of HTML5, you would have probably used a generic division (the div element, covered later in this chapter) in place of every one of these structural elements, and you still can. But a div element is semantically shallow. It's useful for collecting related content into a nonspecific box, but a div says nothing else about what that content means or what purpose it may serve. These new sectioning elements each have a specific meaning and serve a specific purpose.

All of these elements require end tags, and there are no required or optional attributes for any of them, apart from the standard global attributes.

section

The section element defines just what it says: a section of content. But rather than a completely generic box, the section element groups *thematically related content*. It collects content that, when taken together as a whole, serves a single purpose or is related to the same topic. That's still a pretty vague definition, and deliberately so. The section element is multi-purpose, and can be applied in a number of situations. It defines a section of thematically related content, but not any particular *kind* of content.

In Listing 4-1 you see a basic HTML document with its content divided into three sections: an introduction, recent news, and some general information. This document is pretty light on content, but if you imagine it filled with lengthy blocks of text, you can see how breaking it down into a few relevant chunks via section elements could help you keep things organized. A section element should usually begin with a heading (covered later in this chapter) to introduce the content, but that isn't a requirement.

Listing 4-1. An HTML document split into three major sections

```
<!DOCTYPE html>
<html>
  <head>
    <meta charset="utf-8">
    <title>Power Outfitters - Superhero Costume and Supply Company</title>
  </head>
  <body>

    <section class="intro">
      <h1>Welcome, Heroes!</h1>
      <p>Power Outfitters offers top of the line merchandise at
      rock-bottom prices for the discerning costumed crime-fighter.
      From belts to boomerangs, we're your one-stop shop for all
      your specialized gadgetry and costuming needs.</p>
    </section>

    <section class="news">
      <h2>Latest News</h2>
      <p>Small things, big savings. All shrink rays are on sale,
      this week only!</p>
    </section>
```

```
<section class="store-info">
  <h3>Power Outfitters</h3>
  <p>616 Kirby Ave, between Romita and Ditko
  <br>Open Mon-Thu: 8am-10pm, Fri-Sun: 8am-12pm
  <br>24-hour service and repair: call 555-1961</p>
</section>

  </body>
</html>
```

The `section` element requires an end tag and may contain any flow elements, including other sectioning elements. For example, you can nest `sections` within `sections`:

```
<section class="content">
  <section class="intro">
    <h1>Welcome, Heroes!</h1>
    <p>Power Outfitters offers top of the line merchandise at
    rock-bottom prices for the discerning costumed crime-fighter.
    From belts to boomerangs, we're your one-stop shop for all
    your specialized gadgetry and costuming needs.</p>
  </section>

  <section class="news">
    <h2>Latest News</h2>
    <p>Small things, big savings. All shrink rays are on sale,
    this week only!</p>
  </section>
</section>
```

The `section` element's `display` property is `block` by default, so its contents begin on a new line and occupy the full available width, but there is no other default styling. This makes the `section` element a useful container for laying out pages with CSS, but don't get too carried away. Use `sections` appropriately to group related content, not merely for drawing boxes on screen. Think of these sectioning elements first and foremost as content organization devices, not page layout devices.

Required Attributes

The `section` element doesn't require any attributes.

Optional Attributes

There aren't any optional attributes for the `section` element.

article

The `article` element is similar to the `section` element, though with a more refined definition. According to the HTML5 specification (in its current form at the time we write this), an `article` element "represents a self-contained composition in a document, page, application, or site and that is, in principle, independently distributable or reusable, e.g. in syndication." In other words, an `article` element's content should stand on its own and still make sense in different contexts. It might be a blog entry, a comment, a forum post, a letter, a review, a poem, a short story, or indeed an article. Listing 4-2 shows an example of a short, self-contained article, complete with title, author byline, and date.

Listing 4-2. The `article` element containing a complete (if short) article

```
<article>
  <h1>Where Do They Get Those Wonderful Toys?</h1>
  <p>By Norm DePlume</p>

  <p>Power Outfitters Superhero Costume and Supply Company is
  located in a nondescript building on Kirby Ave, a site that
  once housed a large printing plant. Behind their modest
  storefront is an expansive warehouse positively packed to
  the portholes with paraphernalia.</p>

  <p>Posted on August 9, 2011</p>
</article>
```

Like the `section` element, `article` requires an end tag and is styled as a block-level element by default. It can contain any flow elements, including other sectioning elements. When an `article` element contains other `article` elements, the inner `articles` are still self-contained in their own right, but are also related to (and part of) the outer `article` that contains them. For example, an advice column that consists of letters from readers and responses from the author—the entire column could be wrapped in an `article` element and each reader letter wrapped in a nested `article` element of its own.

Required Attributes

There are no required attributes for the `article` element.

Optional Attributes

The `article` element doesn't offer any optional attributes.

header

The `header` element contains introductory or navigational content for a section of a document. It typically appears at the top of a section, but it doesn't have to; calling it a "header" might imply a position at the top, but it's an *introduction* to the section, and can actually appear anywhere within that section (also note that a "section of content" doesn't necessarily mean a `section` element). Even so, it makes plain sense that introductions usually come first. You can use CSS to position a `header` anywhere on the page you like.

The term "header" also commonly refers to a website's overall masthead—where you would usually find the name and logo of the website, some navigation links, perhaps a search form, and so on. If the `header` element's closest sectioning ancestor is the document's `body`, and it isn't a descendant of some other sectioning element, the `header` applies to the entire document and so it might be a suitable element for such a masthead.

When a header occurs within any sectioning element, such as an article, it acts as the introductory header for that section of content only. The header in Listing 4-3 introduces the article, featuring the article's title in an h1 heading and an author byline marked up as a paragraph.

Listing 4-3. A header element introduces the article

```
<article>
  <header>
    <h1>Where Do They Get Those Wonderful Toys?</h1>
    <p>By Norm DePlume</p>
  </header>

  <p>Power Outfitters Superhero Costume and Supply Company is
  located in a nondescript building on Kirby Ave, a site that
  once housed a large printing plant. Behind their modest
  storefront is an expansive warehouse positively packed to
  the portholes with paraphernalia.</p>

  <p>Posted on August 9, 2011</p>
</article>
```

The header element always requires an end tag and can contain any flow content *except* a footer element or another header element.

Required Attributes

The header element doesn't have any required attributes.

Optional Attributes

There are no optional attributes for the header element.

footer

A counterpart to the header element, the footer element contains additional information about its parent sectioning element, such as author contact information, copyright or licensing, related links, supplemental navigation, footnotes, or disclaimers. It typically appears at the end of a section but that's not a requirement. Like header, the name "footer" doesn't necessarily refer to a location—this is footer content by *nature*, not just by position.

Listing 4-4 shows the same article again, this time with a proper footer.

Listing 4-4. An article with a footer element, containing a publication date and copyright notice

```
<article>
  <header>
    <h1>Where Do They Get Those Wonderful Toys?</h1>
    <p>By Norm DePlume</p>
  </header>
```

```
<p>Power Outfitters Superhero Costume and Supply Company is
located in a nondescript building on Kirby Ave, a site that
once housed a large printing plant. Behind their modest
storefront is an expansive warehouse positively packed to
the portholes with paraphernalia.</p>

<footer>
    <p>Posted on August 9, 2011</p>
    <p>&copy; copyright Cape and Cowl Quarterly</p>
</footer>
</article>
```

The footer element requires an end tag and can contain any flow elements, including sectioning elements, but not a header or another footer. If it contains any sectioning elements (section, article, aside, or nav), those sections might be appendices, bibliographies, lengthy license agreements, or extensive footnotes. The footer element has no default styling except to display as a block-level element.

Also like the header element, if a footer appears inside a sectioning element, it relates only to that section. If it appears in the document body without some other sectioning ancestor, it relates to the entire document or even to the entire website.

Required Attributes

There are no required attributes for the footer element.

Optional Attributes

The footer element doesn't have any optional attributes.

> *The header and footer elements aren't true sectioning elements in that they don't necessarily define a self-contained block of content, don't establish a new sectioning root, and don't belong to the sectioning content model. But they're both so closely associated with sectioning elements we felt it was sensible to cover them at this point in the chapter.*

aside

Another new element in HTML5, aside designates a section of tangential content—content that supports and enhances the main content, but isn't an essential part of it. It's optional information that you could easily remove without harming the reader's understanding of the primary content. An aside element might contain additional commentary, background information, a glossary of terms, a collection of related links, a pull quote, or even advertising if the ads are relevant to the content.

The sort of secondary content you would include in an aside element is often called a *sidebar* in publishing, and that term is common in web design as well, but the words "sidebar" and "aside" don't necessarily mean a position on the left or right side of the main content. Use aside appropriately for tangential content, and don't get hung up on the name. With CSS, you can position the aside element anywhere on the page: top, bottom, side, or smack in the middle.

If an aside element appears within an article or other sectioning element, its contents should relate directly to that article or content section. If an aside appears in the body without another sectioning ancestor, its contents are assumed to relate to the entire document or to the entire website. By the same token, if it appears within a section that is itself within an article element, the aside should preferably relate to that particular section of the article.

In Listing 4-5 we've added some supplemental content to the same article, contained in an aside element.

Listing 4-5. Using the aside element in an article

```
<article>
  <header>
    <h1>Where Do They Get Those Wonderful Toys?</h1>
    <p>By Norm DePlume</p>
  </header>

  <p>Power Outfitters Superhero Costume and Supply Company is
  located in a nondescript building on Kirby Ave, a site that
  once housed a large printing plant. Behind their modest
  storefront is an expansive warehouse positively packed to
  the portholes with paraphernalia.</p>

  <aside>
    <p>The historic building at 616 Kirby Ave. was the former
    headquarters of Sinnott Inkworks, a leading printer of
    comic books in America since 1956.</p>
  </aside>

  <footer>
    <p>Posted on August 9, 2011</p>
    <p>&copy; copyright Cape and Cowl Quarterly</p>
  </footer>
</article>
```

There is no default styling for the aside element except to display as a block-level element. It requires an end tag and can contain any other flow content, including other sectioning elements. An aside element might even contain a complete article in an article element, with header, footer and section elements of its own. In theory, that aside article might have an aside of its own, which could also have an aside, which has an aside, and so on, *ad infinitum*... but that way lies madness.

Required Attributes

The aside element doesn't require any attributes.

Optional Attributes

There are no optional attributes for the aside element.

nav

A nav element contains navigation—a group of links that lead to other pages on a website, or to sections of the current page. In a sense, *all* links are navigation, but don't use nav for every collection of links; the nav element is intended only for *major blocks of navigation*. This element should be an important signpost for your visitors to come to when they're trying to find their way to particular areas of interest.

Most websites have a global header or masthead, a prominent banner that features the site name, logo, and usually the primary navigation for the website. That primary navigation almost certainly warrants a nav element. Some lengthy articles may have an internal table of contents, listing the article headings and subheadings with shortcut links to jump directly to that part of the page; that's a job for the nav element, too. If content is spread across multiple pages, like search results or a catalog showing 20 items per page, you'll want to include pagination links to reach those other pages—another perfect use for the nav element.

But sometimes you'll need to mark up a group of links that aren't necessarily vital navigation aids for your users. For example, a sidebar (possibly marked up with an aside element) might feature links to other related articles; useful, yes, but maybe not what you'd consider "major navigation." A footer element might hold similar related links, or links to a privacy policy and contact page; those probably aren't major navigation either. Then again, perhaps they are. There's no rule forbidding nav for such uses, but it's usually not necessary. Think about what your links mean, how they relate to the document or the rest of the website, and how your visitors will use them.

In Listing 4-6 you can see a site's global header, including a list of links to the main pages of the website wrapped in a nav element (the ul element—an unordered list—is covered elsewhere in this chapter).

Listing 4-6. The nav element in a site's global header

```
<header>
  <hgroup>
    <h1>Power Outfitters</h1>
    <h2>Superhero Costume and Supply Company</h2>
  </hgroup>

  <nav>
    <ul>
      <li><a href="/costuming">Costuming</a></li>
      <li><a href="/gear">Gadgets and Gear</a></li>
      <li><a href="/weaponry">Non-lethal Weaponry</a></li>
      <li><a href="/defense">Armor and Defense</a></li>
      <li><a href="/base">Lair and Vehicle</a></li>
    </ul>
  </nav>
</header>
```

Like other sectioning elements, nav has no default styling except display:block. It requires an end tag and can contain any flow elements, including other sectioning elements, even another nav element if necessary.

Required Attributes

There aren't any required attributes for the nav element.

Optional Attributes

The nav element doesn't offer any optional attributes.

Headings

Heading elements (h1 through h6, and the new hgroup element) act as titles to introduce a section of content. They're flow content, but also belong to their own content model: *heading content*. The first child heading element to appear within any sectioning element—section, article, aside, or nav—acts as the heading for the entire parent element, introducing and establishing that block of content, even if other content appears before the heading.

h1, h2, h3, h4, h5, and h6

HTML offers a range of six headings, with each level indicating the heading's relative importance or its rank in the document hierarchy (and, by association, the importance or rank of the content that heading introduces). With these headings, you can organize your content into distinct topics or areas of interest, sorted from the top down in order of importance, and with each section containing subsections of its own.

Listing 4-7 shows some content with headings and short paragraphs, where each heading introduces the content that follows it. The different heading levels imply a clear hierarchy of importance; the top-level heading introduces the entire section, whereas the subheadings beneath it introduce lesser sections within that. The lower headings here simply *imply* subsections under the previous headings, they're not explicit sections defined by nested sectioning elements.

Listing 4-7. Headings and paragraphs

```
<h1>Costume Accessories</h1>
<p>All the trappings and trimmings.</p>

<h2>Masks and Cowls</h2>
<p>Protect your secret identity.</p>

<h3>Masks</h3>
<p>Facial coverage.</p>

<h3>Cowls</h3>
<p>Head coverage.</p>
```

The h1 element designates the top-level heading—the most important one in the section, or even in the entire document. Because there can logically be only one "most important" heading, it's customary for only one h1 to occur within a single section. This isn't a requirement of HTML, just a good semantic rule of thumb. You should also try to keep your headings in the proper sequence—an h5 shouldn't come before an h2 unless you have a really good reason to break their natural order.

Headings always require both a start tag and an end tag. They fall under their own content model—heading content—but are also flow content, and can occur wherever flow content is allowed. Headings can only contain text or phrase elements.

Figure 4-2 shows the previous markup as rendered by a browser with default styling. Graphical web browsers will automatically display headings in a boldfaced font and at different sizes for each level, h1 being the largest and h6 being the smallest, establishing a visual hierarchy to match the semantic hierarchy.

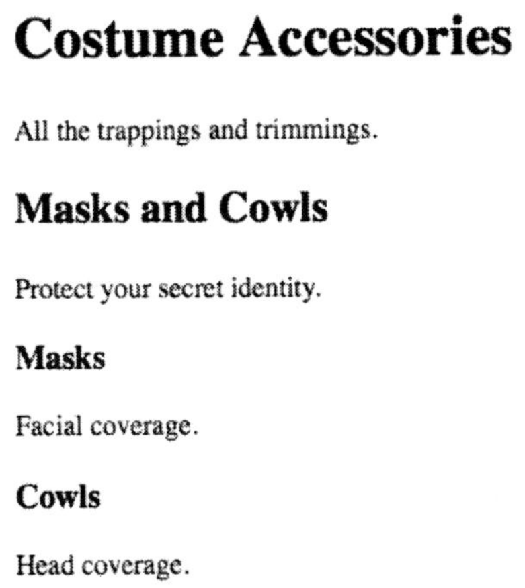

Costume Accessories

All the trappings and trimmings.

Masks and Cowls

Protect your secret identity.

Masks

Facial coverage.

Cowls

Head coverage.

Figure 4-2. Different heading levels appear at different font sizes by default

Because of their default styling, headings have often been abused for their presentational effects. Avoid this mistake and use headings in a meaningful way. An h2 is "the second-most important heading," not "the second largest font." You can use CSS to alter the default appearance of headings, including their font size.

Prior to HTML5 and the new sectioning elements, a document's body acted as the sole sectioning root, forming an outline based only on the hierarchy of its headings. This meant that, if you followed good semantics, only a single h1 would occur per document (often reserved for the site's name or page title), and all other headings on the page ranked below that. It can be difficult to maintain an orderly outline under such circumstances, and if any heading breaks rank—an h4 following an h2, for instance—it could throw off the entire document outline.

But in HTML5, the first child heading within a sectioning element acts as the main heading for that entire section, effectively starting a new hierarchy within that section alone. Now it can be rightly sensible to include multiple h1s in a document, but you should still have only a single h1 per section. Though it might look odd, the markup shown in Listing 4-8 is completely valid and semantically appropriate because each top-level heading marks the beginning of a new section element.

Listing 4-8. Headings within `sections`

```
<h1>Costume Accessories</h1>
<p>All the trappings and trimmings.</p>

<section>
  <h1>Masks and Cowls</h1>
  <p>Protect your secret identity.</p>

  <section>
    <h1>Masks</h1>
    <p>Facial coverage.</p>
  </section>

  <section>
    <h1>Cowls</h1>
    <p>Head coverage.</p>
  </section>
</section>
```

This works because each sectioning element constitutes a new sectioning root, effectively starting a new chain of command in the ranked headings. This nesting of sectioning elements still forms a hierarchical outline even though all four headings are the same element; their rank is implied by the document tree, with each `section` being a subsection of its parent.

However, older browsers—and some current browsers—will render all of these h1 elements at the same size by default. The semantic hierarchy will still be there in the markup, but there will be no visual hierarchy, at least not by default in those browsers. Rather than rely exclusively on default browser styles to establish the sizes of ranked headings, you can use your own CSS to style these nested section headings proportionally, as we'll show you later in this chapter.

Always choose a heading element of the appropriate rank for its importance and position in the outline. The first heading in any sectioning element should be the highest-level heading for that entire section. If you begin an `article` with an h3, that heading acts as the title for the entire section of content so it should be the only h3 in that `article`.

Required Attributes

There are no required attributes for heading elements.

Optional Attributes

Heading elements don't offer any optional attributes.

hgroup

The `hgroup` element can contain a group of headings (h1 to h6) that together act as a heading for a section of content. The highest-level heading in an `hgroup` is taken as the heading for the section, and any other subheadings within the same hgroup don't count towards the document outline. This is perfect for subtitles like the one in Listing 4-9, but not much else.

Listing 4-9. An article's title and subtitle in an hgroup element

```
<article>
  <header>
    <hgroup>
      <h1>Where Do They Get Those Wonderful Toys?</h1>
      <h2>An Insider's Tour of the Cutting Edge Manufacturing
      Wing at Power Outfitters</h2>
    </hgroup>
    <p>By Norm DePlume</p>
  </header>

  <p>Power Outfitters Superhero Costume and Supply Company is
  located in a nondescript building on Kirby Ave, a site that
  once housed a large printing plant. Behind their modest
  storefront is an expansive warehouse positively packed to
  the portholes with paraphernalia.</p>

  <footer>
    <p>Posted on August 9, 2011</p>
    <p>&copy; copyright Cape and Cowl Quarterly</p>
  </footer>
</article>
```

Were it not for the hgroup in this example, the rest of the article would be associated directly with the h2 subtitle, and not with the actual title in the h1. The new hgroup element allows authors to include subtitle headings between a heading and its content without throwing off the document's natural outline.

There's been some debate among web standards sticklers about the usefulness of the hgroup element. It exists solely to hide subtitles from the document outline, and serves no greater semantic purpose. The debate is still going as we write this book, and there are a few open proposals to remove hgroup from the HTML5 spec (w3.org/html/wg/tracker/issues/164), possibly replacing it with another element intended specifically for subtitles, or simply modifying the document outlining algorithm (more on that in a minute) to make better use of the more meaningful header element. But hgroup is still in the spec for now so we've covered it here. That may change by the time you read this so refer to the specs and validate your markup to be certain.

The hgroup element is flow content, but also falls under the heading content model. It can only have heading elements, h1 through h6, as its children; no other elements are allowed as direct children of an hgroup, but those headings can still contain other phrasing elements. The hgroup element also requires an end tag and has no default styling except to display as a block-level element. An hgroup doesn't have to be wrapped in a header element, though it often should be if it's the main heading of a section or article. Don't use an hgroup element at all if you have only a single heading.

Required Attributes

There are no required attributes for the hgroup element.

Optional Attributes

The hgroup element has no optional attributes.

Outlines and Sectioning Roots

A well-structured HTML document should form an orderly outline, organized from the top down in a hierarchy of headings, just like you probably learned when you wrote your first book report. For any given document, the outline begins at the highest-level heading (usually an h1) and descends from there. To begin a new subsection under that heading, simply introduce it with a heading of the next lower rank; if you begin with an h1, follow it with an h2. Use lower-ranking headings for each subsection, creating a hierarchy from h1 all the way down to h6.

User-agents can follow a standard outlining algorithm to find all the headings in a document and automatically generate an outline, which might look something like this:

```
1. Costume Accessories
    1.1 Masks and Cowls
        1.1.1 Masks
        1.1.2 Cowls
    1.2 Belts and Pouches
        1.2.1 Belts
        1.2.2 Pouches
    1.3 Gloves and Bracers
        1.3.1 Gloves
        1.3.2 Bracers
```

Before HTML5, such an outline was formed only by the h1 through h6 elements as they occurred in the body element (and in many cases it still works that way in HTML5). Sections of content were merely implied by the headings, and any and all content that came after a heading was assumed to belong to that heading, whether or not the text itself actually related to the subject. This can make it hard to maintain a logical outline while still using appropriate markup that serves the content. Look at the markup in Listing 4-10, for example.

Listing 4-10. A sequence of ranked headings

```
<h1>Superhero Costume Basics</h1>
<p>Battle for justice in comfort and style.</p>

<h2>Unitards and Leotards</h2>
<p>Freedom of movement with a sleek profile.</p>

<h2>Capes and Cloaks</h2>
<p>For timeless majesty or ominous mystery.</p>

<p>We do tailoring and alterations, too! Fittings are
by appointment only, so please call ahead.</p>
```

Everything seems to be in order until you reach the last paragraph: does that note about tailoring refer only to Capes and Cloaks, or to all costumes? It seems like it should relate to the entire page, but its position in the document hierarchy implies that it relates only to the preceding heading, at least as far as the generated outline is concerned.

HTML5 addresses this problem by introducing *sectioning roots*. Nested sections and subsections could only be implied by the order of headings in past versions of HTML, but now some elements in HTML5 explicitly define a discreet section of content that has its own internal outline. Rather than merely following a straight line of headings from the top down, the new HTML5 outlining formula can also build a hierarchy from the document tree of sections within sections.

Here's the same content, now organized into a few nested `section` elements:

```
<section>
  <h1>Costume Basics for Superheroes</h1>
  <p>Battle for justice in comfort and style.</p>

  <section>
    <h2>Unitards and Leotards</h2>
    <p>Freedom of movement and a sleek profile.</p>
  </section>

  <section>
    <h2>Capes and Cloaks</h2>
    <p>For timeless majesty or ominous mystery.</p>
  </section>

  <p>We do tailoring and alterations, too! Fittings are
  by appointment only, so please call ahead.</p>
</section>
```

The last paragraph is now clearly and explicitly associated with the first heading because they belong to the same sectioning root. In fact, that outermost `section` element might not be necessary because the body element itself is a sectioning root. Elements that define new sectioning roots include:

- the body element, which you've already seen in Chapter 3

- the new sectioning elements: `section`, `article`, `aside`, and `nav`

- `blockquote`, `figure`, `fieldset`, `details`, and `td`—all covered elsewhere in this book

This is pretty cutting-edge stuff and none of the major browsers have fully implemented the new outlining algorithm yet, but that will change in due time. Until then, there are some nagging accessibility concerns about breaking up the heading hierarchy in nested sections.

Some assistive technologies—especially screen-readers for the vision impaired—rely on generating a document outline to aid the user in navigating the document. They can read aloud the headings on a page according to rank and allow the user to skip directly to the part of the page that interests him. But most of those screen-readers haven't yet implemented the outlining algorithm proposed in HTML5, so for now they'll still generate an outline the old-fashioned way, completely ignorant of these new-fangled sectioning roots and their effect on heading hierarchy.

To some extent this is really the problem of the people who make screen-reading software, and you as a developer are still allowed to push the envelope until they catch up. Unfortunately, it's the users who suffer in the interim. To improve accessibility for your web pages, you may prefer to follow a standard hierarchy and choose headings that match their section's nesting level.

> *If this wasn't quite dense enough for you and you'd like to read a technical breakdown of the HTML5 outlining algorithm, consult the W3C's specification at* `w3.org/TR/html5/sections.html#outlines`

Meaningful Portions

Now that you're familiar with some of the elements you'll use to divide your content into general sections and arrange them in a clear order, it's time to delve into those sections and break that content down further into manageable, readable portions.

p

As you probably learned in grammar school, a paragraph is one or more sentences expressing a single thought or idea, or about one aspect of a topic. It's the standard unit of written prose. A `<p>` start tag marks the beginning of a paragraph, and a `</p>` end tag marks its end, though the end tag is optional if the element immediately following a paragraph is another paragraph, a heading, a list, a table, a form or fieldset, any element that is sectioning content, or any of a few other elements (we won't list them all here).

Even though it's perfectly valid in HTML5 to omit the end tag under some circumstances, it's still a good idea to include it. Should you add some other element after a paragraph in a future update, you could easily introduce validation errors or other problems (unless you remember to end the paragraph when you add the new element, of course). Always be considerate and cautious whenever you choose to omit end tags. If in doubt, close your elements.

Listing 4-11 shows two paragraphs in HTML, and we've closed them both with end tags. Blank lines between elements aren't necessary, but they can help make your markup more readable as you work. Paragraphs are flow content, and can only contain phrasing and interactive content.

Listing 4-11. Two paragraphs in HTML

```
<p>Power Outfitters offers top of the line merchandise at rock-bottom
prices for the discerning costumed crime-fighter. From belts to boomerangs,
we're your one-stop shop for all your specialized gadgetry and costuming
needs.</p>

<p>Come browse our wide selection of capes, cowls, masks, boots, belts,
gloves, tights, unitards, and leotards in all the colors of the rainbow.
Our clothiers are on call 24 hours a day, always ready in a pinch to
replace a singed cloak or patch a ripped tunic, because we know crime
doesn't sleep and justice can never rest.</p>
```

Figure 4-3 shows what these paragraphs will look like in a browser. The p element is styled as block-level by default, so each paragraph begins on a new line and is followed by a blank line of white space. In the past, many web designers would inject empty paragraphs (<p></p>) into their documents to add more vertical space on the page. This is the sort of presentational markup you should avoid—an empty paragraph is meaningless. If you need to add vertical white space to your page layout, use CSS.

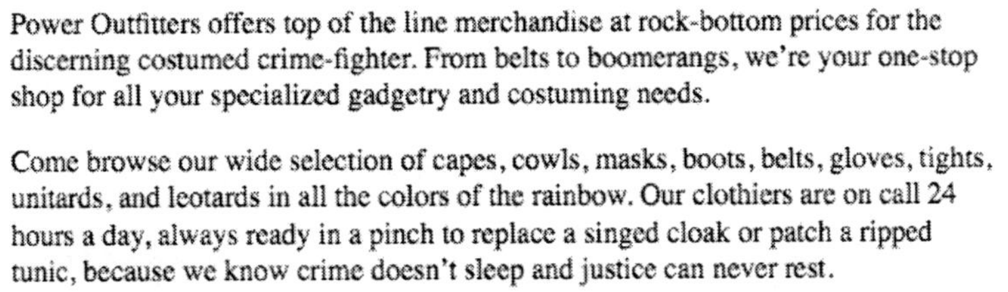

Power Outfitters offers top of the line merchandise at rock-bottom prices for the discerning costumed crime-fighter. From belts to boomerangs, we're your one-stop shop for all your specialized gadgetry and costuming needs.

Come browse our wide selection of capes, cowls, masks, boots, belts, gloves, tights, unitards, and leotards in all the colors of the rainbow. Our clothiers are on call 24 hours a day, always ready in a pinch to replace a singed cloak or patch a ripped tunic, because we know crime doesn't sleep and justice can never rest.

Figure 4-3. A browser displays the two paragraphs as separate blocks

Required Attributes

The p element doesn't have any required attributes.

Optional Attributes

Apart from the standard global attributes, there are no optional attributes for the p element.

blockquote

The blockquote element designates a long quotation, such as a passage from a book or a blurb from a review. This is a flow element that always requires an end tag. Any other flow elements can reside in a blockquote (paragraphs, headings, lists, even other blockquotes), but all of its contents should come from the quoted source.

If you're quoting an online source, even if the quotation is from elsewhere on your own website, you can include the URL of the original source in the optional cite attribute. This attribute's value must be a URL, not a name or title. To mention a source by name, you can use the cite element covered later in this chapter. Listing 4-12 shows a block quotation, including a source URL in the cite attribute.

Listing 4-12. A block quotation

```
<h1>Customer Testimonials</h1>
<p>We love our customers, and our customers love us! Here's just a
small sampling of praise from some of our satisfied champions.</p>

<blockquote cite="http://example.com/blog/2011/manic-monday">
    <p>Having foiled a jewelry store heist on my way to receive a
    medal from the President, imagine my embarrassment to notice
    a nasty laser burn on my cape. There was no time to fly back to
    base and change into my spare costume, even at my speed. Thank
    goodness for Power Outfitters! They had my size and style in stock,
```

```
in just the right shade of red, and at a great price, too. I went
back after the ceremony and bought five more capes, plus matching
gauntlets!</p>
</blockquote>
```

Web browsers will display the blockquote element as an indented block of text, as you can see in Figure 4-4. In the past, some web designers misused this element to create wider margins around their text, whether it was a quotation or not. Once again, that's presentational markup that confuses the content's meaning. You should only use a blockquote for actual quotations and use CSS to control margins.

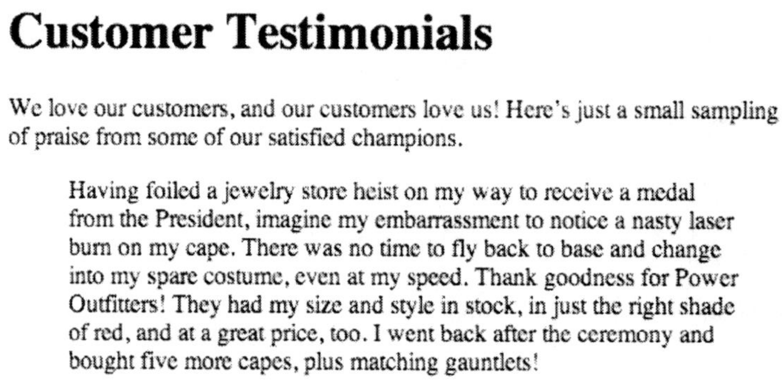

Customer Testimonials

We love our customers, and our customers love us! Here's just a small sampling of praise from some of our satisfied champions.

> Having foiled a jewelry store heist on my way to receive a medal from the President, imagine my embarrassment to notice a nasty laser burn on my cape. There was no time to fly back to base and change into my spare costume, even at my speed. Thank goodness for Power Outfitters! They had my size and style in stock, in just the right shade of red, and at a great price, too. I went back after the ceremony and bought five more capes, plus matching gauntlets!

Figure 4-4. The default rendering of a block quotation as an indented portion of text

HTML 4.01 and XHTML 1.0 specified that a blockquote element could only contain block-level children; plain text or inline (phrasing) elements couldn't appear as direct children of a blockquote. HTML5 has done away with this restriction, but it's always best to use appropriate elements for the quoted content—paragraphs, lists, headings, and so on. The blockquote element also constitutes a sectioning root in HTML, so headings within a block quotation won't interfere with the outline of the surrounding section.

Required Attributes

The blockquote element doesn't have any required attributes.

Optional Attributes

- cite: The URL of the quotation's original source.

address

Contrary to this element's name, address isn't intended for just any postal address; its purpose is to provide contact information for the person or organization responsible for its parent article element (if it occurs within an article), or otherwise for the entire document. An address often belongs in a footer element or possibly in a header, but neither is a requirement.

This element harkens back to the early days when primarily academics and programmers used the Web. A researcher at a university might publish her findings on the Web and include her name, position, website, and e-mail address to stake her claim. In that sense, think of the address element more like a byline or attribution than a physical location on a street in a town somewhere (though it can certainly include a physical addresses as well). An address element says, "This is who is responsible for this article, and here's how to reach them."

The address element is flow content, requires an end tag, and can contain any other flow elements except heading content, sectioning content, or another address. Previous versions of HTML only permitted links and inline phrasing elements within an address, but that restriction has been lifted in HTML5.

Listing 4-13 shows some contact information wrapped in an address element, with a few line breaks (<br>) to provide some additional formatting.

Listing 4-13. Contact info marked up with the address element

```
<address>
  <p><a href="/people/cindy">Cindy Li</a>, Warrior Princess
  <br>1187 Hunterwasser, San Francisco, California
  <br><a href="http://cindyli.com">cindyli.com</a></p>
</address>
```

This example would be semantically appropriate in an article written by Cindy Li, or in an entire document for which Cindy is responsible. If you simply wanted to include Cindy's contact information amidst content she didn't write, some other element would be called for, probably an ordinary paragraph.

Browsers usually display the contents of an address element in an italicized font by default (see Figure 4-5). Of course, if you don't like the looks of it, you can always change its presentation with CSS.

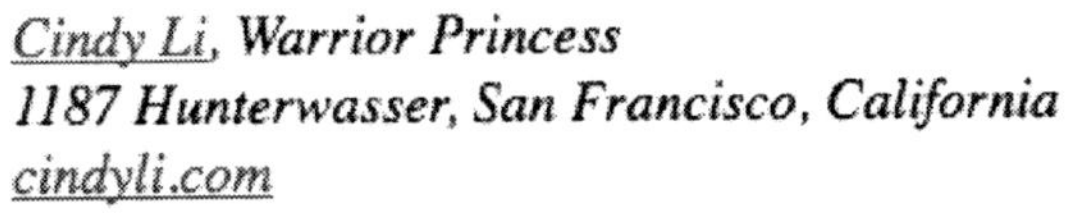

Cindy Li, Warrior Princess
1187 Hunterwasser, San Francisco, California
cindyli.com

Figure 4-5. Most browsers display the address element in italics

Required Attributes

The address element doesn't have any required attributes.

Optional Attributes

There are no optional attributes for the address element.

pre

As you learned in Chapter 2, white space in HTML is "collapsed" when a browser renders the document; multiple spaces are reduced to a single space, and carriage returns are ignored. However, you can use the pre element to define a block of preformatted text in which white space and line breaks should be preserved exactly as they appear in the markup. This element is especially useful for displaying computer code or poetry where line breaks and indention are important, such as in the haiku in Listing 4-14.

Listing 4-14. Poetry wrapped in a `pre` element to preserve its formatting

```
<pre>
        even little things
   can have great impact if they're
              radioactive
</pre>
```

The `pre` element is flow content and it can only contain phrasing elements. Browsers typically render the contents of a `pre` in a monospace typeface, as you can see in Figure 4-6.

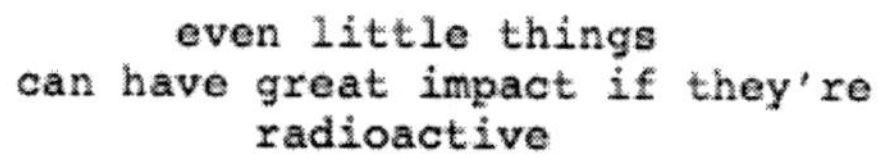

```
           even little things
      can have great impact if they're
                radioactive
```

Figure 4-6. The spaces and returns remain intact on the rendered page

> *Because the `pre` element preserves white space exactly as it's coded, long lines of text will not automatically wrap to fit their container the way ordinary text in HTML does.*

Required Attributes

There are no required attributes for the `pre` element.

Optional Attributes

The `pre` element doesn't offer any optional attributes.

hr

The `hr` element creates a horizontal rule, a dividing line between sections of content. It's largely presentational, but the semantic intent of an `hr` is to indicate a *paragraph-level thematic break* such as a change of topic within a section, or a change of scene in a story. Now that HTML5 has given us the specialized `section` element, you might use separate `section`s to indicate these topic changes, but the `hr` element can still be preferable in some cases.

It's a replaced, void element that can hold no content and has no end tag, though you can optionally close it with a trailing slash (`<hr/>`) as you would in XHTML. Listing 4-15 shows an `hr` element between two paragraphs, marking a change in the story's setting.

Listing 4-15. A horizontal rule marks a change of topic within a section

```
<p>And so the day was saved once again, and the sun sank slowly
in the west, casting its warming glow across a grateful city.</p>

<hr>

<p>Meanwhile, in dank caverns deep below the surface of the Earth,
unrest was stirring amongst the Mole People.</p>
```

The hr element is styled as block-level by default so it will appear on its own line, but the amount of space above and below it will vary slightly in different browsers, as will the appearance of the line itself. Figure 4-7 shows the hr element as Firefox renders it. You can use CSS to specify the top and bottom margins of an hr for some improved consistency across browsers.

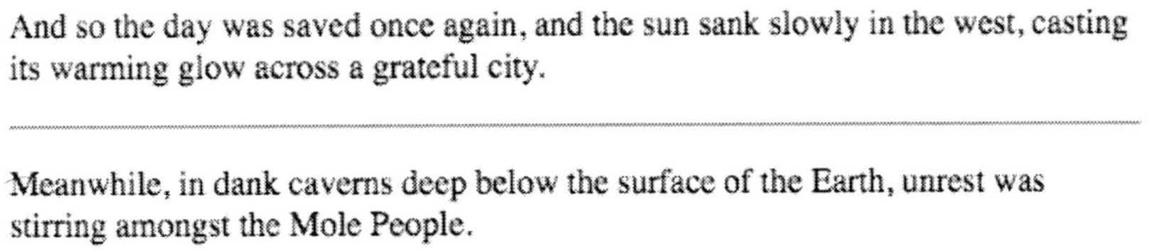

And so the day was saved once again, and the sun sank slowly in the west, casting its warming glow across a grateful city.

Meanwhile, in dank caverns deep below the surface of the Earth, unrest was stirring amongst the Mole People.

Figure 4-7. A horizontal rule rendered by a web browser

Required Attributes

The hr element doesn't have any required attributes.

Optional Attributes

No optional attributes exist for the hr element.

> *Older versions of HTML included a number of presentational attributes for horizontal rules: align to specify the alignment of the rule to the left, right, or center; size to specify the thickness of the rule; width to define its width in pixels; and noshade to override the 3-D shading effect some browsers use when rendering an hr. These are all obsolete in HTML5, and you can better achieve most of their effects with CSS.*

div

The div element creates a general-purpose division in your document, grouping related content and elements together. It's semantically neutral but not entirely meaningless; a div essentially states, "Everything in here belongs together and is separate from everything else," but says nothing specific about the nature of the content within.

Prior to HTML5, the div element was a designer's go-to tool for organizing content into related blocks that could then be styled with CSS or manipulated with JavaScript. But HTML5 has introduced a number of more semantically valuable sectioning elements (covered earlier in this chapter) that can take over that role. Even so, you'll often need to group other elements or related bits of content together without adding the extra layer of meaning that a section, article, aside, nav, or other elements might apply.

In Listing 4-16, a div classified as "legal" wraps around and contains a few related elements, as you might see in a site's footer. This div collects those related elements while also separating them from other adjacent content.

Listing 4-16. A block of content wrapped in a div element

```
<div class="legal">
  <p class="copyright">&copy; 2011-2012 Power Outfitters</p>
  <ul class="nav-legal">
    <li><a href="/legal/terms">Terms of Use</a></li>
    <li><a href="/legal/privacy">Privacy Policy</a></li>
  </ul>
</div>
```

A div is flow content and can contain text and any other elements. Although the div seems similar in function to the section element, a div does *not* establish a new sectioning root in the document hierarchy and doesn't imply any thematic relationship of its contents. A div alone imparts no deeper semantics to its contents, so any text within it should be wrapped in a more meaningful element of its own. The div element's only default styling is to behave as a block-level element; its contents begin on a new line and occupy the full available width.

Because divs are so versatile and act as useful boxes to be styled with CSS, some web designers can show a tendency to overuse them, crowding their markup with an excessive number of otherwise meaningless divs strictly for presentational purposes. This bad habit is sometimes called "divitis" and you should try to avoid it. Use divs wisely to support your content, and always prefer more semantically valuable elements to semantically neutral elements. Like section, the div element is a content-organization device, not just a page-layout device.

Required Attributes

The div element doesn't require any attributes.

Optional Attributes

There are no optional attributes for the div element.

figure

A new addition to HTML5, the figure element represents an image, video, quotation, code listing, or some other content, along with an optional caption, that is self-contained and might be referenced as a single unit from the main flow of content. That isn't to say the figure could be removed entirely; it's not optional content like you'd find in an aside element. A figure is still essential content, but it's the sort of illustrative example that could potentially be removed from the normal flow of content or appear at a different point in the document without harming the readability of the main text.

You've seen many prime examples of figures throughout this book: whenever we include a screen capture or lengthy code listing, we give it a caption and refer to it from the main text. If we were writing this book in HTML, every one of those could be wrapped in a figure element, with its caption in a figcaption element (more on that one next).

Listing 4-17 shows a minimal `figure` element containing a single image without a caption. We'll cover the img element in detail in Chapter 5.

Listing 4-17. A figure element containing a single image with no caption

```
<p>A domino mask covers the area around and between the eyes, and may also
cover the eyebrows and part or all of the nose, as shown below.</p>

<figure>
  <img src="images/domino-mask.jpg" alt="A hero modeling a black and red domino mask">
</figure>
```

In this case, the `figure` element might not seem necessary because it doesn't add a great deal of structural value, but it does imply the figurative nature of the image where an inline image alone would lack that semantic context. The `figure` element really comes into its own when you combine it with the `figcaption` element.

The `figure` element is flow content and can contain any other flow content. It displays as block-level by default, and typically has indented margins the same as `blockquote` (see Figure 4-8), but you can always override those margins in your own style sheet. Also like `blockquote`, the `figure` element is a sectioning root so any headings that appear within it won't affect the generated outline of the parent section.

A domino mask covers the area around and between the eyes, and may also cover the eyebrows and part or all of the nose, as shown below.

Figure 4-8. The figure element is indented on each side by default

Required Attributes

The `figure` element doesn't require any attributes.

Optional Attributes

There aren't any optional attributes for the `figure` element but the usual global attributes still apply.

figcaption

The figcaption element, also introduced in HTML5, represents a caption or legend for the other contents of its parent figure element. It's a flow element and can contain any other flow elements. It can only appear as a child of the figure element, and figcaption must be either the first child or last child of its parent figure. A figure element may only contain a single-child figcaption element.

Listing 4-18 shows a figure element, this time using a code listing instead of an image, like you might see in an online CSS tutorial. We've given it a descriptive figcaption, in this case adding the caption before the rest of the figure content.

Listing 4-18. A code figure with a caption

```
<figure>
  <figcaption>
    These CSS rules will give figures and captions a bit of style
  </figcaption>

  <pre><code>
figure {
  padding: 10px 15px;
  border: 3px double #aaa;
}

figcaption {
  font-style: italic;
  text-align: center;
  padding-bottom: .5em;
  border-bottom: 1px solid #aaa;
  margin-bottom: 1.5em;
}
  </code></pre>
</figure>
```

The figcaption element displays as block-level by default, but has no other default styling so it's ripe for some sprucing up. Figure 4-9 shows the code figure from Listing 4-18, styled with the CSS from that same example (aren't we clever).

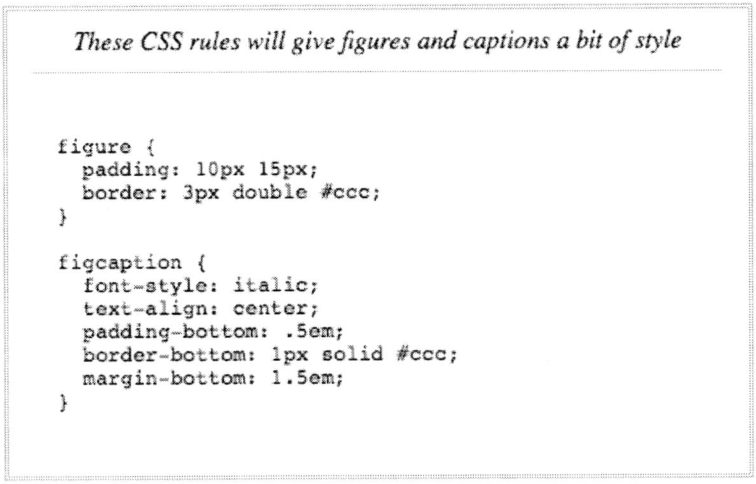

These CSS rules will give figures and captions a bit of style

```
figure {
  padding: 10px 15px;
  border: 3px double #ccc;
}

figcaption {
  font-style: italic;
  text-align: center;
  padding-bottom: .5em;
  border-bottom: 1px solid #ccc;
  margin-bottom: 1.5em;
}
```

Figure 4-9. A lightly styled figure and its caption

A figure element can contain any flow content, and so might actually consist of several elements that act together as one figure with a single figcaption. To take it a step further, a figure could even hold several nested figure elements, each with its own caption, such as the collection of images you see in Listing 4-19. Any one figure element can still only have one child figcaption. All of the nested figure elements together act as one figure, described by a single figcaption. Here the inner captions come after the content they describe, but the group caption appears before its figure content.

Listing 4-19. Multiple figures, each with its own caption, collected as a single figure with another figcaption to describe the group

```
<figure class="product-examples">
  <figcaption>A few of our most popular domino mask designs</figcaption>

  <figure class="product">
    <img src="images/masks/mdts40-th.jpg" alt="" width="192" height="170">
    <figcaption>Model MDTS40<br>"The Colt"</figcaption>
  </figure>

  <figure class="product">
    <img src="images/masks/mdmv77-th.jpg" alt="" width="192" height="170">
    <figcaption>Model MDMV77<br>"The Danvers"</figcaption>
  </figure>

  <figure class="product">
    <img src="images/masks/mddc59-th.jpg" alt="" width="192" height="170">
    <figcaption>Model MDDC59<br>"The Jordan"</figcaption>
  </figure>
</figure>
```

With a bit of added styling, that markup can look something like Figure 4-10.

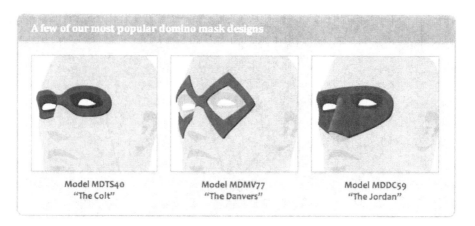

A few of our most popular domino mask designs

Model MDTS40
"The Colt"

Model MDMV77
"The Danvers"

Model MDDC59
"The Jordan"

Figure 4-10. Nested figures after a healthy dose of CSS

Before HTML5 there was no easy way to explicitly associate a picture with a caption. Each of these figures might have been wrapped in a div or perhaps a list item, and each caption might be a heading or paragraph, but the only thing that related each caption to its image was their proximity. Now the figcaption element clearly and emphatically describes the content in its parent figure and can't be mistaken for anything else.

Required Attributes

There aren't any required attributes for the figcaption element.

Optional Attributes

The figcaption element doesn't offer any optional attributes.

iframe

The iframe element designates an *inline frame*, sometimes called a *floating frame*, that can display the contents of a separate document—or even a completely separate website—within a confined space on the rendered page. The spec refers to this as a *nested browsing context*, which is pretty much what it sounds like: a browser within a browser. The content inside the frame exists independent of the surrounding page, and the surrounding page is largely ignorant of anything happening within the frame. The two pages can communicate with each other via JavaScript or server-side programming languages, but for all intents and purposes, the iframe element forms a self-contained window onto another website.

A src attribute specifies the URL of the page to load into the frame, but the iframe element itself may also contain other text or markup as fallback content to be displayed in browsers that don't support the iframe element (such as very old browsers, text browsers, and some mobile devices).

Any CSS styles that apply to the parent document or to the inline frame itself don't apply to the content within the frame, and styles that apply to the embedded content don't have any effect on the parent document. You can embed pages from external websites, but you should only do so with the permission of the external site's owner. Framing someone else's website and passing it off as your own isn't a very nice thing to do, and can be illegal in some cases.

You can specify the size of an inline frame with the optional width and height attributes, or with CSS. The frame typically defaults to around 300 pixels wide and 150 pixels tall if no dimensions are specified, but different browsers will vary. Most browsers also display iframes with a narrow inset border by default, but you can modify or remove the border with CSS.

Listing 4-20 shows a minimal iframe bearing only a src attribute and some simple fallback content for those few browsers that can't display inline frames. In this case, the fallback content includes a link to the framed page so users can still reach that content, even if not in the manner originally intended.

Listing 4-20. A simple iframe with fallback content

```
<section class="news">
  <h2>Latest News</h2>

  <iframe src="newsfeed.html">
    <p>We're sorry, your browser can't display this content in a frame.
    You can still <a href="newsfeed.html">visit the page directly</a>.</p>
  </iframe>

</section>
```

When the contents of an iframe exceed the frame's dimensions, scrollbars will appear allowing visitors to scroll the page within the frame to bring the overflowing content into view. You can disable those scrollbars with CSS and the declaration overflow:hidden, but that will obviously prevent your users from seeing the hidden content. HTML5 has introduced the new seamless attribute, which instructs the browser to render the iframe as if it were part of the parent page, without a border or scrollbars, but no browsers support the seamless attribute at the time of this writing.

Figure 4-11 shows an iframe with only the default styling. This image is from Safari for Mac OSX, which draws the frame at 300 pixels wide and 150 pixels tall by default, though some other browsers may vary slightly.

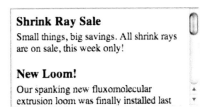

Figure 4-11. An iframe with default styling

An optional name attribute provides a name for the iframe's browsing context, allowing links, forms, and scripts to target the frame and load other pages in the same space, or to interact with the content within.

The optional sandbox attribute applies a set of extra restrictions on the frame's contents as a security measure in case the frame is displaying an untrusted website. When the sandbox attribute is present without a value, the frame's content is limited in its ability to affect the parent document, isolating the framed page in a virtual sandbox so any malicious code within can't harm the page that surrounds it, the website hosting the parent document, the browser, or the user's computer. Supplying values in the sandbox attribute can selectively allow some of the restricted actions: allow-same-origin, allow-top-navigation, allow-forms, and allow-scripts. Only a few browsers have implemented support for the sandbox attribute so far, but the others will catch up soon.

In lieu of a src attribute to provide the URL of the frame's content, the new srcdoc attribute can carry the HTML markup for the framed document. That's right, a complete HTML document acting as an attribute's value. If the src and srcdoc attributes are both defined, the srcdoc attribute takes precedence and the src attribute can still provide a fallback URL for browsers that don't support srcdoc. Right now that's every browser, because none of them have yet implemented the srcdoc attribute.

Required Attributes

The iframe element technically doesn't require any attributes for validation, but without either a src or srcdoc attribute, the frame will have no content to display, showing nothing but a blank, white void.

Optional Attributes

- height: The height of the frame in pixels.

- name: A name for the embedded browsing context (the frame). A valid name can be any single word that does not begin with an underscore (_); names beginning with underscores are reserved for special keywords. The frame name can be used as the value of the target attribute of an anchor or form element, or the formtarget attribute of an input or button element.

- sandbox: If specified as an empty string, this attribute enables extra restrictions on the content that can appear in the inline frame. The value of the attribute can be a space-separated list of tokens that lift particular restrictions. Valid tokens are:

  - allow-same-origin: Allows the content to be treated as being from the same origin as the containing document. If this keyword isn't present, the embedded content is treated as being from a unique origin.

  - allow-top-navigation: Allows the embedded browsing context to load content from the top-level browsing context. If this keyword isn't present, this operation isn't allowed.

  - allow-forms: Allows the embedded browsing context to submit forms. If this keyword isn't present, this operation isn't allowed.

  - allow-scripts: Allows the embedded browsing context to run scripts (but not create pop-up windows). If this keyword isn't present, this operation isn't allowed.

- seamless: A Boolean attribute that, when present, indicates that the browser should render the inline frame in a way that makes it appear to be part of the containing document. For example, a seamless frame might apply CSS styles from the parent document before styles specified in the framed document, and links in the contained document could open pages in the parent browsing context rather than within the iframe (unless another setting prevents this). This effectively embeds the external content into the rendered page, but does not embed the external markup into the current HTML document. There aren't any browsers that support the seamless attribute as of this writing.

- src: The URL of the page to embed. This can be either a relative or absolute URL, and doesn't have to be a page within the same domain as the parent document.

- srcdoc: The content of the page that the embedded context is to contain. If src and srcdoc are both specified, srcdoc takes precedence and src acts as fallback for browsers that don't support the srcdoc attribute.

- width: The width of the frame in pixels.

> The iframe element has been around for a long time, and older versions of HTML offered other, similar framing devices as well. The frameset and frame elements were introduced in HTML 4 and proved popular with web designers, but they were also extremely problematic and inaccessible, and ultimately did more harm than good. Window frames and inline frames were excluded entirely from XHTML 1.0 Strict. Old-school frames are still dead in HTML5 (and good riddance), but iframe has been renewed and revised, largely due to just how very useful it is and how commonplace it is on the Web.

Lists

A list is simply a collection of two or more related items. A list consisting of a single item is perfectly valid and may even be semantically correct in some cases, but normally a list groups several items together. There are three types of lists in HTML: unordered lists, ordered lists, and description lists.

ul

An unordered list, designated by the ul element, is a list wherein the sequence of the items isn't especially significant, such as a list of ingredients—the order in which you fetch them from the pantry doesn't matter so long as you get everything on the list. Each list item is in turn defined by its own li element, all contained by the surrounding <ul> and </ul> tags. The ul element is flow content and only li elements are allowed as its children; no text or other elements can appear in an unordered list unless an li contains them.

Listing 4-21 shows the ingredients for a cake recipe in an unordered list, with each item living in its own li element (more on that one in a moment).

Listing 4-21. An unordered listing of ingredients

```
<ul>
  <li>1/2 cup butter</li>
  <li>1/2 cup milk</li>
  <li>2 eggs</li>
  <li>2 teaspoons vanilla extract</li>
  <li>1 1/2 cups all-purpose flour</li>
  <li>1 3/4 teaspoons baking powder</li>
  <li>1 cup white sugar</li>
</ul>
```

By default, unordered lists are displayed as slightly indented blocks with a bullet marking each list item, as seen in Figure 4-8. Later in this chapter you'll see how you can change the default bullet using CSS, replacing it with a different character or even an image.

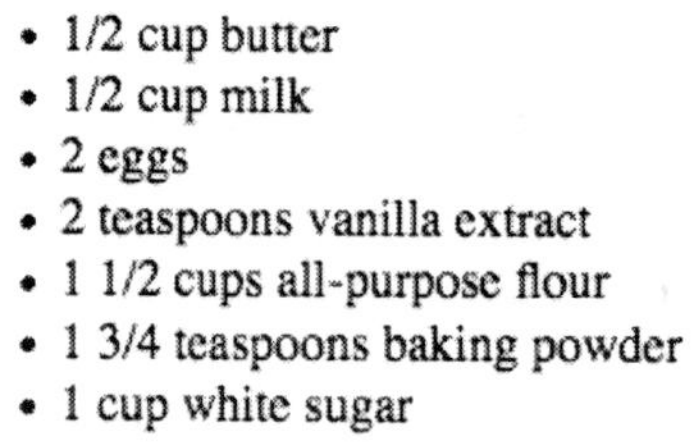

- 1/2 cup butter
- 1/2 cup milk
- 2 eggs
- 2 teaspoons vanilla extract
- 1 1/2 cups all-purpose flour
- 1 3/4 teaspoons baking powder
- 1 cup white sugar

Figure 4-12. A web browser renders the bullets automatically

Required Attributes

The ul element doesn't require any attributes.

Optional Attributes

The ul element doesn't feature any optional attributes.

ol

The ol element defines an ordered list, one in which the items are meant to be read or followed in a specific sequence, such as the steps in a recipe. Listing 4-22 shows an example. Note that the items aren't numbered in the markup—the browser will do the numbering for you.

Listing 4-22. A deliberate sequence of steps marked up as an ordered list

```
<ol>
  <li>Preheat oven to 350 degrees F (175 degrees C). Grease and
  flour a 9x9 inch pan.</li>
  <li>Cream together the sugar and butter. Beat in the eggs one
  at a time, then add the vanilla. Combine flour and baking powder,
  add to the creamed mixture and mix well. Finally, stir in the
  milk until batter is smooth. Pour or spoon batter into the
  prepared pan.</li>
```

```
<li>Bake for 30 to 40 minutes in the preheated oven. Cake is done
when it springs back to the touch.</li>
</ol>
```

As you can see in Figure 4-9, each item in an ordered list is displayed with a number beside it, with those numbers created automatically by the browser. By default, the ol element displays as block-level with some padding on the left side (or right side, in right-to-left languages) to make space for the numbering.

1. Preheat oven to 350 degrees F (175 degrees C). Grease and flour a 9x9 inch pan.
2. Cream together the sugar and butter. Beat in the eggs one at a time, then add the vanilla. Combine flour and baking powder, add to the creamed mixture and mix well. Finally, stir in the milk until batter is smooth. Pour or spoon batter into the prepared pan.
3. Bake for 30 to 40 minutes in the preheated oven. Cake is done when it springs back to the touch.

Figure 4-13. The web browser numbers the list items automatically.

Like unordered lists, the ol element is flow content, requires an end tag, and can only have lis as children.

Required Attributes

There are no attributes required for the ol element.

Optional Attributes

- type: indicates the marker to use when rendering the list. Possible values are 1 (decimal, the default, shows Arabic numerals), a (lowercase English alphabet), A (uppercase English alphabet), i (lowercase Roman numerals), and I (uppercase Roman numerals). All of these have CSS equivalents using the list-style-type property, but sometimes the type of list is essential to the meaning of the content—an alphabetical list of names, for instance—and in those cases it might be preferable to declare the list type in the markup rather than in a presentational style sheet.

- start: a numeral indicating the number from which the list should start counting. The value of this attribute must be a whole integer. A list of five items with the attribute start="3" would be numbered from 3 to 7 when the list is rendered.

- reversed: a Boolean attribute that, when present, reverses the numbering order of the list. For example, a list of five items would be numbered from 5 to 1 when a browser renders it. This is a new attribute in HTML5 so not all browsers support it yet. One possible real-world application for the reversed attribute would be a list that allows a user to sort its items by ascending or descending order; a few lines of JavaScript could simply toggle the reversed attribute rather than rewriting the entire list. If your list should only ever be read in reverse order, you should probably just put the items in that order to begin with.

> *The* type *and* start *attributes existed in older versions of HTML, but were phased out in XHTML because they were considered presentational. They've been brought back in HTML5 because they do have real meaning in some situations. You should only use these attributes when the content demands it, and use CSS when you only want the visual effect.*

li

In both ordered and unordered lists, the li element defines individual list items. A list item can contain text or any flow elements, including more lists. Listing 4-23 shows an elaborate unordered list with more lists nested within it. The containing list has only a single item in this example, but you could add any number of costume accessories within that list, each following the same pattern in its own li.

Listing 4-23. A complex unordered list

```
<h1>Costume Accessories</h1>
<p>All the trappings and trimmings.</p>

<ul>
  <li>
    <h2>Masks and Cowls</h2>
    <p>Protect your secret identity.</p>
    <ul>
      <li>Domino mask</li>
      <li>Half-mask
        <ul>
          <li>Traditional upper face mask</li>
          <li>Lower face "surgical" mask</li>
        </ul>
      </li>
      <li>Full face mask (eye lenses optional)</li>
      <li>Cowl
        <ul>
          <li>Classic loose cowl (hood)</li>
          <li>Fitted cowl</li>
          <li>Fitted cowl with integrated upper half-mask</li>
        </ul>
      </li>
    </ul>
  </li>
</ul>
```

When one list is nested within another, the inner list will, by default, be styled differently according to its level of nesting. Figure 4-10 shows how this list is rendered, and you can see that each nested list is indented a bit further and displayed with a different style of marker. Nested ordered lists inherit their numbering style from their parent, but will begin a new numbering sequence.

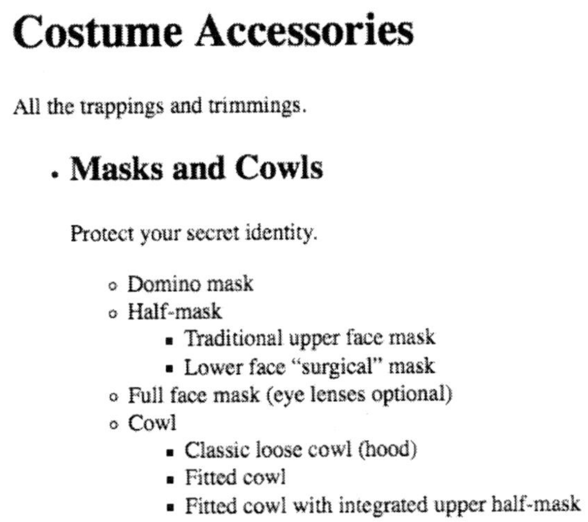

Costume Accessories

All the trappings and trimmings.

• Masks and Cowls

Protect your secret identity.

- Domino mask
- Half-mask
  - Traditional upper face mask
  - Lower face "surgical" mask
- Full face mask (eye lenses optional)
- Cowl
  - Classic loose cowl (hood)
  - Fitted cowl
  - Fitted cowl with integrated upper half-mask

Figure 4-14. The list as it appears in a browser with default styling

You can choose to omit the end tag of a list item if it's immediately followed by another list item, or if there is no more content in the parent element (meaning it's the last item in the list, in which case the very next tag will be the parent list's end tag). An li element can only occur as a child of the ul and ol elements, or as a child of the interactive menu element, which is new in HTML5 and covered in Chapter 8.

Required Attributes

There are no required attributes for the li element.

Optional Attributes

- value: If the li is a child of an ol element, this attribute can specify the item's displayed number in the list, but doesn't change the actual list order. The attribute's value must be a whole integer, and subsequent items will continue the numbering after a previous item's value. For example, in an ordered list of five items where the third item has the attribute value="10", the first two items will be numbered 1 and 2 and the last three items numbered 10, 11, and 12 (assuming they have no value attributes of their own).

dl

A description list isn't merely a collection of items; it's a collection of items and descriptions of each. Unlike ordered and unordered lists, a description list doesn't contain list item (li) elements. Rather, items in a description list are groupings of terms (dt) and descriptions (dd).

In past versions of HTML, the dl element was a *definition list*, intended to list terms and their definitions like you'd find in a glossary. There's an implied semantic connection between a term and its definition, and because of this semantic symbiosis, definition lists were frequently used to mark up content that wasn't technically a list of terms and definitions. A series of questions and their answers, a list of employees and their job titles, or a sequence of events and the dates on which they occurred were all common uses of definition lists. HTML5 has formalized this real-world usage and redefined the definition list as a *description list*, suitable for any case where content calls for a listing of name-value groups. You can still use a dl for a list of terms and definitions, of course.

The dl element is flow content, requires an end tag, and can only contain dt and dd elements as its children. A single term may have several associated descriptions, or a single description may apply to several terms grouped before it. The list is segmented wherever a dt immediately follows a dd, marking the beginning of a new sequence of terms and descriptions.

Required Attributes

The dl element doesn't have any required attributes.

Optional Attributes

There are no optional attributes for the dl element.

dt

The dt element, which can only contain text and/or phrase elements, designates a term or item being described. A description term (or sequence of terms) is associated with every description that follows it until a new dt element appears to begin a new sequence, or until the list ends with a </dl> end tag. You can omit the </dt> end tag if the element is immediately followed by another dt element or a dd element.

Required Attributes

There are no required attributes for the dt element.

Optional Attributes

The dt element doesn't offer any optional attributes.

dd

The dd element contains a description of the dt element (or elements) that immediately precedes it. In the case of multiple descriptions for a single term, each one should be wrapped in its own dd element. The dd element is flow content and can contain text or other flow elements. If your description spans several paragraphs, mark them up as paragraphs (p) in a single dd rather than as separate dds—the entire contents of one dd element should comprise one description. The dd's end tag is optional if the next element is another dd, a dt, or if the next tag is a </dl> end tag.

Listing 4-24 shows the markup for a brief description list. In the example, the first term's description consists of two paragraphs, whereas the second term has two distinct descriptions.

Listing 4-24. A description list featuring two terms

```
<dl>
  <dt>Domino mask</dt>
  <dd>
    <p>A domino mask covers the area around and between the eyes,
    offering maximum comfort, freedom, and visibility, but minimal
    obscurity.</p>
    <p>The name comes from the Latin <i lang="la">dominus</i>, meaning "lord"
    or "master."</p>
  </dd>

  <dt>Cowl</dt>
  <dd>A head covering combining a hood and a collar or mantle.</dd>
  <dd>A streamlined covering around an aircraft engine or personal jetpack.</dd>
</dl>
```

Most browsers will display dd elements slightly indented from their corresponding dt. When a dd contains other structural markup (such as paragraphs), the default margins of that nested element will apply. As you can see in Figure 4-11, the paragraphs in the first term's description have default margins above and below them, whereas the second term's two descriptions have no top and bottom margins at all. You can modify all of this, of course, with CSS.

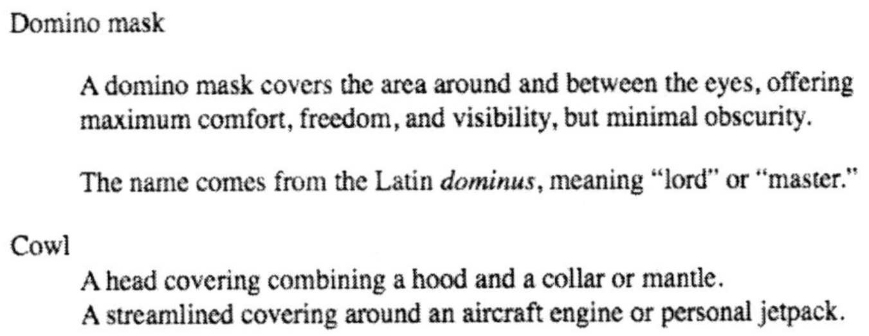

Domino mask

A domino mask covers the area around and between the eyes, offering maximum comfort, freedom, and visibility, but minimal obscurity.

The name comes from the Latin *dominus*, meaning "lord" or "master."

Cowl

A head covering combining a hood and a collar or mantle.
A streamlined covering around an aircraft engine or personal jetpack.

Figure 4-15. The description list rendered with default browser styling

Required Attributes

The dd element doesn't require any attributes.

Optional Attributes

There are no optional attributes for the dd element.

Phrasing Elements

We've covered most of the common elements you'll use to organize your content into sections, and to break it down further into readable portions. Headings, paragraphs, and lists are the basic building blocks of structured text. In this next section, we'll move inside the blocks to pick out smaller morsels of content for special attention.

These elements are called *phrasing elements* because they're intended to wrap around a short string of a few words, or even a single word, to give it added meaning and formatting that sets it apart from the other words that surround it. These elements are all displayed as inline by default, they can only contain text or other phrase elements, and all of them require an end tag.

Emphasis and Importance: em and strong

The em element adds emphasis to a word or phrase, and browsers typically style it in an italicized font. The strong element adds strong emphasis to highlight words or phrases of greater importance than the surrounding text, and it's usually styled in a bold font. Though graphical browsers usually style these elements in italics or bold, don't focus only on appearances; other devices may apply emphasis differently. For example, screen-reading software used by the visually impaired might read the contents of an em or strong aloud with different vocal inflections. These elements have real meaning, not just font styling. A strong element says, "this is important, pay attention," not just, "this text is bold."

Listing 4-25 shows a passage of text with some emphasized phrases. For yet another level of emphasis, you can combine the strong and em elements, effectively declaring that the text is both emphasized *and* important, displayed in a font that is both italicized and boldfaced (see Figure 4-12).

Listing 4-25. A paragraph containing some emphasized phrases

```
<p><strong>Please note:</strong> due to the accelerated decay rate of
phlebotinum isotopes upon activation, <em>we cannot accept returns</em>
of opened vials of youth, growth, intelligence, or strength serums.
<strong><em>All sales are final.</em></strong></p>
```

> **Please note:** due to the accelerated decay rate of phlebotinum isotopes upon activation, *we cannot accept returns* of opened vials of youth, growth, intelligence, or strength serums. *All sales are final.*

Figure 4-16. The contents of em are italicized, the contents of strong are boldfaced, and the combined elements have a combined style.

You can also nest em or strong elements, and the number of parent em or strong elements indicates the relative level of emphasis or importance, as shown in Listing 4-26. An em within an em is extra-emphasized and a strong inside a strong is super-important. The layers of emphasis are purely semantic and browsers don't style these nested elements any differently than their parents, but you can easily change that in your own CSS.

Listing 4-26. Nested em and strong elements imply higher levels of emphasis and/or importance

```
<p><em><strong>Warning!</strong> these premises are protected by
<em>cyborg space gorillas with <em>laser eyes</em></em>.
<strong><strong>Enter at your own risk!</strong></strong></em></p>
```

Required Attributes

There are no required attributes for the em or strong elements.

Optional Attributes

The em and strong elements don't have any optional attributes.

time

Introduced in HTML5, the time element represents either a precise time on a 24-hour clock or a specific date on the calendar (with an optional time as well). The element was introduced to standardize the way dates and times are marked up, so that browsers and web apps can potentially detect and read encoded dates/times and, for example, allow you to add an appointment to your calendar, or alert you when there are five minutes remaining to bid in an online auction. The possible applications for machine-readable dates and times are limitless.

Dates in a time element must follow a specific format that scripts and user-agents can interpret: a four-digit year, two-digit month, and two-digit day, in that order, separated by hyphens (YYYY-MM-DD). Times in a time element must be on a 24-hour clock, not a 12-hour clock, so "2:45 pm" would be written as "14:45". There's no default styling of time elements; they appear as regular text in whatever style they inherit from their parents. Listing 4-27 shows two examples of time elements, marking a date and a time, respectively.

Listing 4-27. Two examples of the time element

```
<p>We'll be closed on <time>2012-05-05</time> but will reopen
at <time>08:00</time> sharp the following morning.</p>
```

The optional datetime attribute can carry the specific date and/or time in a machine-readable format, freeing you to be more vague and human-friendly with your text:

```
<p>We'll be closed on <time datetime="2012-05-05">Saturday, May 5</time>
but will reopen at <time datetime="08:00">8 am</time> the day after.</p>
```

A datetime attribute can include both a date and time, with the time preceded by T:

```
<p>We will reopen on <time datetime="2012-05-06T08:00">Sunday</time>.</p>
```

> There are very specific requirements for formatting dates and times in a datetime attribute, conforming to international standards. See the spec for much more detail: w3.org/TR/html5/common-microsyntaxes.html#dates-and-times

Even with a datetime attribute, you should only use the time element for specific, known dates and times like "August 8, 1961" or "10:02", not for vague terms like "fifty years ago" or "an hour from now," nor for time spans like "77 nanoseconds" or "13.7 billion years." Dates must also be complete—with date, month, and year—so don't use a time element for partial or nonspecific dates like "December 20" or "1690" or

"November, 2019." Furthermore, dates are limited to the modern Gregorian calendar, introduced in the 16th century, so don't use the time element to reference dates in the distant past unless you can accurately convert those dates to the Gregorian calendar. It's hard to pinpoint a date like "October 1, 2975 BCE" because the month of October didn't actually exist back then.

Listing 4-28 is an example of a time element indicating an article's publication date. The datetime attribute has a value machines can interpret, whereas the element's text contents are intended for human readers.

Listing 4-28. A time element indicating a precise date and time

```
<footer>
  <p>Posted on <time datetime="2012-05-05T15:35:42-07:00">↵
  Saturday, May 5, 2012 at 3:35 pm Pacific</time></p>
</footer>
```

Required Attributes

The time element doesn't require any attributes if its contents are properly formatted.

Optional Attributes

- datetime: The precise date and/or time represented, with optional time zone offset. This attribute's value must be a valid date string, a valid time string, or combination of the two.

In late October 2011, the WHAT Working Group announced that the time element was being removed from their working version of the HTML5 specification, to be replaced by a new data element that would allow for the inclusion of more general-purpose, machine-readable data beyond just dates and times. There was a fair bit of public outcry from web developers, citing many real-world uses for encoding times and dates in ways that the generic data element couldn't readily serve as substitute. The decision was quickly reversed and time was restored to the spec, though slightly revised and now lacking the pubdate attribute.

mark

The mark element highlights a segment of text for reference, to indicate its relevance in some other context. The element imparts no further semantic meaning to its contents; it only marks the text as a passage of interest. For example, you might use the mark element in a block quotation to highlight the particular part of the text you're discussing or referencing, to focus the reader's attention on some detail while still including the longer quotation to preserve the original context.

It has long been common practice in journalism and academic writing to mark relevant passages with italics or bold text, along with a disclaimer like, "emphasis added," just to clarify for the reader that the original text didn't stress those phrases. On the Web, this always required some other element (usually em, strong, i, b, or even a span), but now the authors of HTML5 have provided the mark element for just this purpose. Listing 4-29 shows the mark element calling out one part of a longer quotation.

Listing 4-29. Using the mark element in a blockquote

```
<p>After several hours trying to determine why the loom wasn't
powering up, we finally read the instruction manual:</p>

<blockquote>
  <p>Before initializing the fluxomolecular extrusion loom,
  ensure that all interlocks are active and dynatherms are
  properly connected. You may need to <mark>step on the primary
  samoflange several times</mark> before it engages.</p>
</blockquote>

<p>The samoflange was the source of our trouble. Unfortunately,
none of us even knew what a "samoflange" was.</p>
```

When the mark element occurs in regular, unquoted prose, it should call attention to words or phrases that are relevant to the user's current activities. The most common example is a page of search results, where the terms your visitor sought are highlighted with mark elements. Those words might not be of special significance in the original text as it was written, but the mark element points them out because they're the words your searcher was looking for. Automated scripts or server-side applications should usually insert such action-oriented mark elements, and they likely won't be part of any handcrafted markup you author yourself.

This is a new element in HTML5 so not all browsers give it any default styling, but those that do will typically display the contents of a mark with a bright yellow background color and black text color—shown in Figure 4-17—as if the text had been marked with a highlighter pen (of course, this is printed in black and white, but it's really yellow, honest).

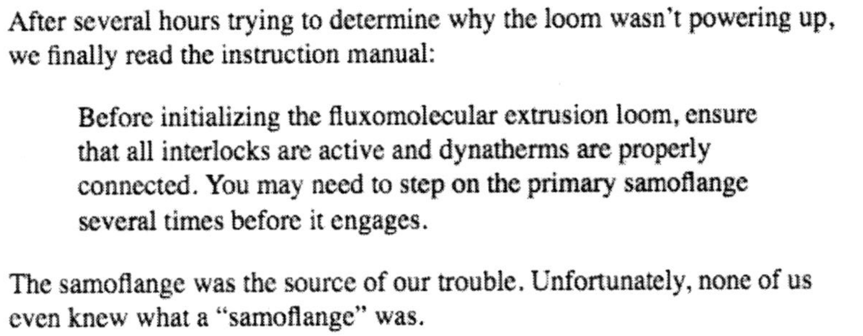

> After several hours trying to determine why the loom wasn't powering up, we finally read the instruction manual:
>
> > Before initializing the fluxomolecular extrusion loom, ensure that all interlocks are active and dynatherms are properly connected. You may need to step on the primary samoflange several times before it engages.
>
> The samoflange was the source of our trouble. Unfortunately, none of us even knew what a "samoflange" was.

Figure 4-17. Text highlighted with the mark element

Required Attributes

The mark element doesn't require any attributes

Optional Attributes

There are no optional attributes for the mark element.

cite

The cite element designates the title of a quoted or referenced work: a book, poem, song, painting, movie, magazine article, blog post, Wikipedia entry, technical specification, or what have you. In previous versions of HTML, the cite element was intended for *any* cited resource, including the names of people. But cite has been redefined in HTML5 to expressly forbid its use for the names of people (or other entities); now you can only use cite for *titles of cited works*.

This decree seems arbitrary and unnecessarily limiting, but even worse, it breaches backward compatibility with existing documents that rightfully used cite for names. But we're in luck: validators can't read. There's no way for any user-agent—be it validator or browser—to tell whether the contents of a cite element are a title or a name, so this is one case where you shouldn't feel too guilty about bending the rules. Use cite for names if you like.

"But what about following the rules?" you ask, shocked at the very suggestion of going against the HTML5 specification. Well, in the case of the cite element, the spec authors based the decision on somewhat flawed reasoning. Because most browsers display cite elements in italics, and titles are usually italicized but names are not, it was decided that cite shouldn't be used for names. This new restriction is based on the *typical default styling* of the element, not on its semantic function or real-world usage.

If you're a stickler for adhering to the theoretical purity of technical specifications, then by all means use cite only for titles and never for names. But if your content includes a citation of a person, group, company, character, or any other entity, especially in the context of a quotation, the cite element is a semantically appropriate choice to mark their name. Perhaps, in time, the spec will be corrected.

> For more on the flawed reasoning behind this limitation of the cite element, and how our civil disobedience can bring about change in the specs, read Jeremy Keith's wonderful rant, Incite A Riot (24ways.org/2009/incite-a-riot)

We've used the cite element three times in Listing 4-30: for a person's name, the title of an article, and the name of a publication. Only the title is "correct" according to the current HTML5 specification, but all three are semantically correct for the content at hand.

Listing 4-30. Three different applications of the cite element

```
<p>Famed reporter <cite>Norm Deplume</cite> had this to say about
our shop:</p>

<blockquote cite="http://example.com/gadgets/PowerOutfitters/">
  <p>Power Outfitters Superhero Costume and Supply Company is
  located in a nondescript building on Kirby Ave, a site that
  once housed a large printing plant. Behind their modest
  storefront is an expansive warehouse positively packed to
  the portholes with paraphernalia.</p>
</blockquote>

<p class="source"><cite>Where Do They Get Those Wonderful Toys?</cite>,
<cite>Cape and Cowl Quarterly</cite>, August 9, 2011</p>
```

Web browsers usually display the contents of a cite element in an italicized font, as shown in Figure 4-18, but—wait for it—you can change that with CSS. In the case of names that should not be italicized, you could use a class attribute to distinguish cited names from cited titles: <cite class="name">, for example.

> Famed reporter *Norm Deplume* had this to say about our shop:
>
> > Power Outfitters Superhero Costume and Supply Company is located in a nondescript building on Kirby Ave, a site that once housed a large printing plant. Behind their modest storefront is an expansive warehouse positively packed to the portholes with paraphernalia.
>
> *Where Do They Get Those Wonderful Toys?*, *Cape and Cowl Quarterly*, August 9, 2011

Figure 4-18. Browsers italicize the cite element by default

Required Attributes

No attributes are required for the cite element.

Optional Attributes

There are no optional attributes for the cite element.

q

The q element marks up short, inline quotations (as opposed to blockquote, which you should use for longer quotations of more than a sentence or two). Like the blockquote element, a q element may carry a cite attribute to include the URL of the quotation's source, as you see in Listing 4-31.

Listing 4-31. The q element with a URL in a cite attribute

```
<p><cite>Norm Deplume</cite>, gadget reporter for <cite>Cape and Cowl↩
Quarterly</cite>, was impressed by our wide selection, saying that
our warehouse is <q cite="http://example.com/gadgets/PowerOutfitters/">↩
positively packed to the portholes with paraphernalia.</q></p>
```

A web browser should automatically render the opening and closing quotation marks at the beginning and ending of a q element, so don't add your own quotation marks with the quoted text. Furthermore, only use the q element for actual quotations from a source, not simply to generate punctuation. Don't use a q element to denote example terms or sarcasm; use regular quotation marks for so-called "mock quotes."

> *Some older browsers (most notably Internet Explorer) didn't generate any punctuation around q elements, so for years many web authors avoided the element entirely. But all current versions of major web browsers—including IE since version 8—display automatic quotation marks for the q element.*

Figure 4-19 shows the quotation from Listing 4-31, complete with automatic punctuation.

Norm Deplume, gadget reporter for *Cape and Cowl Quarterly*, was impressed by our wide selection, saying that our warehouse is "positively packed to the portholes with paraphernalia."

Figure 4-19. The browser generates the quotation marks before and after the q element

Required Attributes

The q element doesn't have any required attributes.

Optional Attributes

- cite: The URL of the quotation's original source.

dfn

The dfn element denotes the defining instance of a term, especially one that may reoccur throughout the rest of the document. If the term is defined in context, the dfn element alone is enough to indicate that a new word has been introduced. If the term's meaning isn't made clear by the adjacent text, you should include a brief definition in a title attribute. Browsers usually display a dfn in an italicized font to set it off from the surrounding text.

Listing 4-32 shows an example of a dfn element that includes a short definition in its title attribute.

Listing 4-32. A dfn element with a definition in its title attribute

```
<p>For added coverage, protection, and identity obfuscation, select
from our wide variety of <dfn title="A head covering combining a hood↪
and a collar or mantle">cowl</dfn> designs. We have cowls with ears,
horns, wings, spikes, lightning bolts, or even plain; whatever your
motif, we can hide your face in style.</p>
```

Required Attributes

There are no required attributes for the dfn element.

Optional Attributes

The dfn element doesn't have any optional attributes.

abbr

The abbr element indicates an abbreviation—a shortened form of a lengthy term. For example, *etc.* is an abbreviation of *et cetera* (the Latin phrase meaning "and so forth"), and *Inc.* is an abbreviation of *Incorporated*. Abbreviations can also be formed from the initial letters of a multiword phrase such as *ATM* for *Automatic Teller Machine* or *CSS* for *Cascading Style Sheets*, or from initials extracted from the syllables of a long word, such as *DNA* for *deoxyribonucleic acid* (these are also called *initialisms*).

An *acronym* is a specific type of abbreviation, being a pronounceable word formed from the first letters of a multiword phrase—*laser* from *light amplification by simulated emission of radiation* and *PIN* from *personal identification number*—or the first portion of each word, as in *retcon* from *retroactive continuity* and *sysadmin* from *system administrator*.

Previous versions of HTML included an `acronym` element specifically for marking up acronyms as a distinct type of abbreviation, but browser support for `acronym` is still inconsistent after all these years, and web authors are often confused about when to use `abbr` or when to use `acronym`. HTML5 has eliminated these problems by eliminating the `acronym` element altogether. Acronyms are abbreviations themselves, so the more general `abbr` element covers acronyms as well.

Use the `abbr` element similarly to `dfn` to point out the defining instance of an abbreviation, the first time it's introduced in a body of text. You can use the abbreviation in text thereafter without any special markup. Of course, not every abbreviation needs to be called out: common ones such as *etc.* and *Inc.* probably don't require explanation. Use your best judgment based on your understanding of the content and your audience.

An `abbr` element can (and usually should) include the expanded form of the term in a `title` attribute. As with the `dfn` element, if the abbreviation is explained in the regular text, expanding it in a `title` attribute isn't necessary. However, if a `title` attribute is present, its value *must* be the expanded form of the abbreviation and nothing else.

Listing 4-33 shows two ways to introduce an abbreviation in text.

Listing 4-33. Abbreviations marked up with the `abbr` element

```
<blockquote>
  <p>After the <abbr title="Electro-Magnetic Pulse">EMP</abbr> incapacitated
  all my electronics, I feared I would be trapped on that rooftop without the
  use of my anti-gravity belt. Luckily I still had my trusty Gravity-Assisted
  Descent Grapple Extension Tool (<abbr>GADGET</abbr>) from Power Outfitters.
  Its double-braided polyfiber construction is purely analog, and thus immune
  to all electro-magnetic disturbances. I rappelled down with ease!</p>
</blockquote>
```

Some browsers (like Firefox for Mac, shown in Figure 4-20) display an `abbr` element with a dotted underline if it carries a `title` attribute, and no decoration if the attribute is absent. Other browsers don't apply any default styling to `abbr` elements at all. Most browsers *do* display the value of the `title` attribute in a "tooltip" when the user's pointer lingers over the element, to reveal the extended form of an abbreviation.

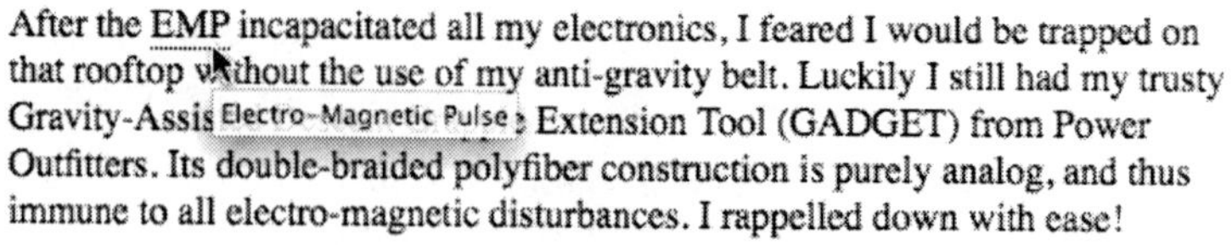

After the EMP incapacitated all my electronics, I feared I would be trapped on that rooftop without the use of my anti-gravity belt. Luckily I still had my trusty Gravity-Assis Electro-Magnetic Pulse Extension Tool (GADGET) from Power Outfitters. Its double-braided polyfiber construction is purely analog, and thus immune to all electro-magnetic disturbances. I rappelled down with ease!

Figure 4-20. Some browsers add a dotted underline to abbreviations, and most show `title` attributes in tooltips

Required Attributes

The `abbr` element doesn't require any attributes.

Optional Attributes

There are no optional attributes for the `abbr` element apart from the standard global attributes.

small

The `small` element indicates a side note or fine print relating to the main text. This might be a disclaimer, clarification, citation, attribution, restriction, or a copyright or licensing notice. It's not intended for long passages of text, only short phrases inline with other text, or sometimes in a footnote at the end of an article or document. The `small` element indicates that its contents are supplemental to the main text but not any less important, and a `small` doesn't serve to "de-emphasize" phrases within a passage already emphasized by the em or `strong` elements.

This element is a carryover from past versions of HTML, where it was essentially a presentational element that only denoted small text. Authors often used the `small` element for such fine print, and so HTML5 has adopted and standardized that practice, giving the element more semantic purpose. Use the `small` element to include these meaningful notes in your content, but don't use it just to make your text appear smaller; that would be presentational markup.

> *Previous versions of HTML offered a counterpart big element, which only denoted larger text and served no purpose beyond presentation. The big element is obsolete in HTML5.*

Listing 4-34 shows a `small` element marking an inline disclaimer.

Listing 4-34. Small print in a `small` element

```
<p>We do tailoring and alterations, too! Our clothiers are the best
in the business and can accommodate even the most anomalous physiques.
<small>Fittings are by appointment only so please call ahead.</small></p>
```

As you'd probably expect, browsers render the contents of a `small` element at a slightly smaller font size than the adjacent text (see Figure 4-21). This is proportional to the font size of the parent element; if you declare a large font size in your style sheet for the parent element, a `small` will be slightly smaller than that, whatever that size happens to be.

We do tailoring and alterations, too! Our clothiers are the best in the business and can accommodate even the most anomalous physiques. Fittings are by appointment only, so please call ahead.

Figure 4-21. The contents of small are proportionally smaller than the surrounding text

Required Attributes

There are no required attributes for the small element.

Optional Attributes

The small element doesn't offer any optional attributes.

span

The span element is a generic phrase element to set apart an arbitrary segment of text, whether to act as a "hook" for CSS styling, or to carry additional information about its contents through attributes in the opening <span> tag. A span is semantically neutral, and imparts no further meaning to its contents except to say, "this text is somehow different." As with its cousin the div, you should use a span only when a more semantically valuable element doesn't fit the bill.

Listing 4-35 shows a span within an h1 heading to distinguish the "last updated" date from the other heading text. You could then style the contents of this span with CSS to appear different from the rest of the heading. Other elements (i or b, perhaps) could serve the same purpose but they might imply unwanted emphasis; this text isn't special, it's just different.

Listing 4-35. A span in a heading

```
<h1>Latest News <span>Last updated on August 14</span></h1>
```

Required Attributes

No attributes are required for the span element.

Optional Attributes

The span element has no optional attributes.

Programming: code, kbd, samp, and var

HTML offers a number of elements specially intended for marking up computer code, allowing computer scientists, programmers, and web developers to publish and share their work.

The code element can designate any sort of computer code. It's not specific to any programming language, so its contents could be HTML, CSS, JavaScript, Python, Perl, C#, or any computer language that needs to be distinguished from surrounding human-language content:

```
<p>You can declare fonts in CSS with the <code>font-family</code> property.</p>
```

The kbd element defines text or commands that the user should enter (usually by keyboard, though it could be a voice or menu command), whereas the samp element illustrates sample output of a program or script:

```
<p>At the prompt, enter your username, <kbd>henchman21</kbd>,
and your password. If it's accepted, the display will read
<samp>ACCESS GRANTED</samp> and the portal will activate.</p>
```

The var element designates a programming variable or argument, or a variable in a mathematical expression. You can also use var in normal prose to mark a placeholder term:

```
<p><var>Something</var>-Man, <var>Something</var>-Man,
does whatever a <var>something</var> can.</p>
```

The code, kbd, and samp elements are frequently combined with the pre element to preserve the formatting of their contents, as you can see in Listing 4-36.

Listing 4-36. A JavaScript function marked up with a code element

```
<pre><code>
function helloWorld() {
  var button = document.getElementById("button");
  if (button) {
    button.onclick = function(){
      alert("Hello, World!");
    }
  }
}
</code></pre>
```

To aid readability, most browsers display code, kbd, and samp elements in a monospace typeface—one in which every character is the same width, such as Courier. The var element is usually rendered in an italicized font. Figure 4-22 shows all the previous examples together.

You can declare fonts in CSS using the font-family property.

At the prompt, enter your username, henchman21, and your password. If it's accepted, the display will read ACCESS GRANTED and the doors will open.

Something-Man, *Something*-Man, does whatever a *something* can.

```
function helloWorld() {
  var button = document.getElementById("button");
  if (button) {
    button.onclick = function(){
      alert("Hello, World!");
    }
  }
}
```

Figure 4-22. Programming-related elements with default styling

Required Attributes

There are no required attributes for these programming-related elements.

Optional Attributes

These programming-related elements don't feature any optional attributes.

Revisions: del and ins

There may be times when you need to update a phrase in your document but would like to clearly indicate what was updated. This is a job for the del and ins elements: del indicates deleted text, and ins indicates inserted text. Both del and ins may optionally include a cite attribute bearing the URL of a page with details about the change and a datetime attribute to mark the date and time the revision was made. You can also include a short note about the change in a title attribute, as Listing 4-37 shows.

Listing 4-37. Revisions noted with the del and ins elements

```
<p>We'll be closed on <del datetime="2012-04-19">Friday</del>
<ins datetime="2012-04-19" title="minor shipping delay">Saturday</ins>
for installation of a new fluxomolecular extrusion loom.</p>
```

Most web browsers display the contents of del as a strikethrough (a horizontal line drawn through the text), and display the ins element as underlined text, as shown in Figure 4-23. It's conventional for inserted text to follow the deleted text.

> We'll be closed on ~~Friday~~ <u>Saturday</u> for installation of a new fluxomolecular extrusion loom.

Figure 4-23. Deleted text is displayed with a strikethrough, and inserted text is underlined

Required Attributes

There are no attributes required for the del and ins elements.

Optional Attributes

- cite: The URL of a document featuring information on why the change was made
- datetime: The date and/or time the change to the document was made

> *As covered earlier in this chapter (see the* time *element), there are strict rules dictating the format of machine-readable dates and times in a* datetime *attribute. You can find much more detailed information in the HTML5 specification:* w3.org/TR/html5/common-microsyntaxes.html#dates-and-times

Offset Text: i, b, u, and s

In the days of yore, before CSS was widely adopted, a number of elements existed in HTML strictly for styling text: i for italic, b for bold, u for underline, and s for strikethrough. None of these elements carried any additional meaning or imparted any real semantic value to their contents; they only affected visual presentation.

Yet they were still sometimes useful, even after CSS came to the fore and authors learned to eschew presentational markup. Sometimes you really do just want to style some text in an italicized font without adding any deeper emphasis. Sometimes bold text is only bold, not important. In a noble effort to avoid all outdated, presentational markup, some authors resort to things like <span class="bold">, which just completely misses the point.

HTML5 has resurrected these presentational elements and imbued them with new meaning. They're still essentially stylistic, but with their newfound sense of purpose they're no longer semantically worthless. The i, b, u, and s elements now represent *offset text*; a word or phrase that is different from the surrounding text for a reason. Even so, you should only use these elements when they really are the most appropriate for the content, and when a more meaningful element would add more meaning than you intend.

The i element represents a word or phrase in an alternate voice, such as a few words in a foreign language, a taxonomic or technical name, or a character's inner monologue. This text is typically styled in an italic font, but doesn't warrant the greater stress or emphasis that the em element would apply.

```
<p>As the saying goes, <i lang="la">Quis custodiet ipsos custodes?</i></p>
```

The b element calls attention to a word or phrase, but doesn't imply the greater importance that a `strong` element does, nor the alternate voice or mood that an `i` element indicates. You might use the b element to mark the key words in a summary, the leading sentence in an article, a "drop cap" at the beginning of a chapter, or product brand names in a review.

```
<p>Our shrink rays operate via <b>transdimensional mass exchange</b>, not
<b>intra-molecular compression</b>, so they're safe for everyday use.</p>
```

The u element underlines text, and can be used for marking text with non-textual annotations such as proper names in Chinese text, or for marking misspelled words. Because links are conventionally underlined, avoid using the u element where it might be mistaken for a link. There are very few cases where a u element would be appropriate at all; another element will almost always be more fitting.

```
<p>She wrote in her letter, <q>my compact <u class="sp" title="sic">lazer</u>
torch has helped me out of more jams than I can count.</q></p>
```

The s element indicates text that is no longer accurate or no longer relevant, and has thus been stricken through or crossed out, like the original price of an item currently on sale. This isn't the same as deleted or replaced text, which calls for the similarly styled `del` element. Stricken text is still there for reading, it's just outdated or inaccurate.

```
<p>V900 Shrink Ray: <s class="reg-price">$10,799</s> <em>marked down to
<strong class="sale-price">$9,799</strong>, this week only!</em></p>
```

Figure 4-24 shows the default styling for all four of these offset text elements. In keeping with their newfound semantic significance, don't assume these elements have to be styled according to the classic browser defaults. A b element doesn't have to be bold and a u element doesn't have to be underlined; you can change these default styles with CSS.

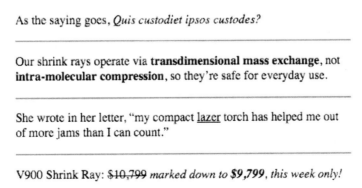

Figure 4-24. Offset text with default styling

Required Attributes

There aren't any required attributes for the i, b, u, or s elements.

Optional Attributes

The i, b, u, and s elements don't have any optional attributes.

Superscript and Subscript: sup and sub

You may occasionally need to include superscript or subscript characters in your text, especially if you're writing about mathematics or chemistry, or in certain languages that require it (French, for example). In these cases, you can use the sup and sub elements, for superscript and subscript, respectively. Superscript text is raised slightly higher than surrounding text, whereas subscripts are slightly lower. Listing 4-38 shows an example of these elements: sup appears in the Pythagorean theorem for calculating right triangles, and sub in the chemical formula for sulfuric acid.

Listing 4-38. Examples of the sup and sub elements

```
<p>a<sup>2</sup> + b<sup>2</sup> = c<sup>2</sup></p>
```

```
<p>H<sub>2</sub>SO<sub>4</sub></p>
```

Figure 4-25 shows how a browser renders these elements. The contents of both elements appear slightly smaller than the ordinary text around them.

$$a^2 + b^2 = c^2$$

$$H_2SO_4$$

Figure 4-25. The sup and sub elements

Whereas the sup and sub elements may seem presentational, when used appropriately they communicate more meaning than a span would. A superscript numeral in a mathematical formula can signify an exponent, so wrapping that numeral in a sup element would be preferable to styling it strictly with CSS; the sup element itself carries that stylistic meaning. The element in that context says, "this is an exponent," not merely "this is raised text." Exercise your own judgment and use these elements only when the content warrants it.

Required Attributes

The sup and sub elements don't require any attributes.

Optional Attributes

There are no optional attributes for the sup or sub elements.

Text Annotations: ruby, rp, and rt

Ruby text is a small annotation that appears alongside other text, most commonly to act as a pronunciation guide in logographic languages like Chinese, Japanese, and Korean. These languages may have thousands of written characters, and even life-long native speakers will often encounter unfamiliar symbols. Furthermore, the same character may have very different meanings in different contexts or when spoken in different tones, so pronunciation hints can be vital to understanding the written text.

You can see an example of Japanese ruby text in Figure 4-26, where the smaller characters act as a pronunciation guide for the larger characters beneath them (ruby annotations are also called *furigana* in Japanese).

Figure 4-26. An example of Japanese ruby text

HTML5 introduces a set of elements specifically to mark up ruby text. The `ruby` element indicates a word or phrase that includes ruby text annotations, and an `rt` element indicates each annotation. Listing 4-39 shows an example in Chinese with *pīnyīn* phonetic pronunciation hints.

Listing 4-39. The Chinese name for San Francisco, with ruby annotations for each character

```
<p lang="zh">
<ruby>
  旧<rt>jiù</rt>
  金<rt>jīn</rt>
  山<rt>shān</rt>
</ruby>
</p>
```

As you see in Figure 4-23, each annotation is rendered above the character(s) preceding it, and at a much smaller font size by default.

Figure 4-27. Ruby text rendered in a supporting web browser (Chrome, in this case)

Ruby text can also offer translations or an explanation of a character's meaning, instead of (or in addition to) pronunciation hints:

```
<p lang="zh"><ruby>旧金山 <rt>San Francisco</rt></ruby></p>
```

These are new elements, so not every browser supports them yet, but there are ways to compensate for lack of browser support and offer a readable fallback. The `rp` element indicates *ruby parentheses*, which are hidden in browsers that support the `ruby`, `rt`, and `rp` elements, but will be visible in browsers that don't recognize these elements. Each single parenthesis should be enclosed in an `rp` element, with the `rt` element in between, as you see in Listing 4-40.

Listing 4-40. The `rp` element hides `ruby` parentheses from supporting browsers

```
<p lang="zh">
<ruby>
 旧<rp> (</rp><rt>jiù</rt><rp>) </rp>
 金<rp> (</rp><rt>jīn</rt><rp>) </rp>
 山<rp> (</rp><rt>shān</rt><rp>) </rp>
</ruby>
</p>
```

In browsers that don't recognize these elements and/or apply no default styling, the annotations will simply appear inline after the base text they reference, just as if the ruby elements weren't present at all (see Figure 4-28).

旧 (jiù) 金 (jīn) 山 (shān)

Figure 4-28. Ruby text as rendered by a browser that doesn't recognize the `rt` or `rp` elements

For even more information on when, how, and why to use ruby text, along with more examples of practical usage, see Oli Studholme's indispensible article at HTML5 Doctor, *The ruby Element and Her Hawt Friends, rt and rp* (html5doctor.com/ruby-rt-rp-element/)

Required Attributes

The `ruby`, `rt`, and `rp` elements don't have any required attributes.

Optional Attributes

There aren't any optional attributes for the `ruby`, `rt`, or `rp` elements.

> *The term "ruby text" is old British typesetter's jargon referring to very small type, roughly 5.5 points, which was often used for between-the-lines annotations. Why they called this particular type size "ruby" is a mystery lost to time. Other sizes of type had names like diamond, pearl, brilliant, great primer, and paragon. Those old printers were an odd bunch.*

Bidirectional Text: bdi and bdo

Written languages are read either from left to right (like English, Spanish, German, Malay, or Hindi) or from right to left (like Arabic, Persian, or Hebrew). Documents written predominantly in one language may still sometimes include words or phrases from other languages, and when that other language is read in another direction from the surrounding text, the result is *bidirectional text* (also known as *bidi text*, for short).

Unicode—a standard for digital text encoding—carries instructions for text direction encoded within the text itself. A user-agent that supports Unicode will follow a standard algorithm to render text in the proper direction. But there are some unusual circumstances in which this algorithm causes adjacent text to be reordered incorrectly. These specialized HTML elements can compensate for calculation errors on those rare occasions when the Unicode bidirectional algorithm produces the wrong rendering.

The bdi element (*bidirectional isolate*) isolates a portion of text so it can be automatically formatted in a direction different from the text surrounding it. This element is most useful when the direction of the text may be unknown, especially user-generated content like usernames or comments. Wrapping such content in a bdi element instructs the browser to treat that span of text's directionality separately from the directionality of its parent, setting the element's direction to "auto" and allowing the Unicode directionality of the content to take over. This is a new element in HTML5 and most browsers don't yet support it, but they will soon.

> For more on the bdi element, including some practical usage examples, see Richard Ishida's aptly-titled post, HTML5's New `<bdi>` Element (*rishida.net/blog/?p=564*).

The bdo element (*bidirectional override*) defines a segment of text where the direction is explicitly reversed from the direction of the text that surrounds it (as inherited from the parent element), or reversed from the calculated direction (as determined by the Unicode bidirectional algorithm). The bdo element requires a dir attribute to carry that explicit direction, with a value of either ltr for "left to right" or rtl for "right to left." This element has been around much longer than bdi and current browsers support it fully.

Listing 4-41 shows the bdo element used as if the offset word were written in a different language from the rest of the document. This example uses English text for demonstration purposes only—you would never do this in reality.

Listing 4-41. The bdo element in action

```
<p>A passage containing one <i lang="en"><bdo dir="rtl">reversed</bdo></i> word.</p>
```

Figure 4-29 shows that the web browser reverses the text automatically

A passage containing one *desrever* word.

Figure 4-29. The contents of the bdo element are displayed in the direction specified by the dir attribute, regardless of language or text encoding

Both of these elements are uncommon (especially the brand new bdi element) and you may go your entire life without ever using them. But if you work with multilingual documents or are building a site that needs to accept bidirectional input from users, these elements may come in handy.

Required Attributes

The bdi element doesn't require any attributes. The bdo element requires a dir attribute:

- dir: The direction in which the enclosed text should be read: either ltr or rtl

Optional Attributes

The bdo and bdi elements don't have any optional attributes.

Line breaks: br and wbr

Long lines of text on a web page wrap naturally to a new line when they reach the edge of their container, with the break occurring in the space between two words. However, you may sometimes need to force text to wrap to a new line at a specific point. The br element creates a line break for just such occasions. It's a void element, so it has no text content and consists of a single tag, which you can optionally close with a trailing slash (<br/>), XHTML-style.

You saw some line breaks when you read about the address element earlier in this chapter. Listing 4-42 shows another address, and this time its contents are all on a single line with brs inserted at strategic points.

Listing 4-42. Contact information with inserted line breaks

```
<address>
  Jon Hicks <br>Illustrator, cheese enthusiast <br>hicksdesign.co.uk
</address>
```

Browsers ignore carriage returns in markup, but will forcefully break a line of text where directed, as you see in Figure 4-30.

Jon Hicks
Illustrator, cheese enthusiast
hicksdesign.co.uk

Figure 4-30. The text wraps to a new line at the specified points

In the past, line breaks were often misused by stacking several in a row to increase white space between elements on the rendered page, to form lists by breaking between items, and to simulate the appearance of paragraphs by forcing line breaks between blocks of text. Don't commit these presentational hacks. Use CSS margins, padding, and positioning to add space, and mark up lists and paragraphs as lists and paragraphs. You should use the br element sparingly and only when the text requires it.

The wbr element represents a *line break opportunity*, a point in an otherwise continuous word where browsers may wrap it to a new line if necessary, to aid readability or prevent text from overflowing its containing element on the rendered page. It's a new element in HTML5 so older browsers don't support it, but most current browsers do. This is also a void element that can't hold any contents and has no end tag.

Listing 4-43 shows a ridiculously long, continuous word with no breaks where a browser can automatically wrap the text to a new line (we've had to force line breaks in this book, so just imagine this was a single line of code). Without a breaking space where the text can wrap to a new line, this word will overflow its container, as you can see in Figure 4-31.

Listing 4-43. A long, unbroken word

```
<section>
  <p>Overcome with sorrow and rage, he broke free of the restraints↪
  and bellowed to the heavens, "NOOOOOOOOOOOOOOOOOOOOOOOOOOOOOOooooo↪
  oooooooooooooooooooooooooooooooooooo!!!"</p>
</section>
```

Overcome with sorrow and rage, he broke free of the
restraints and bellowed to the heavens,
"NOOOOOOOOOOOOOOOOOOOOOOOOOOOOOOooooooooooooooooooooooooooooooooooooooooooooooooooooooooooooooo!!!"

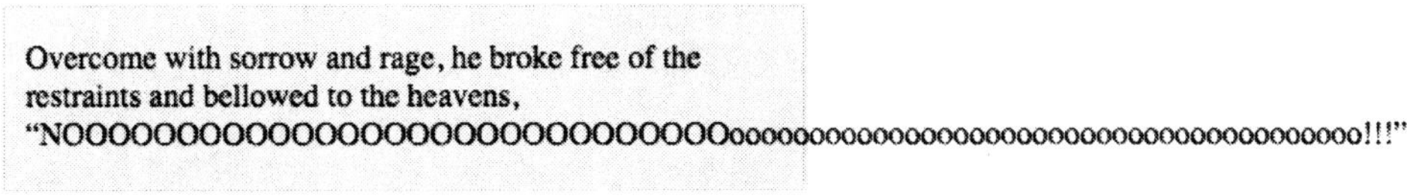

Figure 4-31. The non-breaking word overflows its container

This sort of non-breaking content doesn't come up often, but it does come up. Some URLs can be very long, for example, and don't contain spaces so they're treated as single words. HTML5 has at long last provided a solution. In Listing 4-44, the wbr element adds points where a browser can break the word onto a new line when it needs to. The element itself is completely invisible.

Listing 4-44. Adding wbr elements to an otherwise unbroken word

```
<section>
  <p>Overcome with sorrow and rage, he broke free of the restraints↪
  and bellowed to the heavens, "NOOOOOOOOO<wbr>OOOOOOOOOO<wbr>↪
  OOOOOOOOOO<wbr>oooooooooo<wbr>oooooooooo<wbr>oooooooooo<wbr>↪
  oooooooooo!!!"</p>
</section>
```

You can see the result in Figure 4-32.

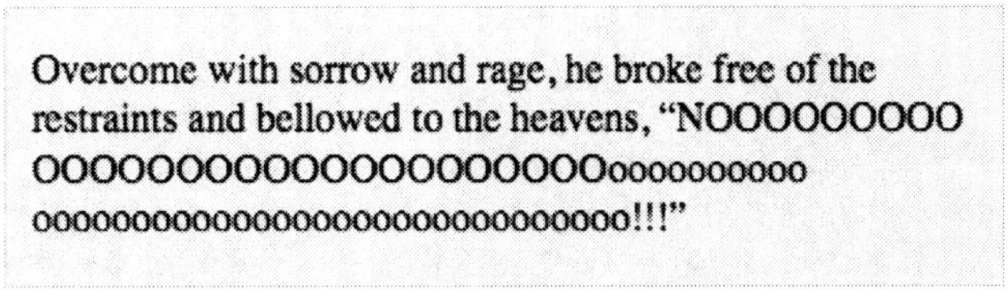

Overcome with sorrow and rage, he broke free of the
restraints and bellowed to the heavens, "NOOOOOOOOO
OOOOOOOOOOOOOOOOOOOOOOOOOoooooooooo
oooooooooooooooooooooooooooooooooooo!!!"

Figure 4-32. The word wraps to new lines where a wbr indicates a breaking point in the markup

Required Attributes

The br and wbr elements don't have any required attributes.

Optional Attributes

There are no optional attributes for the br or wbr elements.

> Older versions of HTML featured a clear attribute for the br element, giving browsers instruction on how text and other elements should flow around the line break. This presentational attribute is obsolete now, replaced by the equivalent clear property in CSS.

Special Characters

You know by now that an HTML document is simply plain text. There's nothing special at all about the file format; it's just written in a language that web devices are programmed to understand. Tags within that plain-text document are enclosed by angle brackets (< and >) to distinguish the tags from ordinary text. When a browser encounters those symbols, it can assume it's dealing with markup and behave accordingly. This raises one issue, of course: what if you need to use angle brackets in your text? If the browser treats them as part of a tag, the entire page might fall apart.

HTML includes a large number of *character references*, which offer a way to encode special characters that aren't part of the regular English alphanumeric set of characters (A-Z, a-z, 0-9, and most common punctuation). A character reference begins with an ampersand (&) and ends with a semicolon (;). Between those symbols there are two different ways to invoke the special character you desire: with a *character entity name* or a *numeric character reference*.

A character entity name is simply a predefined name referring to a particular symbol, like a nickname. The entity for the "less than" symbol (<) is < and its counterpart, the "greater than" symbol (>), is >. You can use these entities to render the symbols in your content and prevent them from being treated as tags.

Your other option, the numeric character reference, refers to a character by its assigned Unicode number, and is specified by an octothorpe (#) after the ampersand. The numeric character reference for the "less than" symbol is < and "greater than" is >. Most of the time, the much-easier-to-remember entity names are sufficient, but some more obscure symbols may not have entity names.

> In XML or XHTML, encoding special characters in this manner is known as escaping, because these embedded codes are excluded from the regular XML parsing. If you're authoring XHTML, one character you must be careful to escape is the ampersand itself; a non-escaped ampersand in your XHTML markup will be treated as the beginning of a character reference. In order to display an ampersand in an XHTML document, encode it with the entity & or the numeric reference &. This also goes for ampersands in URLs within an attribute (such as cite, src, or href). HTML5 is much more forgiving and doesn't require escaping ampersands.

Table 4-1 lists some of the most common (and useful) characters you may need, and you can find more at `entitycode.com`.

Table 4-1. Common character references

Character	Description	Entity	Numeric Reference
&	ampersand	&	&
<	less than	<	<
>	greater than	>	>
'	left single quotation mark	‘	‘
'	right single quotation mark (or apostrophe)	’	’
"	left double quotation mark	“	“
"	right double quotation mark	”	”
	non-breaking space		
…	horizontal ellipsis	…	…
•	bullet	•	•
–	en dash	–	–
—	em dash	—	—
©	copyright	©	©
™	trademark	™	™
®	registered trademark	®	®

Styling Content with CSS

A browser's built-in default style sheet gives most content the simple styling it needs to be at least readable. Headings will appear at different sizes, list items will each appear on their own line with a marker, an em is italicized, a `strong` is bold, and so on. But these minimal styles are just that: *minimal*. They're intended for functional, utilitarian purposes, and aren't exactly attractive. You've seen many examples of default browser styling in this chapter. It hasn't been pretty.

In this section, you'll learn how to override some of these default browser styles with style rules of your own. This is only a starting point, and we can't hope to teach you everything there is to know about CSS in a single book—especially when we're also trying to teach you everything about HTML5 at the same time. But one must walk before one can run.

Establishing New Elements

Every graphical web browser has a built in style sheet that defines the basic default styles for most elements in HTML. That's assuming, of course, the browser recognizes the elements and includes rules for it in its style sheet. The HTML5 standard is still taking shape, and introduces many new elements and attributes that didn't exist in any previous version. Many of the latest versions of web browsers are already integrating support for these new elements, but older versions—and mind you, that "older version" might be only a few weeks old—don't yet recognize the new elements and don't apply any default styling at all.

To make sure those older browsers can properly display your HTML5 pages, you should include a few basic rules at the beginning of your style sheet, just to do what a newer browser's default style sheet will do automatically. The following simple style rule, added at the beginning of your style sheet, will establish many of the new HTML5 elements as block-level elements, priming them for laying out your pages with later style rules:

```
section, article, aside, header, footer,
nav, hgroup, figure, figcaption {
    display: block;
}
```

As you can probably deduce, this simple rule declares that all these elements—section, article, aside, header, footer, nav, hgroup, figure and figcaption—should be rendered on a new line and expand to fill the available width.

The IE Problem

A *rendering engine* is the part of a graphical web browser's program that interprets CSS, applying style rules to elements in the HTML document and converting that code into an on-screen image. The rendering engine reads a selector in a style rule to locate the HTML elements to which that rule applies. When the browser finds a matching element in the document, it will try as hard as it can to style that element according to your instructions. If it doesn't find a matching element, the browser ignores that style rule and moves on to the next one.

Most browsers and their built-in rendering engines are generally element-agnostic, and will happily apply CSS to any element that matches a given selector, regardless of what else it may or may not know about that element. You could, in theory, make up any elements you like—`<animal>cat</animal>`, `<spoiler>Rosebud is the sled</spoiler>`, or `<soundeffect>ZZZAP!</soundeffect>`—and style them with CSS and most browsers will happily oblige you. Go on, try it. The elements won't be valid and won't have any standardized function or semantic value, and you should never commit such shenanigans in reality (unless you're using an extensible markup language that allows that sort of thing). But when it comes to a strictly visual rendering, the browser simply doesn't care.

Internet Explorer for Windows is the notable exception. That browser's rendering engine has a list of HTML elements it recognizes, and if an element doesn't appear on that list, IE will simply refuse to style it at all. Older versions of IE prior to version 9 didn't recognize the new elements introduced in HTML5 such as `section`, `article`, `nav`, `figure`, `time`, `mark`, and so on. These elements didn't exist when those versions of IE were released, so they're not on the list and IE won't let them into the style party.

But all is not lost! There's an interesting quirk in IE's rendering engine: if you use JavaScript to create an element (via the `createElement` method), it's automatically registered in the document object model and IE will suddenly become aware that elements by that name exist. IE will begin styling those previously unrecognized elements just as it would a paragraph or `div` or any other element it already understands. It's as simple as:

```
<script>
  document.createElement("article");
</script>
```

This single line of JavaScript makes IE aware of any instances of the `article` element and it will apply your CSS rules to those elements without complaint. You can repeat the same for all the other new structural elements, but HTML5 wiz Remy Sharp has made it even easier for you. He's concocted a simple and tiny JavaScript library, dubbed the *HTML5 shiv* (`http://code.google.com/p/html5shiv/`), that you can include in the head of any web pages you build with the new HTML5 elements and it will trigger rendering support for all of those new elements in older versions of IE.

The unfortunate downside is that anyone using an outdated copy of Internet Explorer with JavaScript disabled won't experience your website in its fully-rendered CSS glory. Think about your content and your users, and test your pages thoroughly. If you need to offer fully-rendered pages to people using outdated versions of IE who have also turned off JavaScript—a minority, perhaps, but they're out there—you might need to refrain from using these newer structural elements, or at least refrain from styling them with CSS. You could still build them into the document for their semantic utility and for forward compatibility, but you might need to direct your CSS rules to more established elements for your layout and design.

Declaring Base Font Styles

A graphical web browser draws text on-screen using font files installed on your visitor's computer. Unfortunately, this usually limits your options to the few typefaces that are very common in most operating systems—ones with familiar names such as Times New Roman, Helvetica, Arial, Verdana, Georgia, Trebuchet, and Courier. CSS3 brings the `@font-face` rule, a means of embedding third-party fonts in a style sheet that a browser can download and use temporarily to render the page.

We'll cover embedding web fonts in a later chapter, but you should first understand how to use and work with the user's native fonts. You can still achieve great things even with a limited palette. Good typography is about more than just choosing a nice typeface; it's also about how you arrange text on the page.

Font Family

A *font family* is, well, a family of fonts. Also called a *typeface*, a font family consists of a set of variations on a single type design. The typeface known as Times New Roman, for example, includes normal, italic, bold, and bold italic versions in a range of sizes. Each of these variants is actually a distinct font—"12 point Times New Roman bold" is one font within the Times New Roman font family. These days, the terms "font," "typeface," and "font family" are often used interchangeably.

In CSS, a font family is declared using the `font-family` property, followed by a comma-separated list of your desired typefaces, in order of preference. When a browser renders the page, it looks on the user's computer system for the first listed font family. If it doesn't find that one, it will continue to the next, and so on until it finds a font in the stack that your visitor has installed. If it doesn't find any, the browser will simply fall back on its default typeface.

Listing 4-45 shows an example of a CSS style rule declaring a sequence of font families for the body element.

Listing 4-45. Declaring a font family

```
body {
    font-family: Georgia, "Times New Roman", Times, serif;
}
```

> The typeface Times New Roman has a name that includes spaces, so its name appears in quotation marks to group those words together. Font families with single-word names don't require quotes.

One very important aspect of CSS is the concept of *inheritance*. The values of some properties in CSS can be passed down from an ancestor element to its descendant elements, including most font-related properties. Because every element on the page is descended from the body element, they will all inherit their font styles from that common ancestor, without the need to re-declare the same styles over and over. You can then override or alter this base font family for different elements elsewhere in your style sheet.

Revisiting the style rule for the body element, perhaps you've decided you'd prefer a *sans serif* typeface, such as Calibri. Although Calibri is fairly common, not every computer has it installed. If the browser doesn't find Calibri the next best choice might be Helvetica, and if your reader doesn't have Helvetica installed, you might grudgingly accept Arial as a last resort. If your reader has none of these fonts, then you'd at least like the text to be drawn in *some* kind of sans serif typeface, so you should end with the generic family name, `sans-serif` (the phrase "sans serif" must be hyphenated in CSS). Listing 4-46 shows the revised rule.

Listing 4-46. The updated font-family declaration, now with sans serif typefaces

```
body {
    font-family: Calibri, Helvetica, Arial, sans-serif;
}
```

You can see a "before and after" view of a sample web page in Figure 4-33. The left side shows the text in the default browser font (Times, in this case), and the right shows the same text in Calibri after the new CSS has been applied.

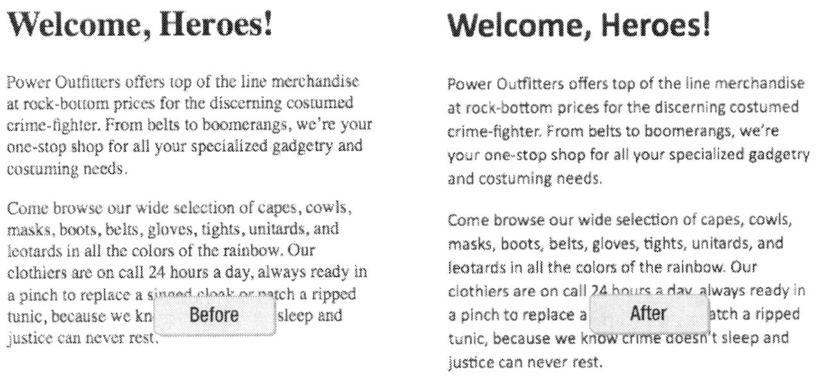

Welcome, Heroes!

Power Outfitters offers top of the line merchandise at rock-bottom prices for the discerning costumed crime-fighter. From belts to boomerangs, we're your one-stop shop for all your specialized gadgetry and costuming needs.

Come browse our wide selection of capes, cowls, masks, boots, belts, gloves, tights, unitards, and leotards in all the colors of the rainbow. Our clothiers are on call 24 hours a day, always ready in a pinch to replace a singed cloak or patch a ripped tunic, because we kn **Before** sleep and justice can never rest.

Welcome, Heroes!

Power Outfitters offers top of the line merchandise at rock-bottom prices for the discerning costumed crime-fighter. From belts to boomerangs, we're your one-stop shop for all your specialized gadgetry and costuming needs.

Come browse our wide selection of capes, cowls, masks, boots, belts, gloves, tights, unitards, and leotards in all the colors of the rainbow. Our clothiers are on call 24 hours a day, always ready in a pinch to replace a **After** atch a ripped tunic, because we know crime doesn't sleep and justice can never rest.

Figure 4-33. Some text rendered in the browser's default typeface, and then in Calibri

GENERIC FONT FAMILIES

There are five generic font family names built into the CSS language. Using any of these in a font-family declaration will instruct the browser to render text in whatever default typeface it's configured to use for that generic family.

- `serif`: A typeface featuring serifs, which are ornamental crosslines at the ends of a character's main strokes. Times New Roman and Georgia are serif typefaces.

- `sans-serif`: Literally, "without serif"; a typeface that lacks those ornamental flourishes. Helvetica and Arial are sans serif typefaces.

- `monospace`: A typeface in which every character, including punctuation, occupies the same width. Courier and Monaco are monospace typefaces.

- `cursive`: A fancy typeface modeled after handwriting. Brush Script MT and Apple Chancery are common cursive typefaces.

- `fantasy`: A decorative or highly stylized typeface. Impact and Copperplate are common fantasy typefaces.

Serif typefaces are best for print, as they remain readable at small sizes. On screen, however, the fine points of the serifs tend to be lost or blocky when rendered in pixels, so sans serif typefaces are generally easier to read on the Web (though serifs can be quite lovely at larger sizes). Monospace typefaces are best for displaying computer code, where it's important to accurately make out each and every character. Cursive and fantasy typefaces are more decorative and can be difficult to read so they should only be used for large headings, or avoided entirely; never use a cursive or fantasy typeface for body text.

Font Size

We've changed the font family, but what about the size? Most browsers today render body text at a default size of 16 pixels, which is a good average size, but might not be exactly what you want. You can change this with the font-size property, and by applying the declaration to the body element every other element on the page will inherit the same value. Listing 4-47 shows the style rule with a font-size declaration added, setting the base size to 14 pixels.

Listing 4-47. A font-size declaration has been added to the body style rule

```
body {
  font-family: Calibri, Helvetica, Arial, sans-serif;
  font-size: 14px;
}
```

Figure 4-34 shows the change in text size.

Welcome, Heroes!

Power Outfitters offers top of the line merchandise at rock-bottom prices for the discerning costumed crimefighter. From belts to boomerangs, we're your one-stop shop for all your specialized gadgetry and costuming needs.

Come browse our wide selection of capes, cowls, masks, boots, belts, gloves, tights, unitards, and leotards in all the colors of the rainbow. Our clothiers are on call 24 hours a day, always ready in a pinch to replace a singed clo   ed tunic, because we know c   p and justice can never rest.

Before

Welcome, Heroes!

Power Outfitters offers top of the line merchandise at rock-bottom prices for the discerning costumed crimefighter. From belts to boomerangs, we're your one-stop shop for all your specialized gadgetry and costuming needs.

Come browse our wide selection of capes, cowls, masks, boots, belts, gloves, tights, unitards, and leotards in all the colors of the rainbow. Our clothiers are on call 24 hours a day, always ready in a pinch to replace a singed cloak or patch a ripped tunic, because we know crime doesn't sleep and justice can never rest.

Figure 4-34. Text rendered at the browser's default size, then at 14 pixels

The heading, an h1, is also just a bit smaller than it was previously. The default font size of headings is relative to the base size for normal text. When the font size changes for the body element, the headings change in proportion to that value. But if you're not happy with the heading at its default size, you can modify it with a new style rule—this time for the h1 element, as you see in Listing 4-48. Thanks to inheritance, there's no need to restate the desired font family, only the font-size property with the new size to use for h1 elements.

Listing 4-48. Adding a new rule to declare the font-size of the h1 element

```
body {
  font-family: "Trebuchet MS", Helvetica, Arial, sans-serif;
  font-size: 14px;
}

h1 {
  font-size: 160%;
}
```

You can see the results in Figure 4-35, with a slightly shrunken heading.

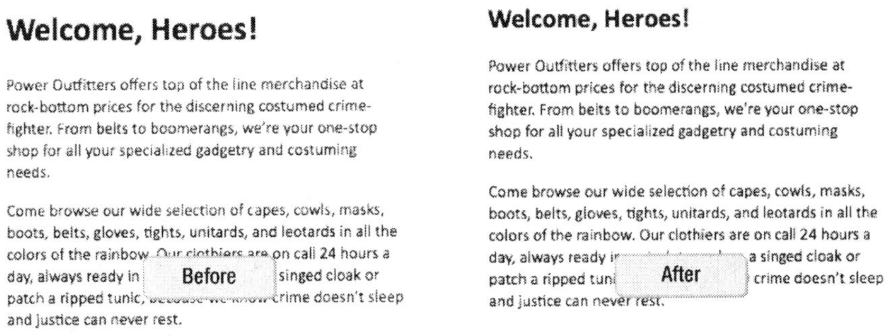

Figure 4-35. The resized heading

The new rule specifies the font size as a percentage of whatever size was inherited from the element's ancestor—160% of 14 pixels in this case, which turns out to be around 22 pixels (22.4 pixels, to be exact, but a browser will round to the nearest whole pixel).

You can declare font sizes using any of several units of measure: pixels, millimeters, centimeters, inches, points, picas, ems (one em is the height of a capital letter from top to baseline), exes (one ex is the height of a lowercase letter from top to baseline), rems (an em relative to the root font-size, skipping inheritance), or a percentage. You can also declare font sizes using a predefined set of keywords: xx-small, x-small, small, medium, large, x-large, and xx-large, or the special relative-size keywords: smaller and larger.

Percentages, smaller, larger, em, rem, and ex are *relative* units, calculated as a proportion of a size declared elsewhere. The others are all *absolute* units: a pixel is a pixel, and an inch is an inch. Some of these units are less practical than others; you'll probably never need to specify a font size in inches, millimeters, or centimeters, whereas points and picas are units used in printing that aren't really appropriate for screen display (though are perfect for an alternative printable style sheet). Most of the time, you'll probably use ems, percentages, keywords, or pixels for font sizes.

Most web browsers allow a user to modify font sizes to suit their own preference, so any size you specify in your CSS is more like a suggestion than a command. Always be aware that your visitors may see text larger or smaller than you originally intended.

Line Height

Line height is the height of a line of text measured from its baseline to the baseline of the preceding line (the *baseline* is the invisible line the text rests on; letters such as g and q have *descenders* that drop below the baseline). Don't confuse line height with *leading*, which is the typographic term for added space between two lines, measured from the bottom of one line to the top of the following line. CSS doesn't offer a means to specify true leading, but you can achieve the same effect by increasing or decreasing the line height of the text.

Returning to the same example, maybe the default line height is a little too close for your tastes. Spreading those lines further apart will help the eye move through the text a bit more easily, so you could add a `line-height` declaration to your CSS rule for the body element, as you see in Listing 4-49. Every other element on the page will also inherit this value.

Listing 4-49. Adding a `line-height` declaration to the body rule

```
body {
  font-family: "Trebuchet MS", Helvetica, Arial, sans-serif;
  font-size: 14px;
  line-height: 1.5;
}
```

You can specify `line-height` with a unit of measure, the same as you would for `font-size`, or omit the unit entirely and the value will be a proportion of the element's `font-size`. A value of `1.5` means the line height will be one and a half times an element's font size, whatever that size happens to be. You could achieve the same effect with the value 150% or `1.5em`, but even proportional units can sometimes lead to tricky inheritance issues down the line.

You can see the result in Figure 4-36—each line of text has a bit more breathing room.

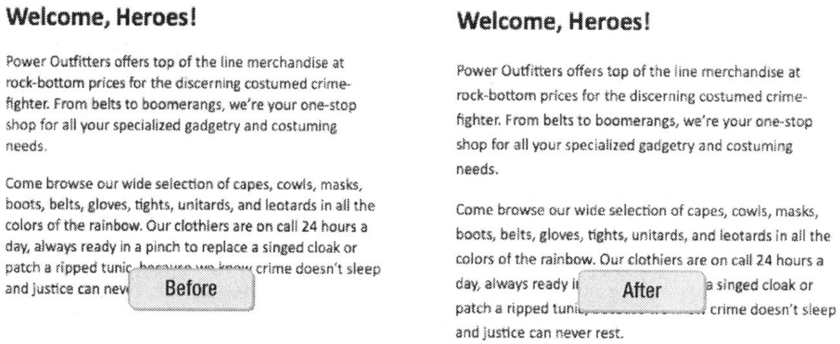

Figure 4-36. Each line of text gets a little more white space by increasing the line height

> *A unitless line-height will always be proportional to the current element's font size, not the font size of the parent element. For a more in-depth and nerdy look at unitless line-heights, see Eric Meyer's appropriately titled article,* Unitless line-heights *(meyerweb.com/eric/thoughts/2006/02/08/unitless-line-heights)*

Shorthand for Fonts

In addition to `font-family`, `font-size`, and `line-height`, there are a number of other CSS properties that apply to typography. The `font-weight` property specifies whether the text is bold, light, or normal, or for some typefaces (and browsers that support it), even a level of boldness. The `font-style` property specifies normal, italic, or oblique text. The `font-variant` property specifies normal text or small-caps.

You can declare all of these properties separately, of course, but that can make for lengthy declaration blocks. Instead, you can condense them to a single declaration with the shorthand `font` property. This single property can carry values for most font styles in a space-separated list, and those values must occur in a specific sequence to be recognized: `font-style`, `font-variant`, `font-weight`, `font-size/line-height`, and `font-family`. Note that a slash (/), not a space, separates the values for `font-size` and `line-height`, binding the two values together.

Any values not declared with `font` will be inherited from an ancestral element, or else the browser will fall back to its default value for that property. However, the `font` property always requires values for `font-size` and `font-family` at a minimum; the declaration will be ignored without both of those values present. Listing 4-50 shows the updated body rule, now with a single shorthand `font` declaration.

Listing 4-50. The shorthand `font` property

```
body {
    font: 14px/1.5 "Trebuchet MS", Helvetica, Arial, sans-serif;
}
```

As another example, this rule sets all h5 elements as Trebuchet italic bold small caps, at 100% font-size (inherited from the parent element) with an inherited line height (because we've omitted a value for that property):

```
h5 {
    font: small-caps italic bold 100% "Trebuchet MS", sans-serif;
}
```

Heading Hierarchy

Earlier in the chapter you learned about sectioning roots and document outlines; an element that establishes a new sectioning root "resets" the heading hierarchy within that element, and the overall document outline can be generated from the nested sections. Visually, headings of descending rank usually become progressively smaller as an indicator of that diminished rank. Some browsers do the same for headings of the same level when they appear in nested sectioning elements, even when those headings are of the same rank. Take the markup in Listing 4-51, for example (it's the same example you saw way back in Listing 4-8).

Listing 4-51. Headings in nested sections

```
<h1>Costume Accessories</h1>
<p>All the trappings and trimmings.</p>

<section>
  <h1>Masks and Cowls</h1>
  <p>Protect your secret identity.</p>

  <section>
    <h1>Masks</h1>
    <p>Facial coverage.</p>
  </section>

  <section>
    <h1>Cowls</h1>
```

```
    <p>Head coverage.</p>
  </section>
</section>
```

You can see how Firefox renders this markup in Figure 4-37, with each descendant heading displayed at a smaller size, even though they're all h1 elements.

Costume Accessories

All the trappings and trimmings.

Masks and Cowls

Protect your secret identity.

Masks

Facial coverage.

Cowls

Head coverage.

Figure 4-37. Firefox displays headings in nested sections at progressively smaller sizes

Figure 4-38 shows the same content rendered by Opera 12. Every h1 is the same size because this version of Opera doesn't include any special default rules for headings in nested sections. That will undoubtedly change in a future update to Opera, but the latest version (at the time we write this) still displays all h1s at the same size.

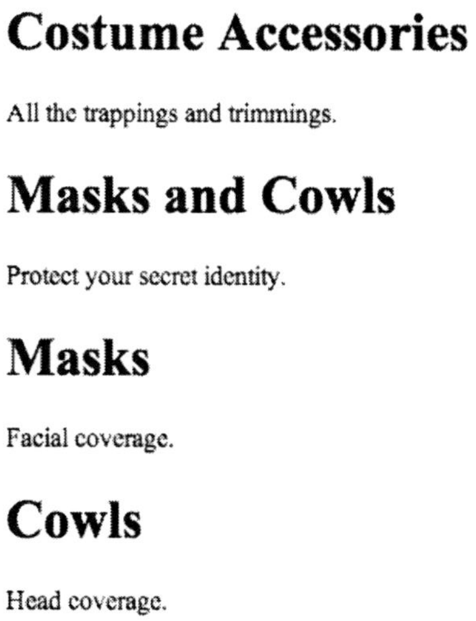

Costume Accessories

All the trappings and trimmings.

Masks and Cowls

Protect your secret identity.

Masks

Facial coverage.

Cowls

Head coverage.

Figure 4-38. The same markup rendered by Opera 12, with all the headings at the same size

For better cross-browser consistency, you can first declare a set of base sizes for common headings in your style sheet. For example:

```
h1 { font-size: 200%; }
h2 { font-size: 150%; }
h3 { font-size: 120%; }
h4 { font-size: 100%; }
```

Then, to preserve some visual hierarchy when headings appear in nested elements, you could expand that set of rules with a few descendant selectors:

```
h1 { font-size: 200%; }
h2, section h1 { font-size: 150%; }
h3, section h2, section section h1 { font-size: 120%; }
h4, section h3, section section h2 { font-size: 100%; }
```

The selector "section h1" selects any h1 element that occurs within any section element. Grouping that descendant selector in the same rule with the h2 selector means any h1 within a section will be the same size as a regular h2. Drilling down one more level with "section section h1" will make any h1 that is a descendant of a section that is itself a descendant of another section the same size as a regular h3.

Figure 4-39 is the same markup in Opera again, now with some visual hierarchy.

Costume Accessories

All the trappings and trimmings.

Masks and Cowls

Protect your secret identity.

Masks

Facial coverage.

Cowls

Head coverage.

Figure 4-39. A few descendant selectors establish some visual hierarchy in nested `sections`

You could take this a lot further, adding complex descendant selectors for `articles` within `sections`, `sections` within `articles`, `articles` within `articles`, `asides` within `sections`, and so on and so forth, but there's no reason to go crazy establishing base styles for every possible markup situation; only those you actually need.

If your particular website frequently calls for nesting an `article` in an `aside` in a `section` in an `article`, then you could include a descendant rule for a heading in that context (`article section aside article h1`). However, that's some pretty deep nesting and an overly complex selector. In those cases you'd be better off using a class or ID selector on a parent element to establish that heading's context.

For example, a deep-nested `article` in an `aside` might be marked up like this:

```
<article>
  ...
  <section>
    ...
    <aside class="notes">
      <article>
        <h1>Note Title</h1>
        <p>Tangential note.</p>
      </article>
    </aside>
  </section>
</article>
```

With the "notes" class as a selector, the style rule for those headings could be much simpler:

```
.notes h1 { font-size: 100%; }
```

Rather than traversing a long series of nested elements, this rule simply styles any `h1` that is a descendant of any element belonging to the "notes" class, whether that element is an `aside`, a `section`, a `div`, or anything else. A good rule of thumb: *use the simplest and least specific selector possible to do the job.*

Complex descendant selectors can be powerful and precise, but they can also be fragile because they demand a very particular markup structure. Simply adding a (hopefully meaningful) class selector is simpler, cleaner, and more flexible.

Styling Lists

Lists are useful elements in HTML. It's the right tool to reach for any time you need to arrange connected portions of content into a sequence of memorable chunks. Unfortunately, lists aren't terribly attractive by default, but you have the power of CSS on your side to compensate for their aesthetic shortcomings.

Changing Unordered List Markers

A special character marks each item in an unordered list to help the reader distinguish one item from the next. The list marker you're probably most familiar with is the *bullet*: a solid dot that's the same color as the list's text. CSS includes a few predefined alternative list markers, declared using the `list-style-type` property: `disc` (this is the default bullet), `circle` (an empty circle), or `square` (a solid square). The size of the marker is proportional to the text size. Listing 4-52 demonstrates the `list-style-type` property, replacing the standard round disc with a small square (see the results in Figure 4-40).

Listing 4-52. Using the `list-style-type` property

```
ul {
  list-style-type: square;
}
```

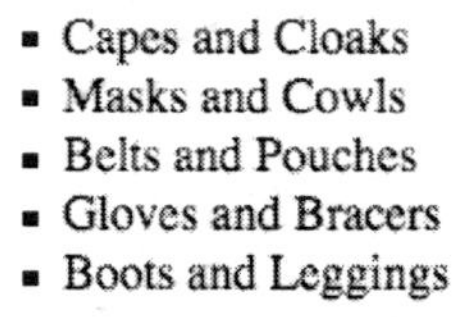

- Capes and Cloaks
- Masks and Cowls
- Belts and Pouches
- Gloves and Bracers
- Boots and Leggings

Figure 4-40. Unordered lists now appear with a small square marking each item

If you like, the declaration `list-style-type: none;` will disable the item markers entirely without affecting the format of the list.

Using an Image As a List Marker

If none of the standard list markers quite satisfies your creative desires, you can provide your own graphic to use via the `list-style-image` property, as shown in Listing 4-53.

Listing 4-53. Using the `list-style-image` property

```
ul {
  list-style-image: url("images/bullet.png");
}
```

The property's value is the URL of the file's location, denoted by the `url` keyword with the URL itself contained in parentheses—the quotation marks are optional. The URL can be either absolute or relative (you learned about absolute and relative URLs in Chapter 1). As you see in Figure 4-41, a browser will load that image file in place of its standard bullet.

> Capes and Cloaks
> Masks and Cowls
> Belts and Pouches
> Gloves and Bracers
> Boots and Leggings

Figure 4-41. The image now appears next to each list item.

Images used for list markers should be small and certainly no taller than the text size. Large images might push your list items apart to make room, as you can see in Figure 4-42.

Figure 4-42. The list items are forced apart by a large image

Changing the Style of Ordered Lists

By default, items in an ordered list are numbered with Arabic numerals (1, 2, 3, etc.). You can change this with CSS, once again using the `list-style-type` property, and this time choosing from another set of accepted values:

- `decimal`: Arabic numerals (this is the default)

- `upper-roman`: Uppercase Roman numerals (I, II, III, IV, etc.)

- `lower-roman`: Lowercase Roman numerals (i, ii, iii, iv, etc.)

- `upper-alpha`: Uppercase English letters (A, B, C, D, etc.)

- `lower-alpha`: Lowercase English letters (a, b, c, d, etc.)

You can see an example in Listing 4-54, with the rendered results in Figure 4-43.

Listing 4-54. Declaring ordered lists to render with uppercase Roman numerals

```
ol {
  list-style-type: upper-roman;
}
```

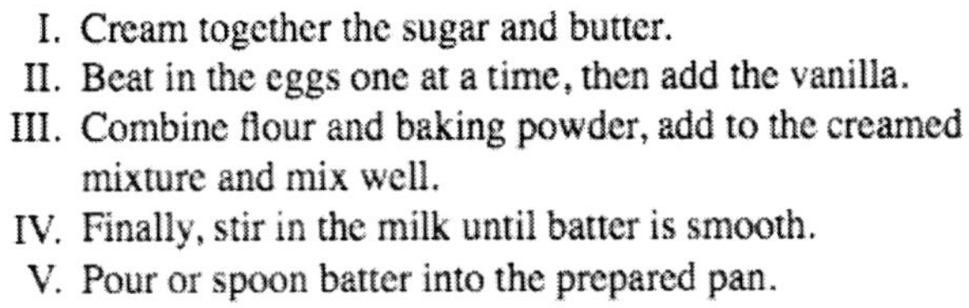

       I. Cream together the sugar and butter.
     II. Beat in the eggs one at a time, then add the vanilla.
   III. Combine flour and baking powder, add to the creamed
        mixture and mix well.
    IV. Finally, stir in the milk until batter is smooth.
     V. Pour or spoon batter into the prepared pan.

Figure 4-43. The browser generates the Roman numerals automatically

As with unordered lists, the declaration `list-style-type: none;` will override the display of any list item markers, while the list remains intact.

Summary

Whew! We've covered a lot of ground in this chapter—a majority of the elements in the entire HTML language, in fact. You learned how to organize your content into bite-sized pieces using meaningful elements that will communicate the true intent of your words, how to insert some useful special characters, and just a few ways you can use CSS to affect the presentation of text. You've also learned a few things you should *not* do when you mark up your content. Be semantically responsible and choose elements for what they mean, not how they look.

Most of this chapter has been about adding text content to your documents, but not all content is text. In the next chapter, you'll learn how to add other media to your web pages—images, audio, video, and plugins—to communicate ideas that text alone just can't get across.

Chapter 5

Embedding Media

Chapter 4 was all about adding text content to your web pages, but now it's time to put the "multi" in "multimedia" with pictures, sound, and motion.

The very first image appeared on the Web in 1992 and they've been with us ever since. It wasn't long before people started finding ways to put audio and video online too, but there has always been one primary obstacle: web browsers couldn't play them. Although the browsers could handle ordinary static images natively, additional plug-in applications were required to handle richer media. That's changing in HTML5. You'll meet the audio and video elements in this chapter, and see how they can join the time-honored img element to enrich your pages with more than just words and pixels.

Playing sound and video without a plug-in is certainly a leap forward for the Web, but plug-ins still serve a purpose for other, more complicated duties. Great things can be accomplished with programs like Adobe's Flash and Microsoft's Silverlight, creating dynamic, interactive, immersive experiences beyond simple sound and motion. Plug-ins aren't going extinct any time soon, and this chapter will show you how to embed that external content into your web pages.

The third-party plug-in isn't dead, but HTML5 does add one more nail to its coffin. The canvas element creates a live surface where, with the help of JavaScript, web authors can draw complex graphics native to the browser, even duplicating some of those dynamic, interactive, immersive experiences that required a plug-in not so long ago. We can't possibly cover all there is to know about creating dynamic graphics with canvas in the pages of this book, but we'll give you a brief introduction to set you on your way.

But first: images.

Imagery of some sort is an important part of most websites, making them more visually stimulating and memorable. The graphical elements of a design can form the basis of your site's branding and visual identity and can set your site apart from the millions of others on the World Wide Web.

Images can decorate, but they can also communicate; pictures are content too, and some ideas are much better communicated visually. Photos, illustrations, logos, icons, maps, charts, and graphs can get your ideas across in ways that text alone might not accomplish.

How Digital Images Work

Like anything else that lives in a computer's electronic memory, a digital image is nothing more than data in the form of ones and zeros (binary code), collected into a virtual file. A computer reads that array of digits (each binary digit is a *bit*) and translates each set of bits into a signal that can be sent to a display device that turns that signal into tiny dots of colored light that human beings can see—bright red, dark blue, pale gray, and so on. The file also includes encoded instructions about how these dots of light (called *pixels*, short for "picture elements") should be arranged, like a mosaic of tiles, to make up a discernable image. You can see the individual pixels if you look closely at a computer or television screen, or you can check out the extreme close-up in Figure 5-1.

Figure 5-1. Zooming in on a digital image reveals the tiny square pixels that comprise it

Because these images are assembled from a "map of bits," they're called *bitmapped* images, and most images on the Web are bitmaps. Storing the color and location of every single pixel adds up to a lot of data, especially when there are hundreds of thousands of pixels in the typical snapshot and millions of possible colors (up to 16,777,216 unique colors in a 24-bit image, to be exact).

Images for the Web are usually *compressed* to decrease the file size so that downloading a web page is tolerable, even on slower Internet connections—and if you've ever downloaded a large file over a slow connection you know how frustrating it can be. By either reducing the number of colors stored or reducing the number of pixels memorized, you can greatly reduce the overall file size as well. The goal of compressing an image is to achieve the smallest possible file without sacrificing too much of the original picture quality.

VECTOR GRAPHICS

In addition to bitmaps, there are also digital images whose data is stored as a set of mathematical instructions that a computer can follow to draw shapes on the screen or on paper. These are called *vector graphics*, and they can be rendered at any size without changing the original image's appearance or quality.

The W3C (and others) have developed a vector graphic format specifically for the Web. Based on XML, the Scalable Vector Graphics (SVG) format still isn't fully supported by some major web browsers, so its practical applications are limited for the time being. Although you can use SVG images in some current browsers, other browsers (including any older versions) won't be able to display them properly. So for the purposes of this book, we'll only be focusing on the old reliable bitmaps. You can learn more about SVG at the W3C website (`w3.org/Graphics/SVG`).

Web-Friendly Image Formats

You can compress digital images for the Web using three common formats: JPEG, GIF, and PNG. Each uses a different means of compression, and each has its own particular benefits and drawbacks. Most web browsers (those that can display images, that is) have built-in software that will interpret and render files in these formats. Web browsers may not be able to render other types of images, so you should stick to JPEG, GIF, and PNG, and almost any program you might use for creating or editing digital images will be able to export files in all three formats.

JPEG

JPEG (pronounced "jay-peg") stands for Joint Photographic Experts Group, the organization that invented the format. The compression scheme reduces the size of the file by sampling the average color values of the pixels and then removing excess redundant pixels from the image. When the image is later decompressed and rendered, those deleted pixels are re-created based on the stored samples.

Because JPEG compression loses some information, the compression is considered *lossy*, and decompressed JPEGs will never be quite the same quality as the originals. JPEG is actually a *variable-loss* format and can be compressed at different levels—more compression means more pixels are discarded to create a smaller file, but the price is paid in quality. Highly compressed JPEGs will tend to appear blurry or with blocky smudges, called *artifacts*, where the pixels have been interpolated. In Figure 5-2 you see three pictures of Jolene, each the same JPEG image saved at a different level of compression (shown here at twice the original size for clarity). The file gets smaller as the image is more compressed, but the quality also declines.

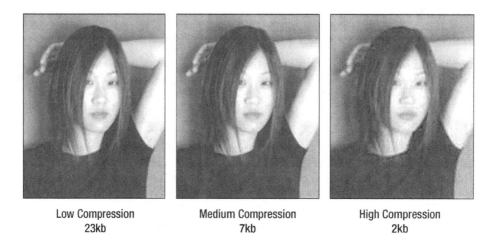

Low Compression	Medium Compression	High Compression
23kb	7kb	2kb

Figure 5-2. The same JPEG image at three different levels of compression. The version on the far right is the smallest file, but the image quality has suffered a lot.

Furthermore, every time you edit and save a JPEG image, you're re-compressing an image that has already been compressed, losing a bit more data in the process. Every generation of JPEG compression will degrade the image quality a little more, like making a photocopy of a photocopy. You should keep original, uncompressed versions of your images to work from, compressing to a JPEG file only when you're ready to put your images on the Web.

The JPEG format saves disk space by sacrificing pixels but will store a lot of color information in a relatively small file, making it ideal for photographs and other images with many different colors, or images where one color blends smoothly into another (called *continuous tone*). JPEG files use the file extension .jpeg or .jpg—the shorter version became customary because some older computer operating systems don't allow four-letter (or more) file extensions.

GIF

GIF stands for Graphic Interchange Format; it compresses images by reducing the overall number of colors saved in the file, but it preserves the color and location of every pixel. Because GIF is considered a *lossless* format, it's a good choice for logos, icons, or graphics that feature text and need to maintain sharp outlines for readability. A GIF image can contain a maximum of 256 different colors but may contain fewer than that; storing fewer colors makes for a smaller file. Graphs, maps, line drawings, and any images with large areas of solid color, or few colors overall, are ideal candidates for GIF.

GIF images may also have some areas that are transparent, allowing whatever is behind the image to show through. Any given pixel is either completely transparent or completely opaque, so there will be a jagged edge where the transparent and opaque areas border each other. Most graphic editing programs enable you to specify a matte color for transparent GIFs, which can be the same as your page's background color to minimize "the jaggies." Figure 5-3 shows a transparent GIF against a checkerboard background. You can see the gray matte surrounding the image, which would blend seamlessly with a solid gray background color.

Figure 5-3. A transparent GIF with a gray matte, shown on a checkerboard background for demonstration

Another special feature of the GIF format is support for rudimentary animation. The image can consist of a number of frames to be displayed in sequence, allowing for some very cool (but also some very annoying) effects. Of course, each frame in an animated GIF is additional information to store that will increase the overall size of the file.

GIF files use the .gif extension. The format and its compression formula were once patented, and the patent holders demanded licensing fees from any software vendor that wanted to produce or display GIF images. Those patents have since expired, but their existence at the time inspired the creation of a free alternative image format: PNG.

> *There's some difference of opinion about just how to pronounce the acronym GIF. Some people (including the people who invented the format) pronounce it like "jif," with a soft g sound. But in common usage it's often pronounced with a hard g, as in "gift," which is arguably more phonetically correct, in English at least. The truth is both ways are equally correct, so say it whichever way sounds most natural to you.*

PNG

Portable Network Graphic (PNG) is a format invented as a free successor to the patented GIF, and it improves on its predecessor in several ways. Like a GIF, a PNG image can also contain a maximum of 256 colors (known as 8-bit color, because 256 different values are the most that can be described using only 8 bits of data per pixel), and it supports transparency the same as GIFs do. Thanks to a different compression scheme, an 8-bit PNG file can sometimes be smaller than its GIF counterpart.

However, another variant of the PNG format can support 24-bit color to produce millions of unique colors; it's similar to JPEG in that respect, though it frequently results in larger files than JPEGs. But the best feature of 24-bit PNG images is their capacity to include a transparent *alpha channel*, like an extra invisible layer embedded in the image to define areas of partial transparency. Whereas the transparent pixels in a GIF or 8-bit PNG are completely transparent, the pixels in a 24-bit PNG can also be *partially* transparent, allowing some of the background to show through the image like a translucent overlay. You can see alpha transparency in action in Figure 5-4. The checkerboard background shows through the translucent parts of the image, allowing this logo to blend smoothly and seamlessly with any background, either a solid color or a pattern, or even overlaying other images.

Figure 5-4. A 24-bit PNG with a transparent alpha channel. The checkerboard background shows through the translucent parts of the image, with no jagged edge.

Unfortunately, some much older browsers (namely Internet Explorer for Windows, prior to version 7) don't fully support PNGs with alpha transparency. If your website needs to support IE 5 or 6, you'll need to be careful if and when you use alpha-transparent PNGs.

Yet another variant of the PNG format allows frame-based animation, similar to animated GIFs, but animated PNG (APNG) images are only supported by a few browsers at this time—others show only a static image of the first frame.

PNG files use the extension .png, whimsically pronounced "ping."

A BIT ABOUT BITS

All data in the world of computers consists of ones and zeros, the "digits" that give us the term *digital*. Those ones and zeros represent two positions of a switch—1 for on, 0 for off—and form the basis of *binary code*, the root language of computers. Each digit is called a *bit* (short for *binary digit*), and they're collected into groups of 8 bits called a *byte*. When dealing with larger collections of bytes, they're measured in multiples of 1,024 (itself a multiple of 8); 1,024 bytes is a *kilobyte*, 1,024 kilobytes is a *megabyte*, 1,024 megabytes is a *gigabyte*, and so on. This is how we measure amounts of digital data.

The color value of every pixel in a bitmapped digital image is described with simple ones and zeros. More colors can be produced as more bits are devoted to describing the color of each pixel. The simplest images use only a single bit of data per pixel to describe two possible colors—each pixel is either 0 or 1, off or on, black or white. Because each bit has two possible values, the total number of possible colors is always 2 to the power of the number of bits. As the number of bits per pixel increases, so does the number of possible colors that can be described. Using 2 bits per pixel provides a total of four possible permutations

(00, 01, 10, and 11), thus producing four possible colors (2^2). Four bits expands the number of colors to 16 (2^4). At 8 bits per pixel, the total possible colors number 256 (2^8).

GIF images store color information at the rate of 8 bits per pixel and hence can contain only a maximum of 256 different colors. JPEGs use 24 bits per pixel and can thus produce 16,777,216 possible colors, approaching the very limits of human vision. The PNG format supports either 8-bit color or 24-bit color.

In an 8-bit GIF or PNG, only a single digit is devoted to describing each pixel's transparency, so any given pixel is either visible or not visible. In a 24-bit transparent PNG, 8 of those bits can be devoted to describing the transparency of the pixel, allowing 256 possible levels of translucency all the way from completely transparent (0) to completely opaque (255).

Embedding Images

The text content of a web page is part of the HTML document, surrounded by tags that indicate the meaning and purpose of each portion of words. Images, on the other hand, are external files and not actually part of the document at all. You can embed an image in your document with the img element (or the object element, though img is more common and reliable). Rendering a web page that includes images is a two-stage process; first the browser downloads the markup, and then it downloads the external images. Wherever the img element occurs in the document, the browser will fetch the referenced file from the web server and display it on the page in place of the element.

Images that are strictly decorative—only for looks and not informative—should usually be applied as a background image in CSS, keeping your presentation separate from your content.

img

The img element (an abbreviation of "image," as you might have guessed) is considered a *replaced element*; the element itself isn't rendered, something else is rendered in its place. It's also a void element with no text content and no end tag, though you can optionally close it XHTML-style with a trailing slash (/>). The img element requires a src attribute to define the source of the graphic file as the URL (either absolute or relative) where that file resides on a web server.

An alt attribute is required in most circumstances, to provide an alternative text equivalent of the image. Browsers can display the alternative text if the image isn't available or if the browser is incapable of displaying images, and the alt attribute is important to improve accessibility for the visually impaired.

Listing 5-1 shows an img element with only the src and alt attributes, the bare minimum required. Browsers treat images as inline elements, so they appear alongside any adjacent text or other inline elements (including other images) on the same baseline, with no other default styling.

Listing 5-1. The simplest incarnation of the *img* element

```
<img src="superhero.jpg" alt="A superhero">
```

Required Attributes

- `src`: Specifies the URL where the graphic file resides on a web server.

- `alt`: Provides an alternative text equivalent of the image. This attribute may be empty to indicate nonessential images. It may be omitted under unusual circumstances, and only if a `title` attribute is supplied or if the `img` is a child of a `figure` element that also includes a `figcaption`.

Optional Attributes

- `width`: Specifies the width of the image in pixels.

- `height`: Specifies the height of the image in pixels.

- `ismap`: Declares that the image is used for a server-side image map.

- `usemap`: Identifies a client-side image map to be used (see Chapter 6 to learn more about image maps).

- `crossorigin`: Cross-Origin Resource Sharing (CORS) settings, specifying that the image file may or may not be served from other domains. This attribute can only have the values anonymous (the default) or `use-credentials`. The attribute with an empty value is equivalent to anonymous. The `crossorigin` attribute is new in HTML5 and mostly useful on secure websites. For more on CORS, see `w3.org/TR/cors`.

The alt Attribute

The `alt` attribute provides a text alternative when the picture can't be seen or isn't available. It could be that your reader is visually impaired, or using a browser or device that doesn't display the image, or the image file couldn't be found at the source URL, or the file was corrupt or in an unsupported format. Including a brief alternative text description preserves some of your image's communicative intent when the image itself isn't visible. There's no explicit character limit for the value of an `alt` attribute, but convention is to limit them to 1,024 characters (including spaces), and ideally less than 256 characters. Shorter is better.

Some browsers, when they encounter a missing image, will display an icon and may show a border indicating the image dimensions (if the dimensions are known), sometimes with the alternative text inside, as Internet Explorer does in Figure 5-5. Other browsers show only the `alt` text as regular inline text, with no border or extra space.

Figure 5-5. Some browsers will display the alternative text if the image isn't available

An alt attribute should be a meaningful substitute for the image, so avoid unhelpful alt texts such as "company logo." Tell your visitors the name of the company, not just that your anonymous company has some sort of logo they're unable to see. If you like, you can specify that the unseen image is, in fact, a logo with alt text like "CorpCo, Inc. (logo)" or something similar. It still replaces the image as well as passing on the extra information that it's a logo. If it's practical, you could even go one better and describe the logo: "CorpCo, Inc. (logo: a yellow sunburst rising behind a blue inverted crescent representing the Earth, above the company name in dark blue, in a heavy, slab-serif font)". Images that are pictures of text (for typographic style) should include that text in their alt attributes.

> Many people use the incorrect term "alt tag" to refer to the alt attribute. This is confusing and misleading because alt isn't a tag at all; it's an attribute of the img element.

A well-written alt attribute might inform the reader that the absent image is a logo, a photograph, an illustration, a portrait, a landscape, a thumbnail, a close-up, a chart, a map, and so on, but you should avoid restating the obvious: "a picture of my cat" tells the reader what it's a picture of but doesn't tell them much else about the scene that picture captures. The alt attribute is a descriptive or functional replacement for the image, so you should try to describe the subject if possible, not just the image itself. And you shouldn't use the image file name as the value of alt; "mycat.jpg" tells the reader nothing meaningful about the picture.

If your web page features a photo of your cat asleep in a grocery bag (as cats are oft wont to do), the appropriate alt text might be "my cat in a bag" or "my gray cat sleeping in a brown paper bag" or even "my gray striped tabby curled up and fast asleep in a brown paper Trader Joe's grocery bag on my red Formica kitchen table." These all describe the content of the picture to help your readers conjure the image in their minds even if they can't see it on their screens.

The rule of thumb for writing alternative text: the content should still make sense if every image on the page were replaced with its text alternative. Imagine reading the page aloud to a friend over the phone. If the picture is important, describe the picture. If it represents an idea, state that idea in words, as briefly as you can. If it's a graph or chart, list the data the chart conveys. And if the image isn't essential to understanding the content, don't mention it at all.

Inline images that aren't essential content—meaning they're just for show and may enhance other content, but aren't informative content themselves—still need `alt` attributes. But rather than describing their ornamental function, including an empty `alt` attribute (`alt=""`) will "hide" those nonessential graphics; it's as if the image doesn't exist at all if its description is blank. An empty `alt` attribute effectively declares that this image isn't vital to the page, so the reader needn't worry about understanding it (screen reading software will also ignore it). For example, you might show a flag icon next to a country's name:

```
<li><img src="/flags/australia.png" alt=""> Australia</li>
<li><img src="/flags/newzealand.png" alt=""> New Zealand</li>
<li><img src="/flags/papuanewguinea.png" alt=""> Papua New Guinea</li>
```

This would be appropriate in a list of countries where the names are the important part and the flags just enhance it. If this list were a gallery of international flags, on the other hand, the flag images would be essential content and each one should carry an `alt` attribute describing the flag's design.

For purely decorative, presentational images, you should use CSS to display them on the page as a background attached to some meaningful element, as you'll see later in this chapter.

For many years, Internet Explorer for Windows, the most common browser on the most common operating system on Earth, inexplicably displayed the contents of an `alt` attribute as a tooltip, a small text bubble that appears when the user's mouse lingers over the image (shown in Figure 5-6).

Figure 5-6. Older versions of IE improperly displayed the value of the `alt` attribute as a tooltip

Because of this, many web designers in years past misused the `alt` attribute to inject the kind of supplemental information they wanted to appear in a tooltip: "this is my favorite picture" or "my cat's name is Neena." Such supplemental information doesn't necessarily describe the image or take its place, so it's probably not a proper value for `alt`. Later versions of IE, starting with version 8, have at last corrected this misbehavior and no longer show `alt` text in tooltips.

The `title` attribute, on the other hand, *will* be displayed as a tooltip in most browsers, and that's the more correct place to include a description of the image's contextual purpose, with the attribute acting as a caption, legend, explanation, or indeed a title. When both `alt` and `title` are present, as in Listing 5-2, even old versions of Internet Explorer will display the `title` text rather than the `alt` text.

Listing 5-2. An *img* element with descriptive *alt* and *title* attributes

```
<img src="images/mask.jpg" title="This heroine wears a domino mask (photo by Ben Hives)"↪
alt="A heroic woman with curly brown hair and black eye mask peers around a corner">
```

Even worse than writing improper `alt` text, some web designers omitted the `alt` attribute entirely, just to avoid unwanted tooltips in Internet Explorer. An `img` element without an `alt` attribute, in addition to being invalid HTML in most cases, is also inaccessible. A screen reader or text browser might simply state "IMAGE" without any further information, or may read/display the file name from the `src` attribute. Omitting the `alt` attribute could render an important image meaningless.

Informative `alt` text is especially critical when you use images in links or as buttons in forms. Such images are functional, not merely informative. If an image features text that acts as a link phrase like "learn more" (or a form button like "buy now"), you must make the link accessible by including the same phrase in an `alt` attribute. If the image doesn't show text and is the *only* content within the link or button (i.e., there's no other descriptive text), the image's `alt` text should describe the purpose or destination of the link, or the function of the button.

To demonstrate, Figure 5-7 shows a site's navigation made up of linked images. A visitor with keen eyesight (and who is able to download the images) can find her way around pretty well, and isn't concerned about `alt` attributes.

Figure 5-7. This site's navigation consists of linked image buttons

However, Figure 5-8 shows the same site as it appears in Lynx, a text-only web browser that displays the image file name when the alt attribute is missing. Without alt attributes for the images, the site's navigation is practically useless. Visually impaired people using screen readers, people using mobile devices with less capable browsers, and even people with limited connections who turn off images to spare their bandwidth—they're all out of luck. The file names don't even provide any clues in this example, and far too many websites are built like this. It's downright shameful.

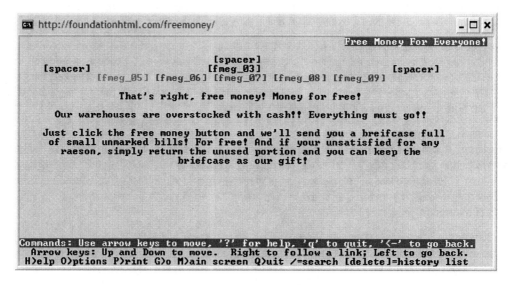

Figure 5-8. Images without alt attributes, as seen in Lynx

The only situation in which you may validly omit the alt attribute is when you don't know the image's content. For instance, you may leave out alt attributes on a web site that allows users to upload images, where you as the host would have no way to describe its content. Even then, alt can only be omitted if certain other conditions are met: if a non-empty title attribute is present (and its value should at least be descriptive of the image's purpose if it can't describe the image itself) or if the image is a child of a figure element that also contains a figcaption but no other content or images (so the figcaption can describe only the one image it shares space with).

An automatic markup validator might not flag missing alt attributes as errors under these circumstances, but remember: validators can't read. Just because your markup might be technically valid doesn't mean your content is appropriately marked up. A title attribute or figcaption isn't really a substitute for accurate, meaningful alt text, even if the validator lets it slide. An img element almost always requires an alt attribute. In those very rare cases where alt is optional, it's a safer bet to include it with an empty value (alt="").

> *For much more on writing proper alt text, as well as many different examples of usage, see the HTML5 spec at w3.org/TR/html5/embedded-content-1.html#alt*

The width and height Attributes

Unless instructed otherwise, browsers will display images at their natural dimensions, but they can't determine those dimensions until they download and analyze the image. Meanwhile, the browser has probably already downloaded and rendered the markup and text, and the images will appear in place as they're downloaded in a second pass. The text will often reflow to accommodate the image once its dimensions are known, which can be jarring if your visitor has already started reading. You can include width and height attributes in an img element to tell the browser to reserve space for the image and draw the text where it should the first time around.

If the width and height attributes aren't the same as the image's natural dimensions, the browser will scale the image to fit to those attributes. However, you should usually avoid resizing images this way. When a web browser scales an image larger than its natural dimensions, it can appear blocky, showing off the individual pixels. If it's scaled significantly smaller, it may still look sharp, but the file size will be larger than necessary and take longer to download. Ideally, the width and height attributes should match the image's natural width and height, and you should do your resizing with a graphic editing program better equipped for the task.

You can also use the CSS width and height properties to describe an image's dimensions. When an img element that includes a width and/or height attribute is further styled by CSS, the CSS dimensions will override the HTML attributes.

The usemap and ismap Attributes

An image map is an image where certain areas are designated as hyperlinks, rather than the entire image being contained in a single link. The usemap attribute identifies the specific map element to use when rendering a *client-side* image map. The ismap attribute declares that this image will be used as a *server-side* image map (which is an inherently inaccessible device that you should usually avoid). We'll cover image maps in more depth in Chapter 6.

Obsolete Presentational Attributes

Older versions of HTML included a number of optional attributes for the img element that have since been eliminated in favor of CSS. None of these are valid in XHTML or HTML5, but we're listing them here so you'll recognize these attributes and know how to achieve their effects with modern CSS:

- align: Specifies how the image should be aligned with adjacent text using the values left, right, top, middle, or bottom. You can achieve left or right alignment with the float property in CSS; the vertical-align property achieves top, middle, or bottom alignment.

- border: Specifies the width of the border that will surround images that act as hyperlinks. This has been supplanted by the border-width property in CSS.

- hspace: Specifies the horizontal space on the left and right sides of the image, replaced by the CSS margin-left and margin-right properties.

- vspace: Specifies the vertical space at the top and bottom of the image, replaced by the CSS margin-top and margin-bottom properties.

Older versions of HTML also included a longdesc attribute for the img element. Its value was a URL leading to a longer text alternative for the image, for those cases where a complete substitute simply couldn't fit into an alt attribute. A complex chart or graph might call for the same data presented in an HTML table, a scan of a Civil War letter might lead to the letter's full text, or a comic book page might need detailed descriptions of the action in each panel along with all the dialog.

However, longdesc was rarely used properly, and many assistive devices (especially screen-readers) still don't fully support it after all this time. And so, as potentially useful as it may be, the longdesc attribute has been dropped from HTML5 simply because it was so often ignored or misused, and other methods exist to fulfill the same need. You can still offer the lengthy text alternative on a separate page and just link to it directly.

Embedding Audio and Video

Although web browsers have had native support for images from the earliest days, incorporating audio or video into a web page has long required a *plug-in*, a separate software component that adds more capabilities to the browser but isn't part of the browser itself, such as Adobe's Flash, Apple's QuickTime, Microsoft's Windows Media Player or Silverlight, and RealNetworks' RealPlayer. These plug-ins work (fairly) well (for the most part) and fill a longstanding gap in the browser landscape, but that gap is closing with HTML5.

The "plug-in" nature of a plug-in also means the application that plays the audio and video content isn't a part of the web browser. A plug-in is locked into a virtual sandbox, with its program isolated from the browser's program, and isolated from other content on the page. Moreover, plug-ins are optional by definition, so you can't always be sure your visitor has the correct software to view your content.

HTML5 introduces the audio and video elements, allowing web authors to embed sound and moving pictures into web pages without requiring proprietary plug-ins. Of course, it follows that the browser itself must be able to play the embedded media, so only the latest browsers support these new elements, but there are ways to provide fallback content for older browsers. There are also lingering issues around the video and audio formats different browsers support, especially because some of the most popular formats themselves are as closed and proprietary as the plug-ins that play them. This playing field should become more level in time, but for the moment you'll have to jump through just a few more hoops to offer rich media to your visitors.

Media Codecs and Formats

Digital audio or video data is processed through a *codec*, a formula that converts and compresses sound or video into a stream of bits for transmission over the Internet (the term "codec" is an abbreviated combination of the words "code" and "decode"). When the data gets to the other end, the player must possess the same codec in order to *decode* the encoded signal and convert it back into sound or video.

Some media codecs are *patent-encumbered*, meaning they're owned and patented by a single company and aren't open standards, and the patent owners typically charge licensing fees for use of their algorithms. Browser makers like Apple, Google, and Microsoft have deep pockets and are willing to license patented codecs for their browsers. Other browser makers like Mozilla and Opera opt instead for open, unencumbered codecs and don't support the patented flavors. Even though the latest versions of all of these browsers support HTML5 embedded media, they don't all agree on which codecs they support.

The codec is only one character in this story. Once the media data is encoded, it must then be encapsulated and packaged for delivery in one of several *formats*. These container formats are the media files that get sent around between servers and clients, carrying data that was encoded through a codec. To play the embedded media, a web browser must first be able to read the container format and then be able to decode the encoded data within it. Just as browsers support different codecs, they also support different container formats for embedded media.

Embedded media must be served with the proper content type for each format, so both the client and the server can know how to treat those files. The web server handles media types automatically, at least for the more common formats. Some newer formats may need a helping hand on the server-side, usually just by adding the new content type to a configuration file.

audio

The audio element embeds a sound file or audio stream in a web page. It's a replaced element, but not a void element, so it may contain other content and elements (as you'll see), and requires an end tag. In its simplest form, the audio element only needs a src attribute pointing to the audio file (or a stream, if it's a streaming source):

```
<audio src="audio/thwip.mp3"></audio>
```

However, it's rarely quite that simple. By default, the audio element has no display properties at all, and is completely invisible. It exists in the document, and can be accessed by the browser or by JavaScript, but simply embedding a sound file doesn't do much without a bit more effort. The optional, Boolean controls attribute will tell a browser to display its native control bar:

```
<audio src="audio/thwip.mp3" controls></audio>
```

These controls, being native to the browser, tend to look very different in different browsers. Figure 5-9 shows the native controls from the latest versions of Firefox, Safari, Chrome, Opera, and Internet Explorer. As you can see, there's quite a variety in the interfaces, but they all offer the same basic functions—a play/pause button, a seek bar with a position indicator, a time display, and a mute/volume control—and all work in much the same way.

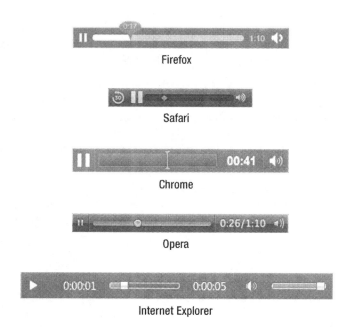

Figure 5-9. Native audio controls from several browsers

You're not limited to the browser's native controls, however. The audio element brings with it a JavaScript API—with methods like play() and pause(), and a volume property—so you can create your own player interface with a bit of scripting and style it however you like. Furthermore, because the audio is now a free resident of the document and no longer locked away in a plug-in, the sound data itself is exposed to the browser and accessible to manipulation with JavaScript. But alas, that's a subject for another book, and we've got more markup to show you.

The audio element also accepts the Boolean attributes autoplay and loop, which do just what they say—the autoplay attribute triggers playback automatically when the page loads, and the loop attribute will replay the audio over and over. One could easily use these attributes for nefarious purposes, especially in combination, and most especially without a controls attribute so a visitor would have no way to shut it off (short of hastily fleeing your website, never to return):

```
<audio src="audio/wilhelm-scream.mp3" autoplay loop></audio>
```

But you're a responsible citizen and a decent human being, so you'd never do such a thing. The Web thanks you.

An optional preload attribute accepts the values auto, metadata, or none. The auto value simply leaves it up to the browser (and hence the user) to determine whether it will begin downloading the sound file before the user chooses to play it. This is left in the hands of the user-agent because different people and devices have different needs. Someone using a mobile device—where transferring large amounts of data is slow and expensive—might not want to preload any media, but someone on a desktop computer with a fast connection might. A preload value of metadata tells the browser to fetch only the file's metadata (title, artist, length, etc.) but not the sound itself, and none tells the browser to not preload any data (this is the default). The `preload` attribute also accepts an empty value, equivalent to `auto`:

```
<audio src="audio/snikt.mp3" controls preload></audio>
```

That all seems easy enough, and it is, except for one significant problem: browsers don't all agree on which audio formats they support.

The most popular and ubiquitous audio format is MP3 (short for MPEG layer 3), which is patent-encumbered. Safari, Chrome, and IE will play MP3 audio, but Firefox and Opera won't. Ogg Vorbis is a free and open audio format, supported by Firefox, Opera, and Chrome, but not by Safari or IE (note that Chrome supports both MP3 and Ogg Vorbis). The unfortunate consequence of all this format and codec and patent business is that to reach the majority of web users, you'll have to offer your audio in at least two formats.

The `audio` element may contain one or more `source` elements, like you see in Listing 5-3, each pointing to a different audio source (you'll find more detail on the `source` element elsewhere in this chapter). A browser will play the first audio source it supports and will simply ignore the rest, and if it doesn't support any of the offered formats it will play nothing. This lets you offer the same piece of audio in both MP3 and Ogg Vorbis formats, covering the majority of browsers on the market.

Listing 5-3. An *audio* element offering the same sound in two file formats

```
<audio controls preload="none">
  <source src="audio/thooom.ogg" type="audio/ogg">
  <source src="audio/thooom.mp3" type="audio/mpeg">
</audio>
```

This still doesn't address the problem of older browsers that don't support HTML5 embedded audio at all. For them, you can still offer a Flash-based player using tried and true plug-in embedding, something like you see in Listing 5-4 (you'll meet the `object` and `param` elements later in this chapter).

Listing 5-4. An *audio* element with a Flash fallback for older browsers

```
<audio controls preload="metadata">
  <source src="audio/Townsville.ogg" type="audio/ogg">
  <source src="audio/Townsville.mp3" type="audio/mpeg">
  <object data="flash/audio-player.swf?soundFile=audio/Townsville.mp3"↵
  width="250" height="25" type="application/x-shockwave-flash">
    <param name="movie" value="flash/player.swf?soundFile=audio/Townsville.mp3">
  </object>
</audio>
```

Browsers that don't support the `audio` element will simply ignore it, and, assuming they have the Flash plug-in installed, will instead embed the plug-in player. And for browsers that support neither HTML5 audio nor Flash, you can at least provide an ordinary text link to download the file directly by including some plain HTML content inside the `object` element, offering a fallback within a fallback:

```
<audio controls preload="metadata">
  <source src="audio/Townsville.ogg" type="audio/ogg">
  <source src="audio/Townsville.mp3" type="audio/mpeg">
```

```
<object data="flash/audio-player.swf?soundFile=audio/Townsville.mp3"↩
width="250" height="25" type="application/x-shockwave-flash">
  <param name="movie" value="flash/player.swf?soundFile=audio/Townsville.mp3">

  <p>Download this delightful tune in either
  <a href="audio/Townsville.mp3">MP3</a> or
  <a href="audio/Townsville.ogg">Ogg Vorbis</a> format.</p>
</object>
</audio>
```

You can find a number of Flash-based media players online, many of them free of charge. Just load up the search engine of your choice and hunt down a player you like. Whatever Flash player you use will have its own parameters for embedding in a web page so just follow the instructions that come with it.

This fallback content is *not* a fallback for browsers that support the audio element but not the particular audio format. If you use an audio element and only offer MP3, for example, browsers that can't play MP3 audio won't fall back to the Flash player; they will still attempt to play the embedded MP3 and just fail silently.

> Apple's Safari browser relies on the QuickTime application to process and play media data. This is no problem for Safari on Mac OS X because QuickTime is already part of OS X right out of the box. But Safari on Windows requires the QuickTime plug-in for Windows in order to play embedded media, so it's not much different than using Flash (though the Flash plug-in is probably more ubiquitous on Windows computers). If Safari on Windows lacks the QuickTime plug-in, it can still fall back to Flash, and if it lacks Flash, it can fall back to the download links. This is a perfect example of graceful degradation.

Required Attributes

The audio element doesn't require any attributes, though it should carry a src attribute if it doesn't contain any source elements. If one or more child source elements are present, you should omit the src attribute from the audio element. An audio element with no attributes is technically valid, but it won't do anything without a media source. Even with no media source, the element still exists in the document and JavaScript can manipulate the object (dynamically adding a media source, for instance).

Optional Attributes

- src: Specifies the URL where the audio file or stream resides on a web server.

- controls: A Boolean attribute that, when present, invokes the browser's standard player interface, typically including a play/pause button, volume control, a seek bar with a position indicator, and the media length or time remaining.

- preload: Suggests to a browser that it may preload the audio data before a user initiates playback. The attribute accepts the values auto (the user-agent, depending on its settings, can preload the audio; this is the default), metadata (load only the audio file's metadata, such as title, artist, track length, etc.), or none (don't preload any data). The attribute with an empty value is equivalent to auto.

- autoplay: A Boolean attribute that, when present, instructs the browser to automatically begin playing the audio when the page loads.

- mediagroup: Can associate multiple media elements (both audio and video) with a single media controller object, allowing multiple sources to be synchronized. For example, a video could be synchronized with a separate audio commentary track. The attribute's value is any name you wish to give to the media group, and all media elements in the group should share the same name in their own mediagroup attributes.

- loop: A Boolean attribute that, when present, instructs the browser to automatically repeat playback from the beginning each time the audio reaches the end, looping forever until you tell it to stop.

- muted: A Boolean attribute that, when present, indicates that the audio defaults to a muted state when it loads.

- crossorigin: Cross-Origin Resource Sharing (CORS) settings, specifying that the video file or stream may or may not be served from other domains. This attribute can only have the values anonymous (the default) or use-credentials. The attribute with an empty value is equivalent to anonymous. The crossorigin attribute is most useful on secure websites. For more on CORS, see w3.org/TR/cors.

video

The video element embeds a digital video in a web page, and is very similar to the audio element, with many of the same optional attributes. As with audio, the video element can include the URL of the video file or stream in a src attribute, assuming there's only a single source:

```
<video src="video/feature.mp4" controls></video>
```

As with audio, the controls attribute invokes the browser's native control bar, which tends to look the same as each browser's audio controls (Figure 5-10 is taken from Chrome). The video element also has a similar set of JavaScript methods, so you can build your own custom control bar if the browser's native controls don't suit you.

Figure 5-10. An embedded video showing Chrome's built-in controls

The video element may also contain one or more source elements, each pointing to a different video source. The battle over competing video formats is as heated as it is for audio formats, and as usual the browsers haven't come to an agreement. The three leading formats are MP4 (which uses the patent-encumbered H.264 codec), the open source Ogg Theora (Theora is the video codec, Ogg is the container format) and WebM (a newer open format quickly gaining ground; it uses a codec called VP8). Safari, IE, and Chrome support MP4, while Firefox, Opera, and Chrome support both Ogg Theora and WebM—once again, Chrome covers all their bases. To reach the widest audience you'll have to offer at least two video sources, if not all three, like you see in Listing 5-5.

Listing 5-5. A video element with three source elements, offering the same video in three formats

```
<video controls>
  <source src="video/laserblast.webm" type="video/webm">
  <source src="video/laserblast.ogv" type="video/ogg">
  <source src="video/laserblast.mp4" type="video/mp4">
</video>
```

A video element can also carry a preload attribute, just like audio, and it accepts the same values: auto, metadata, or none. You should only preload media (either audio or video) if you're relatively certain your users will want to play that media when they arrive at the page, perhaps if they've had to drill down through some navigation to reach it and the media itself is the main reason they're coming. Otherwise you shouldn't tax their bandwidth by automatically sending a lot of data they may not need. You should also avoid preloading media when there are multiple media elements on a page; it's a bit rude to make your users download a dozen videos at once if they didn't ask for it.

So far the video element works just like the audio element, with most of the same attributes. But unlike an audio file, videos take up space on a rendered page. You can include the width and height of your video, just as you would for an image, with the width and height attributes:

```
<video controls preload="auto" width="400" height="300">
  <source src="video/Pod_People.webm" type="video/webm">
  <source src="video/Pod_People.ogv" type="video/ogg">
  <source src="video/Pod_People.mp4" type="video/mp4">
</video>
```

Unless you use the `autoplay` attribute to begin playback as soon as the page loads (usually a bad idea) an embedded video will initially show the first frame of the source video. But more often than not, that first frame won't be much to look at, and may not be indicative of the video's content. You can instead provide a placeholder image with the `poster` attribute, the value of which is the URL of the image:

```
<video controls width="400" height="300" poster="images/Pod_People.jpg">
  <source src="video/Pod_People.webm" type="video/webm">
  <source src="video/Pod_People.ogv" type="video/ogg">
  <source src="video/Pod_People.mp4" type="video/mp4">
</video>
```

Like native audio, native embedded video is a new feature in HTML5 and only supported by the latest browsers. But just like audio, you can offer a Flash-based fallback video player, as well as direct download links for anyone without Flash. Listing 5-6 is a full-featured example of the `video` element, complete with three formats and fallback content for older browsers or those without Flash.

Listing 5-6. The `video` element with fallbacks for less capable browsers

```
<video controls width="468" height="350" poster="images/mechanical-monsters.jpg">
  <source src="video/mechanical-monsters.webm" type="video/webm">
  <source src="video/mechanical-monsters.ogv" type="video/ogg">
  <source src="video/mechanical-monsters.mp4" type="video/mp4">

  <object data="flash/video-player.swf" type="application/x-shockwave-flash" ↪
    width="468" height="350">
    <param name="flashvars" value="file=video/mechanical-monsters.mp4">
    <param name="allowfullscreen" value="true">
    <param name="allowscriptaccess" value="always">

    <img src="images/mechanical-monsters.jpg" alt="">

    <p>Download this exciting video clip in
    <a href="video/mechanical-monsters.webm">WebM</a>,
    <a href="video/mechanical-monsters.ogv">Ogg Theora</a> or
    <a href="video/mechanical-monsters.mp4">MP4</a> format.</p>
  </object>
</video>
```

Required Attributes

The `video` element doesn't require any attributes, though it should carry a `src` attribute if it doesn't contain any `source` elements. If one or more child `source` elements are present, you should omit the `src` attribute from the `video` element. A `video` element with no attributes is technically valid, but it won't do anything without a media source. Even with no media source, the element still exists in the document and JavaScript can manipulate the object (dynamically adding a source, for instance).

Optional Attributes

- `src`: Specifies the URL where the video file or stream resides on a web server.

- poster: The URL of a placeholder image to display before the video is played. Without a specified poster image, browsers display the first frame of the video.

- controls: A Boolean attribute that, when present, invokes the browser's standard player interface, typically including a play/pause button, volume control, a seek bar with a position indicator, and the media length or time remaining

- width: The width of the video in pixels.

- height: The height of the video in pixels.

- preload: Suggests to a browser that it may preload the video data before a user initiates playback. The attribute accepts the values auto (the user-agent, depending on its settings, can preload the audio; this is the default), metadata (load only the audio file's metadata, such as title, artist, length, etc.), or none (don't preload any data). The attribute with an empty value is equivalent to auto.

- autoplay: A Boolean attribute that, when present, instructs the browser to automatically begin playing the video when the page loads.

- mediagroup: Can associate multiple media elements (both audio and video) with a single media controller object, allowing multiple sources to be synchronized. For example, a video could be synchronized with a separate audio commentary track. The attribute's value is any name you wish to give to the media group, and all media elements in the group should share the same name in their own mediagroup attributes.

- loop: A Boolean attribute that, when present, instructs the browser to automatically repeat playback from the beginning each time the video reaches the end, looping forever until it's commanded to stop.

- muted: A Boolean attribute that, when present, indicates that the video's audio track defaults to a muted state when it loads.

- crossorigin: Cross-Origin Resource Sharing (CORS) settings, specifying that the video file or stream may or may not be served from other domains. This attribute can only have the values anonymous (the default) or use-credentials. The attribute with an empty value is equivalent to anonymous. The crossorigin attribute is mostly useful on secure websites. For more on CORS, see w3.org/TR/cors.

source

The source element specifies the address of an embedded media resource. This is a void element that can't hold any content and has no end tag, though you can close it with a trailing slash (/>) if you prefer XHTML syntax. The source element requires a src attribute to provide the media's URL, which may be a file or a stream. This element can only occur as a child of a media element, either audio or video, and should come before any other flow content or track elements. You've seen several examples of source elements already, but here's one more:

```
<audio controls>
  <source src="audio/thwip.ogg" type="audio/ogg">
  <source src="audio/thwip.mp3" type="audio/mpeg">
</audio>
```

It's technically optional, but you should include a `type` attribute specifying the media's content type (content types were introduced in Chapter 3). This allows a browser to quickly determine if the media is in a format it can play, and if not, it shouldn't bother to download any resources. Without the `type` attribute, user-agents have to download at least part of the media and analyze it before they can tell if it's something they can play or not. Including a detailed `type` attribute can save on bandwidth and processing.

In addition to the content type, you can also include the specific codec the media uses. Remember that a browser must use the same codec to decode the encoded media, so informing the browser which codecs are in use is a good thing to do:

```
<audio controls>
  <source src="audio/thwip.ogg" type="audio/ogg;codec=vorbis">
  <source src="audio/thwip.mp3" type="audio/mpeg;codec=mpga">
</audio>
```

Videos usually include two tracks in the same container file: a video track and an audio track. These two tracks will use two different codecs, and a browser must support both if it's to play the complete media. If you include both codecs in a `type` attribute, you can help the browser determine how to handle the media. Multiple codecs appear in a `type` attribute separated by commas, but unfortunately it can be tricky to include those commas without throwing validation errors. To pass validation (for the present, at least) the codecs need to be wrapped in double quotation marks, and the complete value of the `type` attribute needs to appear in single quotes, like this:

```
<video controls>
  <source src="video/Pod_People.webm" type='video/webm; codecs="vp8,vorbis"'>
  <source src="video/Pod_People.ogv" type='video/ogg; codecs="theora,vorbis"'>
  <source src="video/Pod_People.mp4" type='video/mpeg; codecs="avc1.42E01E,mp4a.40.2"'>
</video>
```

It's a bit messy, but it's valid. If you prefer life on the edge, most browsers are happy to accept comma-separated codecs without double quotes, though you'll instead need to omit any spaces, like `type="video/webm;codecs=vp8,vorbis"`. If you want to play it safe and are a stickler for validation, use the nested quotation marks. It's all part of the media encoding thrill ride.

The `source` element can also carry an optional `media` attribute, indicating the media type (screen, print, Braille, aural, handheld, etc.) for which the embedded media (audio or video) is intended. The value of a `media` attribute is a comma-separated list of *media queries*, each consisting of a media type and one or more expressions about the media features, such as screen width or aspect ratio. This way you can offer different audio or video optimized for different displays or devices.

> *Media queries are a concept introduced in CSS3. They extend the functionality of media types and allow a web developer to programmatically check for certain device or media properties, delivering different content or style rules to meet different criteria. You'll learn a bit more about media queries later in this book, and in the mean time you can also read up on them in the CSS specification (w3.org/TR/css3-mediaqueries).*

You can see an example of a media attribute in Listing 5-7. In this scenario, the first source element targets screen media (as opposed to print or Braille, which would have very different needs) on devices at least 600 pixels wide, which we can assume is a computer or tablet with a large enough screen to enjoy the full-size video. The second source element targets screens less than 600 pixels wide, serving those smaller displays a smaller, more mobile-friendly video. You would naturally include the usual multiple formats and fallback content, but we left them out here for the sake of brevity.

Unfortunately, no browsers yet support this technique at the time we're writing this, but it never hurts to begin planning for the future.

Listing 5-7. A video element featuring different sources optimized for different media

```
<video controls poster="images/Gamera.jpg">
  <source src="video/Gamera.ogv" media="screen and (min-device-width: 600px)" ↪
  type='video/ogg;codecs="theora,vorbis"'>
  <source src="video/Gamera-mobi.ogv" media="screen and (max-device-width: 600px)" ↪
  type='video/ogg;codecs="theora,vorbis"'>
</video>
```

Required Attributes

- src: Specifies the URL where the media file or stream resides on a web server.

Optional Attributes

- type: The media source's media type (also called a MIME type). This may optionally include the specific codec(s) used to encode the media.

- media: The output media or devices for which the embedded media is optimized. This attribute's value is a comma-separated list of valid media queries, as taken from the CSS specification (w3.org/TR/css3-mediaqueries). The default value is "all" if the attribute is empty or omitted.

track

A track element specifies the address of an external *timed text track* for a media element, either audio or video. Such a text track can provide accessible captions for the hearing impaired, or subtitles for other languages, additional text descriptions, annotations, or metadata about the media. This is a recent addition to HTML5 and browsers don't support text tracks yet.

The track element is a void element with no end tag, and it can only appear as a child of an audio or video element. Within an audio or video element, track elements should come *after* all source elements and *before* any other flow elements (such as an object, embed, or any other fallback content):

```
<video controls>
  <source src="video/mechanical-monsters.ogv" type="video/ogg">
  <source src="video/mechanical-monsters.mp4" type="video/mp4">

  <track kind="subtitles" src="video/tracks/mechmon-en.vtt" ↵
  srclang="en" label="English subtitles" default>
  <track kind="subtitles" src="video/tracks/mechmon-ja.vtt" ↵
  srclang="ja" label="Japanese subtitles">
  <track kind="captions" src="video/tracks/mechmon-cap.vtt" ↵
  srclang="en" label="English captions for the hearing impaired">

  <p>Download this exciting video clip in
  <a href="video/mechanical-monsters.ogv">Ogg Theora</a> or
  <a href="video/mechanical-monsters.mp4">MP4</a> format.</p>
</video>
```

If there are multiple track elements present, you can mark one of them as the default text track with the Boolean default attribute; without this attribute the first track acts as the default.

Each track element requires a src attribute supplying the URL of the text track data. Also important is the kind attribute, specifying what kind of text track the browser is dealing with. There are only a few different kinds of tracks:

- *Subtitles* are a transcription or translation of dialogue, for cases when the sound is available but may not be understood, especially if it's in another language.

- *Captions* are a transcription of dialogue but also describe any other sounds, music cues, or other essential audio information. Unlike subtitles, captions are intended as a replacement for the audio if the audio isn't available, especially valuable to deaf viewers.

- *Descriptions* provide text descriptions of a video if the video isn't available, or for blind users, in which case the text descriptions might be synthesized as audible speech or printed to a Braille device.

- *Chapters* are titles meant to act as navigation points, to jump to a particular segment of the media source, like the scene selection on a DVD.

- *Metadata* is information about the media, only intended for use by scripts or user-agents, not for display.

The track element has an optional srclang attribute to declare the language of the text track. If the track's kind is set to subtitles, a srclang attribute must be present, though it may have an empty value (srclang="") meaning the track has no language. An optional label attribute offers a title for each text track, which could appear in a menu so your users can select one track from several options.

This is all brand new in HTML5, and is still very much in a state of flux as the specification marches toward completion. As of this writing, only a few of the very latest browsers have implemented support for the track element, but we can hope others add it soon. We've tried to boil it down to a brief introduction here, and although the markup is simple, actually implementing text tracks for rich media is a much more complex matter. One major tangle is defining and standardizing the format of the timed text tracks themselves, and that part is still ongoing.

Required Attributes

- src: The URL of the text track data.

Optional Attributes

- kind: The kind of text track, specified by one of the keywords: subtitles, captions, descriptions, chapters, or metadata. The track's kind defaults to subtitles if the attribute is missing.

- srclang: The language of the text track, specified by a valid language tag (see langtag.net for more on language tags). This attribute must be present if the track element's kind is subtitles, though srclang may have an empty value (in which case the track has no specified language).

- label: A human-readable title for the text track, to assist the user in selecting which track to render. This is especially helpful when there are multiple tracks.

- default: Indicates the default text track for the media element when there is more than one track. This attribute can only appear in one track element per media element.

> *If you'd like to dive much deeper into how text tracks work (or soon will), consult the spec-in-progress at whatwg.org/specs/web-apps/current-work/multipage/the-video-element.html#timed-text-tracks*

Embedding Plug-ins and Other Content

Images have been web-native since the first graphical web browser in the early 1990s, and the new audio and video elements in HTML5 are helping to make sound and moving pictures just as web-native as static pictures. At long last, web users can enjoy musical interludes and funny cat antics without requiring third-party plug-ins. And yet, HTML still can't do everything on its own. Some user experiences simply can't be produced with technology native to the browser environment, and browsers still often require some outside assistance from plug-ins. Though HTML doesn't quite give us unlimited power, it does give us mechanisms to embed external content, for those challenges a browser just can't face on its own.

object

The object element embeds a file or type of media that exists external to the HTML document. The external content could be an image, a video, an audio file, or even an HTML page—but other elements exist for embedding these types of content that a browser can handle natively (img, video, audio, and iframe, respectively). The object element is most often used to embed content that requires a separate plug-in application to render it, such as Flash movies or Java applets.

The object element requires an end tag and may contain one or more param elements, followed by any other flow content. If the embedded content fails to render—if the browser lacks the requisite plug-in, for instance—the nested content is displayed as a fallback.

Earlier in this chapter, you saw some examples of the object element used to embed Flash-based media players inside the audio and video elements, providing a fallback player for browsers that don't support those new elements. Listing 5-8 shows an inversion of that; in this example, the Flash player comes first and a nested audio element provides a fallback for browsers that don't have the Flash plug-in installed but do support native audio (such as every Apple iPad and iPhone).

Listing 5-8. An embedded Flash object with a nested audio element as fallback

```
<object data="flash/audio-player.swf?soundFile=audio/Townsville.mp3" ↵
width="250" height="25" type="application/x-shockwave-flash">
  <param name="movie" value="flash/audio-player.swf?soundFile=audio/Townsville.mp3">
  <param name="allowscriptaccess" value="always">
  <param name="menu" value="false">
  <param name="wmode" value="transparent">

  <audio controls>
    <source src="audio/Townsville.mp3" type="audio/mpeg;codec=mpeg">
    <source src="audio/Townsville.ogg" type="audio/ogg;codec=vorbis">
    <p>Download this tune in <a href="audio/Townsville.mp3">MP3</a>
    or <a href="audio/Townsville.ogg">Ogg Vorbis</a> format.</p>
  </audio>
</object>
```

Required Attributes

The object element doesn't require any attributes. A data attribute is usually required to provide the resource's address, unless that address is provided in a nested param element instead.

Optional Attributes

- data: The URL of the external resource to embed.

- type: The content type of the embedded resource (also called a MIME type). This attribute's value should match the resource's actual content type; a content type mismatch may cause the browser invoke the wrong plug-in to handle the content, and the content may not work.

- name: Provides the object's browsing context, primarily if the embedded object is another HTML document (see w3.org/TR/html5/browsers.html#windows).

- form: Specifies the ID of the form element with which the object is associated (if it's associated with a form). You'll learn more about forms in HTML in Chapter 8.

- width: The width of the object in pixels.

- height: The height of the object in pixels.

- usemap: Identifies a client-side image map to be used, if the object is an image (see Chapter 6 to learn more about image maps).

- typemustmatch: A Boolean attribute that, when present, indicates that the resource specified in the data attribute must match the content type specified in the type attribute; if the resource doesn't match the type, it shouldn't be used or displayed. This is most useful when you're embedding external content from a source you can't control and may not trust, to help prevent the remote host from passing through any malicious code. This attribute can only be present if both the data and type attributes are present as well.

param

A param element appears within an object element to define various object parameters and pass along additional information for the object to use. A single object can contain multiple param elements, though they must appear first before any other nested content. The param element can only appear as a child of an object element. This is a void element with no contents and no end tag. It requires a name attribute and optionally (though usually) features a value attribute as well. This is a multi-purpose element that represents nothing on its own, and actual usage will depend entirely on the particular object you're embedding.

Required Attributes

- name: The name of the parameter.

Optional Attributes

- value: The value of the parameter.

embed

As the HTML5 spec states, the embed element is "an integration point for an external (typically non-HTML) application or interactive content." In simpler terms, this element embeds content that requires a plug-in. It's similar to the object element in that regard, but unlike object, embed is a void element that can't hold any contents, meaning you can't readily provide any fallback content within the element. If the browser lacks the requisite plug-in to process the embedded resource, the embed element won't do anything at all.

Listing 5-9 shows an example of the embed element, here embedding an MP4 video file. Some browsers can play MP4 video natively, but only in a video element. If you embed the file directly with an embed element (or object), the browser will attempt to invoke the appropriate plug-in (such as QuickTime) to handle the media.

Listing 5-9. An MP4 video clip embedded in a document with the embed element

```
<embed src="video/feature.mp4" type="video/mp4" width="394" height="298">
```

The video element is a far better way to embed videos in your web pages. However, you can use embed within a video (or audio) element to include the fallback for older browsers—either embedding a Flash-based media player or embedding the media directly—the same way you would use the object element:

```
<video controls width="468" height="350">
  <source src="video/mechanical-monsters.mp4" type="video/mp4">
  <source src="video/mechanical-monsters.webm" type="video/webm">

  <embed src="flash/video-player.swf" flashvars="video/mechanical-monsters.mp4" ↪
  type="application/x-shockwave-flash" width="468" height="350">
</video>
```

The embed element is newly standardized in HTML5, though it's actually been around for a long time as a non-standard and invalid element. Not so long ago, embed enjoyed better cross-browser support than object, even though embed wasn't part of any standardized HTML specification—it was introduced by Netscape years ago and other browsers imitated Netscape's implementation.

The object element is fully supported in current browsers, but because so many websites used the non-standard embed element for so long, embed became a de facto standard simply through common usage. HTML5 has followed the "pave the cow paths" methodology: observe what people are using in the real world, then tidy it up and make it official. The embed element is now valid in HTML5, but object is still preferable.

Required Attributes

The embed element doesn't require any attributes, though a src attribute is usually required to provide the resource's address. An embed element with no attributes is technically valid, but represents nothing.

Optional Attributes

- src: The URL of the external resource to embed.

- type: The content type of the embedded resource (also called a MIME type). This attribute's value should match the resource's actual content type; a content type mismatch may cause the browser invoke the wrong plug-in to handle the content, and the content may not work.

- width: The width of the embedded content in pixels.

- height: The height of the embedded content in pixels.

- Any other attribute that doesn't have a namespace and isn't one of name, align, hspace, or vspace (these four are obsolete attributes, and are specifically excluded from embed because they have effects beyond passing parameters to the plug-in).

Dynamic Drawings

One of the most exciting innovations in HTML5 is the canvas element and its associated scripting APIs, allowing a browser—with the aid of JavaScript—to natively render imagery in real-time without requiring additional plug-ins. The technology was first introduced by Apple and incorporated into WebKit, the rendering engine that powers both Safari and Chrome. The canvas element was soon adopted by Firefox and Opera, and finally by Internet Explorer as of version 9.

Images are static media—the picture lives on the server in a permanent, unchanging state, and users can download the image to view it in their browsers. It's certainly possible to generate static images programmatically, but once the file is made it remains forever static. Scalable Vector Graphics (SVG) is an image format based on XML, and SVG imagery can be rendered dynamically, but for various reasons SVG wasn't embraced as quickly or as widely as canvas has been. Although SVG offers many of the same capabilities as canvas (and even a few advantages), the current generation of browsers has better support for the canvas element.

canvas

The canvas element creates an empty drawing area for dynamically generated imagery—a metaphorical blank canvas. The markup is incredibly simple:

```
<canvas></canvas>
```

That's it. On a rendered page, the canvas element designates a box 300 pixels wide by 150 pixels high by default, but you can supply your own dimensions with the optional width and height attributes, or with CSS. You may also want to include an ID attribute, to make it easier to target the element with JavaScript:

```
<canvas id="myCanvas" width="460" height="300"></canvas>
```

This is a new element in HTML5 so older browsers won't recognize it, and only the latest browsers support the JavaScript methods for creating canvas drawings. The canvas element requires an end tag and, like the audio and video elements, it can contain any other flow elements and content. Browsers that don't support canvas will show the inner content just as if the outer canvas element didn't exist. The fallback content should preferably be some usable replacement content, such as an image or text equivalent, depending on what you're drawing. For example, if you're using canvas to render charts from numerical data, the fallback content might be the same data presented in a table. If it's a diagram or illustration, you could provide a static image version of it, like you see in Listing 5-10 (Figure 5-11 shows the result). If the canvas drawing is decorative and not essential, leaving the element empty means older browsers won't display anything at all.

Listing 5-10. A `canvas` element containing an image as fallback content for older browsers

```
<figure>
  <canvas id="shrinkray" width="460" height="300">
    <p>We're terribly sorry, but your browser can't display the original
    interactive diagram. Please enjoy this static version instead.</p>

    <img src="images/shrinkray-diagram.png" width="460" height="300" ↪
    alt="A line diagram labeling the key components of the Power Outfitters ↪
    V900 portable shrink ray. It's shaped like a pistol, with a rounded body, ↪
    a beam emitter (barrel), hand grip, and trigger. On the side of the body ↪
    casing are a mode switch and dial control for level adjustment.">
  </canvas>
  <figcaption>
    The Power Outfitters V900 portable shrink ray
  </figcaption>
</figure>
```

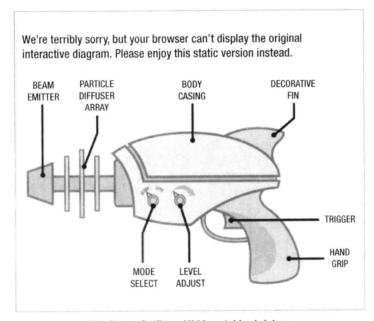

The Power Outfitters V900 portable shrink ray

Figure 5-11. Older browsers that don't support `canvas` will show the static image instead

The `canvas` element is an ordinary citizen of the document so it can be styled similarly to any other element, adding background colors, background images, fonts, borders, margins, padding, and so on. Those CSS styles won't affect the drawings within the rendered box, only the box itself and any fallback content inside it.

Although the markup for the canvas element is very simple, it offers a wide window into a very complex realm. The element itself doesn't do anything more than provide a space where JavaScript can draw, and the script does all the real work. An instance of the canvas element opens up one or more *rendering contexts* with a range of associated JavaScript methods. The only official rendering context at present is 2D, for two-dimensional drawings, but a 3D context is in the works, awaiting wider implementation in browsers. Soon you'll be able to dynamically draw three-dimensional shapes in virtual space, right there in a web browser. But for now you're limited to a flat plane.

Each shape in a canvas drawing is generated and positioned in JavaScript code. For instance, these few lines of script will draw a blue square:

```
var canvas  = document.getElementById("myCanvas");
var context = canvas.getContext("2d");

context.fillStyle = "lightblue";      // Set the fill color
context.fillRect(50, 40, 150, 150);   // Draw the filled rectangle
```

The first two lines establish some variables, first specifying the canvas element on which to draw, then invoking that canvas' 2D rendering context. The next two lines produce the drawing, first declaring a fill color and then drawing the filled rectangle on the canvas, 50 pixels from the left, 40 pixels from the top, 150 pixels wide and 150 pixels tall. That's not so hard, is it? You can see the result in Figure 5-12 (we've added a border to the canvas element here, just so you can see it; a rendered canvas has no border or background by default).

Figure 5-12. A filled square drawn with canvas and JavaScript

Unfortunately, the only shape that's quite that easy to draw is a rectangle. More interesting shapes require some slightly more complex code. We can add an outlined circle like so:

```
context.strokeStyle = "midnightblue";            // Set the stroke color
context.lineWidth = 8;                           // Set the stroke width
context.arc(125, 115, 40, 0, Math.PI*2, true);   // Create the circle path
context.stroke();                                // Add the stroke to that path
```

And you can see the result in Figure 5-13. Shapes are drawn in the order in which they appear in the JavaScript, so the circle overlaps the square because it's drawn later in the script.

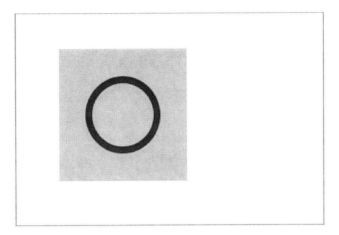

Figure 5-13. Adding a circle to the canvas

More complex shapes are possible, of course, with gradient fills and effects like drop shadows, and integrated bitmap images. With the canvas element and a 2D rendering context, you can produce almost any sort of shape-based illustration you might create with vector drawing software like Adobe Illustrator. It follows that the more complex the drawing is, the more complex the code will be to generate it. It's certainly not quite as easy as dragging a pencil across a sketchpad, but there are tools, frameworks, and code libraries that can help ease the pain.

What's really cool about canvas is that these drawings are generated "on the fly" by JavaScript, and can thus be manipulated by JavaScript in real time, interacting with data and user input. Because the imagery is created before your eyes, a canvas graphic can move and react and respond. Even with two measly dimensions the possibilities are infinite.

Figure 5-14 is a screen capture of a live drawing application called Ghostwriter Art Studio (https://developer.mozilla.org/en-US/demos/detail/ghostwriter-art-studio). Just a few years ago something like this could only be done with plug-ins like Flash or Silverlight, but this app works directly in a browser. It's built entirely with HTML, CSS, and JavaScript, and uses the canvas element as, well, a canvas.

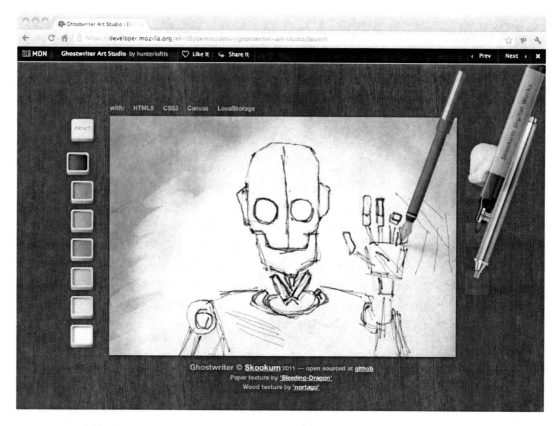

Figure 5-14. Ghostwriter Art Studio is an open-source demonstration of the `canvas` element, with a live drawing surface where you can sketch and doodle by hand.

For something perhaps a bit more practical, Visualize (`filamentgroup.com/examples/charting_v2/`) is a JavaScript widget that reads a well-structured HTML table and automatically generates a chart in a `canvas` element, like you see in Figure 5-15. This is a fine example of progressive enhancement. The table is the original content, fully readable and accessible by any person or user-agent (you'll learn all about tables in Chapter 7). The `canvas`-based chart then further enhances that content when the conditions are right (a graphical browser that supports `canvas` and JavaScript).

Repellant Spray Sales, 2011

	Q1	Q2	Q3	Q4
Shark	167	219	101	41
Crocodile	83	57	45	71
Piranha	112	91	112	175
Giant Squid	44	29	141	113

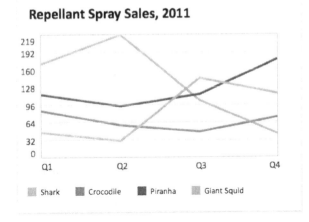

Figure 5-15. The chart on the right is generated in a `canvas` element, derived from the table on the left

Although the possibilities of `canvas` are truly exciting, there are a few unfortunate drawbacks. For one thing, it's entirely reliant on JavaScript, so people who disable JavaScript in their browsers (or are using browsers that don't support scripting) will be excluded from seeing the `canvas`. If the browser supports and recognizes the element but JavaScript is disabled or some other error in the script stops it from running, the browser will still render the `canvas` as a blank box, hiding any fallback content within it. It's a good idea to include some checks in your JavaScript to test for `canvas` support, and it may even be best to generate the `canvas` element itself with JavaScript and insert it into the DOM. That way, without scripting, the `canvas` element won't exist at all and the fallback content can appear in its stead.

Anything drawn in a `canvas` element—including text—exists merely as pixels on screen, not as a true object in the document. Scripts and applications can read and manipulate the code that draws the pixels, but remain ignorant of the shapes those pixels represent. Because in-canvas objects aren't part of the DOM, screen-reading software for the visually impaired has no way to read them, even if the objects are letters and words. The `canvas` element is inaccessible for the time being, but a group within the W3C is working to correct that shortcoming (`w3.org/WAI/PF/html-task-force`). Meanwhile, use `canvas` responsibly and consider your audience. Provide usable, meaningful content and interaction first, and enhance it with `canvas` when it's appropriate.

> We've barely scratched the surface of what can be done with the `canvas` element here, and there are entire books dedicated to the subject. If you'd like to learn more, a good starting point is the `canvas` tutorial from the Mozilla Developer Network (`https://developer.mozilla.org/en/Canvas_tutorial`).

Required Attributes

The `canvas` element doesn't require any attributes.

Optional Attributes

- width: the width of the canvas in pixels.
- height: the height of the canvas in pixels.

Images with Style, Styling with Images

Simply injecting an image into a web page rarely makes for the best visual experience unless you add a bit more panache. With CSS, you can move and manipulate that image, incorporating it into the layout of your content on the screen. You can also use images in CSS itself, filling HTML elements with background patterns, or adding purely decorative images that won't interfere with the structure of your content.

Wrapping Text Around an Image

You've no doubt seen it in hundreds of books, magazines, and newspapers: an image placed in a column of text where the text wraps around the image and continues on its way, like a stream flowing around a boulder. In early versions of HTML, this was accomplished with the now-obsolete align attribute, but the modern way to achieve the same effect is with the float property in CSS.

The float property accepts one of three values: left, right, or none. When an element is "floated," it will be shifted as far to one side (left or right) as possible until its edge comes up against the edge of its containing block (or until it collides with another floating element). Any text or elements that come afterward will then flow upward around the floated element. The default none value is most useful for overriding any float properties that were granted to an element by another rule in your style sheet.

In Listing 5-11, you see the markup for an image followed by a block of text (both are contained in a single paragraph). The img element features a class attribute that will make it easy to apply CSS.

Listing 5-11. An image in a paragraph of text

```
<p><img src="images/avatar.jpg" alt="" class="avatar">
Having foiled a jewelry store heist on my way to receive a
medal from the President, imagine my embarrassment to notice
a nasty laser burn on my cape. There was no time to fly back to
base and change into my spare costume, even at my speed. Thank
goodness for Power Outfitters! They had my size and style in stock,
in just the right shade of red, and at a great price, too. I went
back after the ceremony and bought five more capes, plus matching
gauntlets!</p>
```

The image belongs to the "avatar" class, and Listing 5-12 shows a CSS rule for that class, declaring that the element should float to the left.

Listing 5-12. The CSS rule for the "avatar" class

```
.avatar {
  float: left;
}
```

You can see the results in Figure 5-16; the image floats to the left side of the paragraph and the following text flows upward around it.

Having foiled a jewelry store heist on my way to receive a medal from the President, imagine my embarrassment to notice a nasty laser burn on my cape. There was no time to fly back to base and change into my spare costume, even at my speed. Thank goodness for Power Outfitters! They had my size and style in stock, in just the right shade of red, and at a great price, too. I went back after the ceremony and bought five more capes, plus matching gauntlets!

Figure 5-16. The image floats to the left, allowing the text to wrap around it

An inline image rests on the same baseline as its neighboring text, but when that image floats to one side, its top edge now rests at the top of the line it appears on, descending below the baseline. In the previous example, you'll notice that the wrapped text rubs directly against the right edge of the image, making it harder to read. To create a bit of spacing, you can apply margins to the floating image:

```
.avatar {
  float: left;
  margin-right: 1em;
  margin-bottom: .5em;
}
```

Only the right and bottom sides need margins in this case because the top and left sides don't collide with any text. Leaving those sides with the default `margin` value of 0 will make those edges press right against the invisible edge of the containing paragraph. You can see in Figure 5-17 that the floating image now has a bit more room to breathe; the margins extend the influence of the image's float, and the text now wraps around the margins as well.

Having foiled a jewelry store heist on my way to receive a medal from the President, imagine my embarrassment to notice a nasty laser burn on my cape. There was no time to fly back to base and change into my spare costume, even at my speed. Thank goodness for Power Outfitters! They had my size and style in stock, in just the right shade of red, and at a great price, too. I went back after the ceremony and bought five more capes, plus matching gauntlets!

Figure 5-17. Applying some margins to the floating image separates it from the text

You can float almost any element in HTML, not only images. For instance, a "pull quote" in an article:

```
<p>Power Outfitters Superhero Costume and Supply Company is located
in a nondescript building on Kirby Ave, a site that once housed a
large printing plant. Behind their modest storefront is an expansive
warehouse positively packed to the portholes with paraphernalia.</p>
```

```
<aside class="pull">
<q>&hellip; the most astounding super-science gadgetry ever conceived
on this planet, or several others.</q>
</aside>

<p>You can find all the standard costume components and accessories,
both off the rack and custom tailored. Capes, cowls, tights, belts,
boots, and of course masks in every shape and style. But what you'll
also find at Power Outfitters is some of the most astounding
super-science gadgetry ever conceived on this planet, or several others.
I was lucky enough to receive a tour of the manufacturing wing to see
what goes into making some of their top selling items.</p>
```

With a quick float:right and a few more declarations, this pull quote can easily look something like Figure 5-18.

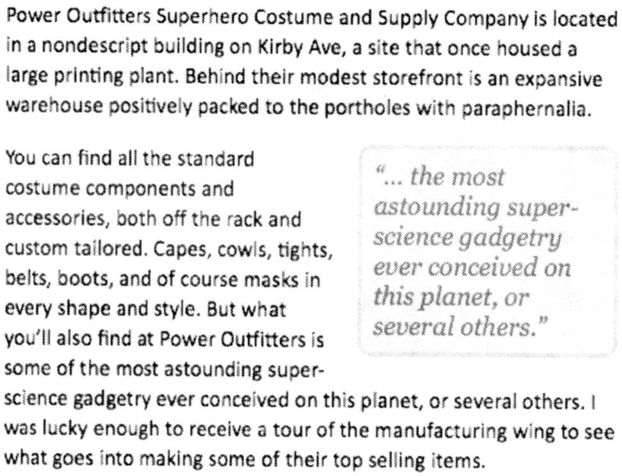

Power Outfitters Superhero Costume and Supply Company is located in a nondescript building on Kirby Ave, a site that once housed a large printing plant. Behind their modest storefront is an expansive warehouse positively packed to the portholes with paraphernalia.

You can find all the standard costume components and accessories, both off the rack and custom tailored. Capes, cowls, tights, belts, boots, and of course masks in every shape and style. But what you'll also find at Power Outfitters is some of the most astounding super-science gadgetry ever conceived on this planet, or several others. I was lucky enough to receive a tour of the manufacturing wing to see what goes into making some of their top selling items.

"... the most astounding super-science gadgetry ever conceived on this planet, or several others."

Figure 5-18. A floating pull quote with some additional style

Background Images

With the CSS background-image property, you can add decorative imagery to your page and still avoid mixing presentation with your content—images that are meaningful content belong in the HTML document with your other content. Almost any element in HTML can carry a background image and the contents of the element will overlay that background. The background image tiles in both directions by default, beginning at the top-left corner of the element and replicating itself horizontally and vertically to fill the space, like the tiles on a kitchen floor.

Listing 5-13 shows a CSS rule that will apply a background image to the body element. The image is specified by its URL, contained in parentheses and denoted by the url keyword.

Listing 5-13. A background image applied to the body element

```
body {
    background-image: url(images/background.png);
}
```

The image tiles to fill the window on the rendered page, as you can see in Figure 5-19.

Figure 5-19. The background image tiles in both directions, repeating as many times as necessary to fill the element's area, the entire browser window in this case.

> *Relative URLs in CSS are relative to where the CSS file resides, not relative to where the HTML document resides. Depending on how you organize your files on the server, you may need to use up-level directives (../) in your CSS URLs, or use site-root-relative URLs with leading slashes if your server is set up that way. If your background image isn't showing up in the browser, check the file path in your image URL.*

You can modify the default tiling with the background-repeat property, specifying whether the image should repeat only horizontally, only vertically, or not at all. Listing 5-14 expands the previous CSS rule, declaring that the background image should only repeat horizontally along the x-axis.

Listing 5-14. Adding a background-repeat declaration

```
body {
    background-image: url(images/background.gif);
    background-repeat: repeat-x;
}
```

You can see in Figure 5-20 that the image now repeats across the top of the page but not downward.

Figure 5-20. The background now tiles horizontally but not vertically

Likewise, a value of repeat-y will tile the image vertically but not horizontally:

```
body {
  background-image: url(images/background.png);
  background-repeat: repeat-y;
}
```

You can see the result in Figure 5-21, where the image now tiles vertically along the y-axis.

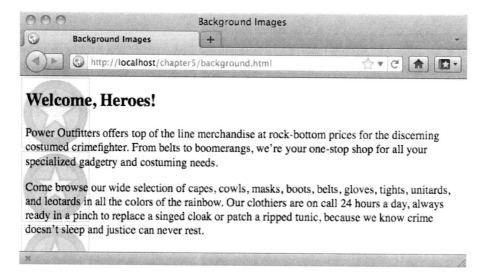

Figure 5-21. The background tiles vertically but not horizontally

The default value of `background-repeat` is `repeat`, which you can use to override another value in another rule if necessary. You can also disable tiling altogether with the value `no-repeat`:

```
body {
  background-image: url(images/background.png);
  background-repeat: no-repeat;
}
```

Figure 5-22 shows the effect of the no-repeat value; the image appears only once and doesn't tile in either direction.

Figure 5-22. The background image appears only once and doesn't repeat

If your background image is larger than the element it decorates, the element's dimensions act like a window defining the portion of the background that can be seen. In Figure 5-23, the background image is much larger than the element in which it appears so part of the image is hidden.

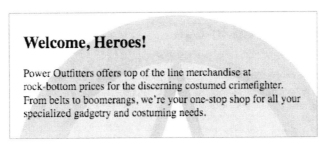

Figure 5-23. Only part of the background image is visible because it's much larger than the element to which it's been applied

If the element expands—if you add more content, increase the text size, or resize the element with CSS— more of the image becomes visible, as in Figure 5-24.

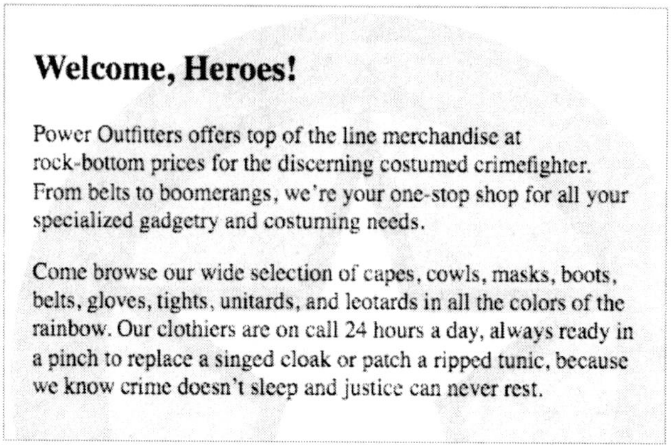

Welcome, Heroes!

Power Outfitters offers top of the line merchandise at rock-bottom prices for the discerning costumed crimefighter. From belts to boomerangs, we're your one-stop shop for all your specialized gadgetry and costuming needs.

Come browse our wide selection of capes, cowls, masks, boots, belts, gloves, tights, unitards, and leotards in all the colors of the rainbow. Our clothiers are on call 24 hours a day, always ready in a pinch to replace a singed cloak or patch a ripped tunic, because we know crime doesn't sleep and justice can never rest.

Figure 5-24. Adding another paragraph expands the container element, revealing more of the background image

Text can be difficult to read when it overlays a complicated background image or when there's not enough contrast between the foreground and background colors. Be wise in your use of background images, ensuring they don't interfere too much with the readability of your text.

Also be sure to specify a solid background color (with the `background-color` property) that provides enough contrast with the foreground text color in the event the image doesn't display. Most modern browsers default to black text on a white background. If your design uses light-colored text against a dark background image, you should declare a dark background color as well—otherwise the browser defaults back to white if the image is missing and your light text could vanish.

Background images are rendered on top of background colors. If the image is opaque, the solid color will show up when the image isn't available. If parts of the background image are transparent, the background color will show through those transparent pixels. You can create some pretty neat layered effects with transparent PNG backgrounds overlaying different colors, or even overlaying other background images.

Positioning a Background Image

By default, a background image appears in the top-left corner of the element, which is also where the tiling begins if the image is allowed to tile. The CSS `background-position` property controls the placement of a background image. If the image is meant to repeat, the value of `background-position` will mark the beginning of the tiling pattern.

The property takes two values: one for the horizontal position and one for the vertical position. The horizontal value always comes before the vertical, and if only one value appears, it will be taken as the horizontal position. Listing 5-15 shows the CSS to place a background image at the bottom of the right side of an element with the class "intro".

Listing 5-15. Adding a `background-position` declaration

```css
.intro {
  background-image: url(images/background.png);
  background-repeat: no-repeat;
  background-position: right bottom;
}
```

Figure 5-25 shows the result—the image appears in the element's bottom-right corner (we've added some padding and a border so you can see the box).

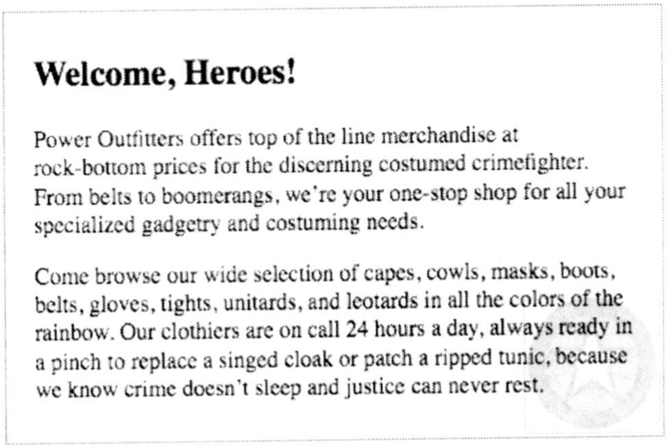

Welcome, Heroes!

Power Outfitters offers top of the line merchandise at rock-bottom prices for the discerning costumed crimefighter. From belts to boomerangs, we're your one-stop shop for all your specialized gadgetry and costuming needs.

Come browse our wide selection of capes, cowls, masks, boots, belts, gloves, tights, unitards, and leotards in all the colors of the rainbow. Our clothiers are on call 24 hours a day, always ready in a pinch to replace a singed cloak or patch a ripped tunic, because we know crime doesn't sleep and justice can never rest.

Figure 5-25. The image now appears in the bottom-right corner (and still doesn't repeat)

You can specify a value for `background-position` in a few ways: keywords, lengths, and percentages. The keywords to use are `left`, `center`, or `right` for the horizontal position and `top`, `center`, or `bottom` for the vertical. Note that you can use the keyword `center` for either horizontal or vertical positioning; vertically, `center` is half the element's height, and horizontally, `center` is half the element's width.

A *length* is simply any number with any unit of measure available, such as 10px, 20mm, or 3.5em, and the two values needn't use the same unit. A unit isn't required for lengths of 0. After all, 0px is the same as 0in or 0em—zero is always zero. Listing 5-16 shows two lengths for the `background-position` property, placing the image 50 pixels from the left and 4 em spaces from the top.

Listing 5-16. Using lengths for `background-position`

```css
.intro {
  background-image: url(images/background.png);
  background-repeat: no-repeat;
  background-position: 50px 4em;
}
```

Figure 5-26 shows the rendered result, with the image positioned 50 pixels from the left side and 4 ems from the top, just as declared in the CSS.

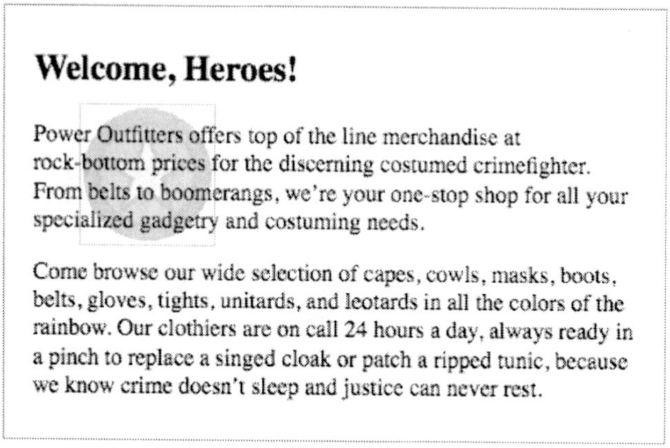

Welcome, Heroes!

Power Outfitters offers top of the line merchandise at
rock-bottom prices for the discerning costumed crimefighter.
From belts to boomerangs, we're your one-stop shop for all your
specialized gadgetry and costuming needs.

Come browse our wide selection of capes, cowls, masks, boots,
belts, gloves, tights, unitards, and leotards in all the colors of the
rainbow. Our clothiers are on call 24 hours a day, always ready in
a pinch to replace a singed cloak or patch a ripped tunic, because
we know crime doesn't sleep and justice can never rest.

Figure 5-26. The background image shows up exactly where the CSS told it to be

When you position a background image with percentages, you must factor in the size of the image as well as the size of the element it decorates. A background image positioned 75% from the left side of the element will move the reference point 75% from the left side of the image as well. This especially makes sense when centering a background at 50%; the background is placed at a point halfway across the element and halfway across the image, as illustrated in Figure 5-27.

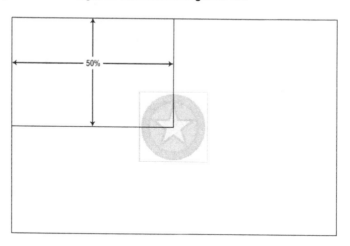

Figure 5-27. A background image positioned 50% from the left and 50% from the top will be perfectly centered, measuring the size of both the element and the image.

This isn't true for lengths; non-percentage lengths always measure the distance from the top and left sides of the element to the top and left sides of the image, as shown in Figure 5-28.

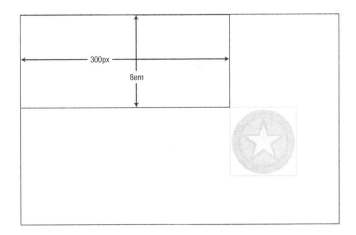

Figure 5-28. Non-percentage lengths position the top-left corner of the background image at the precise point specified in your CSS. This example shows the result of `background-position: 300px 8em;`.

Shorthand for Backgrounds

Instead of writing out each background property separately, you can declare them all in one place with the shorthand `background` property, to reduce the size of your CSS file and spare your carpal tendons from the extra typing:

```
.intro {
  background: #e6f2f9 url(images/background.png) 94% 20px no-repeat;
}
```

The order of the values doesn't matter, with the exception of `background-position`; horizontal must still come before vertical, and nothing else can appear between the two. Any properties not declared simply fall back to their default value. For example, this rule only includes values for `background-repeat` and `background-image` because that's all we need to create a repeating stripe pattern:

```
#sidebar {
  background: repeat-y url(images/stripes.gif);
}
```

All the other, undeclared background properties remain in their default states—`background-color` defaults to transparent (no color) and `background-position` defaults to the top left. However, if you have different rules declaring different values for the same element, and both use the shorthand `background` property, the later declaration can override the earlier one, resetting undeclared values back to their defaults. For example:

```
.intro {
  background: #e6f2f9 url(images/background.png) 94% 20px no-repeat;
}

.intro {
  background: left bottom;
}
```

185

In this instance, the second rule would set the `background-position` to the bottom left, but that doesn't matter because it also completely wipes out the values for `background-image`, `background-color`, and `background-repeat`. You'd end up with a box with no visible background at all. To override just a single background property on an element without affecting any others, declare that property alone in the "longhand" form:

```css
.intro {
  background: #e6f2f9 url(images/background.png) 94% 20px no-repeat;
}

.intro {
  background-position: left bottom;
}
```

Summary

The Web is textual at heart, but it lives a multimedia lifestyle. Images, animation, sound, and video can imbue a humble web page with an energy and vitality that text alone could never achieve. Images have been native to the Web from the beginning, but more complex multimedia has always required some extra help. HTML5 brings us the `audio`, `video`, and `canvas` elements, taking a great leap forward to making rich media as web-native as images have been for years. In this chapter, we briefly introduced these powerful new elements, and showed you how to use them with responsibility, offering accessible fallback content for users and devices that may not be able to enjoy the original media.

Even with these new media elements, HTML still can't do everything, and plug-ins can still add a lot of value when they're used appropriately. This chapter showed you how to embed external plug-in content into your web pages for the jobs a browser can't handle on its own.

Imagery can be instrumental in a well-designed web page and is just one more way to make your site unique and identifiable. But images can also convey meaning in ways words can't. You can embed meaningful images into your content with the `img` element, always including an alternative text equivalent to improve accessibility for people and devices that can't see the picture. You should separate presentational images from your content by using CSS and the `background-image` property. CSS also gives you the power to control the placement and repetition of background images, and the ability to influence the placement of inline images (and other elements) to integrate them into the flow of your page.

You'll make frequent use of the elements and techniques we've covered in this chapter and the previous one to give your content meaning, to make your pages visually attractive, and to bring them to life. But the Web wouldn't be the Web without one essential component: the hyperlink. Chapter 6 will introduce you to hyperlinks and show you how to transform your documents into living, working parts of the World Wide Web.

Chapter 6

Linking the Web

It's not entirely hyperbole when we tell you that links are the most important element in HTML. Without the ability to link from one document to another, the Web wouldn't be the Web. The "H" in "HTML," hypertext, becomes meaningless without the concept of linked documents. Links are the thread that binds the tapestry of the Web together. They allow us, for better or for worse, to spend hours reading articles on Wikipedia, diving into one topic and falling out the other side of a completely different topic. Links are beautiful in their simplicity and awesome in their power.

In this chapter, you'll learn about anchors and their many useful attributes and characteristics. We'll also introduce you to the image map. Over the course of the chapter, there will be plenty of code examples, tips, and tricks. Lastly, we'll show you some common CSS techniques you can employ to spruce up your links.

Anchors

Linking the Web begins with the a, or anchor, element, one of the oldest elements—perhaps *the* oldest element—in HTML. If you take a look at the oldest known HTML document on the Web, still available at www.w3.org/History/19921103-hypertext/hypertext/WWW/Link.html, you'll see that the page includes three elements: title, h1, and a. Functioning hyperlinks were a key component of the Web from the very start!

That page, created by Tim Berners-Lee while in the midst of inventing the Web, amazingly still renders properly in modern browsers. Even in this primordial form, HTML differentiated itself from SGML, the arcane language from which it was loosely derived, by including a facility for linking documents. SGML, itself a descendant of IBM's GML, includes no notion of linked documents. Therefore, linking is one of the fundamental attributes of HTML and is a defining characteristic of hypertext.

The anchor element itself can link to any number of resources: other web pages, images, email addresses, PDFs, and more. Essentially, anything on the Web can be accessed via a hyperlink. In the next section, we'll walk you through a number of facets of the mighty anchor element.

a

The anchor element marks up hyperlinks, those clickable bits of text or images that exist in just about every document on the Web. In previous versions of HTML, the anchor element's content model restricted its content to phrasing (or "inline") content. The HTML5 spec, though, expands the anchor's content model to allow for the inclusion of flow (or "block") content. We'll discuss the reasoning behind this decision later in this chapter.

Thanks to the reworking of the anchor's content model, few restrictions exist on the element. In order to be valid, an anchor element must have both a start and an end tag. Additionally, the anchor element cannot be the child of another anchor element or a child of a button element.

The most basic implementation of an anchor element is shown in Listing 6-1.

Listing 6-1. A sample placeholder hyperlink

```
<a>A placeholder hyperlink</a>
```

As it lacks an href attribute, the example shown in Listing 6-1 is known as a *placeholder* hyperlink. Hyperlinks of this type are functionally useless. However, this is perfectly valid HTML. Browsers will typically render this code the same as plain text, as shown in Figure 6-1.

A placeholder hyperlink

Figure 6-1. A sample placeholder hyperlink as rendered in the browser

Not terribly useful, right? Good thing, then, that we have...

The href attribute

The href attribute ("href" being short for "hypertext reference") of the anchor element adds interactivity and meaning to a placeholder hyperlink. Values for the href attribute are restricted to URLs, which we will cover in great detail in the next section of this chapter. But first, Listing 6-2 illustrates a common anchor element with an href attribute.

Listing 6-2. An anchor element with an href attribute

```
<a href="index.html">Back to homepage</a>
```

Most browsers will render this code as a run of blue, underlined text (see Figure 6-2). Of course, the default styling of a hyperlink can easily be changed using CSS. When you move your mouse over the hyperlink, your computer's cursor will change from its default arrow to a pointer. If you've spent any time at all surfing the Web (and we imagine that you have if you're reading this book), you've no doubt seen this in action.

Back to homepage

Figure 6-2. A hyperlink as rendered by a browser

Required Attributes

There are no required attributes for the anchor element.

Optional Attributes

In addition to the global attributes, the anchor element supports the following attributes.

- `href`: a URL that defines the destination of the hyperlink. This can be a relative URL, an absolute URL, or a fragment identifier.

- `rel`: a space-separated list of tokens that describe the destination document's relationship to the current document.

- `type`: the MIME type of the hyperlink's destination.

- `target`: a name or keyword that is the browsing context that a browser should use when following the hyperlink. Typical values are "_blank", "_self", "_parent", or "_top".

- `media`: defines the media for which the linked document was designed.

- `hreflang`: the language of the linked document.

URLs

If you recall the "Introducing the URL" section in Chapter 1, you'll remember that properly formed URLs generally fall into two categories: absolute URLs and relative URLs.

Absolute URLs contain the complete path (including the protocol; `http://`, `https://`, etc.) to a web page. You'll want to use absolute URLs when linking to a resource that exists on a domain other than your own. For instance, Listing 6-3 demonstrates how you would link to a page on the Power Outfitters website from your own.

Listing 6-3. An anchor element with an absolute URL

```
<a href="http://example.com/about.html">About Power Outfitters</a>
```

Relative URLs, as the name implies, are URLs that reference resources by their location relative to the location of the current document. Assume for a moment that all of the pages of your site are located in the root of your site, as outlined in Listing 6-4.

Listing 6-4. A sample site structure

```
http://example.com/index.html
http://example.com/about.html
http://example.com/links.html
http://example.com/contact.html
```

Creating a link from one page to another in this example is as easy as setting the link's `href` attribute to the file name of the page to which you're linking (see Listing 6-5).

Listing 6-5. An anchor element with a relative URL

```
<a href="about.html">About Power Outfitters</a>
```

This example site structure works great for smaller websites. Assume, though, that you are tasked with creating a much larger website. For this larger web project, you may want to organize your pages in a series of folders. Using that approach, you might organize your pages in a fashion similar to that shown in Listing 6-6.

Listing 6-6. A sample site structure

```
http://example.com/index.html
http://example.com/about/index.html
http://example.com/about/history.html
http://example.com/links/index.html
http://example.com/links/archive.html
```

Let's say you want to add a link from the "links" folder's "index.html" page to the "about" folder's "history.html" page. To accomplish this, you would create a link like that shown in Listing 6-7.

Listing 6-7. An anchor element with a relative URL

```
<a href="../about/history.html">Our History</a>
```

Including the "`../`"characters at the beginning of the relative URL indicates to the browser that it should first navigate up a single directory. After that, the browser is instructed to navigate into the "about" folder and find the file named "history.html." It is possible to chain together several "`../`" characters; each occurrence will instruct the browser to navigate up another folder within the structure of your website.

Fragment identifiers are the third type of link that you can use with the `href` attribute. In the context of a web page, a fragment identifier is a specialized reference to a portion of a page. They are placed at the end of URLs preceded by a hash symbol, as shown in Listing 6-8.

Listing 6-8. A URL with a fragment identifier

```
http://example.com/about.html#products
```

The string "products" that appears after the hash symbol directly correlates to an element on the team.html page that has an `id` attribute with the value "products." The browser recognizes the fragment identifier in the URL and automatically scrolls the page to bring the linked portion into view. You've likely seen fragment identifiers in action if you've ever clicked a "read more" link on a news article.

Fragment identifiers can link to portions of the same page, as well. This technique works exceptionally well if your page has a table of contents at the top with expanded content below. Listing 6-9 illustrates a sample table of contents with some associated content.

Listing 6-9. A table of contents with links to fragment identifiers

```
<ul>
  <li><a href="#products">About Our Products</a></li>
  <li><a href="#faq">Frequently Asked Questions</a></li>
  <li><a href="#villain-policy">Villain Policy</a></li>
</ul>
<div id="products">
  ...
</div>
<div id="faq">
  ...
</div>
<div id="villain-policy">
  ...
</div>
```

The rel attribute

The `rel` attribute of the anchor element consists of a space-separated list of tokens that describe the relationship of the current document to the destination document defined by the anchor's `href` attribute. As such, the `rel` attribute relies on the `href` attribute being a non-empty string. In HTML specification parlance, a token is any string that does not contain space characters. For example, "home" or "home-page" are acceptable tokens, but "home page" is not. A `rel` attribute value of "home page" is interpreted as two discrete tokens.

Listing 6-10 shows an example of an anchor element with a single `rel` attribute value.

Listing 6-10. A sample anchor element with a single `rel` attribute value

```
<a href="secret-lair.html" rel="nofollow">Secret Lair (don't click here!)</a>
```

> The "nofollow" value of the `rel` attribute is interpreted by some search engines (most notably Google) as a directive to not follow the hyperlink to its destination. It's important to note, though, that this is not an effective means of hiding sensitive information from search engines. You can find more information about the "nofollow" `rel` attribute value on this Google Webmaster Tools Help page: www.google.com/support/webmasters/bin/answer.py?answer=96569

Listing 6-11 shows another example of the `rel` attribute in action, this time with multiple attribute values.

Listing 6-11. A sample anchor element with multiple `rel` attribute values

```
<a href="latest-product.rss" rel="nofollow alternate">Latest Products RSS Feed</a>
```

The link in the above example, which points to an RSS feed, has two `rel` attribute values: "nofollow" and "alternate." This tells browsers (and search engine spiders) two things. The first, "nofollow," is aimed at search engine spiders. The second value, "alternate," implies that the linked document is an alternative version of the current document. In this case, it's an RSS feed of the current document's content. If your site is multilingual, any links to translated versions of the current page that you include should also use the "alternate" `rel` attribute value.

At this point, it's worth pausing for a moment and discussing possible values for the `rel` attribute. In the section on Link Types (available at www.w3.org/TR/html4/types.html#h-6.12), the HTML 4 specification details a number of recognized values for the `rel` attribute. In HTML 4, these were referred to as "link types." According to the spec, "user agents, search engines, etc. may interpret these link types in a variety of ways." The implication there is that interpretation of these values is left entirely to the browser, search engine, or other software or device.

The following is a list of common `rel` attribute values:

- `alternate`: Indicates that the linked document is an alternate version of the current document. This value is frequently used to point to versions in different languages and syndicated versions of a document (e.g. RSS or Atom feeds).

- `stylesheet`: Specifies that the linked document is to be used as a stylesheet for the current document. This value is almost universally used on the `link` element. In fact, the WHATWG's HTML Living Standard only allows this attribute value on `link` elements.

- `nofollow`: Implies that the author of the current document does not endorse the linked document. Search engines, in turn, may not follow the link. The WHATWG's HTML Living Standard only allows this attribute value on the `a` and `area` elements.

- `license`: Indicates that the linked document contains information about the copyright or ownership of the current document.

- `next` or `prev`: Specifies that the linked document is the next or previous document in an ordered series of documents. This value is frequently used on pagination links.

- `tag`: Indicates that the link represents a tag that applies to the current document.

These are just a few possible values for the `rel` attribute. As the HTML5 specification does not enumerate a list of potential values, the possibilities are endless. The WHATWG's HTML Living Standard, though, provides a list of defined link types. That list is available at www.whatwg.org/specs/web-apps/current-work/multipage/links.html#linkTypes. Although the WHATWG's HTML Living Standard is not the same as the W3C's official HTML5 specification, you should feel comfortable using the `rel` attribute values described in the Living Standard.

Au revoir, rev attribute

In earlier versions of HTML, there existed a `rev` attribute that was, in effect, the opposite of the `rel` attribute. The `rev` attribute was intended to describe an external document's relationship to the current document. However, due to infrequent and often incorrect usage, the attribute is rendered obsolete in the HTML5 specification.

The current recommendation is to use the `rel` attribute with a value opposite of what would otherwise have been used with the `rev` attribute. If that sounds confusing, don't worry; it is. That confusion is the primary reason the `rev` attribute was removed from the HTML specification.

The type attribute

Often used in concert with the `rel` attribute, the `type` attribute describes the MIME type of the destination of an anchor's hyperlink. The value of the `type` attribute must match a valid MIME type. Listing 6-12 illustrates how to use the `type` attribute, along with the `rel` attribute, to include a link to an RSS feed.

Listing 6-12. A sample anchor element with a `type` attribute

```
<a href="latest-products.rss" rel="alternate" type="application/rss+xml">↵
   Latest Products RSS Feed</a>
```

As you can imagine, including the `type` attribute on all of your anchors would be a tedious task. Thankfully, such a task is entirely unnecessary. Browsers are smart enough to appropriately handle MIME types.

Including the `type` attribute in your markup is entirely optional; no current browsers require you to specify the MIME type of a linked resource. It is, however, a potentially useful inclusion and is one way to future-proof your markup.

Inline vs. Block-level Links

Links are one of a handful of HTML elements that have what's known as a "transparent content model." This means that, depending on context, the element can contain phrasing content or flow content. If the anchor is a child of any element that can only contain phrasing content (such as a span), then the anchor too can only contain phrasing content. This is the traditional, pre-HTML5 interpretation of the anchor element (described in previous versions of HTML as being "inline").

Listing 6-13. An anchor with phrasing content

```
<a href="index.html">
   <em>Go</em> back to our <strong>homepage</strong>!
</a>
```

On the other hand, if the anchor is a child of any element that can contain flow content (such as a `div`), it too can contain flow content. In this context, the anchor is what's commonly referred to as a "block-level link."

Listing 6-14. An anchor with flow content

```
<a href="utility-belts.html">
   <h3>Utility belts</h3>
   <p>For all of your utility belting needs!</p>
</a>
```

The anchor element's transparent content model is a great example of a guiding principle of HTML5: pave the cow paths. For years, web page authors have wrapped anchors around block-level content and browsers have happily rendered those anchors as singular, clickable regions. This behavior, however, was invalid according to the HTML specification. The authors of the HTML5 specification, in turn, deemed this commonplace behavior worthy of codification. Thus, you may now wrap anchors around flow elements or phrasing elements so long as the context is appropriate.

> For more information on HTML5's design principles, check out: www.w3.org/TR/html-design-principles/

Image Maps

The anchor isn't the only element for creating links in a document. You have another tool at your disposal: the image map. Image maps define one or more clickable regions within an image that can be linked to other documents or to other portions of the same document.

Just like real-world maps, image maps are best suited for conveying visual information. An image map is an appropriate choice for creating, say, a clickable, interactive world map. Using an image map to mark up a site's primary navigation, however, is not an appropriate use of an image map.

Image maps have quite a storied history. In the early days of web design, image maps were frequently used to add interactivity to graphically rich designs. At the time, browser support for CSS-based layout was largely non-existent, often resulting in designs that used very large images with complexly defined image maps. As time passed, CSS support improved and the use of image maps fell by the wayside. In their place, we have visually rich layouts that use CSS positioning to achieve similar effects.

Image maps, while still perfectly valid in HTML5, should be used with care. Although image maps are relatively easy to implement, it's also quite easy to misuse them, leaving your users with a bad interactive experience or, worse yet, an inaccessible site. As you know, it is of the utmost importance to always keep accessibility and user experience in mind when considering using image maps—or any other feature of HTML—in your page.

map

The map element, along with its descendant area elements, defines an image map. Unlike some elements in HTML5, the map element must have both a start tag and an end tag. Additionally, the map element's display property defaults to inline, meaning you needn't worry about a map element disrupting the layout of your page. In fact, map elements are essentially hidden from view; browsers typically set a map element's height and width to zero.

Depending on the context, a map element may contain either phrasing content or flow content. Much like the anchor element discussed earlier in this chapter, the map element's content model is transparent. Basically, if the map element is a child of any element that can contain flow content (such as a div), it too can contain flow content. If the map element is a child of any element that can only contain phrasing content (such as a span), then the map element can also only contain phrasing content.

At its most basic, an image map looks like:

```
<map name="crime-map"></map>
```

Currently, no regions exist within the map and it has no association with an image on the page. This image map is ostensibly useless, but it's still perfectly valid.

Let's associate the image map with an `img` element:

```
<img src="crime-map.jpg" alt="Crime Map" usemap="#crime-map">
<map name="crime-map"></map>
```

Easy, right? The `usemap` attribute of the `img` element associates the image map with the graphical image. This means that any `area` elements added to the `map` will be applied to the crime map image. Note that the `usemap` attribute's value must begin with a hash character.

Required Attributes

- `name`: gives the map a name that allows for association with an image via the `usemap` attribute. The value of the `name` attribute must be a string at least one character long and can't contain spaces.

Optional Attributes

Aside from the global attributes available to all elements, there are no additional optional attributes. There is, however, the following caveat relating to the `id` attribute.

Should you define an `id` attribute on the `map` element, its value must be exactly the same as the value of the name attribute:

```
<map name="crime-map" id="crime-map"></map>
```

The `id` attribute isn't required, but when it comes to the `map` element, if both the `name` and the `id` attributes are present, their values must match exactly.

area

The `area` element represents an area on an image map. If the `href` attribute is specified on an `area` element, the corresponding region on the image is clickable. Otherwise, the `area` element defines a dead region on the image map.

`area` elements, like `img` elements, are void elements and don't have an end tag. If you are using HTML-style syntax, you'd write an `area` element like this:

```
<area>
```

If you prefer XHTML-style syntax, you'd include a trailing slash:

```
<area />
```

Either method is appropriate, so long as you generally pick one and stick to it. Consistency counts! For the examples in this chapter, we'll be using the HTML-style syntax with no trailing slash.

> For details on the differences between the HTML syntax and the XHTML syntax in HTML5, check out, "The HTML and XHTML Syntax," on the W3C's website: `http://dev.w3.org/html5/html-author/#the-html-and-xhtml-syntax`

An `area` element must always be a descendant of the `map` element but doesn't have to be an immediate child of the `map` element. As we mentioned earlier, the `map` element can have any number of descendant elements. If it makes sense within the context of your document, you may add additional markup around `area` elements.

Required attributes

There are no required attributes for the `area` element.

Optional attributes

- `shape` and `coords`: specifies the shape of the `area` element and the coordinates of that shape. The shape attribute accepts the following values: `default`, `rect`, `circle`, and `polygon`.

- `href`: a URL that, when present, makes the `area` a clickable hyperlink.

- `alt`: defines fallback content for the `area`. If the `href` attribute is present, the `alt` attribute must also be present.

- `media`, `rel`, `type`, `target`, `hreflang`: These attributes follow the same conventions on `area` elements as they do on a elements, as discussed in the previous section on anchors.

The shape and coords attributes

The `area` element has two important and related attributes that define its shape, size, and location in the image map: `shape` and `coords`.

The `shape` attribute is an enumerated attribute with four possible values: `default`, `rect`, `circle`, and `poly`. As this attribute is optional, you may choose not to include it. In this case, the value defaults to—wait for it—`default` which, in turn, implies a rectangle that contains the entirety of the associated image. If you explicitly set the `shape` attribute to `default`, you cannot include the `coords` attribute. For all other values of the `shape` attribute, you must include the `coords` attribute and correctly specify values.

Listing 6-15 shows an image map with a single area.

Listing 6-15. An image map with a single `area` element

```
<map name="crime-map" id="crime-map">
  <area>
</map>
```

Because no `shape` is specified for the image map's lone `area`, it becomes a rectangle containing the entire image. If you want to make this area clickable, you'd add an `href` attribute as seen in Listing 6-16.

Listing 6-16. An image map with a single, clickable `area` element

```
<map name="crime-map" id="crime-map">
  <area href="crime-junction.html" alt="Crime Junction">
</map>
```

The `href` attribute of the `area` element functions exactly as it does on the a element and can be a full URL, a relative URL (as seen here), or a link to a portion of the current page. You are also encouraged, when supplying an `href`, to include the `alt` attribute which specifies the text of the link.

Next, we'll introduce you to the different shapes you can create using the `area` element.

Rectangles

Creating a rectangular shape on your image map is as easy as setting the value of the `shape` attribute to `rect`, as shown in Listing 6-17.

Listing 6-17. An image map with a rectangular area

```
<map name="crime-map" id="crime-map">
  <area shape="rect" coords="10,5,100,50">
</map>
```

When adding rectangular areas to a `map`, the `coords` attribute must be given four integers. These values are the coordinates, in pixels, of the top left corner of the rectangle (the first pair of integers) and the bottom right of the rectangle (the second pair of integers). Both pairs of values are calculated with respect to the top left corner of the image.

In the example above, we've created a rectangular region that begins ten pixels from the left edge and 5 pixels from the top of the image, extends 90 pixels wide, and is 45 pixels tall. It's important that the first value be less than the third value and the second value be less than the fourth.

Circles

Creating a circular shape on your image map is similarly easy, as you see in Listing 6-18.

Listing 6-18. An image map with a circular area

```
<map name="crime-map" id="crime-map">
  <area shape="circle" coords="50,30,20">
</map>
```

The above example, using the `circle` value of the `shape` attribute, creates a circle whose center point is fifty pixels from the left edge of the image (the first value), is thirty pixels from the top edge of the image (the second value), and has a radius of 20 pixels (the third value).

Polygons

As we've seen so far, creating rectangles and circles is fairly straightforward. Creating polygonal shapes on an image can get very complicated very fast. Polygons, however, can be the most useful shapes.

Listing 6-19 shows a basic example which will create a parallelogram.

Listing 6-19. An image map with a polygonal area

```
<map name="crime-map" id="crime-map">
  <area shape="poly" coords="20,30,100,30,80,60,0,60">
</map>
```

In order to create a polygon, you must provide at least six values (three pairs of coordinates) and the number of integers must be even. Aside from those two conditions, you are free to add as many coordinates to the shape as you like.

Styling Anchors and Image Maps with CSS

Now that you've learned about the features of anchors and image maps, let's dive into some CSS for changing their presentation. In this section, we'll walk you through some common techniques for styling links.

Styling Anchors

As we showed you earlier in this chapter, links, by default, appear as blue, underlined text in the browser. This default styling may work well for Google search results pages, but it doesn't serve the needs of most designs you are likely to dream up or otherwise encounter. Luckily, CSS affords you plenty of opportunity to style anchor elements. For starters, Listing 6-20 contains a little bit of CSS that changes some of the basic presentation of a set of anchors.

Listing 6-20. CSS for styling the default state of an anchor element

```
a:link {
  background: #ddd;
  color: #cc0000;
  font-weight: bold;
  text-decoration: none;
}
```

The results of the code from Listing 6-20 are shown below in Figure 6-3.

Products

- Utility Belts
- Capes
- Potions and Serums
- Evening Wear

Figure 6-3. Browser output of an anchor element styled with CSS

The selector used in Listing 6-20, a:link, instructs the browser to make the default state of links dark red, bold, and underlined.

"But," you ask, "what is that extra code in the selector after the colon?" The :link portion of the selector is what's referred to in CSS as a *pseudo-class*, which we introduced in Chapter 2. Pseudo-classes are the mechanism by which we style various states of certain HTML elements. Anchor elements just happen to be one of those HTML elements with multiple states. Next, we'll guide you through each of the anchor element's pseudo-classes.

Keeping it pseudo-classy

Visited links—anchors that you've previously clicked on in your browser—are generally colored purple (see Figure 6-4). Your web browser will apply visited styling to links by drawing from its own stored history. If, like us, you've ever tried to re-find a page you'd browsed to days or weeks ago, you know how helpful the visited link state can be.

Products

- Utility Belts
- Capes
- Potions and Serums
- Evening Wear

Figure 6-4. Browser output of the default styling of the visited state of an anchor element

The links in Figure 6-4 have no additional styling applied. As such, non-visited links render as blue, underlined text and visited links ("Utility Belts" in this example) render as purple, underlined text. If you're enjoying this example in the printed version of this book, odds are Figure 6-4 appears in various shades of gray. You'll have to trust us that the "Utility Belts" link is purple!

To style the visited state of a link, use the :visited pseudo-class, as shown in Listing 6-21.

Listing 6-21. CSS for styling the visited state of an anchor element

```
a:link {
  color: #cc0000;
  font-weight: bold;
  text-decoration: underline;
}

a:visited {
  color: #00cc00;
}
```

In Listing 6-21, the a:visited selector instructs the browser to style visited links bright green. The visited link state inherits the font-weight and text-decoration properties from the a:link declaration. Figure 6-5 shows this CSS in action.

Products

- Utility Belts
- Capes
- Potions and Serums
- Evening Wear

Figure 6-5. Browser output of the visited state of an anchor element styled with CSS

Physically moving the mouse pointer over an anchor triggers the hover link state. Most browsers don't provide default styling for the hover state, so you'll want to make sure to declare some styles for this pseudo-class (see Listing 6-22).

Listing 6-22. CSS for styling the hover state of an anchor element

```
a:link {
  color: #cc0000;
  font-weight: bold;
  text-decoration: underline;
}

a:visited {
  color: #00cc00;
}

a:hover {
 color: #cccc00;
}
```

With the above bit of code, anchors will turn yellow when hovered over with a mouse. Figure 6-6 shows the output of this code.

Products

- Utility Belts
- Capes
- Potions and Serums
- Evening Wear

Figure 6-6. Browser output of the hover state of an anchor element styled with CSS

Related to the hover state, a link's focus state triggers when the browser gives an anchor focus. This occurs when you use the keyboard's Tab key to cycle through the interactive elements on a page. By default, most browsers will add a one pixel, dotted border to the focused link. Pressing the Enter key on a focused link will activate that hyperlink. Listing 6-23 adds a rule for the :focus pseudo-class.

Listing 6-23. CSS for styling the focus state of an anchor element

```
a:link {
  color: #cc0000;
  font-weight: bold;
  text-decoration: underline;
}

a:visited {
  color: #00cc00;
}

a:hover {
 color: #cccc00;
}

a:focus {
 outline: 1px dashed #cc0000;
}
```

The result of the code in Listing 6-23 is shown in Figure 6-7.

Products

- Utility Belts
- Capes
- Potions and Serums
- Evening Wear

Figure 6-7. Browser output of the focus state of an anchor element styled with CSS

Although you may often style hover and focus states similarly, consider applying additional styles for the focus state that call greater attention to the focused hyperlink. Visitors to your site that use keyboard or other non-mouse navigation will thank you!

A link's active state, the last of the bunch, occurs in the time during which you've pressed down on a link using your mouse or keyboard. In this state, links typically appear styled with a bright red color and may have a one pixel, dotted border. Listing 6-24 shows one example of styling the :active pseudo-class.

Listing 6-24. CSS for styling the active state of an anchor element

```
a:link {
  color: #cc0000;
  font-weight: bold;
  text-decoration: underline;
}

a:visited {
  color: #00cc00;
}
```

```
a:hover {
 color: #cccc00;
}

a:focus {
 outline: 1px dashed #cc0000;
}

a:active {
   color: #0000cc;
}
```

Figure 6-8 shows that this code changes the color of an active link to blue.

Products

- Utility Belts
- Capes
- **Potions and Serums**
- Evening Wear

Figure 6-8. Browser output of the active state of an anchor element styled with CSS

You'll also notice that the :focus styling gets applied to our active link.

It's important to note that the order in which you declare these pseudo-classes matters. It matters so much, in fact, that there's a mnemonic device to help you remember the ordering: LoVe/HAte. Or, LVHA, short for :link, :visited, :hover, and :active. It's silly, yes, but we guarantee you'll remember it.

Ordering of link pseudo-classes is another example of using the cascading characteristics of CSS to our advantage. Using the LVHA mnemonic, an anchor's :visited styles would override its default :link styles and both of those styles would be overridden by :hover and :active styles.

The logic behind this ordering is actually quite simple. During the course of a user's interaction with a website, each link he or she interacts with goes through a particular life cycle. Assuming the user is new to the site, each link exists in its default :link state. This state naturally precedes the :visited state. Similarly, the :hover and :focus states naturally occur before the :active state.

Button-making

If you've spent any appreciable amount of time on the Web—and who hasn't at this point?—you've undoubtedly noticed that not all links are styled as underlined text. The Web is chock full of ornately designed buttons that you can click on. In a lot of these cases, there are anchor elements under the hood styled to look like buttons.

In this example, we'll show you how to style an anchor element to resemble a clickable button. Listing 6-25 and Listing 6-26 detail the markup and CSS needed for this example.

Listing 6-25. An anchor element

```
<a href="index.html">Back to the Power Outfitters homepage</a>
```

Listing 6-26. An anchor element styled using CSS

```css
a {
  border: 3px solid #111;
  background: #666 url("arrow.png") no-repeat 15px 50%;
  color: #fff;
  display: inline-block;
  font-family: Helvetica, Arial, sans-serif;
  font-size: 14px;
  padding: 15px 20px 15px 45px;
  text-shadow: 1px 1px 0 #000;
  text-decoration: none;
}

a:hover {
  background-color: #555;
  border-color: #fff;
  border-style: dashed;
}

a:active {
  background-color: #c99;
  border-color: #c00;
  padding: 16px 19px 14px 46px;
}
```

Figure 6-9 shows the output of the code in the previous two listings.

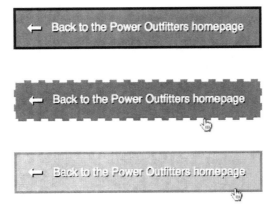

Figure 6-9. Browser output of an anchor element styled with CSS

The markup in Listing 6-25 should look familiar; there's nothing too crazy going on there. We have introduced some interesting style properties in Listing 6-26, though. Let's take a look.

First, we've taken a shortcut in this example by using the a selector instead of declaring separate a:link and a:visited states. You should generally try and declare both states independently of one another, but for the sake of this example, we've cut that corner. Do as we say, not as we... You know the rest.

Second, we're adding a background image using the shorthand background property. This property is a rolled up version whose value contains the background-color, background-image, background-repeat, and background-position properties.

Third, the display property has a value of inline-block. This property value allows an element to have properties similar to that of a block-level element while still displaying inline and adjacent to other content. Thus, you can add properties such as margin, padding, width, and height that are otherwise limited to block-level elements. Support for this property value has only recently gained widespread support in all major browsers.

Lastly, the text-shadow property, as you can probably divine, adds a text shadow to the button. This property is new to CSS3 and, as such, may not render in every browser. Don't worry, though: browsers that don't understand the text-shadow property will happily ignore it. The text-shadow property accepts four values:

- A positive or negative integer (with an appropriate CSS unit of measure) defining the horizontal offset of the shadow. Positive values place the shadow to the right of the text and negative values place the shadow to the left of the text.

- A positive or negative integer (with an appropriate CSS unit of measure) defining the vertical offset of the shadow. Positive values move the shadow down (relative to the text) and negative values move the shadow up (relative to the text).

- A positive integer (with an appropriate CSS unit of measure) defining the blur radius of the shadow. The larger the integer, the blurrier the shadow.

- A CSS color definition.

There you have it: an anchor element styled to resemble a button!

A Word of Caution

What you've done in this example is take one of the defining elements of the Web—the mighty anchor element—and completely reconfigured its appearance. Gone is the underlined blue link of the past! In with the flexibility of CSS!

With this power, though, comes a certain degree of responsibility. Users have grown to expect links on a web page to look like, well... links. Particularly, the expectation is that links are underlined text of a color different from that of the surrounding text. What we've introduced to you in this example breaks that mental model.

Now, there's nothing fundamentally wrong with styling certain links to look like buttons. In fact, well-designed anchor elements can increase usability by providing clear calls to action. You do, however, have to keep your users in mind. Always take care when choosing presentation styles for anchors.

Styling Image Maps

Unfortunately, there exists no easy or consistent way of styling either the map or area elements using only CSS. Google search results pertaining to styling either of these elements are littered with the shattered hopes and dreams of many a poor soul. Techniques using JavaScript do exist, but fall outside the purview of this book. Should you find yourself in a situation where you need to add styling or enhanced interactivity to an image map, we encourage you to investigate some of the JavaScript solutions cooked up by intrepid web developers.

Summary

In this chapter, you were introduced to one of the fundamental concepts of the Web: linking documents together. You learned how to create anchor elements and how to appropriately point them to documents both local and remote. You also learned about the history of the image map and about its place in modern web development. As if that wasn't enough, we showed you some common styling techniques of links that you can apply in your own work.

Thus far, you've learned the essentials of creating documents, marking up content, and linking documents together. In the next chapter, we introduce you to data tables.

Chapter 7

Building Tables

In Chapter 4, you learned how to mark up all kinds of content: headings, paragraphs, lists, and more. You've also learned how to embed images and other multimedia into your web pages. So far, so good, right? If you can believe it, we're still not done introducing you to ways of marking up types of content in HTML. In this chapter, we introduce you to the powerful—and often maligned—data table.

But, before we do that: a brief history lesson.

The Table's Lament

From time to time, you may hear some seasoned developers decry the use of the table element. They speak not out of ignorance of the table's legitimate use, but out of remembrance for a time long since passed.

Beginning a scant five years after Tim Berners-Lee created the Web, the metaphorical Browser Wars erupted when Microsoft, with its Internet Explorer browser, went toe-to-toe (and feature-for-feature), with Netscape's Navigator browser. This "war," lasting from roughly 1995 through the early 2000s, marked a period of incredibly rapid advances in web technology, particularly HTML.

In an effort to attract a larger share of the burgeoning web audience, browser makers invented their own, non-standard HTML elements and attributes with reckless abandon. If Netscape added support for a new, custom HTML element, Microsoft would add support for that element in addition to support for another of its own creation.

HTML was both the victor and the victim of this war. In some sense, the Web greatly benefited from the rapid development sparked by fierce competition. Exciting new features meant web developers had more tools at their disposal. On the other hand, developing the Web at such a rapid, haphazard place left web developers with a difficult choice: to which browser do they cater? With the glut of non-standard features and elements, HTML support was fragmented to such a degree that building effective websites often meant choosing a side.

At the time, the newly formed W3C struggled to keep pace with the rapidly changing markup language. It wasn't until long after the dust settled on the Browser Wars that the W3C caught up, made sense of the situation, and codified some of the non-standard elements created by browser makers. The early W3C was a reactive organization in this regard, folding features into new versions of the specification as those features gained traction. Some features survived the war while others died on the battlefield.

The table element just happens to be one of the notable survivors of the Browser Wars.

table

Originally introduced by Netscape in early 1994, the table element provides a markup-based structure for tabular data. "Tabular data" is the fancy way of referring to content that you might find in a spreadsheet, calendar, quarterly sales report, or train schedule. Not just any data thrown into a table is tabular data, though. Tabular data is data that *belongs* in a table so that it may be accurately understood.

HTML tables, like spreadsheets, are made up of cells organized into columns and rows. Based on the elements outlined in the spec, HTML takes a row-centric approach to tabular data. There are, however, a few elements that give you some degree of columnar control.

Specifications long-since-passed allowed for tables to be used for page layout. Before widespread support for CSS-based layout, web developers had few options other than tables for creating complex visual designs. This led to all manner of bad practices, less-than-accessible web pages, and bloated, hard-to-maintain code. Thankfully, those days are behind us. The HTML5 specification explicitly states that the table element represents tabular data.

To create a data table, we start with the basics.

Listing 7-1. A basic table with a single row

```
<table>
  <tr>
    <td>Utility Belts</td>
  </tr>
</table>
```

Nothing too crazy, right? The table element, which must have both a start and an end tag, may be a child of any element that can contain flow elements. We'll be covering the additional elements in the example above shortly.

The table element acts as a container for a number of elements that organize the data within. We'll be covering each of these elements and the rules surrounding their usage in the rest of this chapter.

Required Attributes

There are no required attributes for the `table` element.

Optional Attributes

In addition to the global attributes, the `table` element has the following optional attribute:

- `border`: indicates that its `table` element is not being used for layout. The value of this attribute must be either an empty string or "1".

To be frank, the inclusion of this presentational attribute somewhat muddies the waters regarding proper use of the `table` element. According to the specification, the entirely optional `border` attribute may be used to explicitly declare that the `table` element is not being used for layout. But, as you know from earlier in this section, tables are not to be used for layout anyway.

The HTML5 specification does indicate, however, that certain user agents use this attribute to determine whether or not to draw borders around cells within the table. For completion's sake, we've included information about this attribute but believe you'd rarely need to use it.

> *In previous versions of the HTML specification, the `table` element had a number of presentational attributes: `width`, `align`, `cellpadding`, `cellspacing`, etc. Although these attributes have been rendered obsolete in the HTML5 specification, you may still encounter them in the wild. These attributes were at one time valid but are now deprecated and shouldn't be used.*

tr

Tables are composed of cells organized into rows and columns. In HTML, you mark up tables one row at a time using the `tr` element which is short for "table row."

Listing 7-2. A basic table with a single row

```
<table>
  <tr>
    <td>Utility Belts</td>
  </tr>
</table>
```

A `tr` element must have a start tag. The end tag, however, is optional if the `tr` element's next immediate sibling is another `tr` element *or* if its parent contains no further content. For example, Listing 7-3 shows a table with `tr` end tags omitted.

Listing 7-3. A table with an end-tag omitted row

```
<table>
  <tr>
    <td>Utility Belts</td>
</table>
```

Throughout this chapter, we'll make mention of rules regarding tag omissions you can take advantage of when coding tables. However, tables can become very complex once you start dealing with large numbers of rows and columns, so we recommend including both start and end tags whenever possible. You'll find the resulting markup easier to read and less prone to errors of omission. For all remaining examples in this chapter, we'll include both start and end tags while making note of opportunities for tag omissions.

Required Attributes

There are no required attributes for the `tr` element.

Optional Attributes

Aside from the global attributes, there are no additional attributes for the `tr` element.

td

The `td` element, the workhorse of any HTML table, represents an individual cell in a data table. The element's name, which is short for "table data," gives you an indication of its expected content. Listing 7-4 marks up a table with a single row and a single cell.

Listing 7-4. A simple table with a single row and a single cell

```
<table>
  <tr>
    <td>Utility Belts</td>
  </tr>
</table>
```

The example in Listing 7-4, a table with a single row and a single cell, is technically valid but doesn't really represent tabular data. A proper table consists of multiple rows containing multiple cells of information that relate to one another in some fashion. Listing 7-5 expands on the previous example by adding several rows and cells to the table.

Listing 7-5. A table with three rows, each with two cells

```
<table>
  <tr>
    <td>Utility Belts</td>
    <td>9</td>
  </tr>
  <tr>
    <td>Grappling Hooks</td>
    <td>27</td>
  </tr>
  <tr>
    <td>Smoke Pellets</td>
    <td>623</td>
  </tr>
</table>
```

The td element must be a child of a tr element and must have a start tag. The end tag, though, is optional, and the rules here are similar to those for the tr element. You may omit the end tag if the td element is immediately followed by either another td element or by a th element (more on this one later!) *or* if its parent contains no further content (meaning it's the last cell in its row).

Required Attributes

The td element has no required attributes.

Optional Attributes

In addition to the global attributes, the following are optional attributes of the td element.

- colspan: a positive integer indicating the number of adjacent columns to be spanned by the table cell.

- rowspan: a positive integer indicating the number of adjacent rows to be spanned by the table cell.

- headers: a space-separated list of unique IDs referencing th elements with those IDs that act as headers for the table cell.

The colspan attribute

The colspan attribute accepts a positive integer and instructs the browser to create a cell that spans as many columns of the table as the attribute's value indicates. Listing 7-6 demonstrates this.

Listing 7-6. A table demonstrating usage of the colspan attribute

```
<table>
  <tr>
    <td colspan="2">Utility Belts</td>
  </tr>
  <tr>
    <td>New</td>
    <td>Used</td>
  </tr>
  <tr>
    <td>9</td>
    <td>27</td>
  </tr>
</table>
```

Figure 7-1 shows the rendered output of this code. For illustrative purposes, we've added a background color to the spanned cell.

Utility Belts

New Used

9 27

Figure 7-1. Browser output of a table with a cell spanning two columns

As you can see, the first row contains a single cell whose `colspan` attribute is set to span two columns. The second row still holds two cells, as does the third. Browsers, recognizing that the cell in the first row should stretch across two columns, generally center content in spanned cells.

Introducing the `colspan` attribute into your table adds complexity to the design and layout of the table. In the example shown here, that complication is minimal. But with larger data sets and, thus larger tables, you can imagine how introducing multiple instances of spanned columns can complicate the markup.

We're certainly not trying to scare you away from using the `colspan` and `rowspan` attributes (we'll be discussing the `rowspan` attribute next)—quite the opposite, in fact. What we want to impress upon you is the importance of planning out a table structure ahead of time so that you can make the best possible markup decisions.

The rowspan attribute

Similar in usage to the `colspan` attribute, the `rowspan` attribute accepts a positive integer as its value. The higher the specified value, the more rows your cell will span. Listing 7-7 shows an example of the `rowspan` attribute in action.

Listing 7-7. A table demonstrating usage of the `rowspan` attribute

```
<table>
  <tr>
    <td rowspan="2">Utility Belts</td>
    <td>New</td>
    <td>9</td>
  </tr>
  <tr>
    <td>Used</td>
    <td>27</td>
  </tr>
</table>
```

Looking at the code, you see that the first row has three cells, the first of which is set to span two rows. The second row, accordingly, has only two cells. Because the first cell of the first row spans its row and the following row, we've included one fewer cell in the subsequent row. The browser understands that what would have been the first cell in the second row is occupied by the first cell from the first row.

Figure 7-2 shows the output of this code with a background color added to the spanned cell for clarity. By default, most browsers will vertically center cells that span multiple rows. This default presentation can be changed easily using a touch of CSS. We'll be demonstrating techniques for this and more near the end of this chapter.

New 9
Utility Belts
Used 27

Figure 7-2. Browser output of a table with a cell spanning two rows

th

Any well-crafted spreadsheet, in addition to its cells, rows, and columns of data, has headers that describe those cells, rows, and data. As luck would have it, HTML provides an element for marking up table headers. The th element represents a table header cell. Listing 7-8 adds table headers to the same table structure from earlier portions of this chapter.

Listing 7-8. A table demonstrating usage of the th element

```
<table>
  <tr>
    <th>Product</th>
    <th>Quantity</th>
  </tr>
  <tr>
    <td>Utility Belts</td>
    <td>9</td>
  </tr>
  <tr>
    <td>Grappling Hooks</td>
    <td>27</td>
  </tr>
  <tr>
    <td>Smoke Pellets</td>
    <td>623</td>
  </tr>
</table>
```

Figure 7-3 shows what this table looks like in a browser.

Product	Quantity
Utility Belts	9
Grappling Hooks	27
Smoke Pellets	623

Figure 7-3. Browser output of a table with table column headings

By default, browsers tend to embolden header text and center it within its th element. We've added column headers in this example to make it easier to understand the tabular data, clearly labeling the data in each column. In Listing 7-9, we've added another set of headers, this time labeling the data in each row by converting those td elements to th elements.

Listing 7-9. Note that the first table cell in each row is now a table heading

```
<table>
  <tr>
    <th>Product</th>
    <th>Quantity</th>
  </tr>
  <tr>
    <th>Utility Belts</th>
    <td>9</td>
  </tr>
  <tr>
    <th>Grappling Hooks</th>
    <td>27</td>
  </tr>
  <tr>
    <th>Smoke Pellets</th>
    <td>623</td>
  </tr>
</table>
```

Product	Quantity
Utility Belts	9
Grappling Hooks	27
Smoke Pellets	623

Figure 7-4. Browser output of a table with table row headings

Required Attributes

Similar to the td element, the th element has no required attributes.

Optional Attributes

The th element has the following optional attributes in addition to the global attributes.

- scope: an enumerated attribute defining the scope of a table header. There are four explicit values for this attribute and one implied, default state. Those values are:

    - row: the table heading applies to some of the succeeding cells in the same row.

    - col: the table heading applies to some of the succeeding cells in the same column.

    - rowgroup: The table heading applies to the remaining cells in the same row.

    - colgroup: The table heading applies to the remaining cells in the same column.

    - auto: the table heading applies to a set of cells based on context. This attribute value is implied in the absence of any of the other four attribute values and shouldn't be used explicitly.

- `colspan`: a positive integer indicating the number of adjacent columns to be spanned by the table heading.

- `rowspan`: a positive integer indicating the number of adjacent rows to be spanned by the table heading.

- `headers`: a space-separated list of unique IDs referencing `th` elements with those IDs that act as headers for the table heading.

Setting scope

Looking back at Figure 7-4, you can see that the `th` elements are presented in a bold font and centered. For sighted users, this makes comprehending a table's structure fairly easy. Unfortunately for other users, including those with disabilities, our table structure lacks important cues as to the nature of its layout. Luckily, there exists a helpful attribute unique to the `th` element that defines what it labels.

The `scope` attribute provides information about the context of a table header. From the example in Listing 7-8, you know that the table headers "Product" and "Quantity" act as column headers. As such, you would use the value `col` with the `scope` attribute, as you see in Listing 7-10.

Listing 7-10. A table demonstrating usage of the `scope` attribute's `col` value

```
<table>
  <tr>
    <th scope="col">Product</th>
    <th scope="col">Quantity</th>
  </tr>
  <tr>
    <th>Utility Belts</th>
    <td>9</td>
  </tr>
  <tr>
    <th>Grappling Hooks</th>
    <td>27</td>
  </tr>
  <tr>
    <th>Smoke Pellets</th>
    <td>623</td>
  </tr>
</table>
```

The browser now understands that the "Product" and "Quantity" table headings act as column headers. Assistive software such as screen readers can take advantage of this attribute and better describe the information presented in the table.

Similarly, you can add a `scope` attribute with a value of `row` to the remaining headers in the table (as shown in Listing 7-11).

Listing 7-11. A table demonstrating usage of the scope attribute's row value

```
<table>
  <tr>
    <th scope="col">Product</th>
    <th scope="col">Quantity</th>
  </tr>
  <tr>
    <th scope="row">Utility Belts</th>
    <td>9</td>
  </tr>
  <tr>
    <th scope="row">Grappling Hooks</th>
    <td>27</td>
  </tr>
  <tr>
    <th scope="row">Smoke Pellets</th>
    <td>623</td>
  </tr>
</table>
```

While the scope attribute has no impact on the visual presentation of the table, it adds a healthy dose of semantics and is a boon to assistive technologies. Remember, not every visitor to your website will be using a visual web browser to interact with your content.

Table Row Groups

Now that you know how to build a basic table, we'll introduce you to a collection of elements whose job is to increase the semantic value of your data tables. As an added bonus, using these grouping elements will result in a more accessible data table. All of the elements in this section are optional, but given the semantic and accessibility gains from their inclusion, we recommend that you use them whenever it's practical.

Each of these row group elements—thead, tbody, and tfoot—must appear as direct children of their parent table element.

thead

The thead element, also known as a *table heading row group*, contains the row or rows that act as column headings for its parent table element. Based on its prescribed function, the thead element may only have tr elements as its children. Listing 7-12 shows a table with a heading row group.

Listing 7-12. A table with a table heading row group

```
<table>
  <thead>
    <tr>
      <th scope="col">Product</th>
      <th scope="col">Quantity</th>
```

```
      </tr>
    </thead>
    <tr>
      <th scope="row">Utility Belts</th>
      <td>9</td>
    </tr>
    <tr>
      <th scope="row">Grappling Hooks</th>
      <td>27</td>
    </tr>
    <tr>
      <th scope="row">Smoke Pellets</th>
      <td>623</td>
    </tr>
</table>
```

The thead element adds semantic value to the data table by explicitly designating the headers that apply to the entire table. As a child of the table element, the thead element should appear after any caption and colgroup elements (more on these elements later in the chapter) and before any tbody, tfoot, or tr elements. There can be only one thead element per table.

The thead element may contain multiple rows, so long as those rows contain headings that act as headings for the entire table. Additional rows containing more headings or cells with supportive content are also permitted. You could, for instance, add a second row containing td elements that provide more information about the columns to which they belong.

You may choose to omit a thead element's end tag only if the thead is immediately followed by a tbody or tfoot element. The end tag is required in other cases. But as we've mentioned before, including end tags, even when optional, makes your code more readable and less prone to parsing errors.

As you can see in Figure 7-5, the thead element has no visual impact on the table to which it belongs. It can, however, be used as a hook using descendant selectors to style its child elements. We'll show an example of this technique near the end of this chapter.

Product	Quantity
Utility Belts	9
Grappling Hooks	27
Smoke Pellets	623

Figure 7-5. Browser output of a table with a table heading row group

Required Attributes

There are no required elements for the thead element.

Optional Attributes

Aside from the global attributes, the thead element has no additional optional attributes.

tbody

The tbody element, also known as a *table row group*, represents one or more rows that make up the body of data of its parent table element. The tbody element may only have tr elements as its children and the tbody itself must be a direct child of a table element. You can see an example in Listing 7-13.

Listing 7-13. A table with a table row group

```
<table>
  <thead>
    <tr>
      <th scope="col">Product</th>
      <th scope="col">Quantity</th>
    </tr>
  </thead>
  <tbody>
    <tr>
      <th scope="row">Utility Belts</th>
      <td>9</td>
    </tr>
    <tr>
      <th scope="row">Grappling Hooks</th>
      <td>27</td>
    </tr>
    <tr>
      <th scope="row">Smoke Pellets</th>
      <td>623</td>
    </tr>
  </tbody>
</table>
```

The unique thing about this element is that there can be multiple tbody elements within a single table. Odds are you'll encounter a situation where, when dealing with a significantly large data set, it makes sense to break that data set into distinct, logical groupings. To do so, you could simply wrap those groupings of table rows into their own tbody elements. For example, an alphabetized list of names could be organized in separate tbody elements for each letter of the alphabet.

If you add multiple tbody elements to your table, they must be siblings of one another; no nesting tbody elements allowed! Another caveat worth noting: tbody elements and tr elements can't be siblings. If your table includes one tbody element, any other rows need to be grouped in their own tbody as well, even if it's a single row. For instance, the code in Listing 7-14 isn't valid.

Listing 7-14. An invalid table with sibling tr and tbody elements

```
<table>
  <tr>
    <td>Utility Belts</td>
    <td>9</td>
  </tr>
  <tbody>
    <tr>
      <th scope="row">Grappling Hooks</th>
```

```
        <td>27</td>
      </tr>
      <tr>
        <th scope="row">Smoke Pellets</th>
        <td>623</td>
      </tr>
    </tbody>
</table>
```

Basically, the rule to remember here is that if you're using table row groupings—thead, tbody, and tfoot—try to use as many of them as makes sense for your table. We recommend using table row groupings for all but the simplest tables; the organizational and accessibility benefits are worth it!

The tbody element, like the thead and tfoot elements, must appear as a direct child of its parent table element. Additionally, tbody elements must be included after any caption, colgroup, and thead elements, should they be present.

The rules governing start tag omission for the tbody element are slightly more elaborate than most tag omission rules. The tbody element's start tag may be omitted if its first child is a tr element and if the immediately preceding tbody, thead, or tfoot element does not have its end tag omitted. Most browsers will insert an implied tbody element into the DOM. Our best-practice recommendation to you is this: if you're going to use the tbody element, always include the start tag, particularly if you're using the other row grouping elements.

Less confusingly, the tbody element's end tag may be omitted if it is immediately followed by a tbody or tfoot element, or if there is no more content in the table. But including end tags is always a safe bet.

Required Attributes

There are no required elements for the tbody element.

Optional Attributes

Beyond the global attributes, there are no additional optional attributes for the tbody element.

tfoot

The optional tfoot element, known as a table footer row group, represents a row or rows whose content consists of the column summaries for its parent table element. A large table containing sales data for, say, superhero supplies, may include a tfoot row grouping containing a row of cells with sums denoting inventory, similar to that shown in Listing 7-15.

Listing 7-15. *A table demonstrating usage of the* `tfoot` *element*

```
<table>
  <thead>
    <tr>
      <th scope="col">Product</th>
      <th scope="col">Quantity</th>
    </tr>
  </thead>
  <tbody>
    <tr>
      <th scope="row">Utility Belts</th>
      <td>9</td>
    </tr>
    <tr>
      <th scope="row">Grappling Hooks</th>
      <td>27</td>
    </tr>
    <tr>
      <th scope="row">Smoke Pellets</th>
      <td>623</td>
    </tr>
  </tbody>
  <tfoot>
    <tr>
      <th scope="row">Totals</th>
      <td>659</td>
    </tr>
  </tfoot>
</table>
```

Figure 7-6 shows how a browser renders the code from Listing 7-15. Note that the `tfoot` element itself doesn't add any particular visual styling to the resulting output; it's simply a grouping element that adds semantic value and improves the table's accessibility.

Product	Quantity
Utility Belts	9
Grappling Hooks	27
Smoke Pellets	623
Totals	659

Figure 7-6. *Browser output of a table with a table footer row group*

Previous versions of HTML required that the `tfoot` element appear in markup immediately following a `thead` element, despite the element being rendered visually at the bottom of the resulting table. As a requirement, this was confusing for authors and, as such, has been amended in HTML5. The current specification allows the `tfoot` element to appear in one of the following two places:

1. After any `caption`, `colgroup`, and `thead` elements but before any `tbody` or `tr` elements, or

2. After any `caption`, `colgroup`, `thead`, `tbody`, and `tr` elements.

In either of the above cases, only one `tfoot` element is permitted per table. An example of the `tfoot` element placed in code before a `tbody` element is shown in Listing 7-16.

Listing 7-16. A table demonstrating an alternative placement of the `tfoot` element

```
<table>
  <thead>
    <tr>
      <th scope="col">Product</th>
      <th scope="col">Quantity</th>
    </tr>
  </thead>
  <tfoot>
    <tr>
      <th scope="row">Totals</th>
      <td>659</td>
    </tr>
  </tfoot>
  <tbody>
    <tr>
      <th scope="row">Utility Belts</th>
      <td>9</td>
    </tr>
    <tr>
      <th scope="row">Grappling Hooks</th>
      <td>27</td>
    </tr>
    <tr>
      <th scope="row">Smoke Pellets</th>
      <td>623</td>
    </tr>
  </tbody>
</table>
```

Figure 7-7 shows the output of the code from Listing 7-16. As you can see, the table renders exactly the same as the code used in Listing 7-15 and shown in Figure 7-6. A `tfoot` element will always be rendered at the bottom of the table to which it belongs.

Product	Quantity
Utility Belts	9
Grappling Hooks	27
Smoke Pellets	623
Totals	659

Figure 7-7. Browser output of a table with a table footer row group

Like the thead and tbody elements, the tfoot element may only have tr elements as children. Those tr elements, in turn, may only have th or td elements as children. The tfoot element's end tag is optional if the element is immediately succeeded by a tbody element or if there is no more content in the table.

Like the thead element, the tfoot does not directly impose any styling on its children. It can, however, be used as a hook for styling its child elements with descendant selectors in CSS.

Required Attributes

There are no required elements for the tfoot element.

Optional Attributes

There are no additional optional attributes for the tfoot element other than the global attributes.

Columns

This chapter has thus far dealt with the structure and semantics of tables largely in terms of rows. An HTML table is composed of a collection of rows containing headers and cells that can be organized into row groups. But what if you need to add information on a column-by-column basis? Or, what if you need to style cells that appear in a particular column a certain way? For these cases, there are two elements at your disposal that prescribe meaning to a table's columns: colgroup and col.

colgroup

The colgroup element represents a logical grouping of one or more columns in a table. Defining one or more column groups, when sensible, also provides you with an opportunity for richer styling of the table element and its child elements. You can, for instance, define a column group that contains three or four columns and use CSS to set the width of that column group. The browser would then take that width and distribute it amongst the columns within the group.

The colgroup has a conditional content model, which means that the rules governing what elements the colgroup can or can't contain can change depending on the condition of the element. For instance, if the span attribute is defined, then the element should be empty, as shown in Listing 7-17.

Listing 7-17. A table with an empty colgroup

```
<table>
  <colgroup span="2">
  <tr>
    <th scope="row">Utility Belts</th>
    <td>9</td>
  </tr>
</table>
```

If the span attribute is not defined, then the colgroup must contain one or more col elements (see Listing 7-18). We'll discuss the col element in detail shortly.

Listing 7-18. A table including a colgroup and two col elements

```
<table>
  <colgroup>
    <col>
    <col>
  </colgroup>
  <tr>
    <th scope="row">Utility Belts</th>
    <td>9</td>
  </tr>
</table>
```

You may define multiple column groupings in your table if the size of the data set and organization of the table warrants. Listing 7-19 shows an example of a complex table with multiple colgroup elements.

Listing 7-19. A complex data table including multiple colgroup elements

```
<table>
  <colgroup>
    <col>
  </colgroup>
  <colgroup span="2">
  <colgroup>
    <col>
    <col>
  </colgroup>
  <thead>
    <tr>
      <th scope="col">Product</th>
      <th colspan="2" scope="col">Quantity</th>
      <th colspan="2" scope="col">Price</th>
    </tr>
    <tr>
      <td></td>
      <th scope="col">New</th>
      <th scope="col">Used</th>
      <th scope="col">New</th>
      <th scope="col">Used</th>
    </tr>
  </thead>
  <tbody>
    <tr>
      <th scope="row">Utility Belts</th>
      <td>9</td>
      <td>27</td>
      <td>6</td>
      <td>23</td>
    </tr>
  </tbody>
</table>
```

Figure 7-8 shows the rendered output of the code from Listing 7-19. Column groupings, much like the row groupings discussed in the previous section of this chapter, have no default visual impact on the table.

Product	Quantity		Price	
	New	Used	New	Used
Utility Belts	9	27	6	23

Figure 7-8. Browser output of a table with column groupings

The start tag of the `colgroup` element may be optional if the first element within the `colgroup` is a `col` element *and* if the element is not immediately preceded by another `colgroup` element whose end tag has been omitted. A `colgroup` element's end tag may be omitted so long as it is not immediately succeeded by a space character or an HTML comment. Phew! Remember what we were saying earlier about confusing tag omission rules? These are generally odd cases, but they're worthy of note nonetheless.

The `colgroup` element must be an immediate child of the `table` element and should be included after the `caption` element, if present, and before any `thead`, `tbody`, `tfoot`, and `tr` elements.

Required Attributes

There are no required attributes for the `colgroup` element.

Optional Attributes

In addition to the global attributes, the `colgroup` element has an additional optional attribute.

- `span`: a positive integer that describes how many columns the column group contains.

col

The `col` element, a void element with no content, represents one or more columns in a column group. The `col` element appears as a child of a `colgroup` element that lacks a `span` attribute as shown in Listing 7-19 in the previous section on the `colgroup` element.

Place as many `col` elements within a `colgroup` element as you need to create a logical column grouping. The `span` attribute of a `col` element informs the browser of how many columns the element spans. You can even combine `col` elements that have the `span` attribute set with those that don't.

As the `col` element is a void element, it must have a start tag and does not have an end tag. If you prefer XHTML syntax, you can close the `col` element with a trailing slash: <col />.

Required Attributes

There are no required attributes for the `col` element.

Optional Attributes

In addition to the global attributes, the `col` element has an additional optional attribute.

- span: a positive integer that defines how many columns are spanned by the `col` element. Properties of the `col` element are shared across all of the columns it spans.

One more thing...

Did you ever imagine there could be so many unique elements needed to build a semantic, accessible table? We've introduced you to rows, cells, headings, row groups, and column groups. The last two—row groups and column groups—add great semantic and accessibility value to a table but largely function behind the scenes. We have one last element to introduce to you that adds semantic value and increases accessibility in a manner that is apparent to all.

caption

The `caption` element defines a title for its parent `table` element. The addition of a `caption` element can provide clarity and context to a table that it may otherwise be lacking. The `caption` element, a part of HTML since version 3.2, receives a bit of a promotion in HTML5. Previous versions of HTML limited its content model to inline elements and recommended that authors keep its content relatively short. The `summary` attribute of the `table` element was intended for longer descriptions of a table and its content.

HTML5 changes most of this. For starters, the `summary` attribute of the `table` element is no longer with us. Farewell, dear `summary` attribute; we hardly used ye. As part of its promotion, the `caption` element now accepts flow elements as children and has no implied restriction on the length of its content.

The `caption` element, if included, must be the first child of a `table` element and must have both a start and an end tag. Listing 7-20 shows an example of the `caption` element in use.

Listing 7-20. A table with a caption

```
<table>
  <caption>
    <h2>Power Outfitters Inventory</h2>
    <p>Power Outfitters continues to stock only the finest products ↪
        for all your crime-solving needs.</p>
  </caption>
  <thead>
    <tr>
      <th scope="col">Product</th>
      <th scope="col">Quantity</th>
    </tr>
  </thead>
  <tbody>
    <tr>
      <th scope="row">Utility Belts</th>
      <td>9</td>
    </tr>
    <tr>
      <th scope="row">Grappling Hooks</th>
      <td>27</td>
    </tr>
```

```
  <tr>
    <th scope="row">Smoke Pellets</th>
    <td>623</td>
  </tr>
</tbody>
<tfoot>
  <tr>
    <th scope="row">Totals</th>
    <td>659</td>
  </tr>
</tfoot>
</table>
```

Figure 7-9 shows the browser output of the code in Listing 7-20 using only the browser's default styling.

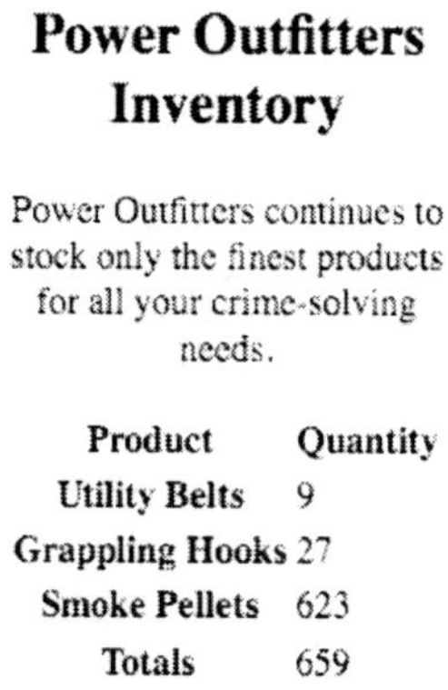

Power Outfitters Inventory

Power Outfitters continues to stock only the finest products for all your crime-solving needs.

Product	Quantity
Utility Belts	9
Grappling Hooks	27
Smoke Pellets	623
Totals	659

Figure 7-9. Browser output of a table with a caption

In most browsers, the caption element appears above its table and with center-aligned text. Placement of the caption element can be adjusted in CSS using the caption-side property and we'll show you examples of this in the section on styling tables later in this chapter.

While the caption element is optional, we strongly recommended that you include one for accessibility purposes and as a general best practice. You can sometimes get away with omitting the caption element if the table is introduced in the content with an h1-h6 heading or in a preceding paragraph.

Required Attributes

There are no required attributes for the caption element.

Optional Attributes

There are no additional optional attributes for the caption element other than the global attributes.

Styling Tables with CSS

Tables, when processed by CSS, conform to a complicated set of algorithms referred to in the CSS specification as the *CSS table model*. The CSS table model defines special display characteristics for each of the elements within a table.

> If you'd like to read through the CSS table model yourself, you can find it in the W3C's CSS specification at `w3.org/TR/CSS21/tables.html`.

You're most familiar at this point with two possible values of the CSS `display` property: `block` and `inline`. Unfortunately, tables in HTML don't fit neatly into either of these categories. Thus, a handful of `display` property values exist that apply specifically to tables. The list of these property values includes:

- `table`
- `inline-table`
- `table-header-group`
- `table-row-group`
- `table-footer-group`
- `table-row`
- `table-cell`
- `table-column`
- `table-column-group`
- `table-caption`

As you can see from the list above, the property values map pretty closely in naming to the elements we've introduced in this chapter. In the examples in this section, we'll be building up a data table featuring a list of products for our favorite super hero supply store, Power Outfitters.

Styling Rows and Cells

We'll begin with the basic `table` shown in Listing 7-21.

Listing 7-21. A simple table

```
<table>
  <thead>
    <tr>
      <th scope="col">Product</th>
      <th scope="col">Quantity</th>
      <th scope="col">Price</th>
      <th scope="col">Totals</th>
    </tr>
```

```
    </thead>
    <tbody>
      <tr>
        <th scope="row">Utility Belts</th>
        <td>9</td>
        <td>$129.99</td>
        <td>$1,169.91</td>
      </tr>
      <tr>
        <th scope="row">Grappling Hooks</th>
        <td>27</td>
        <td>$79.99</td>
        <td>$2,159.73</td>
      </tr>
      <tr>
        <th scope="row">Smoke Pellets</th>
        <td>623</td>
        <td>$4.99</td>
        <td>$3,108.77</td>
      </tr>
    </tbody>
    <tfoot>
      <tr>
        <th scope="row">Totals</th>
        <td>659</td>
        <td></td>
        <td>$6,438.41</td>
      </tr>
    </tfoot>
</table>
```

The output of that block of markup with only the default browser styling applied can be seen in Figure 7-10.

Product	Quantity	Price	Totals
Utility Belts	9	$129.99	$1,169.91
Grappling Hooks	27	$79.99	$2,159.73
Smoke Pellets	623	$4.99	$3,108.77
Totals	659		$6,438.41

Figure 7-10. It's not much to look at, but it's a serviceable table.

Adding just the little bit of CSS, shown in Listing 7-22, will have a dramatic effect on the display of the table.

Listing 7-22. Basic CSS for the table structure detailed in Listing 7-21

```
table {
  width: 600px;
  font-size: 14px;
  font-family: Helvetica, Arial, sans-serif;
  border-collapse: separate;
  border-spacing: 10px 5px;
```

```
    table-layout: auto;
    empty-cells: hide;
}

thead th,
tfoot th,
tfoot td {
  background: #eee;
}

th,
td {
  border: 1px solid #ccc;
  padding: 10px;
}

thead th:first-child {
  text-align: left;
}

tbody th,
tfoot th {
  text-align: left;
}

tbody tr:nth-child( even ) {
  background: #ddd;
}
```

Before diving into the particulars of the CSS you've just seen, take a look at the results in Figure 7-11. In this example, we're using basic element selectors, which means that these styles will be applied to **all** tables. If you want to be more specific, you could use a class attribute to distinguish some tables from others or an id attribute to single out just one table. In these cases, you would need to adjust the CSS in these examples to match your markup.

Product	Quantity	Price	Totals
Utility Belts	9	$129.99	$1,169.91
Grappling Hooks	27	$79.99	$2,159.73
Smoke Pellets	623	$4.99	$3,108.77
Totals	659		$6,438.41

Figure 7-11. A basic table transformed in grand fashion by some carefully applied CSS

Pretty impressive, right? There's a lot going on here, so hang in there as we walk you through each rule in our CSS. First up, the table rule and its declarations:

```
table {
  width: 600px;
  font-family: Helvetica, Arial, sans-serif;
  font-size: 14px;
  border-collapse: separate
  border-spacing: 10px 5px;
  table-layout: auto;
  empty-cells: hide;
}
```

You're no doubt familiar with the font and width declarations, so no need to explain those. What's new—and unique to tables—are the border-collapse, border-spacing, table-layout, and empty-cells properties.

The border-collapse property

The border-collapse property determines the table's *border model*. Possible values for this property are collapse, separate, and the cascaded value inherit. Supplying a value of collapse will trigger the table's *collapsing border model*, wherein the spacing between cells is collapsed and the browser recalculates any border property applied to table cells and headings. Declaring border-collapse: separate—as the code in Listing 7-22 does—triggers the *separated borders model*, wherein each table cell is spaced apart from its neighboring cells.

The border-spacing property

The border-spacing property controls the amount of separation between the borders of adjacent cells. The property can accept one or two length values (or a value of inherit). If one value is present, then cells are spaced apart evenly using that value around all four sides of the cell. If two values are supplied, the first value represents the horizontal spacing between adjacent cells in the same row and the second value represents the vertical spacing between rows. While there is no official default value for this property, most browsers will add two pixels of spacing between cells if the border-spacing property is not explicitly set.

The empty-cells property

The empty-cells property tells the browser whether or not to render styling on cells that have no content. Possible values for this property are show, hide, and inherit. By default, most browsers opt for the show value, so even empty cells will appear with whatever borders or background they would have if they carried content. In the table resulting from the CSS laid out in Listing 7-22, though, empty table cells are hidden and thus appear to be a completely empty break in the table.

The table-layout property

Lastly, the table-layout property determines which layout algorithm a browser should employ as it renders the table. Possible values are fixed, auto, and inherit. Using a property value of fixed triggers the *fixed table layout algorithm* which relies only on the table's overall width—supplied in CSS or inferred from the width of the table's content—and divides the width equally amongst all columns. The auto property value takes into account the overall width of the table, the contents of each of the table's cells, and any specified cell or column widths and divides width amongst columns as determined by the browser's own algorithm.

Browsers will render tables using table-layout: auto by default. This value triggers a more complex layout algorithm that requires the browser to first load the entire contents of the table and scan over every cell, generating a record of each cell's width. The table's layout is then determined based on the browser's findings. While this method is more computationally complex, there's no need to be concerned about browser performance.

The :first-child and :nth-child pseudo-classes

If you look back at the code in Listing 7-22, you'll notice the following two declarations:

```
thead th:first-child {
   text-align: left;
}

tbody tr:nth-child( even ) {
   background: #ddd;
}
```

In the example above, the :first-child and :nth-child pseudo-classes are structural pseudo-classes that select elements based on where they occur in the markup. The :first-child pseudo-class is left-aligning the text of the table heading that is a first-child descendant of the table heading. More generally, the :first-child pseudo-class refers to an element that is the first child of another element such as the first li in an unordered list or the first paragraph in an article.

The :nth-child pseudo-class matches an element or set of elements based on the keyword or formula passed to it in parenthesis. In the example above, only even-numbered rows are matched by the selector. As Figure 7-11 shows, the second table row in the body of the table has a background color. The keywords even and odd are equivalent to the formulas 2n and 2n+1, respectively. Older browsers may not support these selectors but should render the table in an attractive, usable format, just with slightly fewer bells and whistles.

> For a greatly detailed description of :first-child, :nth-child, and other pseudo-class selectors, see the W3C's section on Pseudo-classes in the Selectors Level 3 module at w3.org/TR/css3-selectors/#pseudo-classes.

Styling Columns

Now that we've successfully styled a table and its rows, headings, and cells, we'll show you some options for styling columns. As we mentioned earlier in this chapter, tables in HTML and CSS are predominately row-based creatures. Unfortunately, styling tables from a column-based approach is a bit more complicated, with fewer options available.

The first step is to add some column information to our table, as shown in Listing 7-23.

Listing 7-23. A basic table with column groupings added

```
<table>
  <colgroup>
    <col id="products ">
    <col id="quantities">
    <col id="prices">
    <col id="totals ">
  </colgroup>
  <thead>
    <tr>
      <th scope="col">Product</th>
      <th scope="col">Quantity</th>
      <th scope="col">Price</th>
      <th scope="col">Totals</th>
    </tr>
  </thead>
  <tbody>
    <tr>
      <th scope="row">Utility Belts</th>
      <td>9</td>
      <td>$129.99</td>
      <td>$1,169.91</td>
    </tr>
    <tr>
      <th scope="row">Grappling Hooks</th>
      <td>27</td>
      <td>$79.99</td>
      <td>$2,159.73</td>
    </tr>
    <tr>
      <th scope="row">Smoke Pellets</th>
      <td>623</td>
      <td>$4.99</td>
      <td>$3,108.77</td>
    </tr>
  </tbody>
  <tfoot>
    <tr>
      <th scope="row">Totals</th>
      <td>659</td>
      <td></td>
      <td>$6,438.41</td>
    </tr>
  </tfoot>
</table>
```

The browser's output of this code is identical to that in Figure 7-10. The CSS in Listing 7-24 includes some styling for our newly created column groups. For this example, we've dropped the borders on cells, left out background colors on even rows, and omitted the empty-cells rule.

Listing 7-24. CSS with additional styling for column groupings

```
table {
  width: 600px;
  font-family: Helvetica, Arial, sans-serif;
  font-size: 14px;
  border-collapse: separate;
  border-spacing: 5px;
  table-layout: auto;
}

thead th,
tfoot th,
tfoot td {
  background: #eee;
}

th,
td {
  padding: 10px;
}

thead th:first-child {
  text-align: left;
}

tbody th,
tfoot th {
  text-align: left;
}

#quantities {
  width: 200px;
}

#prices {
  background: #ddd;
}
```

The output of the CSS in Listing 7-24 is shown in Figure 7-12.

Product	Quantity	Price	Totals
Utility Belts	9	$129.99	$1,169.91
Grappling Hooks	27	$79.99	$2,159.73
Smoke Pellets	623	$4.99	$3,108.77
Totals	659		$6,438.41

Figure 7-12. The quantities column and the prices column are both styled uniquely

In this example, the #quantities column is set to 200 pixels in width and the cells in the #prices column are set to have a background color of #ddd. Note, though, that the cells in the thead and tfoot portion of the table retain their background color of #eee. This is due to the influence of *table layer stacking*.

As it pertains to determining a table cell's background color, there are six layers of stacking. Assume for a moment that each of the following six layers has a unique background color specified on one of its elements.

1. The lowest layer, the table element itself, is superseded by column groups;

2. Column groups, in turn, are superseded by columns;

3. Columns lose out to row groups;

4. Row groups bow down before individual rows; and finally,

5. Cells are king of the mountain.

In the example code, cells—in this case, headings in the header and cells in the footer—beat out the background color declaration on the column. This is one rare case where CSS specificity takes a back seat to stack order. The column's ID selector *should* overpower the cell's generic element selector, but the table layer model tells the browser to give preference to stacking order over specificity.

> For a detailed explanation of the table layer model, including a handy diagram, see the section on "Table Layers and Transparency" available on the W3C's website at w3.org/TR/CSS21/tables.html#table-layers.

Styling Captions

The caption element, as you saw earlier, will generally appear above its parent table element. Its position is determined by the caption-side property. Using the markup in Listing 7-25 and the CSS in Listing 7-26, you'll see the ease with which you can style a table's caption.

Listing 7-25. A table with an added caption element

```
<table>
  <caption>
    <h2>Power Outfitters Inventory</h2>
    <p>Power Outfitters continues to stock only the finest products ↰
        for all your crime-solving needs.</p>
  </caption>
  <colgroup>
    <col id="products-column">
    <col id="quantity-column">
    <col id="price-column">
    <col id="totals-column">
  </colgroup>
  <thead>
    <tr>
      <th scope="col">Product</th>
      <th scope="col">Quantity</th>
      <th scope="col">Price</th>
      <th scope="col">Totals</th>
    </tr>
  </thead>
  <tbody>
    <tr>
      <th scope="row">Utility Belts</th>
      <td>9</td>
      <td>$129.99</td>
      <td>$1,169.91</td>
    </tr>
    <tr>
      <th scope="row">Grappling Hooks</th>
      <td>27</td>
      <td>$79.99</td>
      <td>$2,159.73</td>
    </tr>
    <tr>
      <th scope="row">Smoke Pellets</th>
      <td>623</td>
      <td>$4.99</td>
      <td>$3,108.77</td>
    </tr>
  </tbody>
  <tfoot>
    <tr>
      <th scope="row">Totals</th>
      <td>659</td>
      <td></td>
      <td>$6,438.41</td>
    </tr>
  </tfoot>
</table>
```

Listing 7-26. CSS for styling the table and its caption from Listing 7-25

```css
table {
  width: 600px;
  font-family: Helvetica, Arial, sans-serif;
  font-size: 14px;
  border-collapse: separate;
  border-spacing: 5px;
  table-layout: auto;
}

caption {
  background: #444;
  caption-side: top;
  color: #fff;
  font-weight: bold;
  line-height: 1.4;
  margin: 0 5px;
  padding: 15px;
}

caption h2 {
  font-size: 20px;
  margin: 0 0 10px 0;
}

caption p {
  font-size: 16px;
  margin: 0;
}

thead th,
tfoot th,
tfoot td {
  background: #eee;
}

th,
td {
  padding: 10px;
}

thead th:first-child {
  text-align: left;
}

tbody th,
tfoot th {
  text-align: left;
}

#quantity-column {
  width: 200px;
```

```
}
#price-column {
  background: #ddd;
}
```

Rendering the code from the previous two listings in a browser should look something like Figure 7-13.

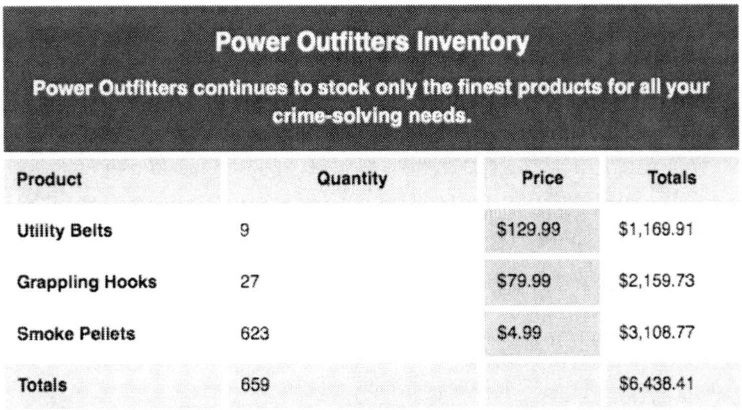

Power Outfitters Inventory			
Power Outfitters continues to stock only the finest products for all your crime-solving needs.			
Product	Quantity	Price	Totals
Utility Belts	9	$129.99	$1,169.91
Grappling Hooks	27	$79.99	$2,159.73
Smoke Pellets	623	$4.99	$3,108.77
Totals	659		$6,438.41

Figure 7-13. That ominous-looking thing above the table? That's the caption element in action.

The caption-side property

The caption-side property accepts one of three possible values: top, bottom, and inherit. As most browsers default to a value of top, you can safely leave out the caption-side declaration if you prefer to let your table captions ride high. If, however, you want to reposition your table captions, simply supply the table-caption property with a value of bottom and the caption moves visually below the table:

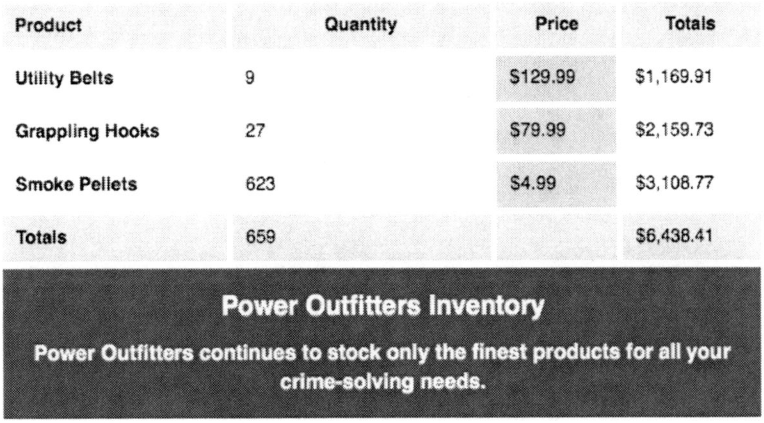

Product	Quantity	Price	Totals
Utility Belts	9	$129.99	$1,169.91
Grappling Hooks	27	$79.99	$2,159.73
Smoke Pellets	623	$4.99	$3,108.77
Totals	659		$6,438.41
Power Outfitters Inventory			
Power Outfitters continues to stock only the finest products for all your crime-solving needs.			

Figure 7-14. The caption now appears below the table.

Remember: regardless of the visual position of the table caption, the `caption` element must always be the first child of its parent `table` element.

Summary

In this chapter, we introduced you to the `table` element and its supporting cast of child elements. You learned about the differences between rows, columns, cells, and headings. We also introduced you to logical row groupings and how to take advantage of column groupings.

While its history is marred by misuse, the `table` element remains a powerful means of conveying a wide range of data. Whether you're marking up a simple two-column, two-row table or the most complicated sales spreadsheet you can imagine, you should always keep in mind the values of semantics and accessibility. From what you've learned in this chapter, you now have the know-how to bring even the most boring set of data to life.

Coming up in Chapter 8, we'll introduce you to HTML forms, including some of the exciting new developments in HTML5.

Chapter 8

Assembling Forms and Applications

We've referred to the Web as a conduit for the movement of information, distributing ideas around the world to anyone who wants to find them. It's this far-reaching scope and wide-open range that makes the Web so captivating and philosophically marvelous. But information doesn't flow only downhill. Your visitors might arrive at your website to passively absorb, but, if allowed, they can also participate in the exchange of information, offering their own ideas and reactions.

But how can you receive such feedback from your visitors? How can readers and viewers become valued contributors? The simplest, most common, and perhaps most powerful means of moving ideas uphill onto the Web is through a *form*. In the analog world, a form is just a printed document with predefined, labeled blanks where people can write information. Forms standardize the formatting of data for easier handling; when a clerk knows exactly where to look to find a customer's name on a slip of paper, it saves precious time and makes his or her job that much easier. If you take this concept a step further, a web form becomes more than just a stodgy way to force your formatting expectations onto your visitors. Forms are the means by which an anonymous user becomes an active participant.

If you've ever used a search engine, made an online purchase, created a personalized login to a website, posted a comment, uploaded a photo, or updated your status on a social network, you've already seen and used web forms; the Web simply wouldn't be what it is without them. They're ubiquitous and a fundamental cornerstone of online living, so you'll inevitably need to include forms in some of the pages you build. This chapter explores the HTML elements you'll need to construct functional, usable, and accessible forms for your web pages, as well as a few ways to use CSS to make your web forms more visually appealing.

The still-growing HTML5 specification first germinated as two other specifications, originally dubbed "Web Forms 2.0" and "Web Applications 1.0." Those early specs were an effort to extend and expand upon long-standing HTML features that were becoming outdated in a Web desperately trying to innovate beyond them. For example, before HTML5, there was no simple means for a form to validate that a required field had been filled in, and no simple means for a user to enter something as common as a date of birth.

Another thing the spec authors of times past didn't anticipate was the rise of web applications—dynamic and interactive applications accessed through a web browser and built with browser-supported coding languages (especially HTML, CSS, and JavaScript). Web developers have long had to use heavy-handed scripts and semantically dubious markup to render common interface widgets like progress bars, boxes that can open and close, and dropdown lists of suggested field values. HTML5 has at last answered the call for more interactive elements, paving the way for the next generation of web apps.

> *As always, you should test your web pages thoroughly in as many different browsers as you can get your hands on. That's especially important if you plan to use newer form controls and interactive elements that may not be widely supported. Don't make your forms and applications entirely dependent on the bleeding edge features of a still-in-progress spec. Practice progressive enhancement and use these newer elements and attributes wisely.*

How Forms Work

Defined in simplest terms, a *form* is any section of a web page where a user can input information (though sometimes form elements only display information rather than collect it). Your visitors can enter text into blank fields, make choices by checking boxes, select options from menus, and then click a button to send it all away for processing. These interactive devices are called *controls*, and each control's data is its *value*.

To modify the value of a control, a user must first bring the control into *focus* so it becomes active and primed to accept input. A control is usually given focus by clicking it with a mouse or using the Tab key to move the cursor from one control to the next. Entering a value usually requires typing text or performing some other deliberate action—clicking a mouse button, pressing the Enter key, and so on. Your visitor can then shift her browser's focus to another control, enter another value, and continue on in that fashion, modifying controls (or skipping over the optional ones) until she reaches the end of the form.

A form isn't really complete until the user submits it. The information she entered gets transmitted to the server in a *form data set* comprising the names of all the form controls and their values. The job of processing the data set falls to a *form handler*: a script or program designed to interpret and use the submitted data. Many form handlers are also designed to *validate* the entered values, making sure all the required information has been entered and properly formatted.

Handling submitted form data is another matter entirely; it delves into the complex subjects of scripting, programming, database design, and application design, and raises issues of encryption, privacy, and security. Such advanced topics are well beyond the scope of a book about front-end HTML and CSS.

Instead, the rest of this chapter focuses on the markup you'll need to be familiar with to assemble forms for display and use. Actually making them *work*... well, that's a subject for another book.

The form Element

As its name implies, the `form` element defines a portion of an HTML document that can receive input from the user. It acts as a container for other interactive form elements, as well as any other elements needed to give the form structure. The `form` element is flow content and can contain any other flow elements except another `form`. To include multiple, separate forms within a single document, each must be contained by its own `form` element—you can't nest a form within a form. However, as of HTML5, you can now associate a control anywhere in the document with a different form elsewhere on the same page using the `form` attribute.

> *The new* form *attribute for form controls compensates for the inability to nest forms. Without it, any controls outside the* form *element aren't included in that form's data set. A* form *attribute explicitly associates a control with a form, even when the control isn't inside that* form *element. Many current browsers support* form *attributes already, but alas, not yet all of them at the time we're writing this. For the time being you should still keep all your controls within the same* form *element.*

The optional `action` attribute, if present, carries the URL of the form handler, or in other words, the address where the data is going to end up. That form handler may be a document or script elsewhere on the website, a back-end application, or the very same document the form resides in if its data will be handled exclusively on the client side by JavaScript, or if the HTML document has been integrated with some kind of scripting language such as PHP, Ruby, Python, or ASP.NET. If the `action` attribute is missing from the `<form>` start tag, and if no other controls specify an action, then the browser assumes the form's handler is the current document. If the document lacks any form handling code and no other form handler is specified, the form won't do anything at all.

A `method` attribute is optional and can accept two values, `get` or `post`, to indicate the particular HTTP method to use when the form is submitted. If the `method` attribute is missing, the default method is `get`.

When the form's method is `get`, the submitted data will be appended to the form handler's URL (taken from the `action` attribute, or else the current document's URL) in a *query string* consisting of all the form's name-value pairs. You may have seen URLs with query strings that look something like `http://example.com/watch?video=funnycats.mp4&width=480&height=320` (this is just an example we made up; there are no funny cat videos on the Internet). The question mark (?) in the URL marks the beginning of the query string, with each name-value pair connected by an equal sign (=), and additional values are appended with an ampersand (&). A form handler can interpret and process that URL, extracting values from the exposed query string.

The `get` method is best for requesting static data from the server for temporary use—for example, searching the Web for a definition of the word "idempotent"—especially when the URL, including its query string, might be reused in a link or bookmark.

By contrast, the post method sends the data set directly to the form handler application (not in a visible URL query string) for processing at the server. The post method sends data to the server where it can be saved for use in the future, for example, submitting a comment or uploading a video. It can also be useful when a URL with a visible query string isn't desirable for reasons of security and privacy, for instance when you submit your password to log into a secure website.

> HTTP stands for HyperText Transfer Protocol, the set of program rules used for transferring electronic data over the Web. The two most basic methods of HTTP are "get" to send data from a server to a client and "post" to send data from a client to a server. Whenever you download something from a web server, be it an HTML document, a cascading style sheet, a video, an image, or anything else, your browser sends a request to "get" that file. Many forms use the opposite "post" method, sending data from your browser to the server. Other HTTP methods exist, but "get" and "post" are the only ones used with forms in HTML.

Listing 8-1 shows the markup for a simple form, including the action and method attributes in the opening `<form>` tag. This example contains two input elements (an e-mail field and a submit button) and a text label wrapped in a label element. You'll learn more about all of these elements in this chapter.

Listing 8-1. *A simple form with an e-mail field and a submit button*

```
<form method="post" action="/apps/subscribe.py">
  <p><label for="email">Enter your e-mail address to
  subscribe to our newsletter.</label></p>

  <p><input type="email" name="email" id="email" required>
  <input type="submit" value="Subscribe"></p>
</form>
```

Figure 8-1 shows how this form is rendered in a web browser with default styling, Firefox for Mac OS X in this case. Some form controls will look different in different browsers and on different operating systems, but in the end they all send their data the same way.

Enter your e-mail address to subscribe to our newsletter.

Subscribe

Figure 8-1. The same simple form as it appears in Firefox for Mac OS X

> The label element is extremely important in forms. It provides a text label for a form control that assistive technologies can read to make the form more accessible and easier to use. You'll learn about it in detail later in this chapter.

Required Attributes

The form element doesn't require any attributes. Previous versions of HTML required an action attribute to specify the form handler URL, but in HTML5 that attribute can appear on another control such as a submit button, or it can be omitted entirely and the current document will act as the default form handler.

Optional Attributes

- accept-charset: Specifies the accepted character encoding for data submitted through the form. When the attribute is missing, the accepted character encoding is assumed to be the same as that of the parent document.

- action: Specifies the URL of the form handler, which is the script or application that will process the submitted form data.

- autocomplete: This attribute is new to HTML5 and specifies whether browsers should be allowed to automatically complete the controls within the form. This attribute only accepts the values on or off, with on being the default value if the attribute is missing.

- enctype: Specifies the type of encoding to use when the form is submitted, one of three possible values: application/x-www-form-urlencoded (the default), multipart/form-data (if the submitted form will include files uploaded via an input type="file" control), or text/plain (which performs no additional encoding).

- method: Specifies which HTTP method will be used to submit the form data, either get or post. The method defaults to get if this attribute is missing.

- novalidate: Indicates that the form data should *not* be validated when submitted, bypassing any field requirements or formatting rules, though any JavaScript or server-side validation might still be performed. This Boolean attribute is new in HTML5, and doesn't require a value, but you can provide a value in XHTML syntax as novalidate="novalidate".

> *Previous versions of HTML included an accept attribute for the form element that indicated the file types accepted by the form via an input type="file" control, covered later in this chapter. This attribute is obsolete for form elements in HTML5, but can instead appear on the input element itself.*

The input Element

Most common form controls are instances of the input element, with each type of input control indicated by a corresponding type attribute. The input element is styled as inline by default so several can appear on the same line. It's also a void element, so it can hold neither text nor any other elements. A browser replaces the input element with a functional form control when it renders the page. This is a diverse element that performs many different duties. It also has loads of optional attributes, though some are only for use with certain input types.

Every input element—those you intend to process, at least—requires a name attribute so it can be associated with its value when a user submits the form. Technically, name is an optional attribute, and isn't required for a valid document so a validator may not indicate an error if it's missing. But a markup validator won't know what you intend to do with the form data so it can't automatically determine which inputs require names.

The type attribute specifies the particular type of control the element represents, from simple text fields to checkboxes to image buttons, tailored for particular types of data. A number of new input types (or *states* of the input element, as the spec refers to them) have been introduced in HTML5, as well as many new attributes that extend and enhance the functionality of the humble form field.

Browser support for some of the new input types is inconsistent at the time of this writing, but browsers are updating rapidly and adding new features in every release. Even so, HTML5 has been designed from the ground up to be *backwards compatible* with older user-agents, and any unrecognized input type simply reverts to an ordinary text field that can still accept any value your users might enter. In this section we'll cover the full range of input types, both old and new.

Required Attributes

- name: Identifies the control so it can be matched with its value when the form is submitted. A markup validator may not generate an error if this attribute is missing, but it's required in order to successfully handle the form. Notable exceptions are input type="submit" or input type="reset", which don't always require names because their values aren't necessarily submitted with the data set.

Optional Attributes

- accept: Includes a comma-separated list of accepted file MIME types (only for input type="file").

- alt: Specifies an alternative text description for an image when the image isn't available (only for input type="image").

- autocomplete: This attribute is new in HTML5 and specifies whether browsers should be allowed to automatically complete the input field, either by filling in locally stored values or by suggesting previously entered text as the user types. This will only work if you also enable auto-completion for the parent form element. The attribute accepts the values on or off, with on being the default when the attribute is missing. Auto-completion is really handy for often-entered information such as a shipping address, but you could disable it for a more sensitive field such as a credit card number.

- autofocus: This Boolean attribute is new in HTML5 and indicates that the control should automatically receive focus when the page loads.

- checked: A Boolean attribute that, when present, sets an initial checked state for checkboxes or radio buttons (only for input type="checkbox" and input type="radio").

- disabled: A Boolean attribute that disables the control so it can't receive focus or be modified. The value of a disabled control is not submitted. Many browsers will display disabled controls in a "grayed-out" style by default.

- form: This is new in HTML5 and allows the label to be associated with one or more additional forms. The form attribute accepts a value of one or more form IDs, separated by spaces. This feature allows authors to work around the lack of support for nested form elements.

- formaction: This attribute is new to HTML5 and overrides the form's action attribute in defining the control's handler. The value is the URL of the form handler where the data is sent when a user submits the form.

- formenctype: This is a new attribute in HTML5 and overrides the form's enctype attribute. It specifies how the data from this control should be encoded before it's sent to the server. The attribute only accepts the values application/x-www-form-urlencoded, multipart/form-data (for input type="file"), or text/plain (the default if the attribute is missing).

- formmethod: This is new to HTML5 and overrides the form's method for sending data to the URL defined in the action attribute. The two possible values are get and post.

- formnovalidate: A new Boolean attribute in HTML5, this allows a form to be submitted while bypassing the form's validation (only for input type="submit"). Indicating this on an input instead of for the entire form allows some buttons to bypass validation while others don't. For example, a "save" button might submit a partially completed form to let users save their progress, but without going through the validation process the form will undergo when it's finally submitted at the end.

- formtarget: This is new to HTML5 and overrides the form's target attribute, which specifies the target window to use when the form is submitted. This attribute can only appear on input type="submit" and its value is the name of the target window or frame, or one of the keywords _blank, _self, _parent, or _top.

- height: Specifies the height of an input type="image" in either pixels or as a percentage. This is new in HTML5; image inputs couldn't previously carry dimension attributes.

- ismap: A Boolean attribute declaring that the control is a server-side image map (only for input type="image").

- list: This attribute is new to HTML5 and references the ID of a datalist element that contains predefined options for the control.

- max: Specifies the maximum value allowed for the control, either a number, a date, or a time. This is new in HTML5 and only for use with a number input or any of the date and time input types. If a min attribute is also present, the value of max can't be less than the value of min.

- maxlength: Specifies the maximum number of characters (including spaces) that can be entered in a text field (any input type that can receive text). Browsers may not give any indication that a field has a maximum length, and will simply stop accepting input when the limit is reached. If you include a maxlength attribute you should also provide some visible hint to your visitors to let them know how many characters the control will accept.

- min: Specifies the minimum value allowed for the control, either a number, a date, or a time. This is new in HTML5 and only for use with a number input or any of the date input types. If a max attribute is also present, the value of min can't exceed the value of max.

- multiple: A Boolean attribute that, when present, indicates that multiple values can be entered. This is new in HTML5 and typically appears in combination with a datalist element (covered later in this chapter).

- pattern: This is new to HTML5 and allows an author to define a *regular expression* against which the input's value can be checked. For example, pattern="[1-5]" specifies that the input's value must be an integer between 1 and 5, and pattern="[A-Za-z]" accepts only upper- and lowercase letters (no numbers or other symbols). Far more complex patterns are possible. See regular-expressions.info for a good starting point with regular expressions.

- placeholder: This new attribute introduced in HTML5 allows the author to include a short text hint to advise the user on what value is expected for the input. The browser hides the placeholder label automatically when the control is in focus (or when the user begins typing) and, if there was no value entered in its place, the placeholder reappears when the field loses focus.

- readonly: Specifies that the control may only display an initial value and can't be modified. This differs from disabled in that a read-only control can still receive focus and its value is still submitted with the form.

- required: This Boolean attribute is new to HTML5 and indicates that the control must have a value in order to submit the form.

- size: Specifies the width of a rendered text control as a number of characters, so the actual rendered width will depend on the font size. By default, most browsers will display text controls around 20 or 25 characters wide.

- src: Specifies the source URL of an image file (only for input type="image").

- step: This is new in HTML5 and specifies the number intervals for a numeric input (input type="number"). For example, given the attribute step="3", the number control will accept -3, 0, 3, 6, 9, and so on, stepping in multiples of 3.

- tabindex: Specifies, by number, the control's position in the tabbing order when a user cycles through active controls using the Tab key. Typically (and by default), the tabbing order follows the source order, with each stroke of the Tab key advancing focus to the next active control in the document. The tabindex attribute can change that natural order if needed. For example, a control with tabindex="1" appears first in the tabbing order, regardless of where it might occur in the document's source order.

- type: Specifies the type of form control the input element represents. The default input type is text if the attribute is missing or if its value isn't recognized. Older browsers that may not recognize the new input types introduced in HTML5 will gracefully degrade to a text input.

- usemap: Specifies the URL of a client-side image map (only for input type="image").

- value: Specifies the initial value of a control before it has been modified by the user.

- width: Specifies the width of an input type="image" in either pixels or as a percentage. This is new in HTML5; image inputs couldn't previously carry dimension attributes.

> Note that many of the optional attributes available for the input element are specific only to certain types of form inputs (as indicated by the type attribute). Also, many of the new attributes in HTML5 can override the equivalent attribute settings in the parent form element.

Next we'll go through each of the different input types in more detail, one by one.

input type="text"

This type of input element creates a single-line field in which your visitor can type whatever text you might require, such as a name, address, or a short answer to a question. It's usually rendered in browsers as a white, rectangular box with a thin inset border, though CSS can easily change its appearance.

These single-line text fields are best for very short bits of text, no more than a few words. If the entered text exceeds the width of the field, the excess characters will run off to one end of the field so the end of the text string is visible and the first portion appears truncated. Rest assured that the complete value is still there, it's just not all visible. Longer, multi-line passages of text call for the textarea element, covered later in this chapter.

An input type="text" element may carry an optional maxlength attribute, defining the maximum number of characters (including spaces) that can be entered into the field. Unfortunately, web browsers offer no indication that a text field has a maximum allowed length; when you reach the limit, it simply stops accepting anything you type. If you paste an overlong string of text into a field with a maxlength attribute, the text will be truncated. If you need to use a maxlength attribute on a text field (for example, a username field to log into a system that restricts usernames to 12 characters or less), it's helpful to indicate the maximum length in a note near the form control.

An optional value attribute allows you to set the initial text of the field, which a user can delete or modify, or she can it leave alone and the default value will be submitted with the form. It's especially useful for automatically "prepopulating" forms with stored information that a user can edit. Text fields that are meant to be blanks where your users can enter new information should, in fact, be blank when initially rendered. You shouldn't use value to provide hints or instructions; there are other elements and attributes for that, as you'll soon see.

Listing 8-2 shows the markup for a basic text control. We've included a maxlength attribute along with a note about the maximum allowed length, as well as a size attribute. Because this example asks a user to update previously saved information, we've also prepopulated the field using the value attribute.

Listing 8-2. *A text control with a prepopulated value attribute*

```
<p><label for="zip">Update your ZIP code <i>(maximum 5 characters)</i></label>
<input type="text" id="zip" name="postcode" size="5" maxlength="5" value="94710"></p>
```

Figure 8-2 shows how this would look in a browser (this is in Firefox on Mac OS X; other browsers might differ slightly).

Update your ZIP code *(maximum 5 characters)* 94710

Figure 8-2. The text field as it appears in a browser with default styling

This example also has an optional (and largely presentational) `size` attribute, defining the width of the field as a number of characters. By default, most browsers will display text fields around 20 or 25 characters wide. You can also modify the width of a text field with the CSS `width` property using any unit you like (ems, pixels, a percentage, etc.) and a CSS width will override the `size` attribute, if present.

input type="search"

The search input type is new in HTML5 and, as you might suspect, indicates a text field where visitors can enter search terms. In years past this was accomplished with an ordinary `input type="text"`, but by adding a dedicated type for search fields, browsers can treat those fields differently than ordinary text fields. For example, a browser might save terms you've previously searched for and offer to autocomplete terms from your own search history as you type into the same field on later searches, which can be especially handy on mobile devices where typing is cumbersome. Older browsers—as well as current browsers that don't yet give any special treatment to search inputs—treat a search control as an ordinary text control and it still works just as well, though without any extra features.

Listing 8-3 shows a search input with a `placeholder` attribute offering a suggestion of what you might search for. An `input type="text"` would be just as functional and processed the same way by a form handler, but using the new search type garners some special treatment in the latest browsers.

Listing 8-3: *A search input bearing a placeholder attribute*

```
<p><label for="search">Search for products</label>•
<input type="search" id="search" name="q" placeholder="utility belts"></p>
```

The `placeholder` attribute is also new in HTML5. It lets the author supply some short instructional text in the control itself, suggesting a value to enter, or an example of how the user should format the data they provide. The placeholder text disappears when the field is in focus, and reappears when the field loses focus if there is no other value to display. If the element includes a `value` attribute, the supplied value will override the placeholder.

In the past, many developers accomplished this feat using the `value` attribute and automatically clearing it with JavaScript when the field was focused, but that meant the placeholder text could be submitted with the form. The `placeholder` attribute eliminates that problem; placeholder text is never submitted, it's strictly for visual feedback and improved accessibility. We're introducing the `placeholder` attribute here with a search input, but you can also use it with any of the textual input types, including URL, e-mail, and telephone controls, as well as the `textarea` element covered later in this chapter.

Figure 8-3 shows the search input showing off its placeholder text. This image is taken from Safari for OS X, which also styles search inputs with rounded corners by default. Older browsers that don't support `placeholder` will simply ignore the attribute and display a plain, empty field. Because some browsers can't display it, always think of placeholder text as an optional hint, and you should display any really vital information some other way (in a `label`, perhaps).

Figure 8-3. How the search field appears in Safari, including placeholder text. Safari styles search inputs with rounded ends by default, in keeping with Apple's general style for search boxes on OS X, but other browsers will differ.

Some browsers already recognize search inputs and will display a dropdown of recent search terms as you type, matching the text you've entered and narrowing the suggestions as you enter more letters. Safari and Chrome—and possibly other browsers in the near future—also add a small clearing button at the end of search fields when a user enters a value (as in Figure 8-4). This makes it easy to empty the control with a single click, clearing the field for the next search. Not every browser does this; it's just an extra touch WebKit adds.

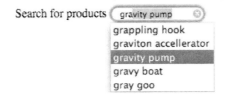

Figure 8-4. Safari adds a small clearing button to search fields, and recalls previous searches in a dropdown while also offering to auto-complete the text as you type.

input type="password"

This control is similar to a text field; it's a single-line field and will usually appear as a rectangular box with a white background and an inset border. But unlike a regular text field, a password field obscures the entered text, usually as a series of solid dots or asterisks (*). This offers a bit of added security and privacy, preventing someone from peering over your shoulder to sneak a peek at your secret password when you're logging into a secure system. But this is *very light* security, protecting your password from a casual glance only. A properly secured form should be encrypted when it's submitted to the server; don't count on just visually obscuring passwords to keep a determined crook at bay.

> Encryption *is a means of mathematically scrambling data so that anyone who might intercept it won't be able to read or use the information. Unscrambling, or decrypting, encrypted data requires an* encryption key *that should be extremely difficult to guess. Any sensitive information, such as passwords and credit card numbers, sent over the Web through a form should be encrypted to protect the security and privacy of your users. Encryption usually happens between the browser and the server, and is much too complicated to be addressed in detail in this book.*

Listing 8-4 shows an example of a simple login form, with a text field for a user name and a password field for a password. We've also added some new attributes: autofocus and required.

Listing 8-4. *Part of a typical login form, with both a text input and a password input*

```
<p><label for="username">Your user name</label>
<input type="text" name="user" id="username" autofocus required></p>

<p><label for="password">Your password</label>
<input type="password" name="pass" id="password" required></p>
```

Figure 8-5 shows how a browser renders the markup, with the entered password obscured as a string of dots.

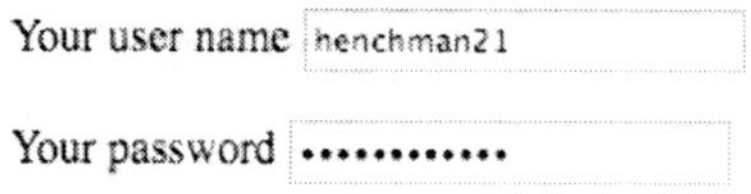

Your user name   henchman21

Your password   •••••••••••

Figure 8-5. Text entered into a password field is obscured from sneaky onlookers

The autofocus attribute is new in HTML5. It automatically sets focus to the control when the page loads. This should usually appear in the first field of a form and only when that form is the primary content of the page, such as a dedicated login page, or the front page of a search engine that only has one big field. It should also only appear on one control in the document. If several controls carry an autofocus attribute only the first one will actually receive focus; a browser can only focus on one control at a time. Try not to annoy your visitors by automatically setting their browser's focus into a form field they might not be planning to use right away, such as a comment form at the end of a long article or a search field on a page where someone may not want to begin searching immediately. Older browsers that don't recognize the autofocus attribute will simply ignore it and the form will still work as usual.

The required attribute is also a new addition to HTML5 and indicates that the form shouldn't be submitted unless the control in question has a value. When more than one field in a form is required, *all* of them must have a value before the user can submit the form. However, because this is a new attribute in HTML5, older browsers—and even some current browsers at the time we write this—don't support the required attribute, so it's still no substitute for proper form validation.

Special Text: URLs, E-mail Addresses, and Phone Numbers

Similar to the new input type for search controls, HTML5 introduces specialized input types for URLs (input type="url"), e-mail addresses (input type="email"), and phone numbers (input type="tel"). They typically look just like ordinary text fields, but browsers can give these special fields a bit of special treatment. Older browsers that don't recognize these new input types still fall back to a standard text field.

A URL or e-mail address should follow a certain format: complete URLs should begin with a protocol such as http:, https:, ftp:, mailto:, and so on, and e-mail addresses should comprise a username followed by an @ symbol followed by a domain name (or possibly an IP number). Browsers that recognize and support input type="url" and input type="email" can automatically check that the entered value conforms to the expected format and display a warning if it doesn't, preventing the user from submitting the form until she corrects the field. It's up to the browser how it displays the errors, and different browsers indicate errors in very different styles.

Listing 8-5 shows part of a comment form like you might find on a typical weblog, with fields for an e-mail address and website URL. The e-mail field also carries a required attribute so browsers that recognize this attribute won't allow the form to be submitted until all required controls carry a value. The URL field isn't required here, but if a commenter does enter a value, the browser will require that value to be a complete URL before submitting the form.

Listing 8-5. *A partial comment form featuring inputs for an e-mail address and a URL*

```
<ul>
  <li>
    <label for="name">Your name (required)</label>
    <input type="text" id="name" name="name" required>
  </li>
  <li>
    <label for="email">Your e-mail address (required, not published)</label>
    <input type="email" id="email" name="email" required>
  </li>
  <li>
    <label for="url">Your website</label>
    <input type="url" id="url" name="url">
  </li>
</ul>
```

This form can't be submitted until the name and e-mail fields are filled, and the e-mail field must hold a formatted e-mail address. However, a browser can't verify that the provided e-mail address actually exists or that it belongs to the person entering it; the browser can only check that the data conforms to the general format of an e-mail address (x@y). The URL field validation is even more rudimentary, only requiring some kind of protocol prefix followed by a colon (:) and after that the field will accept any other text; the browser won't verify that the rest of the URL is complete or if it's a working Internet address (and it may not even be a real protocol—any character followed by a colon will usually pass the URL test).

> *Because the browser-level validation for these input types is so simplistic and, more importantly, because not all browsers yet support these elements and attributes, you should still have some additional form validation in place, either client-side using JavaScript or server-side when the form data is processed—ideally both.*

Figure 8-6 shows how Chrome indicates an empty required field on the left, in the middle you see how Opera indicates a malformed e-mail address, and on the right you see how Firefox indicates an incomplete URL (these are all on Mac OS X). The styles vary widely across the different browsers, but they all function the same way.

Figure 8-6. Different browsers indicate errors in very different styles. This shows the same form in Chrome, Opera, and Firefox.

Another new input type—input type="tel"—is akin to the e-mail and URL inputs, though browsers may not perform any checking of the value's format. A phone number can be written in many different ways, with many different telephone systems around the world, so a user-agent can't enforce one particular format for a phone number input. That might lead you to think a standard input type="text" would be best for entering phone numbers (and it had to be sufficient for many years). But a telephone number is a special kind of data and well deserves its own input type.

With the ever-increasing number and popularity of sophisticated mobile devices, allowing millions of people to access the Web from their phones, a specialized input type="tel" (like the one in Listing 8-6) can differentiate a phone number field from an ordinary text field.

Listing 8-6. *A telephone input*

```
<p>
  <label for="home">Your home phone number</label>
  <input type="tel" id="home" name="tel-home">
</p>
```

When entering text into a telephone field, many touchscreen smartphones will automatically invoke a numeric keypad—as you can see in Figure 8-7—instead of their usual onscreen keyboard. Otherwise a telephone input behaves just like a text input, and desktop browsers may not give them any special treatment at all (at least not yet; even less-mobile desktop and laptop computers can access telephone networks electronically, so future desktop browsers could certainly support telephone inputs).

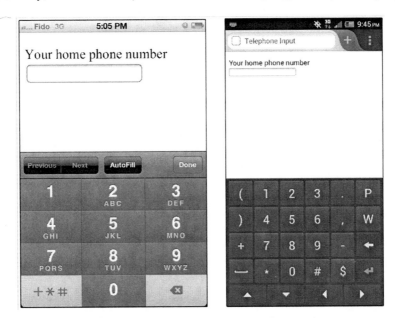

Figure 8-7. A telephone input invokes a numeric keypad in some mobile browsers, such as the iPhone's Mobile Safari on the left and Firefox for Android on the right.

Dates and Times

Like phone numbers, dates and times can be written many different ways: "19th of June, 1996", "May 22", "10/24/1999", "2012-Mar-3", "4:15pm", "09:44:16 PST", "quarter past midnight on the autumnal equinox"... the variations are endless. But web apps and databases tend to be very particular and require a consistent, machine-readable format so they can accurately handle dates and times. It's always been difficult to impose a standard date or time format on web users, and for years developers have made use of JavaScript calendar widgets or forced users to step through multiple text fields or dropdown menus to enter a year, month, and day separately. HTML5 makes a web developer's—and a web user's—life a little bit easier with a number of input types built especially for collecting date and time data.

- `input type="date"`: For a complete date comprising a year, month, and day. Example: 2012-07-22

- `input type="datetime"`: For year, month, day, hours, minutes, and coordinated universal time zone (UTC). Example: 2012-07-22T08:45Z

- `input type="datetime-local"`: The same as `datetime`, but minus the time zone. This input assumes the time given is in the user's local time zone, whatever that may be (perhaps provided separately or derived from geolocation data). Example: `2012-07-22T08:45`

- `input type="month"`: For the year and month. Example: `2012-07`

- `input type="week"`: For the year and calendar week, indicated as a number between 1 and 53). Example: `2012-W29` (the twenty-ninth week of 2012)

- `input type="time"`: For hours and minutes, but not seconds, and without any time zone information. Example: `08:45`

Each of these new input types automatically carries its value in a machine-readable format while presenting the user with a simplified, human-friendly interface. That is, in browsers that support these input types, and that's a short list at the time we write this. Opera is farthest in the lead, having supported the various date and time inputs since version 10.62 (released in late 2010). For example, current versions of Opera display a pop-up calendar (Figure 8-8) for `date`, `month`, `week`, `datetime`, and `datetime-local` inputs.

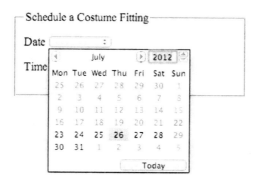

Figure 8-8. Opera displays a calendar interface when a date field receives focus. A user can select a year, month, and day with a few clicks and the browser will automatically enter the date in a machine-readable format.

Some current browsers may recognize these input types but don't yet offer a special interface, and others don't yet recognize these input types at all, falling back to a basic text field. Unfortunately this means older and non-supporting browsers can't automatically format the data and will just accept whatever text they're given. Until browser support is more widespread and consistent, one interim solution is to offer a JavaScript date or time picker (like the ones websites have been using for years) only to browsers that don't support these new HTML5 inputs, and more advanced browsers can use their built-in interfaces. If you use these new date and time inputs in your web forms, plan accordingly and test thoroughly

Date and time inputs can carry optional `min` and `max` attributes, specifying the control's minimum and maximum values. The attribute's value is a date or time (or full datetime) in the same format as the particular input type accepts. Time inputs don't differentiate between AM and PM, so you may need to specify a 24-hour clock instead of a 12-hour clock.

Listing 8-7 is an example of a reservation form with separate inputs for date and time. Because you can't make an appointment in the past (unless you're a time traveler), the date field has a minimum value that is the same as today's date, which would probably need to be generated automatically by a script or server-side code (just pretend you're reading this on July 22 of 2012... unless you're a time traveler).

Listing 8-7. *Using date and time inputs in a reservation form*

```
<fieldset>
  <legend>Schedule a Costume Fitting</legend>
  <p><label for="fit-date">Date</label>
    <input type="date" id="fit-date" name="fit-date" min="2012-07-22"></p>
  <p><label for="fit-time">Time</label>
    <input type="time" id="fit-time" name="fit-time" min="08:00" max="18:00"></p>
</fieldset>
```

This time field has both a minimum and maximum value so this form can only accept appointments during business hours. However, time inputs don't carry any indication of AM or PM, so we've specified a 24-hour clock instead of a 12-hour clock. Otherwise a maximum value of 06:00 (for 6 PM) would be treated as *less* than the 08:00 (8 AM) minimum, which isn't allowed. When the min and max attributes are both present, a minimum can't be greater than a maximum, and a maximum can't be less than a minimum. It just makes sense.

input type="color"

This new-in-HTML5 input type allows a user to provide a color value via a handy color picker interface. The input's value is a hexadecimal color code, but the graphical interface of the control is left up to the browser; the HTML5 spec doesn't prescribe any particular design for the color picker. At the time we write this, Opera is the only major desktop browser that supports input type="color" and their picker interface is quite simple (see Figure 8-9).

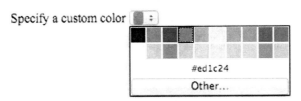

Figure 8-9. A color input as displayed by Opera (this is on OS X)

When the input is in focus, Opera displays a small dropdown palette of color swatches for a predetermined set of common, basic colors (black, white, red, yellow, blue, etc.) or you can provide a customized set of swatches using the datalist element, covered later in this chapter. The swatch palette also includes an "Other..." button that invokes the operating system's native color picker. The input's current hex code value appears in the palette as well. The unfocused input manifests as a small selection control, filled with a single swatch displaying the current color.

Browsers that don't support the color input fall back to a default text field that can still accept a hexadecimal color code. In fact, the value of an input type="color" *must* be a hexadecimal color code; no other value is valid, so entering the word "blue" wouldn't be correct. For that reason, you might opt to provide a JavaScript-based color picker such as JSColor (jscolor.com) for browsers that don't support color inputs, while browsers that do support it can use their native interface.

input type="number"

A number input is for—you guessed it—entering numbers. This input type is new in HTML5 but already supported by several browsers, though not yet all of them. Some mobile browsers will automatically invoke a numeric keyboard for number fields, and desktop browsers will typically render the field with a set of up and down arrows (called a *spinner control*, shown in Figure 8-10) making it easy to increase or decrease the value one digit at a time. You can also specify a different increment in the optional step attribute and each click of the spinner will raise or lower the value by that number, though users can still enter a value by hand. The optional min and max attributes can specify the minimum and maximum values, as you would expect.

A number field won't accept any non-numeric characters, with just a few exceptions. If the number entered begins with a minus symbol (-) it indicates a negative number, so that symbol is allowed but only as the first character in the value. A valid number may also include a single period (.) as a decimal point. Any other letters, symbols, or punctuation are invalid, but a browser might not indicate any error, instead opting to just ignore and strip away those characters when the form is submitted.

A number input isn't intended for any arbitrary numerals; it's specifically made for indicating a *count* for calculation purposes, such as a number of items or an amount of currency. Use a number input for numbers where an incremental spinner control would make sense. For other kinds of numeric input that people would typically enter by hand, like addresses, measurements, or a credit card number, use an ordinary text field.

Listing 8-8 shows a number input with a min attribute that prevents entering any negative numbers (values less than 0 aren't allowed) and a step attribute that increments (or decrements) the value by 2 with each click of the spinner. The up and down arrow keys on a keyboard can also increment the value by the same step.

Listing 8-8. *A number input with min and step attributes*

```
<label for="order-count">How many? (sold only in matched pairs)</label>
<input type="number" name="count" id="order-count" min="0" step="2">
```

Figure 8-10 shows the rendered result, taken once again from Opera. Browsers that don't support the number input will fall back to an ordinary text field with no spinner control and no restrictions on what value it will accept. Some additional client-side or server-side validation could catch any non-numeric characters and either reformat the value or display an error so the user can correct it.

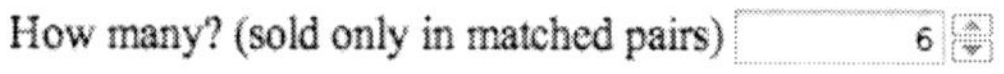

How many? (sold only in matched pairs) [6]

Figure 8-10. Opera displays a number input with a spinner control and the number aligned to the right within the field.

input type="range"

A range input generates a slider widget, useful for entering numbers where the precise value isn't important. The default range is 0 to 100, but you can define your own range with the optional `min` and `max` attributes, including negative numbers and decimals. Like a number input, a range control also accepts a `step` attribute to specify the incremental value (the default step is 1 if the attribute is missing).

Moving the slider handle along the path automatically changes the control's value, but the user won't necessarily see the actual number the slider represents—hence this control is best for approximate numbers or estimates, not for precise values. In left-to-right languages, sliding the handle to the left decreases the value and sliding it to the right increases it. Right-to-left languages reverse the direction.

Similar slider controls have been seen on the Web for years, but they always relied on JavaScript to render the widget and pass a value into a separate field. The new `input type="range"` in HTML5 brings this functionality to the masses without the need for fancy scripts or heavy code libraries.

Listing 8-9 shows an example of a range input, including `min` and `max` attributes. Omitting the `step` attribute allows this control to fall back to the default step value (1); the control's value will be a positive whole number in the range of 0 to 10.

Listing 8-9. *A range input lets users enter an approximate numeric value within a given range*

```
<p><label for="power">Indicate your power level</label>
<input type="range" id="power" name="power" min="0" max="10"></p>
```

At the time we're writing this, Opera, Safari, and Chrome all support range inputs, as will Internet Explorer 10 (which might be out by the time you read this). Firefox hasn't implemented range inputs yet, but hopefully will soon. Meanwhile, non-supporting and older browsers still fall back to a regular text field, and you might opt to provide a JavaScript-based slider interface for those browsers that don't provide a native slider of their own.

Browsers that do fully support range inputs will render a slider widget like the one you see in Figure 8-11, taken from Opera on OS X (other browsers and platforms will look a bit different). The rendered slider isn't very susceptible to CSS; you can specify a width with the `width` property, but not much else. A browser will automatically place the slider handle in the middle of the range, indicating a default mid-range value. You can specify your own initial value with the `value` attribute.

Figure 8-11. Opera renders range inputs as a slider widget. Sliders may look different in other browsers.

input type="checkbox"

A checkbox control is a choice toggle in the form of a small square filled with a check mark (or sometimes an x) when the control is selected. Use checkboxes when several options are available and more than one can be selected, in the sense of "check all that apply," or to represent a single decisive action, like "check this box to accept the terms."

A checkbox input may have a value attribute corresponding to whatever the selected option is, and this value is passed along when the form is submitted. Without a specific value, all that will submit is the state of the box—a value of "on" if it's checked or nothing at all if it's not checked. That could be enough information in some cases, so an explicit value attribute might not always be necessary.

Once checked, a checkbox can be unchecked by simply selecting it again. Furthermore, it can be "prechecked" using the Boolean checked attribute, which requires no value though you can write it as checked="checked" if you prefer XHTML syntax.

Listing 8-10 shows an example of several checkbox input elements, two of which have been prechecked. This is a simple checklist and each control has a meaningful name attribute, so value attributes probably aren't necessary here; just ticking an item tells us everything we need to know. We've also organized these options in an unordered list for a bit of added structure.

Listing 8-10. *A set of multiple-choice options using checkbox controls*

```
<ul>
  <li>
    <label><input type="checkbox" name="grapgun" checked> Grapple gun</label>
  </li>
  <li>
    <label><input type="checkbox" name="minilaser"> Mini laser cutter</label>
  </li>
  <li>
    <label><input type="checkbox" name="smokepel" checked> Smoke pellets</label>
  </li>
  <li>
    <label><input type="checkbox" name="xrayspecs"> Terahertz imaging goggles</label>
  </li>
  <li>
    <label><input type="checkbox" name="microcam"> Micro-camera</label>
  </li>
</ul>
```

Figure 8-12 shows this checklist in a browser with default styling, Safari on Mac OS X in this case. Checkboxes may look different in other browsers and on different platforms. You could, of course, remove the default list item markers with CSS, as you learned in Chapter 4.

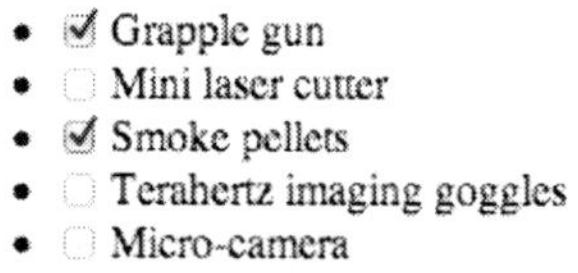

- ☑ Grapple gun
- ☐ Mini laser cutter
- ☑ Smoke pellets
- ☐ Terahertz imaging goggles
- ☐ Micro-camera

Figure 8-12. The list of checkboxes as it might appear in a browser (this is from Safari on OS X).

input type="radio"

A radio button control is somewhat like a checkbox, but only one option in a set can be selected. Radio buttons get their name from the station preset buttons on old-fashioned car radios; since you can listen to only one radio station at a time, pushing one button in would cause the previous button to pop back out.

The radio buttons in a web form work the same way; selecting a button will automatically deselect whichever one in the list was previously selected. Hence, radio buttons are ideal when you need to offer a multiple-choice list of options where only one choice is allowed (unlike checkboxes, which allow multiple choices). Once a radio button has been checked, it can't be unchecked unless another button in the set is checked in its stead.

To define a set of radio buttons, each one must share the same name attribute, and the value of the selected radio button is taken as the value for the entire set when the form is submitted. As with checkboxes, each radio button control can carry a value attribute to pass along additional information about the selected option, and in this case a value is essential. Without a value attribute, the submitted value would simply be "on" for the entire set of options, without any indication of which option was selected. You could have a set with only one option, but in that case a radio button probably isn't the right control for the job; use a checkbox for a single option.

Also like checkboxes, you can preselect a radio button by including the checked attribute. However, only one radio button in a set may be preselected. In the event of multiple preselected radio buttons, only the last one in the set will be checked when a browser renders the form.

Listing 8-11 shows a set of radio buttons, each with the same name attribute to define the set and a different value attribute to distinguish the options.

Listing 8-11. *A set of radio buttons*

```
<ul>
  <li>
    <label>
      <input type="radio" name="cape-length" value="S"> Short (36")
    </label>
  </li>
  <li>
    <label>
      <input type="radio" name="cape-length" value="M"> Medium (48")
    </label>
  </li>
  <li>
    <label>
      <input type="radio" name="cape-length" value="L"> Long (72")
    </label>
  </li>
  <li>
    <label>
      <input type="radio" name="cape-length" value="XL"> Extra-long (96")
    </label>
  </li>
</ul>
```

Figure 8-13 shows this set of radio buttons in Internet Explorer on Windows 7, and we've removed the list item markers with a simple CSS rule (ul { list-style: none; }). As with most other form controls, radio buttons may appear different in other browsers or on other operating systems. In this example, one

259

of the options has been selected, filling the circle with a solid dot. Choosing a different option will automatically uncheck the previous choice.

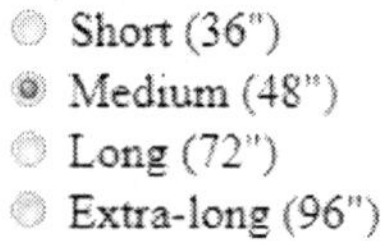

◎ Short (36")
◉ Medium (48")
◎ Long (72")
◎ Extra-long (96")

Figure 8-13. The set of radio buttons as it might be rendered in a browser, now with one option selected.

input type="file"

A file input renders a file upload control—usually consisting of a text field alongside a "choose file" or "browse" button—allowing the user to locate a file on her computer's hard drive or local network and upload that file when she submits the form. Clicking the button invokes a computer's built-in file browser, and once a file is located, the local file path appears in the text field (or some browsers show only the file name without the full path). As with other text fields, an optional size attribute can specify the width of the file field as a number of characters. Browsers that don't display a text field with a file input simply ignore the size attribute.

An input type="file" control can include an optional accept attribute, where the value is a comma-separated list of the accepted file types (specified by their MIME types). If you're asking your users to upload an image, for example, the accept attribute can restrict the field to accept only standard image formats; any other file type would be rejected.

> *Previous versions of HTML also allowed the accept attribute on the form element itself, but that's no longer valid in HTML5, partly because file inputs are no longer required to reside in a form element. HTML5 allows form controls to appear anywhere in the document and be directly associated with a form elsewhere in the document by way of the new form attribute.*

Listing 8-12 presents the markup for a file control, including an accept attribute that limits uploaded files to GIF, JPEG, or PNG images.

Listing 8-12. *A file control with an accept attribute*

```
<p>
  <label for="photo">Send us your action shots and show off your new gear!</label>
  <input name="photo" id="photo" type="file" accept="image/gif, image/jpeg, image/png">
</p>
```

Figure 8-14 shows how this looks in Firefox for Mac OS X. We've already selected a file by browsing the local hard drive, and its path appears in the text field. Only the first portion is visible because the full path is longer than what the text field can display. The button's text is left up to the browser; you can't supply your own label. File controls are also largely immune to CSS, unfortunately, so you can only alter a few aspects of their styling.

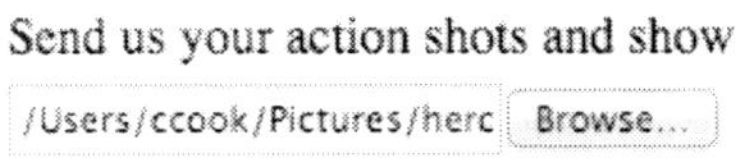

Send us your action shots and show off your new gear!

/Users/ccook/Pictures/herc Browse...

Figure 8-14. The file control as it appears in Firefox for OS X.

Some browsers display a file control like you see in Figure 8-14, as a text field with a button to its right. However, Safari and Chrome—both based on the WebKit rendering engine—display file controls in a very different way. As you can see in Figure 8-15, these browsers don't show a writable text field, instead offering only the browse option with the button on the left side of the control. To the right of the button, Safari and Chrome display only the name of the selected file (once the file has been selected) instead of the full path. Along with the file name, Safari will also display a small icon to indicate the type of file, if the type is known. As is usually the case, the function of the control is the same across browsers, even if its presentation isn't.

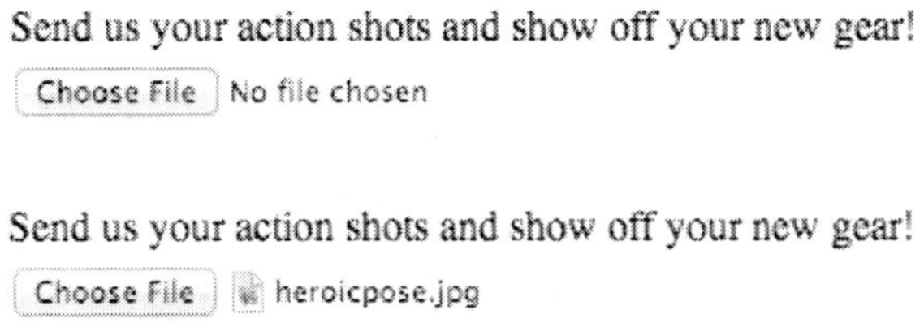

Send us your action shots and show off your new gear!

Choose File No file chosen

Send us your action shots and show off your new gear!

Choose File 🖼 heroicpose.jpg

Figure 8-15. A file control as rendered by Chrome on top and Safari below, both on Mac OS X. They're practically identical because both browsers are built on the same rendering engine. The buttons will look different on other operating systems, including older versions of OS X.

input type="submit"

An input type="submit" control creates a button that will submit the entire form data set—all the data entered in the various controls—when clicked. The control's value attribute sets the text label for the rendered button, which defaults to "Submit" (or "Submit Query" in some browsers) if a value attribute is omitted. The button's value isn't submitted with the rest of the form; it's strictly a label. When the button is activated and the form is submitted, the form handler takes over to process the data.

You can see the markup for a simple login form with a submit button in Listing 8-13. In this example the label "Log In" will appear on the rendered button rather than the default text.

Listing 8-13. *A simple login form with a submit button*

```
<ul>
  <li>
    <label for="username">Your username:</label>
    <input type="text" id="username" name="username" required>
  </li>
  <li>
    <label for="password">Your password:</label>
    <input type="password" id="password" name="password" required>
  </li>
  <li>
```

```
    <input type="submit" value="Log In">
  </li>
</ul>
```

Figure 8-16 shows the rendered form. As you know by now, form elements may look different in other browsers and on other operating systems, and that's especially true of buttons (this image is from Internet Explorer on Windows 7).

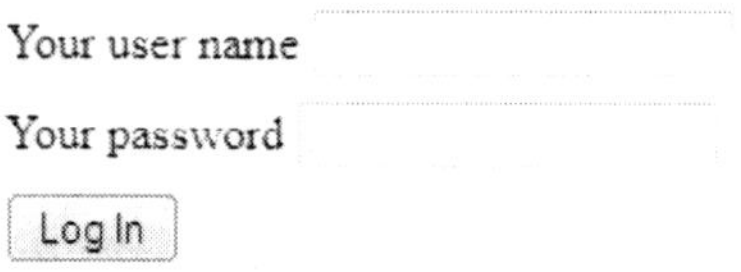

Your user name

Your password

Log In

Figure 8-16. The input element's value attribute specifies the button's text label

input type="reset"

This control generates a button that, when clicked, resets the entire form, blanking out any data the user has entered and setting all controls back to their initial values. Reset buttons were much more common in the past, but a few years of practical use has shown them to rarely be of much value. It's far too likely that a user will accidentally reset the form and irretrievably lose all the information he's carefully entered— especially frustrating when there's no mechanism to undo such a mistake. These days reset buttons are generally discouraged; if you decide to use one, do so with care and only when it can actually help people use your forms.

As with a submit button, the reset button's value attribute determines the button's text label, usually defaulting to "Reset" if the attribute is missing.

input type="button"

A button input is just that: a generic button. It has no inherent function; it merely serves as a clickable widget that can trigger a client-side script. You can set the button's text via the value attribute, or it typically defaults to "Button" if you don't provide a value. Instead of embedding these scripted buttons in your markup, you might prefer to use JavaScript to generate the button itself. After all, the button won't function without a client-side script to imbue it with purpose, and a control that only works with a script needn't be displayed if the script isn't available.

input type="image"

An image control behaves essentially like a submit button: activating the control will submit the form. But an input type="image" allows you to substitute the standard button with a more decorative graphic. As with other images in HTML, an image input requires a src attribute to specify the image file's URL and an alt attribute to provide an alternative text description when the image isn't available (see Chapter 5 for more about the src and alt attributes). Alternative text is especially vital for image form controls, to ensure that the form can be successfully completed even when the image can't be seen. Without a useful alt attribute, people using text browsers or screen readers will have difficulty identifying the button, making it nearly impossible for them to submit the form. You wouldn't want to turn away thousands of paying customers simply because they can't see your "Buy Now" button, would you?

When your visitor uses a mouse (or other pointing device) to click an image control, the precise location of that click is included in the data set as X and Y coordinates (with the control identified by its name attribute, if present). A script or form handler can use this information to determine exactly which part of the button was clicked and thus treat an image control like an image map (which you learned about in Chapter 6), with different regions of the button triggering different actions. However, since this requires the button to be clicked by a pointing device, people using their keyboard to submit the form will be at a disadvantage. It's usually best to use separate, distinct submit or image controls to trigger those different actions rather than a single image button.

You can see the markup for an image control in Listing 8-14 and the rendered result in Figure 8-17. Like the img element, the width and height attributes are optional here but it's usually best to include the dimensions.

Listing 8-14. *An image input offers more decorative choices than a standard submit button*

```
<input type="image" src="images/order-button.png" alt="Place Your Order!" ↪
width="320" height="70">
```

Figure 8-17. An image control inserts a graphical button that might be more (or sometimes less) attractive than the native buttons.

input type="hidden"

As you might have guessed, a hidden input isn't displayed on the rendered page. It exists simply as a vehicle to pass along extra data with the submitted form that a user doesn't need to see or modify—such as an order number or internal tracking ID—via the element's value attribute.

More Form Controls

As multitalented as the input element is with its wide variety of types—including all the fancy new ones introduced in HTML5—it's not the only way to enter and submit data in a web form. In this section we'll round out the collection of form controls with selection menus, blocks of text, and more versatile buttons.

select

The select element creates a selection control—a menu of options from which to choose. The control may be displayed either as a single line that can "drop down" and expand to show all the options or it may occupy multiple lines as specified by the optional size attribute (the size defaults to 1 if the attribute is missing). Each option in the select element is wrapped in its own option element, and we'll get to that momentarily.

A single-line selection control, often called a *drop-down menu*, will show the selected option when in its collapsed, inactive state, with a small arrow at one end as a visual cue that the control can be expanded. Selected options in a multi-line select are usually highlighted with a different background color.

A selection control will only allow one option to be selected by default, especially obvious if it's a single-line drop-down menu. Adding the Boolean multiple attribute automatically converts the select element to a multi-line control and also allows the user to choose more than one option, usually by holding down the Shift, Control, or Command key while making his choices. In the absence of a size attribute, some browsers will automatically expand the multi-line menu to show 10 or even 20 options, or to show all of them if there are only a few. Other browsers only show three or four options regardless of how many are in the list. You can achieve a bit more cross-browser consistency by including a size attribute whenever you allow multiple selections, but it isn't required. If the size attribute is greater than the number of options, the rendered height honors the attribute and the remaining lines will be empty.

When a user submits the form, the selected options are passed as the value of the selection control. As with most other form controls, a name attribute identifies the select element to associate the control with its value (or values).

The display and behavior of a single-line selection can be somewhat unpredictable, largely dependent on the browser and operating system, as well as the location of the control on the screen. If the control appears near the bottom of the screen, the open menu will usually expand upward rather than downward to prevent it from extending past the lower edge of the display where it can't be reached. A menu might expand both up and down if the selected option is near the middle of the list. When expanded, a selection control will overlap other content on the page and can even escape the boundaries of the browser window if it needs to.

When the list of options is exceptionally long, a vertical scroll bar will appear in the expanded menu, allowing the user to scroll up and down to see the entire list. The number of items visible in the expanded list can change depending on the size of the screen or browser window, automatically determined by the browser and operating system. A multi-line select element will display a vertical scroll bar if the number of the options exceeds the number of visible lines, and many browsers reserve space on one side for a scroll bar even when the box isn't scrollable.

> *So far we've been focusing on how desktop browsers render the select element, but mobile phones and tablets may treat selection controls very differently, perhaps by showing a scrolling popup dialog with radio buttons or checkboxes to make the selection. Interacting with forms on a small touchscreen is a very different experience from the traditional keyboard-and-mouse combination.*

The width of a selection control is determined by the longest option in the list, even if that option isn't selected. You can modify the element's natural width with the CSS width property, and any text that exceeds that declared width will appear truncated, but most browsers will automatically expand the width of the menu when it's opened. Each option appears on a single line; text doesn't wrap in a selection control. Ideally, each option in the list should have a short text label of no more than a few words to avoid overly wide menus. If your options require lengthy descriptions, then the `select` element probably isn't the right choice and you should use a set of checkboxes or radio buttons instead.

The `select` element is a non-empty element that requires an end tag, and it acts as a container for one or more `option` or `optgroup` elements; the `select` element must contain at least one `option`. Listing 8-15 shows a `select` element containing three `option` elements. Without a `multiple` or `size` attribute, this control defaults to a single-line selection and only allows one option to be selected.

Listing 8-15. *A select element containing four option elements*

```
<select name="cape-length">
  <option>Short (36")</option>
  <option>Medium (48")</option>
  <option>Long (72")</option>
  <option>Extra-long (96)</option>
</select>
```

You can see what this control will look like in Figure 8-18. This image is from Safari for OS X, with the selection closed on the left and expanded on the right. Some browsers (including Safari) also indicate the currently selected option with a check mark to the side of the label, but other browsers don't. The first option in the list is the initial selection by default unless some other option is preselected (more on that when we cover the `option` element next). In its open state, the focused option in the list—that is, the option the user is about to select—is usually indicated with a highlight color.

Figure 8-18. The same selection control in both inactive and active states

Adding a `multiple` attribute to a `select` element, as in Listing 8-16, converts the control from a single-line drop-down menu to a multi-line box and allows the user to choose more than one option. This example also carries a `size` attribute to set the height of the menu at five lines (thus the actual rendered height depends on the size of the text).

Listing 8-16. *A select element with size and multiple attributes*

```
<select name="suit-options" size="5" multiple>
  <option>Thruster boots</option>
  <option>Repulsor gauntlets</option>
  <option>Multi-spectrum HUD</option>
  <option>Therm-optic camouflage</option>
  <option>Rust-proofing undercoat</option>
</select>
```

Figure 8-19 shows the result: a scrolling box displaying the options, with selected options highlighted on a darker background color. A scroll bar isn't needed in this case because there are only five options in the list, the same number of lines specified by the `size` attribute, but this browser (Firefox) reserves space for a scroll bar anyway.

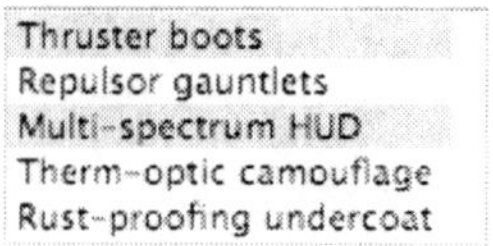

Thruster boots
Repulsor gauntlets
Multi-spectrum HUD
Therm-optic camouflage
Rust-proofing undercoat

Figure 8-19. A multi-line selection menu with two options selected

Required Attributes

- name: Identifies the control so that it can be associated with its value when the form is submitted. A markup validator may not generate an error if this attribute is missing, but it's required to successfully handle the form.

Optional Attributes

- autofocus: This Boolean attribute is new in HTML5 and specifies that the button should automatically receive focus when the page loads.

- disabled: A Boolean attribute that disables the control so it can't receive focus or be changed. Many browsers will display disabled controls in a "grayed-out" style.

- form: This is new in HTML5 and allows the control to be associated with one or more additional forms. The form attribute accepts a value of one or more form IDs, separated by spaces. This feature allows authors to work around the lack of support for nested form elements.

- multiple: A Boolean attribute that, when present, indicates that multiple options may be selected, usually by holding down a Shift, Control, or Command key while selecting or deselecting options.

- required: This Boolean attribute is new to HTML5 and indicates that the control must have a value in order to submit the form; i.e. at least one option must be selected.

- size: Specifies the height of a multi-line selection control as a number of lines; the value must be a positive whole numeral, such as size="15".

option

Each option in a select element is represented by an option element, though as of HTML5 the option element may also appear within a datalist element, and there are some slightly different rules about its use with datalists. We'll go into more detail on that later in this chapter when we cover the datalist element, but for now let's focus on options within a selection control.

When it appears in a select element, option is a non-empty element that requires an end tag and can only contain text, which acts as a label that will be displayed in the selection menu. Each option in the selection control appears on a single, non-wrapping line within the menu. That text content is also the value that will be sent with the form unless you specify a different value with an optional value attribute.

You can preselect an option by including a Boolean selected attribute, and you can preselect more than one option, but only when the parent selection control has a multiple attribute.

We've given each of the `option` elements in Listing 8-17 a `value` attribute that will be submitted in place of the element's text label. This way a back-end system can receive whatever machine-friendly values it's been programmed to handle while the user still sees sensible text labels. In this example, the first option acts as a label for the control and shouldn't be submitted with the form (it's also been preselected by adding a `selected` attribute). An empty `value` attribute prevents the first option's text from being submitted as its value, allowing the automatic validation indicated by the `required` attribute to kick in—a user can't submit this form with an empty value (in browsers that support the `required` attribute for `select` elements, at least).

Listing 8-17. *option elements with value attributes; one is preselected*

```
<select name="cape-length" required>
  <option value="" selected>Choose a length</option>
  <option value="S">Short (36")</option>
  <option value="M">Medium (48")</option>
  <option value="L">Long (72")</option>
  <option value="XL">Extra-long (96")</option>
</select>
```

Required Attributes

The `option` element doesn't require any attributes.

Optional Attributes

- `disabled`: When present, disables the option so it can't be selected. Many browsers will display disabled options in a "grayed-out" style.

- `label`: Provides a shorter alternative text label, displayed in place of the element's contents to improve accessibility when the regular value is too verbose. Not every browser supports this attribute so it's usually best to keep your option text short.

- `selected`: Indicates an initially selected option.

- `value`: Specifies a value to pass with submitted form data. If no `value` attribute is present, the selected `option` element's text contents are passed as the selection's value.

optgroup

You can collect `option` elements into related sections or categories by enclosing them in an `optgroup` element, so named because it forms a "group of options." An option group can only contain `option` elements; no other elements are allowed, and you can't nest an `optgroup` within an `optgroup`.

In browsers, the value of the required `label` attribute will be displayed as a title at the top of the group with the options listed beneath it, usually indented. All browsers display `optgroup` labels in some distinctive fashion, but the particular style varies and isn't very susceptible to CSS. Firefox and Internet Explorer render them in a boldfaced and italicized font, while Chrome, Safari, and Opera render them in a gray color. Furthermore, some browsers change the label's style when the `select` is multi-line instead of single-line—Chrome and Safari go from gray text in a single-line select to bold, black labels when the selection is multi-line, and Opera goes from plain gray to bold, black, and italicized optgroup labels.

The optional disabled attribute will disable the entire group, preventing the user from selecting any of those options. Most browsers will display disabled options as "grayed out" text, and some will gray out the group label as well. The optgroup label itself isn't a selectable option.

You can see an example of optgroup elements in action in Listing 8-18, which groups different styles of superhero masks into logical categories. Although the "Lower Half-masks" category is a group of one, that's perfectly logical and semantically correct in this situation.

Listing 8-18. *A select element containing several option groups*

```
<select name="mask-style">
  <option value="" selected disabled>Select a style</option>
  <optgroup label="Domino Masks">
    <option value="MDTS40">The Colt</option>
    <option value="MDMV77">The Danvers</option>
    <option value="MDRD66">The Gorshin</option>
    <option value="MDDC40">The Grayson</option>
    <option value="MDMV79">The Hardy</option>
    <option value="MDDC59">The Jordan</option>
  </optgroup>
  <optgroup label="Upper Half-masks">
    <option value="MUDC09">The Kane</option>
    <option value="MUMV74">The Logan</option>
    <option value="MUMV41">The Rogers</option>
    <option value="MUDC37">The Wayne</option>
  </optgroup>
  <optgroup label="Lower Half-masks">
    <option value="MLSH31">The Cranston</option>
  </optgroup>
  <optgroup label="Full Face Masks">
    <option value="MFDC86">The Kovacs</option>
    <option value="MFMV62">The Parker</option>
  </optgroup>
</select>
```

Figure 8-20 shows the same selection control in two different browsers: Firefox and Opera. You can see that it looks a very different in each, but they both work the same way.

Figures 8-20. The control in Firefox (left) and Chrome (right), both on OS X. The menus appear quite different, but both browsers do make the group labels clearly distinguishable from the options beneath them.

Required Attributes

- `label`: Specifies a text label or title for the option group, usually displayed in some distinctive style to set it apart from the selectable options.

Optional Attributes

- `disabled`: A Boolean attribute that, when present, disables the entire group so none of its options can be selected. Most browsers will display disabled options in a "grayed-out" style, and may gray out the group label as well.

textarea

The `textarea` element creates a multi-line field for entering passages of text too lengthy for a single-line text field (`input type="text"`). You can define its rendered size with CSS, or with the optional `rows` and `cols` attributes; the value of `rows` is the vertical number of text rows and `cols` is the number of characters (or columns, hence the shortened name, `cols`) on a horizontal line. Left to its own devices, most browsers will display a `textarea` as a white box, two or three rows tall and about 20 columns wide.

Because the size of the box is based on the size of the text, a larger or smaller font size will obviously influence the dimensions of the `textarea` element. If the `rows` and `cols` attributes are present, CSS can still override them and apply a different width or height. Vertical and horizontal scroll bars will appear if the amount of text entered into a `textarea` exceeds what can fit within its given dimensions.

This is a non-empty element that requires an end tag. It can contain only text—no HTML allowed—that will be displayed as the control's initial value, and a user can easily delete or edit that initial text. Any initial text within the `textarea` element will be displayed with all whitespace intact, including tabs and returns, exactly as it appears in the document's markup. This element also allows an optional placeholder attribute to display instructions or hints about what content the user is expected to provide (placeholders aren't submitted as form values; they're for display only). If the element has no initial text content and no placeholder attribute, the box will be blank when a browser renders it.

Some browsers render the text in a textarea in a monospace typeface—one in which every character is the same width, such as Courier—but you can easily change the font with CSS if you prefer (and you'll see how later in this chapter). Listing 8-19 shows a textarea element already filled with text as its initial value.

Listing 8-19. *A textarea element containing initial text*

```
<textarea name="message" rows="8" cols="50">
Dear Power Outfitters,

I recently had to replace my trusty grappling gun after years of faithful service ↪
(and I'm still kicking myself for leaving it in that cab, believe me). I ordered ↪
the latest model, the Dreiberg 4000, from your website and it arrived the very next ↪
day. Well I couldn't be more pleased! Not only is it smaller and lighter than my old ↪
one, but it has twice the range and the new winching system is three times faster. ↪
I'm scaling buildings like a teenaged sidekick again! I should have upgraded years ago.

Thanks!
</textarea>
```

You can see this box rendered with default styling in Figure 8-21. The scroll bar appears when the length of the text exceeds the height of the box, and some browsers will automatically reserve some space for a scroll bar along the box's right edge even when scrolling isn't necessary. This image is taken is from Firefox for Windows.

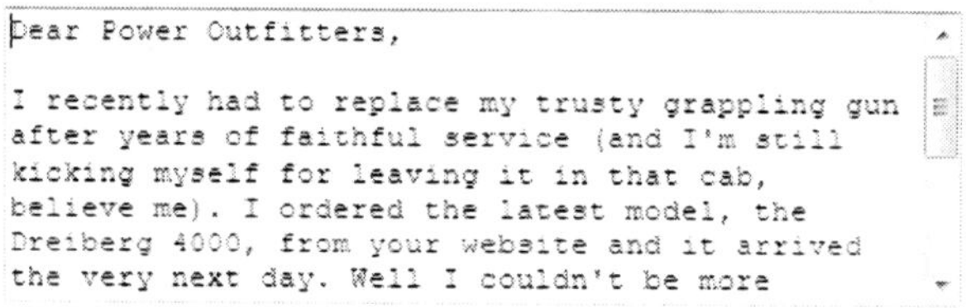

Figure 8-21. The textarea as seen in Firefox

Required Attributes

- name: Identifies the control so it can be associated with its value when the form is submitted. A markup validator may not generate an error if this attribute is missing, but it's required in order to successfully handle the form.

Optional Attributes

- autofocus: This Boolean attribute is new in HTML5 and indicates that the field should automatically receive focus when the page loads.

- `cols`: Specifies the number of characters to display on a single horizontal line, thus defining the width of the rendered box. Text will automatically wrap to new lines as needed or will invoke a horizontal scroll bar (crawl bar) if a long line doesn't include word spaces to facilitate wrapping.

- `dirname`: This attribute, new in HTML5, allows the control to automatically indicate the directionality of its text value when the form is submitted. For example, in a document with a default left-to-right direction, a user could enter text in a right-to-left language into a form control. The `dirname` attribute can carry that additional direction information so a form handler can process or store text of a different directionality than that of the original form. This attribute's value is a secondary name for the control and the content direction is automatically assigned on submission, either `rtl` or `ltr`.

- `disabled`: A Boolean attribute that disables the control so it can't receive focus or be modified. The value of a disabled control is not submitted. Most browsers will display disabled controls in a "grayed-out" style by default.

- `form`: This is new in HTML5 and allows the control to be associated with one or more additional forms. The `form` attribute accepts a value of one or more form IDs, separated by spaces. This feature allows authors to work around the lack of support for nested `form` elements.

- `maxlength`: Specifies the maximum number of characters (including spaces) that can be entered in the `textarea`. Browsers may not give any indication that a field has a maximum length, and will simply stop accepting input when the limit is reached. If you include a `maxlength` attribute you should also provide some visible hint to your visitors to let them know how many characters the control will accept.

- `placeholder`: This new attribute introduced in HTML5 allows the author to include a short text hint to advise the user on what value is expected for the text area. The browser hides the placeholder label automatically when the control is in focus (or when the user begins typing) and, if there was no value entered in its place, the placeholder reappears when the field loses focus.

- `readonly`: A Boolean attribute specifying that the control may only display a value and can't be modified. This differs from `disabled` in that a read-only control can still receive focus and its value is still submitted with the form.

- `required`: This Boolean attribute is new to HTML5 and indicates that the control must have a value in order to submit the form.

- `rows`: Specifies the number of lines of text to display before scrolling vertically, thus defining the height of the rendered box. The browser will automatically produce a vertical scroll bar when the length of the text exceeds this given height.

- `wrap`: Specifies how the text value should be wrapped when the form is submitted. The `wrap` attribute only accepts two values: `soft` (the text is not wrapped at submission, but may still be wrapped when displayed) or `hard` (the browser inserts returns at the `textarea`'s column width to force long lines to wrap). If the `wrap` value is `hard`, the `cols` attribute must be defined. This attribute is new in HTML5, and the default value is `soft` if the attribute is missing.

datalist

The datalist element, introduced in HTML5, contains a set of suggested, predefined values for an input element that appear as a list of options. But unlike a select element, the control can still accept other values besides those in the datalist. Using the datalist element with an input element effectively combines the features of a freeform text field that accepts any text entered and a select element that presents an explicit set of options.

> In user interface terminology, such a combined text-entry-plus-list-component device is commonly known as a combo box. They've been part of software and operating systems for decades, but HTML didn't have a web-ready equivalent until now.

You can associate an input element with a datalist element by way of the list attribute, whose value is the ID of the particular datalist element you're targeting (hence the datalist element requires a unique id attribute). When a user activates the input, either by clicking the field with a pointer or by typing into it, the list of options will appear. In most browsers—those that support the datalist element, at least—the options shown will be pattern matches for the text typed, and the list updates automatically as the user continues typing, narrowing the available options. If the list appears after a click instead of a keystroke and the text field is still empty, the entire list will appear (usually with only five to ten options visible, and a scroll bar to reach the full list).

Each option within a datalist element is an option element, formerly an exclusive child of the select element but now serving double duty in HTML5. A datalist element can't contain any other elements besides options, not even optgroup. When an option element appears in a datalist it takes on some slightly different rules and properties. Inside a datalist, the option element no longer requires an end tag, and can instead be treated as a void element, but only if it carries its value in a value attribute. If the option contains text and also bears a value attribute, the text label will appear in the menu but, once selected, the value attribute is inserted into the text field for submission with the form; an option element's value attribute always trumps its text label. Unlike most other void elements in HTML5, an option element lacking an end tag cannot be self-closed with a trailing slash.

Listing 8-20 shows an example of an input element associated with its supporting datalist element. Here we've omitted any text inside the option elements, treating them as void elements with value attributes. A person filling in this form would be able to type the name of a city into the field and, if the first few letters match some of the options in the datalist, that list would appear, saving the user a few keystrokes.

Listing 8-20. *A text input and its associated* datalist

```
<label for="city">Base of operations</label>
<input type="text" name="city" id="city" list="citieslist">

<datalist id="citieslist">
  <option value="Attilan">
  <option value="Bludhaven">
  <option value="Coast City">
```

```
<option value="Fawcett City">
<option value="Kandor">
<option value="Mega-City One">
<option value="Neo-Tokyo">
<option value="Platinum Flats">
```
</datalist>

You can see this control in action in Figure 8-22, taken from Firefox. The datalist element isn't widely supported by browsers yet, but those that don't support it will still get the fully functional, tried-and-true text input. It's another fine example of progressive enhancement—improving the utility of a simple form control for those browsers that are capable, but less-capable browsers and devices aren't left out in the cold.

Figure 8-22. The datalist element holds suggested values for the text field, automatically matched to the text already entered. A user can choose from the list or continue to enter a different value.

Required Attributes

- **id**: Identifies the datalist control so it can be associated with an input element by way of a list attribute.

Optional Attributes

The datalist element doesn't offer any optional attributes apart from the standard global attributes that apply to all elements.

button

The button element works just like a submit, reset, or button input, or even an input type="image"— activating a button element (with the click of a mouse or press of a key) will submit or reset the form, or trigger a scripted response.

The button element requires a type attribute with a value of submit, reset, or button. However, unlike the input element, a button element is not empty; it can contain text or other elements, offering many more design and semantic options than a void input element. In fact, a button *must* hold some content, because an empty button element will have no default label. And because it contains text or other elements, a button requires an end tag. Web developer Aaron Gustafson gives an informative overview of the button element's usefulness and flexibility in his 2006 article, "Push My Button" (digital-web.com/articles/push_my_button/).

Listing 8-21 shows an example of a button element like you might see in a multi-step "wizard" style form. This button also bears a formnovalidate attribute, allowing the form to be submitted without checking for required fields (controls with required attributes) or imposing any formatting rules (for e-mail or URL fields, or any controls with `pattern` attributes). Note that this button contains some emphasized text and an image, something you couldn't do with an ordinary `input` element.

Listing 8-21. *A `button` element containing some emphasized text and an image*

```
<p>
  <button type="submit" name="save" formnovalidate>
    <em>Save and continue</em>
    <img src="images/next.png" width="28" height="20" alt="">
  </button>
</p>
```

When a browser renders this on-screen (as shown in Figure 8-23), the entire element and its contents becomes an active push-button to submit the form. By default, a `button` element will have the same appearance as an `input` button, but because it can contain other HTML elements, it creates many more opportunities for styling with CSS.

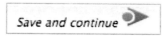

Figure 8-23. The button as it appears in Firefox for OS X without any additional styling

It's not much to look at with default styling, and because the button contains some non-text content (the arrow image), OS X gives it a slightly different style than the typical rounded, glassy look most other buttons receive. But with a bit of CSS enhancement this humble element can look like Figure 8-24, an effect that would be impossible with an `input` element.

Figure 8-24. The same `button` element, now with more pizzazz

Required Attributes

- `type`: Specifies the type of button control the element represents—submit, reset, or button.

Optional Attributes

- `autofocus`: This Boolean attribute is new in HTML5 and indicates that the button should automatically receive focus when the page loads.

- `disabled`: A Boolean attribute that disables the control so it can't receive focus or be activated. Many browsers will display disabled buttons in a "grayed-out" style by default.

- `form`: This is new in HTML5 and allows the control to be associated with one or more additional forms. The `form` attribute accepts a value of one or more form IDs, separated by spaces. This feature allows authors to work around the lack of support for nested `form` elements.

- `formaction`: This attribute is new to HTML5 and overrides the form's `action` attribute in defining the control's handler (only for `button type="submit"`). The attribute's value is the URL of the form handler where the data is sent when a user submits the form.

- `formenctype`: This is a new attribute in HTML5 and overrides the form's `enctype` attribute. It specifies how the data should be encoded before it's sent to the server, but only when submitted by the button bearing this attribute (and only for `button type="submit"`). The `formenctype` attribute only accepts the values `application/x-www-form-urlencoded`, `multipart/form-data`, or `text/plain`.

- `formmethod`: This is new to HTML5 and overrides the form's method for sending data to the form handler. The two possible values are `get` and `post` (only for `button type="submit"`).

- `formnovalidate`: A new Boolean attribute in HTML5, this allows a form to be submitted while bypassing the form's validation (only for `button type="submit"`). Indicating this on a button instead of for the entire form allows some buttons to bypass validation while others don't. For example, a "save" button might submit a partially completed form to let users save their progress, but without going through the validation process the form will undergo when it's finally submitted at the end.

- `formtarget`: This is new to HTML5 and overrides the form's `target` attribute, which specifies the target window to use when the form is submitted. This attribute can only appear on a `button type="submit"` and its value is the name of the target window or frame, or one of the keywords `_blank`, `_self`, `_parent`, or `_top`.

- `value`: Specifies the value of the button to be submitted along with the form data. This value is only submitted if the button itself is used to submit the form; another submit button or submitting a form by pressing "Enter" won't submit this value.

keygen

The keygen element generates a matched pair of encryption keys when the form is submitted—one public, sent to the form handler for use by the website or application, the other private and stored locally in the browser. This mathematically matched pair of keys allows the browser and the original website or application to securely identify each other on subsequent visits.

Netscape first introduced this element years ago and other browsers (apart from Internet Explorer) copied Netscape's implementation, but keygen wasn't part of any official HTML specification until it was included in HTML5. Microsoft has stated that they have no plans to implement keygen support in Internet Explorer—and have even asked for it to be taken out of the HTML5 specification—so this type of form encryption won't work with any past, current, or future version of IE. You may prefer to use a more universally supported encryption method, such as Transport Layer Security (TLS) or Secure Sockets Layer (SSL).

We won't explain all the ins and outs of public key cryptography here, as it's well beyond the scope of this book (see wikipedia.org/wiki/Public-key_cryptography for a brief introduction, if you're still curious). And because the keygen element is so specialized and obscure, you can have a long and fruitful career in web development without ever seeing it. We're not even going to cover the element in any further depth in this book. You can learn more about keygen at the Mozilla Developer Network (https://developer.mozilla.org/docs/HTML/Element/keygen).

Structuring Forms

Now that you've been introduced to all the myriad form controls you'll need, you might be thinking about how to put them all together. Controls are merely component parts, and the form in its entirety is more than the sum of its controls. A usable and accessible form needs a meaningful structure, just as the rest of your document does. And because the form element can contain almost any structural markup, you have a broad HTML arsenal at your disposal.

When you construct a form, as with any other content, you should think about the meaning and purpose of the content and wrap it in the most semantically appropriate tags. A list of options with checkboxes or radio buttons should probably be marked up as a list, with each option held in a separate list item (the li element). If the order of those options is significant—option 1, option 2, option 3, and so on—the list should probably be an ordered one (the ol element). If your form is split into distinct sections, perhaps each section could be wrapped in a section element with a heading (h1 through h6) as its title. If each control in that form represents a separate thought, it may be sensible to wrap them in paragraphs (the p element).

With that in mind, remember that forms aren't actually read like normal content. They exist to engage the user—to open the door and invite your visitors in. Think about the meaning behind the information you're requesting of them, and consider the often-tedious procedure of stepping through a series of controls and entering data into them. Arrange and organize your form with an eye toward optimal usability and accessibility.

In addition to the headings, paragraphs, lists, and tables you already know, a few special elements are designed specifically for use with forms.

fieldset

The fieldset element encompasses a set of related controls, collecting them into a logical group. The fieldset can in turn contain any other structural markup you might need to further arrange and support each control (paragraphs, lists, and so on), and even nested fieldset elements to establish groups within groups (but keep nesting to a minimum). By default, most web browsers will display a thin border around a fieldset, though the exact appearance of the border will vary from browser to browser. We'll show you how you can remove this default border with CSS later in this chapter.

The fieldset element doesn't do much on its own, it's simply a container, but it has more semantic value than the semantically neutral div element; if you're inclined to use a div or even a section to group controls together, a fieldset might be a better choice. Consider the meaning and purpose of your fields and gather them into sets appropriately.

Listing 8-22 demonstrates the markup for a simple form, much like the one you saw in Listing 8-1 way back at the beginning of this chapter. This time, the two form controls have been wrapped in a fieldset element to bind them together and establish their semantic relationship (we'll introduce the legend element next).

Listing 8-22. *A simple form with its controls wrapped in a fieldset*

```
<form method="post" action="/apps/subscribe.py">
  <fieldset>
    <legend>Subscribe to our newsletter</legend>
    <p>
      <input type="email" name="email" id="email" required>
      <button type="submit">Subscribe</button>
    </p>
  </fieldset>
</form>
```

You can see how a browser displays this form in Figure 8-25. The browser draws the border automatically, along with a bit of padding to create space between the border and its contents. You can adjust or remove the border and padding with CSS.

Figure 8-25. The form as it appears in Chrome for OS X

Required Attributes

The fieldset element doesn't require any attributes.

Optional Attributes

There aren't any optional attributes for the fieldset element, only the usual global attributes.

legend

The legend element provides a text title or caption for a set of form fields, hence it can appear only within a fieldset element. When it does appear, it must be the *first child* of the fieldset, coming before any other content or elements. It's a phrasing element that can only contain text and other phrasing elements, but most browsers will position a legend so that it overlaps the fieldset's top border (as shown in Figure 8-15), deviating from typical inline styling. Text in a legend element usually doesn't wrap to multiple lines like ordinary text, so keep your legends short.

Unfortunately, the legend element is notoriously difficult to style consistently with CSS. Browsers simply refuse to apply some CSS properties to legends, even those they'll willingly apply to almost any other element. You can usually influence a legend's font family, size, weight, and color, but attempting to apply a background image, border, margins or padding, or to reposition the legend via CSS will be next to impossible in some common browsers, especially older versions.

It's often best to leave the browsers to render form legends with most of their default styling intact, and keep the CSS artistry to a minimum. If your design requires more stylistic power than the legend element allows, you might opt for a heading instead, though the legend element is more semantically fitting and improves your form's accessibility. Styling limitations might not be a good enough justification to forego such an otherwise useful element.

Listing 8-23 shows a fieldset featuring a legend element, in this case acting as both a title to announce the purpose of the controls and some instructional text to help the visitor figure out what to do.

Listing 8-23. *A set of form fields labeled by a legend element*

```html
<fieldset id="accessories">
  <legend>Select additional accessories</legend>
  <ul>
    <li>
      <label><input type="checkbox" name="grapgun"> Grapple gun</label>
    </li>
    <li>
      <label><input type="checkbox" name="minilaser"> Mini laser cutter</label>
    </li>
    <li>
      <label><input type="checkbox" name="smokepel"> Smoke pellets</label>
    </li>
    <li>
      <label><input type="checkbox" name="xrayspecs"> Terahertz imaging goggles</label>
    </li>
    <li>
      <label><input type="checkbox" name="microcam"> Micro-camera</label>
    </li>
  </ul>
</fieldset>
```

Figure 8-26 shows a legend as rendered by Firefox, and most other browsers will display it much like this with their default styling. The legend is indented from the edge and centered vertically over the fieldset's top border, with a small gap of white space on each side. One interesting oddity is that older versions of Internet Explorer for Windows inexplicably colored legend elements blue by default, but you can override that color easily with CSS.

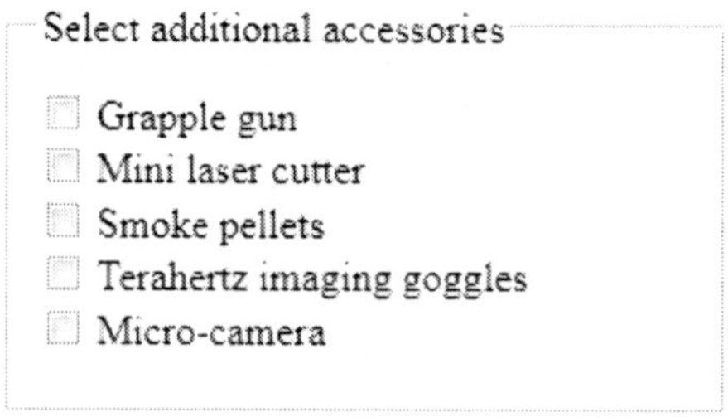

Figure 8-26. The legend element as seen in Firefox for Windows with default styling. This rendering is fairly typical, though you might see slight variations in some browsers.

Required Attributes

There are no required attributes for the legend element.

Optional Attributes

The legend element doesn't have any optional attributes.

label

Perhaps the most useful and meaningful element for structuring forms, the label element designates a text label for a specific control. A label element may enclose both the control and its text label, in which case the connection between the two elements is implied only by context. Alternatively, the label element may carry an optional for attribute whose value corresponds to the control's unique ID, explicitly declaring the connection between the two elements. Even if the label element encloses both the text and the control, the for and id attributes reinforce the connection; neither attribute is required, but both are good to have. It's possible (but rare) for more than one label to share the same for value, in which case all those labels are associated with the same control.

When a label is properly associated with a control, most browsers will make the entire label area clickable to give focus to the specified control. This feature especially makes checkboxes and radio buttons easier to use because the text label enlarges the clickable area, and those controls can present very small targets for a mouse pointer to land on. Screen readers will announce each field's label as the user moves from control to control, and forms can be very difficult for visually impaired visitors to negotiate without proper labels.

When laying out a form, labels for text fields and selection menus typically appear above or to the left of the control, while labels for checkboxes and radio buttons should appear to the control's right (in left-to-right languages; right-to-left languages reverse the directions). These aren't rules dictated by web standards, just usability conventions established over time.

Listing 8-24 expands our newsletter subscription form, this time adding some more structural markup. We've added options to choose either plain text or HTML e-mails and wrapped them in a nested fieldset because those controls are a subset of the complete set. They're in an unordered list because it's a list of two options in no particular order, so that markup makes good sense. We've added labels to identify the e-mail address field as well as the radio buttons for choosing a format, and all of them are explicitly connected to their controls with for attributes. It might look like a lot of extra markup for such a simple form, but the benefits gained in improved usability, accessibility, and meaningful structure are worth it.

Listing 8-24. *A form structured with* fieldsets, *lists, paragraphs, and* labels

```
<form method="post" action="/apps/subscribe.py">
  <fieldset>
    <legend>Subscribe to our newsletter</legend>
    <p>
      <label for="email">Your e-mail address</label>
      <input type="email" name="email" id="email" required>
    </p>
```

```
<fieldset>
  <legend>Select your preferred format</legend>
  <ul>
    <li>
      <label for="text">
        <input type="radio" id="text" name="format" value="text"> Plain text
      </label>
    </li>
    <li>
      <label for="html">
        <input type="radio" id="html" name="format" value="html"> HTML
      </label>
    </li>
  </ul>
</fieldset>
<p><button type="submit">Subscribe</button></p>
</fieldset>
</form>
```

The label element describing the e-mail field doesn't enclose its associated input element, but they're connected by the for and id attributes. The labels for the format options contain both their label text and their inputs, so their for attributes aren't strictly necessary but are still worth including. A label element that lacks a for attribute and doesn't contain a control won't do much good at all; there's nothing to relate that label to a form control.

You can see the final product in Figure 8-27. Alas, it's not very pretty when you see it with the browser's default styling. Fortunately you have the power of CSS on your side, and you'll learn just a few ways to improve the looks of your forms before the end of this chapter.

Figure 8-27. The form isn't the prettiest thing when rendered with a browser's default style sheet, but its markup is semantically sound and will be accessible to a wide range of people and devices.

Required Attributes

The label element doesn't require any attributes.

Optional Attributes

- `for`: Explicitly associates the `label` with a single control when the attribute's value matches the control's unique ID.

- `form`: This is new in HTML5 and allows the label to be associated with one or more additional forms. The `form` attribute accepts a value of one or more form IDs, separated by spaces. This feature allows authors to work around the lack of support for nested `form` elements.

INDICATING REQUIRED FIELDS

Not every control in every form is essential for the form's completion. Some fields may be required while others will be optional, so it's polite and advisable to clearly indicate the difference. In the relatively short life of the Web so far, it's become a convention to indicate required fields with an asterisk (*), a small graphical dot or icon, or the word "required" next to the control (preferably in a `label` element).

In addition to an indicator of some sort, you should also include an informational statement to introduce that notation to anyone who might not be familiar with it. A sentence such as "Required fields are marked with *" at the beginning of the form will suffice. If a particular form has no optional fields, it could become redundant to indicate every single control as required, so simply stating "All fields are required" might be preferable. An instructional statement probably isn't necessary if required fields are individually flagged with the word "required."

Some web designers opt for indicating required fields with an italicized or boldfaced label, but that cue is essentially visual and hence problematic for non-sighted users. If you choose to alter the presentation of label text to indicate required fields, do so by wrapping the text in an em or `strong` element so even non-visual devices can suitably emphasize it. If you use an image as a required field indicator, adding `alt="required"` will assist non-sighted visitors using screen-reading software. You shouldn't indicate required fields purely through the use of color either; color-blind users might be unable to distinguish them, and unsighted users will obviously run into problems. Don't indicate required fields visually through CSS alone (with a background image or some other decoration); the indicator has real meaning and it belongs in the HTML.

Displaying Output

Along with all the new and interesting ways to input data into a form, HTML5 has introduced a few new elements specifically intended for displaying data to users. These elements aren't strictly related to forms, though they're often very useful in conjunction with forms to display and visualize the results of a user's input.

output

The output element displays the result of a calculation in a form, such as a total price in a virtual shopping cart, or an interest rate adjusted for a credit score. In the past, web developers usually used an input type="text" to display such results, but HTML5 has added the output element as a more appropriate counterpart to the input element—especially complementary to the new number input type. The output element by itself doesn't do much, but it's a much more semantically meaningful and accessible alternative to an input element or a generic span or div.

Listing 8-25 shows a simple calculation form, adding two number inputs to arrive at a total, to be displayed in the empty output element. A bit of basic JavaScript does the math (triggered by the oninput inline event handler in the form's start tag); these elements can't perform any calculations on their own. The output element's optional for attribute carries the IDs of the two controls that contributed to its value, establishing a semantic link and aiding accessibility.

Listing 8-25. *A very simple calculation form, displaying the results in an output element*

```
<form oninput="sum.value = parseInt(a.value) + parseInt(b.value)">
  <input name="a" id="a" type="number"> +
  <input name="b" id="b" type="number"> =
  <output name="sum" for="a b"></output>
</form>
```

This is a phrasing element that requires an end tag and can only contain text and other phrasing elements. The entire contents of the output element are the element's value, so any initial value—including any nested elements—is replaced when the value changes. An empty output element has no value. This is also a form-associated element, but doesn't necessarily have to appear within a form element—the optional form attribute can associate an output element with one or more forms elsewhere in the same document. It displays as an inline element but doesn't have any default styling otherwise.

Figure 8-28 shows our simple calculator in Chrome on OS X, but it's not much to look at. The output element has no default styling at all so its value is ordinary text. You could make this form a lot fancier with a little CSS wizardry. In previous versions of HTML you might have used a simple span to display such results, but output is much more semantically meaningful.

Figure 8-28. The simple addition form as seen in Chrome for Mac OS X. The output element has no default styling so its value is just ordinary text.

Required Attributes

The output element doesn't require any attributes.

Optional Attributes

- for: contains a space-separated list of IDs of form controls that contributed to the output element's value. This attribute establishes an explicit relationship between one output element and one or more `input` elements and can aid accessibility, especially if the `output` appears elsewhere in the document, separated from its associated controls.

- `form`: allows the `output` to be associated with one or more forms in the same document. The `form` attribute accepts a value of one or more form IDs, separated by spaces. This feature allows authors to work around the lack of support for nested `form` elements.

- `name`: the name of the `output` element, useful for targeting the element with JavaScript. The `output` element holds a value but that value isn't submitted with the form; it's for display only.

meter

Introduced in HTML5, the `meter` element represents a measurement on any scale with a known range, meaning the scale has both a minimum and a maximum. The measurement can be anything you like, and the scale can be anything as well, so long as the ends of the scale are known figures. A `meter` element could represent a distance in a range from 25 to 50 miles, a time interval between 0 and 60 seconds, the temperature of a star between 1,000 and 3,700 degrees Kelvin, or the concentration of helium in the atmosphere of Neptune between 0% and 100%—anything that can be expressed as a number on a finite scale might be expressed with a `meter` element.

The `meter` element isn't appropriate for scales without a known minimum and maximum, as there's no way to determine where one number falls on an infinite scale. Even assuming a minimum of zero, don't use `meter` for measurements without a specific maximum, such as a person's height or weight, or how long you've been waiting for your pizza—you could be waiting forever, and there's no way to represent that on a scale.

The `meter` element falls into the phrasing content model, and requires both a start and an end tag along with a `value` attribute specifying the measurement. This element can appear anywhere in the document where flow content is allowed. It isn't exclusive to forms although it can be related to a form if it appears within a `form` element or carries a `form` attribute. It can only contain text or other phrasing elements (but not another `meter` element) and its contents should indicate the same measurement as its `value` attribute:

```
<p>Rating: <meter value="0.75">0.75</meter></p>
```

By default, the scale ranges from 0 and 1, so the measurement can be expressed as any decimal number within that range (this also translates nicely to percentages from 0% to 100%). If decimals aren't what you want, you can instead specify your own minimum and maximum values with the optional `min` and `max` attributes:

```
<p>Rating: <meter min="0" max="5" value="4">4 out of 5</meter></p>
```

The contents of the element don't have to be a number, but they should reflect the same information as the `meter`'s value. With the measurement explicitly declared in a `value` attribute, the element's contents could be some other, human-readable text that gets the same idea across:

```
<p>Rating: <meter min="0" max="5" value="4">pretty good, but not perfect</meter></p>
```

If the specified value is less than 0, a min attribute must be present, and a max attribute must be present if the value exceeds 1. As long as the minimum and maximum values are indicated, the actual value can be any number within that range. You can even use negative numbers:

```
<p>Rating: <meter min="-1000" max="100" value="-1000">Worst. Episode. Ever.</meter></p>
```

The meter element also accepts optional high, low, and optimum attributes, so you can indicate not only a measurement on a scale, but the relative quality of that measurement:

```
<p>Your score: <meter min="0" max="100" value="63" low="20" high="80" optimum="60">
  63%, slightly above average</meter></p>
```

That's all well and good for marking up scalar measurements with semantically rich metadata, but now comes the cool part: in place of the meter element's text contents, a supporting browser will display the measurement as a graphically rendered bar, like you see in Figure 8-29. The filled portion of the bar represents the meter's value.

Your score:

Figure 8-29. A browser replaces meter elements with a rendered bar (this image is taken from Chrome on Windows)

Chrome and Opera both present meter gauges as a gray box filled with a green bar representing the value. The bar turns yellow when the value is either high or low (if those attributes are present) or if it's equal to the min or max attributes, to indicate that the gauge has crossed the specified threshold. Unfortunately you won't have much influence over the bar's styling, so bear that in mind when you use the meter element. Different browsers render the bar in different ways, with differing levels of support for CSS to change its appearance. You can declare a width and height for the bar and perhaps add a few other decorations such as a border or a shadow, but for the most part you're stuck with the color and style the browser gives you, at least for now.

For a more complete and elaborate example, Listing 8-26 presents a collection of scores rated on a scale of zero to ten, where anything above 8 is considered a high score and anything below 2 is considered low (we haven't implied any optimum score here). We don't need to include a min attribute because the minimum score is 0, the default low end of the scale. The entire set of scores is marked up in a description list (the dl, dt, and dd elements are covered in Chapter 4).

Listing 8-26. *Displaying a set of scores with meter elements*

```
<h2>Power Levels</h2>
<dl class="power-levels">
  <dt>Strength:</dt>
  <dd><meter max="10" high="8" low="2" value="6">6</meter></dd>
  <dt>Agility:</dt>
  <dd><meter max="10" high="8" low="2" value="9">9</meter></dd>
  <dt>Stamina:</dt>
  <dd><meter max="10" high="8" low="2" value="7">7</meter></dd>
  <dt>Energy Projection:</dt>
  <dd><meter max="10" high="8" low="2" value="0">0</meter></dd>
  <dt>Combat Skills:</dt>
  <dd><meter max="10" high="8" low="2" value="7">7</meter></dd>
```

```
</dl>
```

After styling the list with a bit of CSS, that block of scores can easily look something like Figure 8-30. The `meter` element is new in HTML5 and not widely supported yet, so not every browser will render such lovely bars (this screenshot is from Opera, one of the few browsers that does support `meter` at the time we're writing this). But that's okay; browsers that don't recognize the `meter` element will simply show the element's text content.

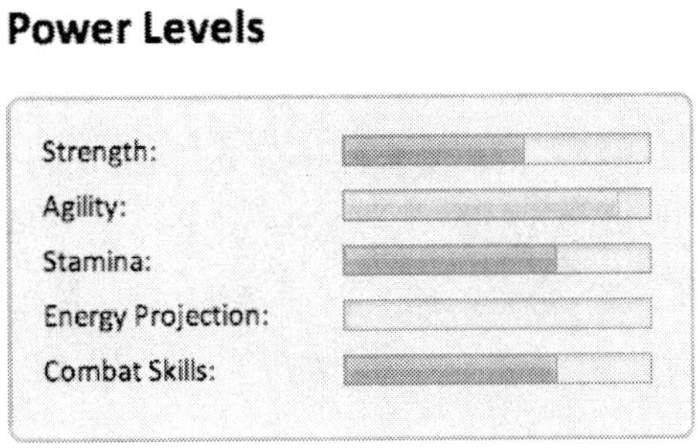

Figure 8-30. The list of scores becomes a styled box with filled gauges

Because the `meter` element results in such a graphical rendering, it's most useful for displaying general proportions and isn't necessarily appropriate for every measurement you might come across. A graphical bar is swell for visualizing a ballpark figure, but precise and specific measurements that need to be clearly understood by a reader are best expressed with plain old numbers.

Required Attributes

- `value`: specifies the current numeric value. This must be between the minimum and maximum values (`min` attribute and `max` attribute) if they are specified. If unspecified or malformed, the value is 0. If specified, but not within the range given by the `min` attribute and `max` attribute, the value is equal to the nearest end of the range.

Optional Attributes

- `min`: specifies the lower numeric boundary of the measured range. This must be less than the maximum value (`max` attribute), if specified. If unspecified, the minimum value is 0.

- `max`: specifies the upper numeric bound of the measured range. This must be greater than the minimum value (`min` attribute), if specified. If unspecified, the maximum value is 1.

- `low`: defines the upper numeric bound of the low end of the measured range; a value between the `low` and `min` attributes is considered a low measurement. This attribute's value must be greater than the minimum value (`min` attribute), and it also must be less than the high value and maximum value (`high` attribute and `max` attribute, respectively), if they are specified. If unspecified, or if less than the minimum value, the low value is equal to the minimum value.

- `high`: defines the lower numeric bound of the high end of the measured range; a value between the `high` and `max` attributes is considered a high measurement. This attribute's value must be less than the maximum value (`max` attribute), and it also must be greater than the low value and minimum value (`low` attribute and `min` attribute, respectively), if they are specified. If unspecified, or if greater than the maximum value, the high value is equal to the maximum value.

- `optimum`: indicates the optimal numeric value. It must be within the range as defined by the `min` and `max` attributes. When used with the `low` and `high` attributes, it gives an indication where along the range is considered preferable. For example, if the optimum value falls between the `min` attribute and the `low` attribute, then lower values are considered preferable.

- `form`: associates the element with a `form` element that has ownership of the `meter` element. For example, a `meter` might display a range corresponding to an `input type="number"`. The `form` attribute is only necessary if the `meter` element is being used as a form-associated element; even then, it may be omitted if the element appears as a descendant of a `form` element.

progress

Somewhat similar to the `meter` element (and also new in HTML5), the `progress` element represents the current stage in the completion of a task, rendered as a graphical bar with a filled portion to indicate the progress completed. This element is most useful in combination with JavaScript to dynamically update its value as progress is made in an application, animating the bar filling up to completion.

The progress can be indeterminate with no specified value, indicating that progress is being made but that it's not yet clear how much work is left before the task is done. For example, you might display an indeterminate progress bar while waiting for a response from a server before a process can begin:

```
<p>Upload: <progress>starting...</progress></p>
```

Or the progress can be a number in the range of zero to a maximum, giving the portion of work that has been completed thus far, specified by the optional `value` and `max` attributes:

```
<p>Processing: <progress max="100" value="77">77%</progress></p>
```

The `progress` element doesn't have a `min` attribute; the minimum is always 0. The maximum can be any positive number you like, and the `value` attribute must fall within the specified range. For rendering purposes, any value less than 0 is treated as 0, and any value greater than the maximum is treated as equal to the maximum. The default maximum is 1, hence the value must be a decimal in the range of 0 to 1 if the `max` attribute is absent.

This is a phrasing element that requires both a start and end tag, and may contain only text and other phrasing elements. As with the `meter` element, browsers that support the `progress` element will render a graphical bar, shown in Figure 8-31. Older and non-supporting browsers will display the element's contents, so that content should communicate the same value to offer a readable fallback:

```
<p>Check out: <progress max="5" value="3">Step 3 of 5</progress></p>
```

Figure 8-31. Progress bars—both indeterminate and determined—as rendered by Firefox for Mac OS X on the left and by Firefox for Windows 7 on the right.

The style of the rendered bar depends on the browser and operating system. Chrome and Firefox, for example, use the operating system's native progress bar styling (complete with animated effects in some cases), so they'll look quite different between platforms. Opera renders its own progress bar in a style similar to its style for meter elements, so Opera's bars look roughly the same on Windows, Mac, and Linux. Safari and Internet Explorer don't yet support the progress element at the time we're writing this book, but they probably will soon.

As with the meter element, styling progress bars with CSS is currently difficult and inconsistent, with some browsers honoring some CSS properties or providing their own proprietary properties and selectors, while other browsers don't currently allow any styling of progress bars at all. Not every browser yet supports this element, so be mindful when and if you choose to employ it.

Required Attributes

The progress element doesn't require any attributes. Without any attributes it represents an indeterminate progress state. Some operating systems will render indeterminate progress bars with a sweeping or scrolling animation to indicate that something is happening.

Optional Attributes

- value: a number specifying how much of the task has been completed. This attribute's value cannot be less than 0 or greater than the maximum indicated by the max attribute, or, in the absence of a max attribute, the value can't be greater than the default maximum of 1.

- max: specifies how much work the task requires in total, represented by a positive number. For example, max="100" could indicate a percentage scale, max="5" could indicate a series of 5 total steps, or max="12595.2" could indicate 12,595.2 total kilobytes (12.3 megabytes) to download a file.

Interactive Elements

The HTML language started out with an emphasis on static text documents, and to a large degree that remains its primary purpose. HTML is a fine way to mark up a limitless variety of content for easy reading. But the Web hasn't been entirely static for a long time; these days it's much more than a collection of academic research papers. The advent of the web app has advanced the Web beyond its roots as a cross-referenced document repository.

Previous versions of HTML didn't provide meaningful elements for all the different kinds of interactive content web apps call for. Developers have long made due with the elements at hand, thrusting new functionality onto elements that weren't specifically designed for it. Part of the evolving HTML5 specification began its life as a spec originally dubbed "Web Applications 1.0," which was intended to standardize a set of elements and methods for managing interactive content in web pages.

details and summary

The details element represents a collapsible block of content from which a user can obtain additional information or, when used in a form or application, additional controls or interactive functions. The details element can contain any kind of content or other elements—including nested details elements—and a user or script can expand or collapse the containing element to show or hide its contents.

This sort of "expand and collapse" effect was previously only possible with JavaScript, but the details element makes such behavior native to the browsers without the need for additional scripts. However, only a few browsers have yet implemented support for the details element, so you'll still need JavaScript to achieve the expand-and-collapse effect in other browsers.

Listing 8-27 shows an example of a details element containing additional product information that can be hidden from view when the page loads, but the user can show it if they'd like to see more information.

Listing 8-27. *Collapsible product information in a details element*

```
<div class="item">
  <h3>V900 Portable Shrink Ray</h3>
  <p>Shrink and unshrink inanimate objects with point-and-shoot simplicity!</p>
  <p><strong class="price">$10,799</strong></p>
  <details>
    <summary>Product info</summary>
    <dl>
      <dt>Colors</dt>
      <dd>Midnight black, cherry red, powder blue, violet mist, seafoam green</dd>
      <dt>Dimensions</dt>
      <dd>10.8 x 4.3 x 8.5 inches (27.5 x 10.9 x 21.6 cm)</dd>
      <dt>Shipping Weight</dt>
      <dd>2.8 pounds (1.27 kg)</dd>
      <dt>Power Supply</dt>
      <dd>4.4mW quantum fusion battery (included)</dd>
    </dl>
  </details>
</div>
```

A details element is initially closed when a browser renders the page. Alternatively, the Boolean open attribute can instruct the browser to automatically show the contents of the details element when the page loads, and a user can hide it if they so desire. Browsers that don't support the details element will always show it in an opened, visible state.

The nested summary element acts as a title or legend for its parent details element. Browsers that support these elements (such as Chrome, shown in Figure 8-32) will automatically add a visual indicator to the summary to indicate whether the details are open or closed. If a summary element is absent, supporting browsers will supply their own default show/hide toggle with a default text label such as

"Details" or a localized equivalent (in browsers localized in other languages). The summary element can only contain text or phrasing elements; sorry, no headings allowed.

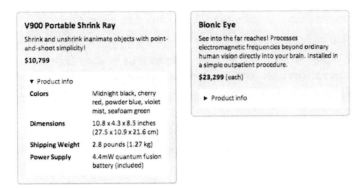

Figure 8-32. Two examples of the details and summary elements in Chrome, with a bit of additional styling. The box on the left shows a details element in the opened state and the one on the right is closed.

Chrome is the only browser to support collapsing details elements without JavaScript at the time we're writing this. These elements are still very new and there are lingering questions about styling, interaction, and accessibility that need to be hammered out, but more browsers should implement these elements soon.

Required Attributes

Neither the details nor summary elements require any attributes.

Optional Attributes

- open: a Boolean attribute indicating that the details element should be open when the page initially loads.

menu

The menu element represents a list of commands or actions the user can trigger. In a supporting browser, the menu might be presented in a contextual "right click" menu, as a menu in the browser's toolbar, or as an ordinary list on the page (which could be styled any number of ways with CSS). You can indicate the type of menu with the optional type attribute and the values context, toolbar, or list, with list being the default type if the attribute is missing or empty.

This element was first introduced long ago, but was formally deprecated in HTML 4, only to be resurrected and redefined in HTML5. Unfortunately it's rather difficult for us to demonstrate how the menu element works because not a single browser in the land has properly implemented it at the time of writing. Some browsers (Firefox, for example) do support a form of contextual menus using the menu element, but the particular implementation is outdated and not compliant with the current state of the HTML5 specification. So we're afraid our coverage of the menu and command elements will be pure theory from here on.

A menu element is flow content and requires both a start and end tag. It can contain any other flow content, including nested menus, or if the menu is a list, its commands can each be contained in an li element (covered in Chapter 4). The commands in a menu element can take the form of command elements (which we'll cover next), but they can also be links, buttons, or other form controls.

Although there are some surface similarities, don't confuse the menu element with the nav element (also covered in Chapter 4). A nav element contains navigational links to other pages on the Web or sections of the same page, whereas a menu element contains executable commands, not navigation links (even if those commands are represented by a elements).

Required Attributes

There aren't any required attributes for the menu element.

Optional Attributes

- type: indicates the type of menu being declared, either list, context, or toolbar. If this attribute is missing or empty, list is the default menu type.
- label: a text label for the menu that browsers will display in a contextual menu or toolbar.

command

The command element represents an executable command in a menu element, or it can appear anywhere else in a document to represent a keyboard shortcut. It's a void element that can contain no text and must not have an end tag, but you can self-close it with a trailing slash if you're a stickler for XHTML syntax. A label attribute provides the text label that will be visible to the user, and an optional icon attribute can include a graphic icon for the command (the attribute's value is the icon image's URL).

There are three types of commands, indicated by the optional type attribute: command (the default if type is missing or empty), radio (similar to a radio button in that it represents an option in a set where only one choice is allowed), or checkbox (represents a toggle or an option in a set that allows multiple selections, much like a form checkbox).

Listing 8-28 shows a menu element containing a set of commands. This is a contextual menu, as indicated by the menu element's type attribute, so it would appear when a user right-clicks on the page or on a target element that carries the menu's ID in its contextmenu attribute, first mentioned way back in Chapter 2 (Go on, flip back to it. We'll wait.). Each command is a mutually exclusive radio option, all belonging to the same "colors" set. Selecting one of the commands triggers the chColor JavaScript function (which we just made up for this example).

Listing 8-28. *A contextual menu using the menu and command elements*

```
<menu type="context" id="color" label="Change color">
  <command type="radio" radiogroup="colors" label="Black" onclick="chColor('black')">
  <command type="radio" radiogroup="colors" label="Red" onclick="chColor('red')">
  <command type="radio" radiogroup="colors" label="Blue" onclick="chColor('blue')">
</menu>
```

We would love to show you a screen capture of what this menu looks like in a browser, but because no browsers yet support these elements, you'll just have to use your imagination. The current lack of browser support also means the `menu` and `command` elements aren't really practical to use right now, but hopefully they'll be usable in the very near future.

Required Attributes

- `label`: the name of the command as shown to the user.

Optional Attributes

- `checked`: a Boolean attribute that, when present, indicates that the command is preselected when the page initially loads (or has been toggled by some other action, if the attribute is added dynamically).

- `disabled`: a Boolean attribute indicating that the command can't be selected.

- `icon`: an image representing the command or decorating its text label. This attribute's value is the URL of an image file.

- `radiogroup`: gives the name of the group of commands (with a type="radio"), that will be toggled when the command itself is toggled. This attribute can only be present when the command's `type` attribute is `radio`.

- `type`: indicates the type of command the element represents, either `command` (the default), `radio`, or `checkbox`.

Styling Forms with CSS

As we've said before, form controls will appear slightly different in just about every browser on the planet. This is true partly because they're not strictly web elements; they're basic elements of any graphical user interface. Many web browsers that run on desktop computers or mobile devices don't possess any ingrained presentation logic for rendering form controls. Rather, they call upon the local operating system to display those controls in whatever visual style is native for that operating system.

Most browsers for Mac OS X rely on that operating system's standard rendering of form controls, so buttons, checkboxes, and selection menus on a Mac appear in glossy, candy-coated splendor. Internet Explorer is such a deeply entrenched part of the Windows operating system that form controls will look completely different under Windows 7 compared to what you'd see in the same browser running under Windows Vista. Firefox, Chrome, and Opera—all available for Windows, Macintosh, and Linux—render form controls in different ways on each of those platforms because they employ different native controls.

Figure 8-33 shows the same form in both Safari for the latest Mac OS X and Internet Explorer 7 for Windows XP (long outdated, but many people around the world still use it). You can see just how differently these controls are presented.

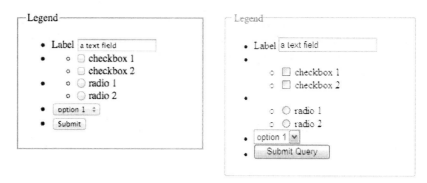

Figure 8-33. A comparison of common form elements as rendered by two very different browsers: Safari on the left and Internet Explorer on the right.

In the end, web designers must accept the inescapable fact that forms—like many other elements on a web page—will never look the same in every browser. With that acceptance comes a Zen-like relinquishing of control. In many cases, it's simply best to leave form controls alone and allow the browsers to display them in whatever style they will. This isn't to say that form controls can never be styled, just that perhaps sometimes they shouldn't be.

A person who regularly uses a particular browser on a particular operating system tends to grow accustomed to a consistent presentation of form-related interface elements. They'll become trained to recognize text fields, drop-down selections, and buttons in that familiar style because they see them every day. Deviating too far from that norm—by making a submit button look like a text link, for example—may breach your visitor's expectations and make the form more difficult to use ("I'm looking for the submit button, but all I can find is a text link!").

Despite these admonitions against overly styling form controls, and despite warnings that not all browsers will equally honor CSS rules applied to those controls, it's still usually possible to affect their appearance. Many browsers do, in fact, allow extensive alteration of a form control's rendering; its color, typography, borders, and background can all be modified through CSS, and pretty consistently in the current generation of browsers. Browsers that don't honor those style properties will simply display the control in its default style. In keeping with the principles of progressive enhancement and graceful degradation, browsers that support the CSS will display the control as designed, and those that don't support the CSS…won't. The control will still function just as it should.

As a guiding principle, try not to overdesign your form controls, and those form controls should still look like what they are. A text field should still look like a text field, and a button should look like a button.

> *Roger Johansson has explored the rendering of form elements in a wide range of browsers on several operating systems, including tests of how those browsers honor or disregard CSS rules applied to those elements. See his extensive collection of tests and demonstrations at 456bereastreet.com/lab/styling-form-controls-revisited/*

With all of that said, a web designer can easily, through artful application of CSS, influence the overall layout and design of the form and the page in which it resides. The presentation of the controls themselves may sometimes be beyond the designer's reach, but the elements around them are fair game for styling.

Removing the Border from fieldsets

The majority of web browsers display a `fieldset` element with a border and a bit of padding by default. The border exists for a reason—to visually indicate the boundaries of the group—but it's not always a desirable part of a design. Luckily you can disable the border very easily with CSS, as you see in Listing 8-29.

Listing 8-29. *The `border` property with a value of none*

```
fieldset {
  border: none;
}
```

The none keyword instructs the browser to override any default or inherited values for border-style; if the style is none, there's no border at all. You can accomplish the same feat with border:0, declaring 0 as the value for border-width, and saving a few bytes in the process by eliminating three more characters from your style sheet.

The border property is CSS shorthand, automatically applying the same value to all four sides of an element without the need to call out each side individually. There is also an equivalent padding shorthand property, shown in Listing 8-30, affecting the padding on all four sides of a box with a single declaration.

Listing 8-30. *The `border` and `padding` properties set to 0*

```
fieldset {
  border: 0;
  padding: 0;
}
```

You can see the result in Figure 8-34. This is the same form you saw in Figure 8-27, only now the fieldsets vanish into white space. The elements still exist in the markup, bringing all their semantic and accessibility benefits with them, but their presentation has been altered to reduce visual clutter. We've also removed the standard bullets from the unordered list, as you saw in Chapter 4, and we've shifted the list items to the left to align with the other elements. It still isn't pretty, but it's a start in the right direction.

Figure 8-34. The form as it appears without borders or padding around the field sets

Aligning Labels

Being a phrasing element and styled as inline by default, a `label` will be only as wide as its text content, and that text will rest on the same baseline as its adjacent content, just as any ordinary text would. But what if your form has a stack of several controls with labels of different widths? By default, it will look something like Figure 8-35. Surely we can tidy this up a bit.

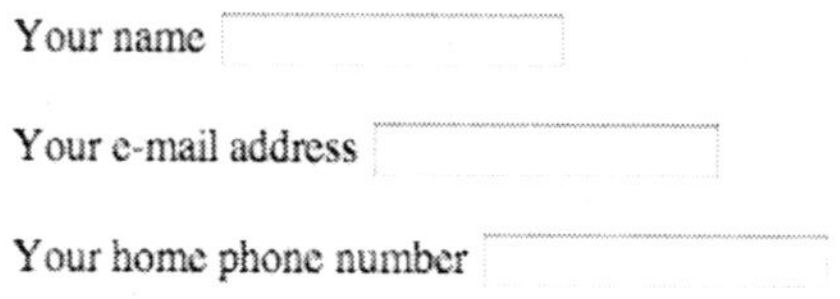

Your name

Your e-mail address

Your home phone number

Figure 8-35. Labels of different widths are staggered and unsightly

Inline phrasing elements can be treated as block-level with the simple CSS declaration `display:block`, overriding the browser's default style (`display:inline`). However, that will also cause the `label`s to each appear on its own line—as any other block-level element would—rather than to the left of the control. If the `label` element is instead floated to the left, the text field can then flow up onto the same line. It so happens that any floated element is automatically styled as a block-level element as well, so the `display:block` declaration isn't even necessary in combination with `float:left`.

Once the `label`s have become floating blocks, giving each of them the same width will push their related text fields to the right, aligning them in a straight column. The text will still be aligned to the left of the label, resulting in varying gaps of white space between the labels and their controls. You can align the text to the right instead, and a margin will put some distance between the labels and their controls. Listing 8-31 shows the final CSS rule, converting all `label` elements within the element with the class "info" (whatever that element may be, even the parent `form` itself) to floating blocks 200 pixels wide.

Listing 8-31. *A CSS rule aligning the labels and controls into columns*

```
.info label {
  float: left;
  width: 200px;
  text-align: right;
  margin-right: 15px;
}
```

You can see the results in Figure 8-36, where the labels and text fields now align in two neat columns. The label text is aligned to the right, and the margin creates some space between the label and its control.

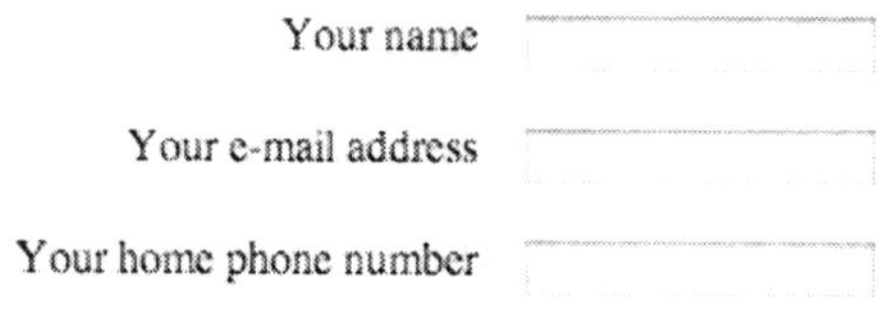

Your name

Your e-mail address

Your home phone number

Figure 8-36. The same form with the CSS applied

If that layout isn't to your liking and you'd prefer the labels above the controls, a simple `display: block`, as in Listing 8-32, does the trick. There's no need for floats or widths; simply styling the `label` element as block-level will put it on its own line. A small bottom margin adds a bit of space to keep things clean, and we've declared the margin with an em unit so it's proportional to the size of the text (0.25em is one quarter of the font size).

Listing 8-32. *A CSS rule styling all label elements as block-level*

```
label {
  display: block;
  margin-bottom: 0.25em;
}
```

Figure 8-37 shows the results, with the labels above their associated fields.

Figure 8-37. The labels are now styled as block-level so each appears on its own line

Changing Fonts in Form Controls

Browsers typically render text in an `input`, `select`, `textarea`, or `button` element in a default size and typeface that may differ from the default font for regular body text. Furthermore, this default form font persists in spite of any base font you've declared for the rest of the document (as you learned in Chapter 4). That's because the browser's built-in style sheet declares fonts specifically for form elements rather than allowing them to inherit their font settings as other elements do. There are good reasons for this, since it's especially important for form elements to be readable and render consistently, but it can still be a thorn in a designer's side.

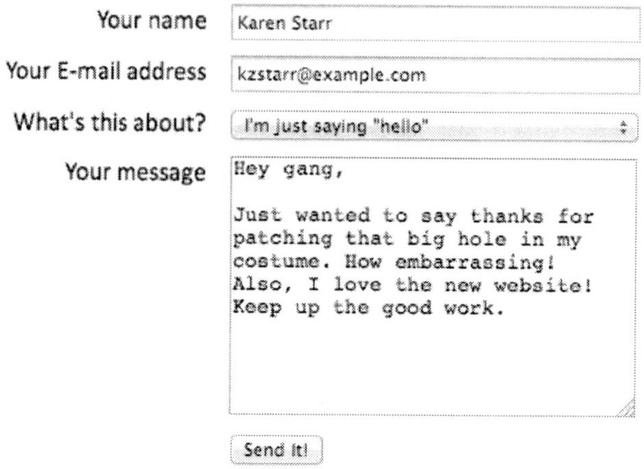

Figure 8-38. The label text is rendered in Calibri, as inherited from the body element, but text in the various form elements is in a different font and at a different size.

To overcome the default typeface, you could declare the font-family property specifically for the input, select, textarea, and button elements. However, if you'd like those elements to share the same font family as the rest of your page, you needn't re-declare the same font properties you applied to the body element; you can instead use the inherit keyword, as shown in Listing 8-33.

Listing 8-33. *A simple CSS rule instructing form controls to inherit values for font-family and font-size*

```
input, select, textarea, button {
  font-family: inherit;
  font-size: inherit;
}
```

Some properties in CSS—including most font properties—are *inherited*, passed down from parent elements to child elements. The inherit keyword instructs the browser to use the same value for this property that was applied to the element's parent. Because the value of font-family is automatically inherited by every other element (except these pesky form controls), the browser will follow the document tree all the way up to the body element to determine what font and size values to use, assuming no other ancestor along the way has been assigned a different value.

This CSS rule also combines all four elements into a single selector, separated by commas. Whenever the same set of declarations is meant to apply to several elements, you can merge them into a single CSS rule to minimize redundancy and keep your style sheet clean.

Figure 8-39 shows the same form, now with a consistent font family and size in all the form controls. The controls have also grown in size a bit because their size is determined by the font size.

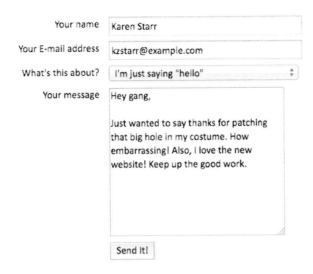

Figure 8-39. The controls now inherit their font styles—16px Calibri, in this case—from their parent element.

Summary

Forms are a vital and integral part of the World Wide Web. They open the flow of communication so information can move in both directions—from the website to the user and from the user back to the website. They're also the transit system that makes Internet commerce possible; there would be no e-commerce in a Web without forms. A form in HTML is composed of a wide variety of controls, each with a distinct purpose and function, designed for gathering and processing different types of data. You can (and should) enhance the structure and utility of a form by grouping controls into field sets and giving each control a clear label.

HTML5 introduces a number of new form controls, tailored for common types of data beyond ordinary, freeform text. We now have access to specialized input types for searching, e-mail addresses, URLs, phone numbers, dates and times, numbers and ranges, and even colors. HTML5 also brings new elements for displaying form-related data, and new interactive elements for the next generation of web apps.

Although the components of a form are fairly straightforward, constructing an attractive, usable, accessible, and functional form can be a real challenge, especially if that form is long and complex. By putting yourself into your visitors' shoes and thinking about the meaning and purpose of your forms, you can assemble forms and applications that will meet all of these goals. Usable forms improve the interactive Web experience. Your visitors will appreciate it.

Different browsers running on different operating systems render form elements in very different styles. Even so, the structural markup around those form controls can be extensively styled with CSS. You can use CSS to influence the visual organization and arrangement of your forms, making them more attractive for most of your visitors without harming the underlying structure. You'll learn a lot more about using CSS to control and enhance the visual layout of your web pages in the next chapter.

Chapter 9

Page Layout with CSS

Over the last eight chapters you've become familiar with all the HTML elements you'll need to build your own web pages. Along the way you've picked up a healthy dose of CSS, learning how to give your content a bit more style and learning a few useful effects and techniques. Most of the CSS tips we've shown you so far have been on a relatively small scale, styling individual elements or limited aspects of your content. In this chapter we're finally going to tackle the bigger picture and show you a few ways you can use CSS to lay out your web pages.

In years past, before CSS was widely supported or adopted, web designers used HTML tables to lay out their pages (and many still do, sadly). As you saw in Chapter 7, a table forms a natural grid making it relatively trivial to arrange content into aligned rows and columns. But that was never the intended purpose of tables in HTML. Tables are for tabular data, where all the information in a row is related in some way, and all the information in a column is related in another way. The intersection of a row and a column in a table forms a single point of data combining the meaning of its row and its column. That's how tables work, that's what tables are for, and that's how tables are read.

Using a table to create arbitrary rows and columns for purely presentational purposes is an abuse of the element's natural function. It's equivalent to using the blockquote element to artificially indent content that isn't a quotation at all—another crime many web designers committed before they learned CSS. A layout table repurposes and misappropriates a browser's standard display of one element to achieve a visual effect for a completely different kind of content. It's the epitome of presentational markup, using HTML only for how it looks and completely ignoring what it means.

Layout tables also tend to require a lot of extraneous markup, enforce their own rules for how you order your content, and can seriously hinder accessibility for people who use screen readers or use a keyboard to navigate. They can also be difficult to maintain and modify when you want to alter your layout during the next redesign—and pretty much every website *will* be redesigned eventually, you can count on it.

Thankfully you have the power of CSS at your fingertips. It's a language specifically designed for describing the presentation of content, and much more suited to arranging elements on the page. But even as powerful as CSS is, it still isn't really ideal for describing page layout, at least in its current state. Something you can easily draw on paper or in Photoshop can be a real challenge to achieve in a browser using clean markup and CSS, and the more complex the design the more challenging it can be. If you're just starting out it's going to take some time to learn all the ins and outs and tricks of the trade.

We can't possibly cover every nuanced facet of laying out a complex design with CSS in this one chapter, or even in one book. As with so many aspects of computing and web development, designing with CSS is something you'll pick up gradually through reading other books and tutorials, or from attending classes and lectures. Most importantly, you'll learn a lot through practice and experimentation. This chapter will help to set you on the right path.

The Box Model

Every rendered element on a web page resides in a rectangular box, whether you can see it or not. The box in turn has a number of associated properties in CSS, all of which are described in the *box model*—the formatting rules for how browsers should draw these boxes and how they interact with other boxes on the page. Laying out a page with CSS is essentially an exercise in arranging boxes, so it's worth taking a little time to understand the box itself. You can see a diagram of the CSS box model in Figure 9-1.

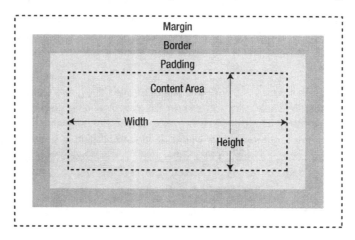

Figure 9-1. The parts of the CSS box model

Block-level elements (those styled with `display:block` in either a browser's default style sheet or in your own) form boxes that expand horizontally to the width of their parent box and vertically to the height of their contents. Working from the inside out, *padding* is the transparent space between a box's content area and its edge, and any background colors or images will fill the padding space as well. The *border* is a decorated line drawn around the outer edge of the padding space (or around the content area if there is no padding), and the *margin* is transparent spacing between the border (or edge of the box, if it has no border) and the box's neighboring content.

The width and height properties in CSS can define—no surprise here—the width and height of a box. Somewhat less self-explanatory is that the width and height properties apply only to the *content area* of the box, and any padding or borders are *added to* any declared dimensions. This seems counter-intuitive at first, and has confused many designers when they start using CSS for page layout. After all, when you buy a new appliance, they put the foam padding *inside* the box. When you declare dimensions in CSS you're actually declaring the size of the *content area* and not the box drawn around it.

A box 300 pixels wide with 5 pixels of padding on each side and a 5 pixel border will take up 320 pixels on the rendered page; 5px + 5px + 300px + 5px + 5px = 320px. If you wanted a box exactly 300 pixels wide, including the 20 pixels of padding and borders, you would need to give it a width of 280 pixels (width:280px;).

You can specify box dimensions with the value auto (the default, which just lets a browser calculate the size of the box automatically), a percentage of the box's parent element, or a length using any unit of measure available in CSS—px (pixels), pt (points), pc (picas), in (inches), cm (centimeters), mm (millimeters), em (equal to the element's font size), or ex (the x-height of the element's font).

If the contents of a box exceed its specified dimensions, those contents will overflow the boundaries of the box. Text will automatically wrap to fit within the width you specify, assuming the box is wide enough to accommodate the longest word; long, unwrapping words will overflow horizontally. Heights, though, can be harder to predict. Fonts and font sizes can (and will) vary depending on user preferences and the fonts they have installed. Different browsers also render text in subtly different ways, so, for example, a sentence that fits neatly on one line in Chrome might wrap to a second line in Internet Explorer. Given the fluid nature of text on the web, it's usually best to avoid declaring a height for any element containing text, instead allowing the box to automatically adjust to the height of its contents.

Margins and Padding

Margins are transparent space between the outside edge of a box and the content or elements that surround it. You can specify margins for each side of a box separately, using a different value for each side, if you like:

```
.intro {
  margin-top: 20px;
  margin-bottom: 2em;
  margin-left: 5%;
  margin-right: 5%;
}
```

To apply the same margin to all four sides at once, the shorthand margin property will spare you a lot of repetition:

```
.intro { margin: 20px; }
```

The margin property can accept up to four values, separated by spaces, applying each value to each side in clockwise order: top, right, bottom, left:

```
.intro { margin: 20px 5% 2em 5%; }
```

With two values, the first will apply to the top and bottom and the second will apply to the left and right. For example, this rule adds a 20 pixel margin to both the top and bottom of the box, and a 5% margin to both the left and right sides:

```
.intro { margin: 20px 5%; }
```

When there are three values, the first sets the top margin, the second applies to both the right and left sides, and the third value sets the bottom margin:

```
.intro { margin: 20px 5% 2em; }
```

Padding is space between the content area and border, and you can specify padding in much the same way as margins, with a separate declaration for each side of the box:

```
.intro {
  padding-top: 1em;
  padding-bottom: 1.5em;
  padding-left: 20px;
  padding-right: 40px;
}
```

Or use the shorthand padding property, with two, three, or four values. This rule applies no padding to the top of the box, 10% padding to the left and right sides, and 1.5 ems of padding (which is one and a half times the height of the current font size) to the bottom:

```
.intro { padding: 0 10% 1.5em; }
```

Borders

A border is a decorative line drawn around the outside of a box and it has three distinct characteristics: a width, a style, and a color. You can declare each of them separately for each side of a box:

```
.intro {
  border-top-width: 3px;
  border-top-style: dashed;
  border-top-color: red;
  border-right-width: 1em;
  border-right-style: dotted;
  border-right-color: blue;
}
```

You can see that this might become a pretty verbose style rule by the time you make it all the way around a four-sided box. Thankfully there are a number of shorthand properties for borders to save you a lot of typing. You can declare all three traits in a single declaration, declaring each side separately:

```
.intro {
  border-top: 3px dashed red;
  border-right: 1em dotted blue;
  border-bottom: 1px solid orange;
  border-left: 0.25in double green;
}
```

Or declare all four sides at once with the shorthand `border` property (note that the order of the three values doesn't matter):

```
.intro { border-top: purple 3px double; }
```

Furthermore, you can declare a single border trait for each side of the box the same way you can declare padding and margins, going clockwise around the box in order: top, right, bottom, left:

```
.intro {
  border-width: 3px 1em 1px 0.25in;
  border-style: dashed dotted solid double;
  border-color: red blue orange green;
}
```

As with padding and margins, these shorthand border properties also take two or three values for matching sides, or one value for all four sides:

```
.intro {
  border-width: 6px;
  border-style: dashed solid;
  border-color: red blue green;
}
```

Border widths can't be specified as percentages, but you can use any unit of measure, or use the keywords `thin`, `medium`, or `thick`. The value `thin` is usually equal to 1px, `medium` is usually 3px, and `thick` is usually 5px, but these may vary across browsers. A border width of 0 will effectively disable the border, useful for removing borders that are present by default or that carry over from some other rule in your style sheet.

Borders come in a variety of styles, designated by keyword:

- `none`: no border.

- `hidden`: no border, the same as `none`, but this value is specifically intended to resolve rendering conflicts in table elements. For elements that aren't part of a table, use `none`.

- `dotted`: a line of evenly spaced dots. The dots may be round or square in thicker borders, depending on the browser.

- `dashed`: a dashed line. Thicker borders have longer dashes, in proportion to the border width.

- `solid`: a solid line.

- `double`: two solid, parallel lines. The lines plus the space between them totals the border width.

- `groove`: a solid border with highlights and shading as if it were engraved into the page surface.

- `ridge`: the opposite of `groove`, this border reverses the lighting effect so the border appears raised from the page surface.

- `inset`: appears as if the box is set into the page, with the top and left borders shaded and the right and bottom borders highlighted, as though it were three dimensional and lit from the top left.

- outset: the opposite of inset, this reverses the lighting effect so the box appears raised from the page surface.

Figure 9-2 shows examples of these border styles—all except none and hidden, of course.

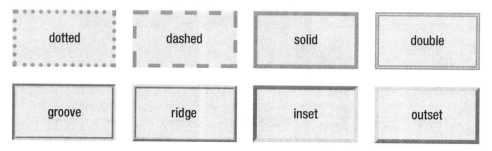

Figure 9-2. CSS border styles. These each have a width of 5 pixels.

Page Width: Fixed vs. Liquid

At a point early in the process of designing and assembling any website with CSS, you'll have to make an important decision: will your site's layout have a fixed width that is always the same no matter how wide the browser window is, or will its width be liquid and adjust dynamically to the window's width? This has been a topic of much lively debate among web designers for years.

Many designers create sites with a fixed width because it allows for precise alignment of the page elements in a predictable, rigid grid. Other designers prefer liquid widths that flex automatically, letting viewers set their browsers as wide or as narrow as they like while the page layout adjusts to their preferences.

Fixed Width

A fixed width layout (sometimes called a *static* layout) has its overall page width declared in an absolute unit of measure, usually pixels, and that width stays the same regardless of the size of the browser window. This is appealing to many designers because it affords them more control over how elements line up and how they fit within the page space.

To be honest, fixed width layouts are also easier to build. That may be the real reason they're so common and popular. A fixed layout is rigid and predictable—a pixel is always a pixel. You can set all your widths, padding, and margins in pixels and know they won't shift at the whim of the user. It eliminates one more variable from the complicated job of designing a website with CSS.

But a fixed width doesn't allow for a browser window that's narrower than the design, forcing part of the page to run off to one side, obscuring valuable content and causing the dreaded horizontal scroll bar (perhaps more properly called a *crawl bar*). Users with narrow windows have to drag the bar to the left or right to see all the content. On the other hand, narrow fixed layouts intended for small screens can waste a lot of screen real estate in wider windows that could easily display more content. That may be an aesthetic choice by the designer, but it disregards the choice of the viewer.

Figure 9-3 shows a fixed width web page in three windows. The page doesn't fit into a very narrow window, and it sits in the middle of a very wide window, leaving a lot of space that could otherwise be put to use.

Figure 9-3. A fixed width layout at three different window widths

Liquid Width

A liquid width layout (also called *fluid* or *dynamic*) has its width specified using percentages rather than fixed lengths. The outermost containing element—perhaps the body element but it could be some other container—is given a width that is a percentage of the browser window, and any elements inside it are given percentage widths based on the width of that container. The entire page can automatically adjust to fit whatever window width each viewer prefers (or that her device dictates), returning some control to the user. Figure 9-4 shows the same liquid layout page in three different windows, each time adjusting to the environment and rearranging the content to fit. But allowing for that much flexibility can be a chore for the developer; there are many more ways it can go wrong.

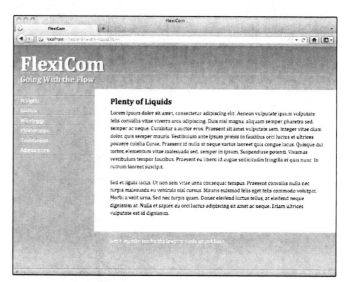
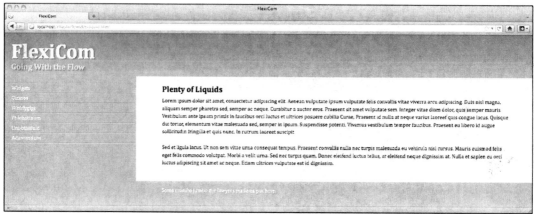

Figure 9-4. A liquid width layout in three different window widths

Liquid layouts require some additional planning and testing to build in some allowances for boxes to contract and expand and for content to reflow. Very narrow windows can become uncomfortably cramped and elements might collide and overlap. Very wide windows can cause text to stretch out to long lines that are harder to read, and can leave elements stranded in too much white space. It's no wonder many beginning web developers throw their hands up in frustration with liquid layouts, only to fall back on a simpler fixed layout.

> *Although liquid layouts offer a lot more flexibility, you can still run into trouble when the page is squeezed too narrow or stretched too wide. There are elegant solutions to these extreme situations, and we'll investigate some of them in Chapter 10. Stay tuned.*

Although fixed width layouts are easier to build, there's something intrinsically un-web-like about the fixed approach. A printed page is a tangible thing wrought from wood pulp and ink, with a predetermined width and height that will never change. You know exactly what you're in for when you lay something out on paper. But a web page isn't tangible; it's a constantly changing mosaic of pixels living in a browser portal of unknowable dimensions. The Web as a medium is unpredictable by its very nature. Rather than fight that fact and attempt to impose print-like precision on an imprecise canvas, perhaps it's better to embrace the natural fluidity of the Web and design *for* it instead of *against* it.

So in the end, which is better: fixed or liquid? The answer is easy: *it depends*. Some sites lend themselves better to a liquid layout, and others may work best with a fixed width. Consider your content and your audience, weigh the options, and make an informed choice. With that said, it's almost impossible to go wrong with a liquid layout, even if it's a bit trickier to build. In an age when people are carrying three-inch-wide computers in their pockets and web surfing on eight-foot-wide televisions in their living rooms, a bit more forethought in the design and construction phase can make your web sites work better for everyone.

Floating Columns

Many—if not most—web pages organize content into more than one vertical column. It's a design tradition that goes way back to the earliest days of written language and will probably remain in fashion for a long time to come (though you'll find many single-column layouts on the Web, too). A typical web page layout often consists of a main content area and one or more sidebars for supplemental content, navigation, advertising, and so on. Arranging content into columns is the most common layout challenge you'll face, and you will face it time and time again. One of the most tried and true solutions to this common predicament employs the `float` property, which we first introduced back in Chapter 5.

Unless otherwise specified, block-level elements stack one on top of another in the same order in which they occur in the markup. Text and inline elements lay down in courses, fitting as many words onto a line as possible before the excess words wrap to the next line, stacking more courses like bricks. This is the *normal flow* of content; wrapping lines of text filling the width of block boxes stacked up in source order. CSS lets you break away from that normal flow, singling out elements, altering their dimensions, and moving them around on the page.

The original purpose of the float property was simply to wrap text around an image, just as you've seen before. A floated element is partially removed from the normal flow of content and shifted to the left or right as far as it will go, until it runs into the edge of its containing box (inside any padding or border) or into another floated element. Any content that appears after a floated element then flows up and around that floating block like a stream around a boulder.

We can repurpose this shifting and flowing behavior of floating boxes to form vertical columns of content. In a nutshell, simply wrap each block of content in a box and float those boxes in opposite directions (or even the same direction) and they'll line up side by side in tidy columns. Of course, it's just a *little* bit more complicated than that.

To begin, Listing 9-1 shows the markup we'll be working with. In this case it's a section element containing the main content of the page, and another section element containing supplemental content. These could be different elements, such as an article and an aside, or two divs, or a section and a figure, and so on, but we'll use sections for this demonstration. We've given each section an appropriate class—"main" and "extra", respectively—to describe how they differ semantically and also to make them easier to target in our CSS.

Listing 9-1. Two sections of content

```
<section class="main">
  <h1>Welcome, Heroes!</h1>

  <p>Power Outfitters offers top of the line merchandise at rock-bottom
  prices for the discerning costumed crime-fighter. From belts to boomerangs,
  we're your one-stop shop for all your specialized gadgetry and costuming
  needs.</p>

  <p>Come browse our wide selection of capes, cowls, masks, boots, belts,
  gloves, tights, unitards, and leotards in all the colors of the rainbow.
  Our clothiers are on call 24 hours a day, always ready in a pinch to
  replace a singed cloak or patch a ripped tunic, because we know crime
  doesn't sleep and justice can never rest.</p>
</section>

<section class="extra">
  <p><strong>Power Outfitters</strong>
  <br>616 Kirby Ave, between Romita and Ditko
  <br>Mon-Thu: 8am-10pm
  <br>Fri-Sun: 8am-12pm
  <br>24-hour service and repair: call 555-1961</p>
</section>
```

By assigning each of these sections a width and floating them in opposite directions, as we've done in Listing 9-2, we can achieve the coveted two-column layout. We'll add some background colors as well so you can clearly see the two boxes in Figure 9-5.

Listing 9-2. Applying opposite floats to form adjacent columns

```
.main {
  width: 60%;
  float: left;
  background-color: #e6f2f9;
}

.extra {
  width: 40%;
  float: right;
  background-color: #c3deee;
}
```

Welcome, Heroes!

Power Outfitters offers top of the line merchandise at rock-bottom prices for the discerning costumed crime-fighter. From belts to boomerangs, we're your one-stop shop for all your specialized gadgetry and costuming needs.

Come browse our wide selection of capes, cowls, masks, boots, belts, gloves, tights, unitards, and leotards in all the colors of the rainbow. Our clothiers are on call 24 hours a day, always ready in a pinch to replace a singed cloak or patch a ripped tunic, because we know crime doesn't sleep and justice can never rest.

Power Outfitters
616 Kirby Ave, between Romita and Ditko
Mon-Thu: 8am-10pm
Fri-Sun: 8am-12pm
24-hour service and repair: call 555-1961

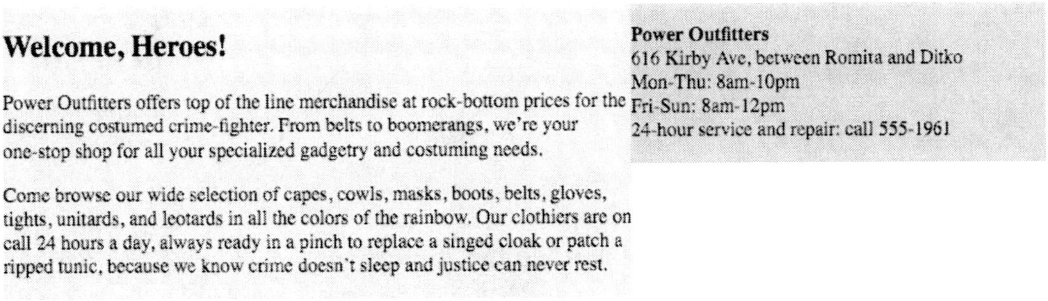

Figure 9-5. The two floated `sections` form two columns

Not a bad start, but those boxes look a bit cramped and in need of some padding. We'll use percentages for the side padding, to keep our overall width liquid:

```
.main {
  width: 60%;
  float: left;
  background-color: #e6f2f9;
  padding: 15px 3%;
}

.extra {
  width: 40%;
  float: right;
  background-color: #c3deee;
  padding: 15px 3%;
}
```

But now there's a problem, as you can see in Figure 9-6: the second box drops below the first. That's because padding is *added to* the declared width, so our two boxes are each now wider by 6% (3% padding on each side). Added together, the two boxes are wider than the available space—66% plus 46% is 112%—so the second box wraps under the first.

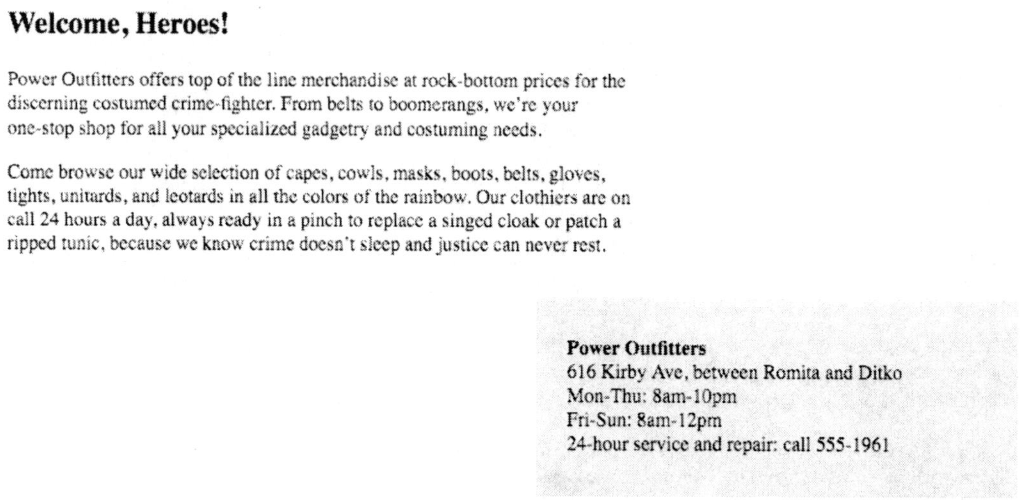

Welcome, Heroes!

Power Outfitters offers top of the line merchandise at rock-bottom prices for the discerning costumed crime-fighter. From belts to boomerangs, we're your one-stop shop for all your specialized gadgetry and costuming needs.

Come browse our wide selection of capes, cowls, masks, boots, belts, gloves, tights, unitards, and leotards in all the colors of the rainbow. Our clothiers are on call 24 hours a day, always ready in a pinch to replace a singed cloak or patch a ripped tunic, because we know crime doesn't sleep and justice can never rest.

Power Outfitters
616 Kirby Ave, between Romita and Ditko
Mon-Thu: 8am-10pm
Fri-Sun: 8am-12pm
24-hour service and repair: call 555-1961

Figure 9-6. When floating elements are too wide to fit in the available space, later floating elements drop under previous floating elements.

If two elements are floating next to each other and one (or both) of them becomes too wide for the containing element to accommodate them together, the floating boxes will collide and whichever element comes later in the source order will wrap under the previous element. Think of the boxes as two giant words and you'll see they wrap to new lines the same way text does when it runs out of room. (This is also true with any number of floating boxes; if there isn't enough width for all of them to line up, later boxes will wrap under previous boxes.)

You can prevent disastrous "float drop" by ensuring that the elements' combined widths never exceed their container's width. To make sure these floating boxes remain side by side, we'll need to adjust their widths to accommodate the padding. We can even make them a bit narrower than strictly necessary to leave a nice gutter between the columns (see Figure 9-7):

```
.main {
  width: 52%;
  float: left;
  background-color: #e6f2f9;
  padding: 15px 3%;
}

.extra {
  width: 32%;
  float: right;
  background-color: #c3deee;
  padding: 15px 3%;
}
```

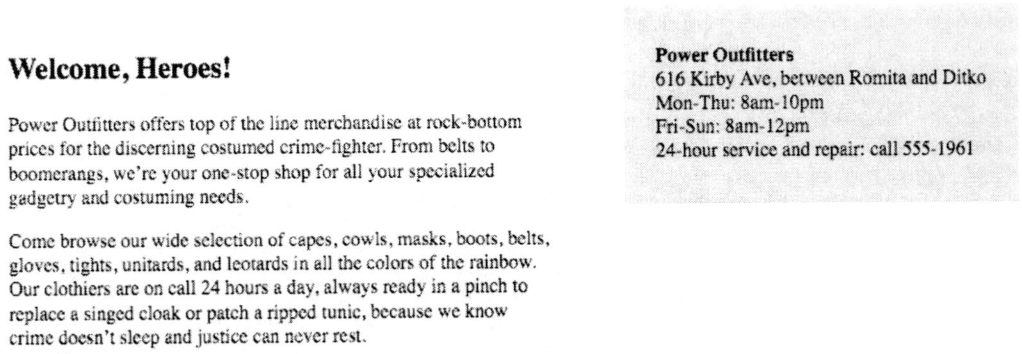

Welcome, Heroes!

Power Outfitters offers top of the line merchandise at rock-bottom prices for the discerning costumed crime-fighter. From belts to boomerangs, we're your one-stop shop for all your specialized gadgetry and costuming needs.

Come browse our wide selection of capes, cowls, masks, boots, belts, gloves, tights, unitards, and leotards in all the colors of the rainbow. Our clothiers are on call 24 hours a day, always ready in a pinch to replace a singed cloak or patch a ripped tunic, because we know crime doesn't sleep and justice can never rest.

Power Outfitters
616 Kirby Ave, between Romita and Ditko
Mon-Thu: 8am-10pm
Fri-Sun: 8am-12pm
24-hour service and repair: call 555-1961

Figure 9-7. *The columns float side by side with more room to breathe*

Clearing Floats

This is working out pretty well so far, with our columns floating side by side in perfect harmony. But a new problem arises when we add more content *outside* the floating boxes, perhaps a `footer` element to include some sort of tagline and a copyright statement.

A floated element is partially removed from the normal flow of content, allowing subsequent content to flow upward and wrap around the floating box. However, when two adjacent boxes are both floating, there's nothing to tell the browser where to draw their lower boundary. Content can flow upward around those boxes, squeezing into whatever space is available. It's what floats are supposed to do, but in this case it's not what we want. You can see an example of this phenomenon in Figure 9-8; because the two content boxes are floating, the footer content flows up into whatever space it can find, even wedging itself into the gutter.

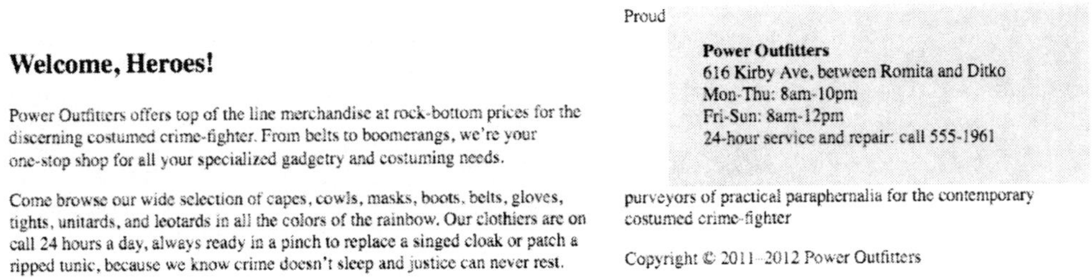

Proud

Welcome, Heroes!

Power Outfitters offers top of the line merchandise at rock-bottom prices for the discerning costumed crime-fighter. From belts to boomerangs, we're your one-stop shop for all your specialized gadgetry and costuming needs.

Come browse our wide selection of capes, cowls, masks, boots, belts, gloves, tights, unitards, and leotards in all the colors of the rainbow. Our clothiers are on call 24 hours a day, always ready in a pinch to replace a singed cloak or patch a ripped tunic, because we know crime doesn't sleep and justice can never rest.

Power Outfitters
616 Kirby Ave, between Romita and Ditko
Mon-Thu: 8am-10pm
Fri-Sun: 8am-12pm
24-hour service and repair: call 555-1961

purveyors of practical paraphernalia for the contemporary costumed crime-fighter

Copyright © 2011–2012 Power Outfitters

Figure 9-8. *Content flows around floating elements, even when you don't want it to*

To remedy the situation, you must *clear* the floats by drawing an invisible line across their lower border beyond which no content will flow. In this particular example, the tagline and copyright statement are in an element that should span the whole page width, so that element itself can form the invisible clearing line with a simple declaration:

```
footer { clear: both; }
```

311

The clear property instructs the browser to not allow any floats to descend below the element, nor or any content to flow above it. The property accepts four values: left (clear on the left side, while the right side flows normally), right (clear to the right while the left flows normally), both (clear content to both sides), and none (don't clear floats at all, most useful for overriding any other clearing value applied elsewhere). Clearing the flow of content around both sides of the footer element solves our flow problem.

As you can see in Figure 9-9, the footer clears the floating boxes and rests at the bottom of the tallest column, pushed down by the boxes above it, and ready to receive some further styling to make it look nicer (we added a dotted border just for this illustration).

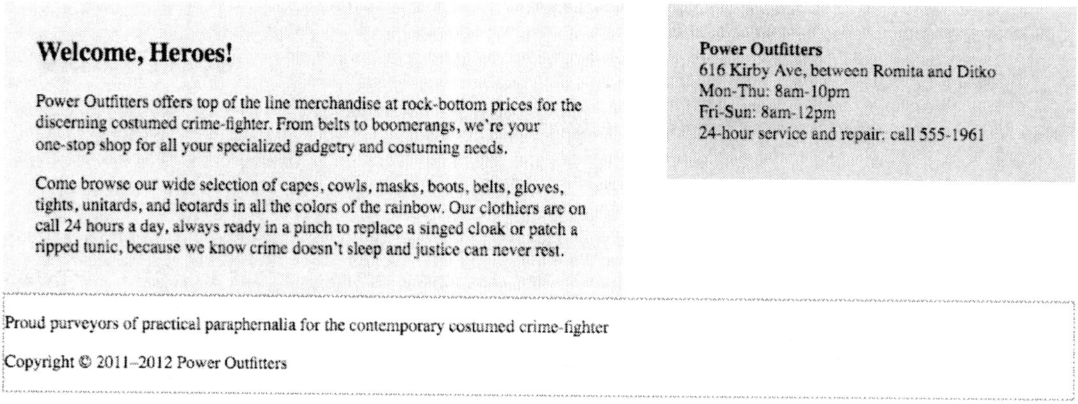

Welcome, Heroes!

Power Outfitters offers top of the line merchandise at rock-bottom prices for the discerning costumed crime-fighter. From belts to boomerangs, we're your one-stop shop for all your specialized gadgetry and costuming needs.

Come browse our wide selection of capes, cowls, masks, boots, belts, gloves, tights, unitards, and leotards in all the colors of the rainbow. Our clothiers are on call 24 hours a day, always ready in a pinch to replace a singed cloak or patch a ripped tunic, because we know crime doesn't sleep and justice can never rest.

Power Outfitters
616 Kirby Ave, between Romita and Ditko
Mon-Thu: 8am-10pm
Fri-Sun: 8am-12pm
24-hour service and repair: call 555-1961

Proud purveyors of practical paraphernalia for the contemporary costumed crime-fighter

Copyright © 2011–2012 Power Outfitters

Figure 9-9. The footer now clears the floats above it rather than flowing upward around them

Applying a clear property to an element is a foolproof way to clear floats, but sometimes you don't have an element available to carry that property. In Listing 9-3 we've added another element that wraps around and contains both our floating columns. You could use different elements, naturally, but we've gone with another section for this example. We've also omitted the text to keep the printed markup short.

Listing 9-3. Wrapping a containing element around two floating columns

```
<section id="content">
  <section class="main">
    <!-- main content -->
  </section>

  <section class="extra">
    <!-- extra content -->
  </section>
</section>
```

Without an explicit declared height, an element will only be the height of its contents (plus any padding or borders). Because floated elements allow content to flow around them, and with nothing else inside the container to clear the floating boxes, the container has no height at all and will collapse vertically, just as if it had no contents. Its floating children will spill out the bottom and any (uncleared) content that comes after will flow up around those protruding floats. We've illustrated this effect in Figure 9-10, and added some padding, a darker background, and a dotted border so you can see the collapsed container that would otherwise be invisible.

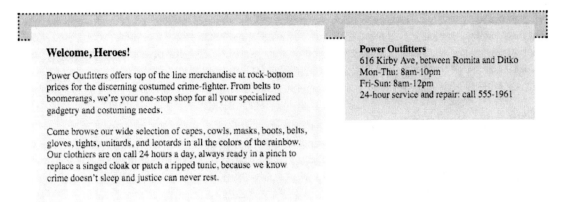

Figure 9-10. Uncleared floats overflow their container

If your design calls for a visible container with a background or border, you'll certainly want the container to wrap around and enclose its contents. You could simply add some element inside the container to clear the floats—an empty div or a line break—but that's just the sort of meaningless, presentational markup you should try to avoid. Luckily there are a few ways to clear floats without adding an extra element.

Floats Within Floats

A floating element will automatically expand to contain any floating elements within it. Adding a float property to the container and floating it to the left or right clears its inner floating boxes and the container expands to enclose them (see Figure 9-11):

```
#content { float: left; }
```

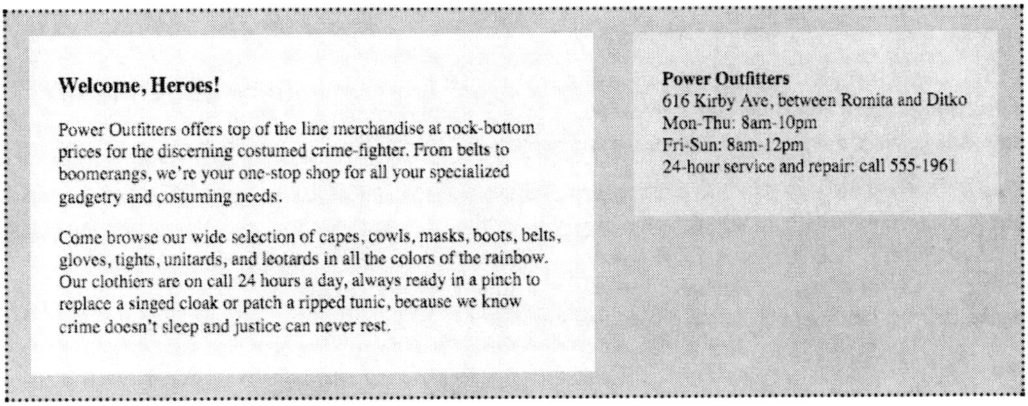

Figure 9-11. Floating the container makes it enclose its floating children

This works like a charm, except for one major drawback: the outer floated container may then need clearing of its own if there is other content it might run into. Depending on your particular layout and design, it might be as simple as adding clear:both to another element, or even to the container itself. You can produce complex layouts by floating nearly every element on the page and applying clear properties where necessary, hopefully to an already meaningful element rather than resorting to presentational markup. Overly complicated float-based layouts, with lots of elements floating in every direction, can be problematic and fragile. They can also have problems in older browsers, especially earlier versions of Internet Explorer.

Overflow

If floating the container isn't feasible, another option might be to apply an overflow property with a value of either hidden or auto. The overflow property in CSS instructs a browser in how to deal with content that is too big for its container. A block-level element with no declared width or height (the default state being width:auto and height:auto) will automatically expand vertically to enclose its contents, and expand horizontally to fill its container. If you declare your own explicit width or height to override that standard rendering, the browser needs to know what to do with overflowing content. By default, the content just runs out of its container and remains visible, like you see in Figure 9-12. Text wraps to fit within the width (assuming the text has room to wrap), but it can overflow vertically beyond the specified height, spilling out of the bottom of the box.

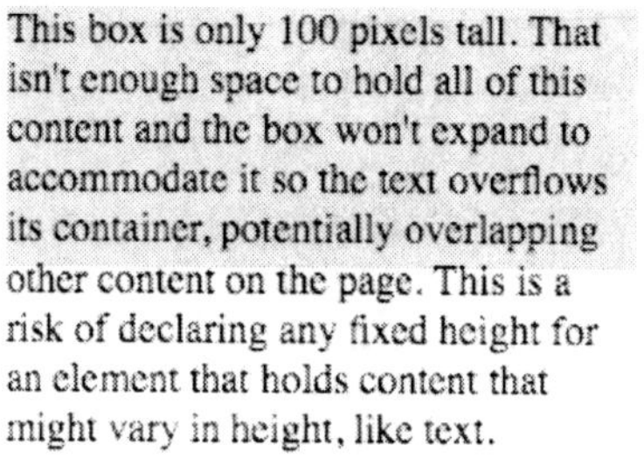

This box is only 100 pixels tall. That isn't enough space to hold all of this content and the box won't expand to accommodate it so the text overflows its container, potentially overlapping other content on the page. This is a risk of declaring any fixed height for an element that holds content that might vary in height, like text.

Figure 9-12. Content is visible when it overflows its container

The CSS overflow property accepts the values visible (the default), hidden (overflowing content is hidden beyond the edge of the container), scroll (adds scrollbars in both directions), or auto (overflowing content invokes scrollbars when necessary). But what does this have to do with floats?

There's an interesting side effect of altering an element's overflow property: applying a value of hidden or auto to an element containing floats will make that element expand around its floating children (overflow:scroll has the same effect but also adds scrollbars, which you usually don't want to see). It's as if the overflow property "reminds" the element that it should enclose its contents. Returning to our example, we can set the overflow of the containing element and it will automatically clear the floats inside it:

```
#content { overflow: auto; }
```

We could show you a screen capture of the results, but it looks exactly like Figure 9-11. The `overflow` declaration makes the container expand around the floating boxes within. It's not exactly what the `overflow` property was meant for, but it works reliably in all compliant browsers.

Using the `overflow` property to contain floats can work well in many cases, but isn't always infallible. The trick only works when the containing element has a `height` value of `auto` (the browser default), allowing it to automatically expand vertically to accommodate its contents. An explicit height combined with `overflow:hidden` or `overflow:auto` triggers the expected overflow behavior, clipping or scrolling the overflow rather than expanding the element around the floats. As for width, sometimes it's preferable to let overflowing content be visible rather than hiding it or invoking scrollbars, so using `overflow` to contain floats might have some negative side effects when the content is too wide for its box.

Generated Content

Among the many innovations that were introduced in CSS level 2 are the `:after` pseudo-element selector and the `content` property to generate content on the rendered page. You can cleverly combine these two features of CSS to clear floats without any additional markup.

A *pseudo-element* is a CSS selector that targets an element that doesn't actually exist in the document but is implied by its structure. Combined with another selector, the `:after` pseudo-element selects an imaginary element immediately after the reference element. Then you can apply any other CSS properties to that non-existent pseudo-element.

The `content` property renders the text of its value onto the page at the position of the selected element. This *generated content* doesn't actually exist in the document; it's merely displayed, so this property is only appropriate for decorative or presentational content, never for anything that should be meaningful or accessible.

In Listing 9-4 we've used these features together to create a presentational pseudo-element at the end of the containing block, and that new element can clear the floats above it. Its text content can really be anything because it'll be hidden anyway, but a single dot will suffice. It must be declared block-level for the `clear` property to take effect, and we can minimize the layout effects of this pseudo-element on its surroundings by giving it zero height and making it invisible. All it does is clear the floats and nothing else.

Listing 9-4. This CSS rule clears floats without adding any presentational markup

```
#content:after {
  content: ".";
  display: block;
  clear: both;
  height: 0;
  visibility: hidden;
}
```

Once again, we could show you a screen shot of the result, but it looks just the same as the previous clearing methods. This technique, first devised by Tony Aslett, is written up in much greater technical detail at `positioniseverything.net/easyclearing.html`. The approach is relatively foolproof and it's well supported by all the current browsers, but older browsers didn't support generated content or the `:after` pseudo-element. If you need your float-based layout to display properly in web browsers more than a decade old you might need to choose an alternative method for clearing floats.

> Versions 6 and 7 of Internet Explorer for Windows didn't support pseudo-elements or generated content, so this float clearing technique doesn't work for those versions. Unfortunately, those outdated versions are still in use in some corners of the Web, so you'll often have to make some special concessions for them (though their numbers are dwindling as people and companies gradually update their software).
>
> However, those versions of IE included a mysterious and proprietary concept in their rendering engines called "hasLayout." A container block that "has layout" will automatically expand to contain floating contents. You can learn more about the weirdness of hasLayout, what it does in IE 6 and 7, and how to invoke it to compensate for numerous CSS layout bugs at satzansatz.de/cssd/onhavinglayout.html

A float-based layout seems simple enough once you get the hang of it, but there are a few downsides as well. A floating element is taken out of the normal flow of content and shifted to one side, but it doesn't move up or down; the floated element's top edge will remain more or less where it would have been if it wasn't floating. Sometimes you'll have to order elements in your document according to where they should wind up when they float, which may not be ideal; you probably don't want a sidebar appearing before the main article, for example. But with a bit of skill and craft, the float property is one of the best layout tools at your disposal.

Positioning Elements

In addition to float, the position property is the other key layout tool in your CSS toolbox. With the accompanying offset properties left, right, top, and bottom, you can move a positioned element anywhere on the page and place it exactly where you want it to be. But like floating elements, positioned elements have a few idiosyncrasies that you'll need to become familiar with.

The position property accepts four values: static, relative, absolute, and fixed. The default value is static, which simply means the element has no special positioning, and appears on the page according to its place in the normal flow. Because static is the default, automatically assigned to every element, you'll rarely need to declare it in your own style sheets except to override a different position value declared elsewhere. Adding position:static to a rule simply resets the element back to its normal place in the flow. The other positioning schemes—relative, absolute, and fixed—are where it starts to get interesting.

Relative Positioning

When an element's position is relative, it's initially laid out according to the normal content flow. From there you can shift the element to a different position with the left, right, top, or bottom offset properties, any of which will take a percentage or a length as their value, or auto to revert to the normal flow position with no offset. The element's new position is *relative* to where it would have been before it was repositioned, but any surrounding content will still flow as if the element were in its original spot.

To demonstrate relative positioning we'll start with the markup in Listing 9-5, just a bit of text with an inline image, wrapped in an `article` element.

Listing 9-5. The markup we'll be styling with relative positioning

```
<article class="comment">
  <img src="images/avatar.jpg" alt="" class="avatar">
  <p>Having foiled a jewelry store heist on my way to receive a
  medal from the President, imagine my embarrassment to notice
  a nasty laser burn on my cape. There was no time to fly back to
  base and change into my spare costume, even at my speed. Thank
  goodness for Power Outfitters! They had my size and style in stock,
  in just the right shade of red, and at a great price, too. I went
  back after the ceremony and bought five more capes, plus matching
  gauntlets!</p>
</article>
```

First we'll give the containing `article` element a bit of style with a background, padding, and a border. We'll also set some margins on the paragraph inside, overriding any default margins with values of our own (most browsers add margins to both the top and bottom of paragraphs, but we want a margin on the bottom only). And finally we'll float the image, just like you saw back in Chapter 5:

```
.comment {
  background-color: #e6f2f9;
  padding: 15px 15px 0;
  border: 1px solid #98b8cd;
  margin: 0 0 15px;
}

.comment p {
  margin: 0 0 15px;
}

.avatar {
  float: left;
}
```

Figure 9-13 shows you what we have so far.

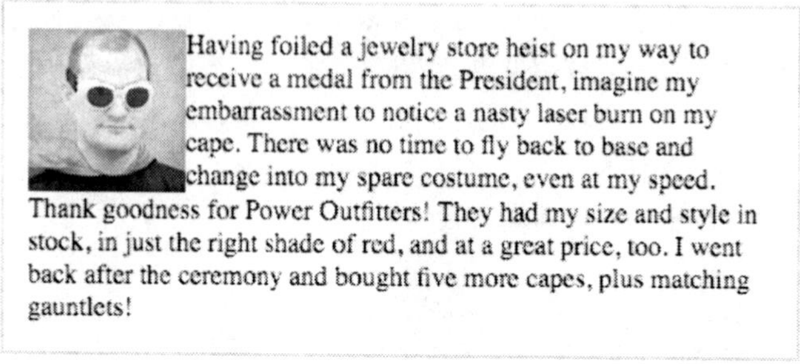

Having foiled a jewelry store heist on my way to receive a medal from the President, imagine my embarrassment to notice a nasty laser burn on my cape. There was no time to fly back to base and change into my spare costume, even at my speed. Thank goodness for Power Outfitters! They had my size and style in stock, in just the right shade of red, and at a great price, too. I went back after the ceremony and bought five more capes, plus matching gauntlets!

Figure 9-13. Our starting point for the positioning to come

We can offset that image from its current location by adding a `position:relative` declaration. With the `right` and `bottom` properties, we can push the image into the space created by the container's padding:

```
.avatar {
  float: left;
  position: relative;
  right: 17px;
  bottom: 17px;
}
```

Figure 9-14 shows the result, with the image offset from its initial position. You can even position elements outside of their containers. The surrounding box in our example has 15 pixels of padding and 2 pixels of border, so the 17 pixel offset we've added to this image lets the element escape its container and overlap the outer border. Also note that we haven't added any margins to the image; the space between the image and the text appears because the text still wraps around the area where the image *used to be*, still honoring the `float` property.

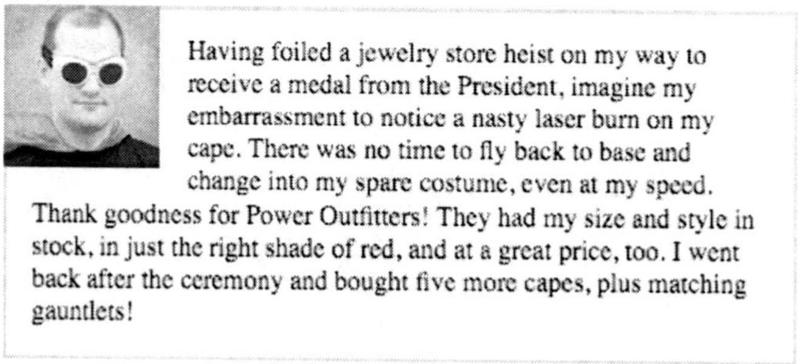

Having foiled a jewelry store heist on my way to receive a medal from the President, imagine my embarrassment to notice a nasty laser burn on my cape. There was no time to fly back to base and change into my spare costume, even at my speed. Thank goodness for Power Outfitters! They had my size and style in stock, in just the right shade of red, and at a great price, too. I went back after the ceremony and bought five more capes, plus matching gauntlets!

Figure 9-14. The image is re-positioned 17 pixels from the right and 17 pixels from the bottom, relative to its initial position

We can use this border overlap to our advantage to create a "notched" effect—as if the corner of the box were cut away and the image rests in that notch—by adding some padding to the image and a background color the same as the page background (white, in this case). A right and bottom border matching the outer container's border completes the effect:

```
.avatar {
  float: left;
  position: relative;
  right: 17px;
  bottom: 17px;
  padding-right: 15px;
  padding-bottom: 15px;
  background: #fff;
  border-right: 2px solid #98b8cd;
  border-bottom: 2px solid #98b8cd;
}
```

Figure 9-15 shows the finished result. The padding and border we added to the image has also affected the text flow. Whatever space an element would occupy in its original position remains in place after the element is offset with relative positioning. The text wraps and flows around an empty, avatar-sized area as if the image were still occupying that space.

Having foiled a jewelry store heist on my way to receive a medal from the President, imagine my embarrassment to notice a nasty laser burn on my cape. There was no time to fly back to base and change into my spare costume, even at my speed. Thank goodness for Power Outfitters! They had my size and style in stock, in just the right shade of red, and at a great price, too. I went back after the ceremony and bought five more capes, plus matching gauntlets!

Figure 9-15. The positioned image with some padding and borders creates an effect as if a notch were cut out of the corner of the box

Absolute Positioning

Absolute positioning goes a step further than relative positioning, allowing you to completely remove an element from the normal flow of content and place it in any location. Instead of leaving behind an element-sized hole of whitespace, the other content on the page flows and behaves as if the positioned element isn't even there.

Rather than offsetting the element relative to its starting position, the top, right, left, and bottom properties specify the element's new location relative to its *nearest positioned ancestor*. The first containing element that has any position value other than static defines the *positioning context* for the absolutely positioned descendant. If the element has no positioned ancestors, then the positioning context is the browser window itself.

We'll demonstrate with the same comment box and avatar image as before, setting it back to the starting point you saw in Figure 9-13. This time we'll apply position:absolute to the avatar image and place it in the bottom right corner, 15 pixels from the right and 15 pixels from the bottom:

```
.avatar {
  position: absolute;
  right: 15px;
  bottom: 15px;
}
```

Figure 9-16 shows the result—perhaps not quite what you expected. The positioning context here is the browser window, not the comment box, because the box itself isn't positioned and there are no other positioned ancestors.

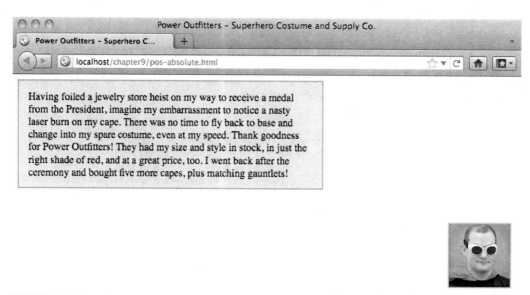

Figure 9-16. The image is positioned in the bottom right corner of the window, which acts as the default positioning context when there are no other positioned ancestors.

Of course there will be times when this is exactly what you want—an element positioned in the window exactly where you told it to go—but it's not the effect we're going for here. We need to change the element's positioning context by adding a `position:relative` declaration to the comment box:

```
.comment {
  background-color: #e6f2f9;
  width: 445px;
  padding: 15px 15px 0;
  border: 2px solid #98b8cd;
  margin: 0 0 15px;
  position: relative;
}
```

Without any offset values, the box stays just where it is in the normal content flow, but now it establishes a new positioning context for any positioned descendants inside it. As you can see in Figure 9-17, the image is in the bottom right corner of the box.

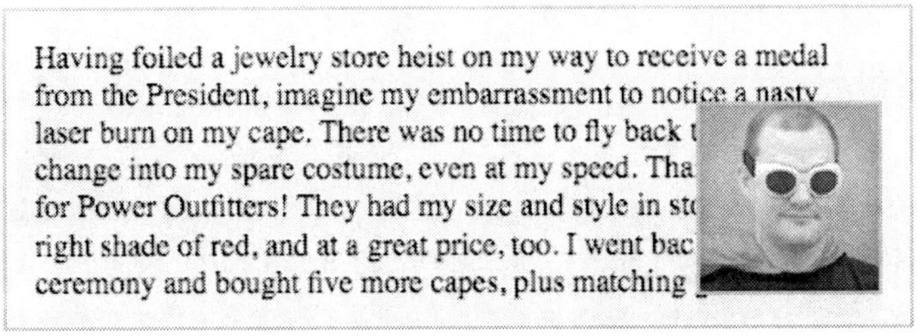

Figure 9-17. The positioned image is now inside the box due to its new positioning context

The positioned element overlaps the other content because it was removed from the flow and no longer takes up space; the text flows normally, completely unaware that there's an image in its midst. We can make some space for the image by padding the box, remembering to adjust its width accordingly:

```
.comment {
    background-color: #e6f2f9;
    width: 325px;
    padding: 15px 135px 0 15px;
    border: 2px solid #98b8cd;
    margin: 0 0 15px;
    position: relative;
}
```

In Figure 9-18 you'll see that the box now has reserved space for the positioned image. Padding counts as part of the box when determining the location of an absolutely positioned descendant. The element is offset from the *calculated edge* as the browser draws it, including any padding, but inside any borders or margins.

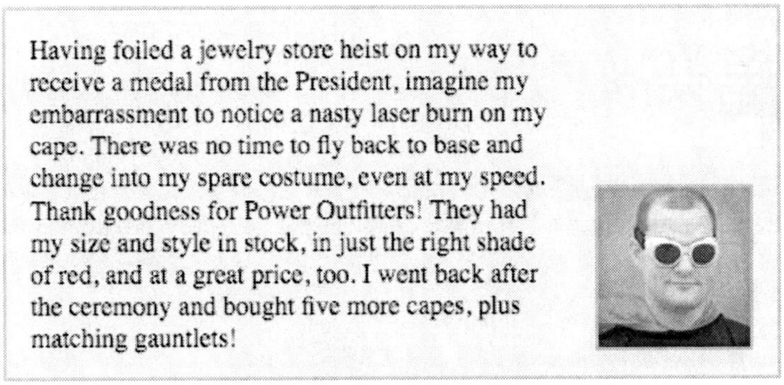

Figure 9-18. Padding creates space for the positioned image. The content reflows within the confines of its narrower width.

All is well and good, as long as the containing box is tall enough to accommodate the positioned element's height. An absolutely positioned element doesn't affect the flow of surrounding content, so it has no effect on the size of the box around it. If the box is short due to shorter content, and the positioned element simply overlaps it, like you see in Figure 9-19.

Laser burns are the worst!

Figure 9-19. Absolutely positioned elements aren't part of the normal content flow, so containers will behave as if the element isn't even there

It appears to be a similar problem as what you saw with floats earlier in this chapter, but this element isn't overflowing its container, it's *overlapping* an element that no longer contains it, at least as far as the browser's rendering is concerned. There's no way to "clear" a positioned element and make the box expand around it. The only way to ensure the box will always be tall enough to visually frame the image is to change the box's height. You could specify a fixed height to make the box exactly the right size, but then any added text could overflow and spill out of the box, so a fixed height is a bad idea. Clearly what we need here is a way to tell the box to be *at least* as tall as the image, but still let it expand vertically when it needs to. And, sure enough, we can do just that.

The min-height property specifies an element's minimum height. The element can expand naturally beyond that height when it needs to accommodate more content, but it won't collapse any smaller than that minimum height. If we add a min-height to our comment box that matches the height of the avatar image (plus any padding or borders), the box will always be at least that tall, even if its text contents are shorter:

```
.comment {
  background-color: #e6f2f9;
  width: 415px;
  padding: 15px 135px 0 15px;
  border: 2px solid #98b8cd;
  position: relative;
  min-height: 115px;
}
```

You can see the result in Figure 9-20. The first comment box expands around its content as usual, and the second comment box collapses to the minimum height so it can still frame the positioned image.

Having foiled a jewelry store heist on my way to receive a medal from the President, imagine my embarrassment to notice a nasty laser burn on my cape. There was no time to fly back to base and change into my spare costume, even at my speed. Thank goodness for Power Outfitters! They had my size and style in stock, in just the right shade of red, and at a great price, too. I went back after the ceremony and bought five more capes, plus matching gauntlets!

Laser burns are the worst!

Figure 9-20. The `min-height` property ensures there's always room for the positioned image

CSS also offers a similar `min-width` property as well as `max-width` and `max-height`, and you'll see them put to good use in Chapter 10.

As a consequence of being excluded from the normal content flow, absolutely positioned elements will collapse to the width of their contents. Ordinarily, a block-level element defaults to the width of its parent element, but once the element is out of flow, it loses that parental context and, in a sense, forgets how wide it should be. In our example we didn't need to include a `width` property because we were positioning an image, an element with an inherent width already, so its invisible box can collapse around it without incident. If you're positioning other types of elements, especially any that contain text that can wrap and change size, you'll probably need to define a width as well.

Fixed Positioning

In the fixed positioning model, an element is placed at a precise location in the browser window and remains fixed to the spot, even when a viewer resizes or scrolls the window—the element won't budge from its assigned position. Like absolute positioning, fixed positioning removes the element from the normal content flow so other content on the page will behave as if the positioned element isn't even there. The fixed element can overlap other content, including other positioned elements.

However, unlike absolute positioning, the positioning context for a fixed element is always the browser window, even when it has a positioned ancestor. You can't offset a fixed element relative to some other block of content on the page, nor to its initial position; offset properties relate to the edges of the browser window itself. Because the fixed element no longer relates to any other content on the page, fixed positioning is rarely useful for the classic page layout situations like creating columns or moving an element within its container. However it can be useful for menus or messages that you want to remain visible as your user scrolls down the page, and fixed positioning can be put to creative use for some pretty nifty scroll-based effects.

Listing 9-6 is the markup we're starting with for this demonstration. It's a site-wide masthead appearing above a long article (we haven't included the entire article in this example), and we'll use fixed positioning to make the masthead "stick" to the top of the window when a visitor scrolls down the page.

Listing 9-6. The masthead and article that we'll style with fixed positioning

```
<header id="masthead">
  <hgroup>
    <h1>Cape and Cowl Quarterly</h1>
    <h2>Online Edition | August, 2011</h2>
  </hgroup>
</header>

<article>
  <header>
    <h1 class="title">Where Do They Get Those Wonderful Toys?</h1>
    <p class="byline">By Norm DePlume</p>
  </header>
  <!-- article text -->
</article>
```

Figure 9-21 shows our starting point. We've already added some style rules to establish some coloring and typography, and to define the column width, but we haven't yet positioned the masthead (it's still defaulting to position:static for now). As you scroll down the page, the masthead will scroll up and out of view just like you'd expect.

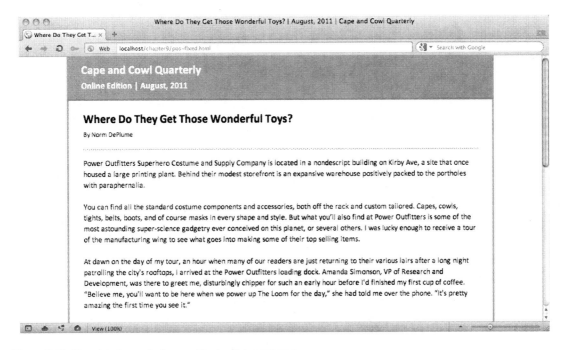

Figure 9-21. The styled page before positioning the masthead

Adding a `position:fixed` declaration to the masthead rule changes its positioning model, but by omitting any offset properties (`left`, `right`, `top`, or `bottom`) and leaving them to their default `auto` values, the element remains just where it would be otherwise:

```
#masthead {
  background-color: #b88c53;
  border-bottom: 4px solid #a67a40;
  color: #fff;
  padding: 10px 30px;
  position: fixed;
}
```

Giving the masthead a fixed position takes the element out of the normal content flow, so now all the subsequent content can move up into the space the masthead previously occupied, as shown in Figure 9-22. The masthead overlaps the content now, hiding part of the title and byline, and has also collapsed to the width of its content (plus padding). Obviously, this just won't do.

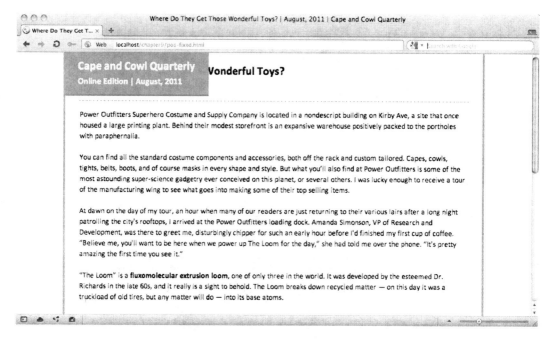

Figure 9-22. After positioning the masthead out of the normal flow, the masthead collapses and the rest of the content flows up under it

Without a declared width, positioned elements collapse to the width of their contents. This "shrink-wrap effect" isn't always obvious because the contents may still follow the normal flow; if our title were longer, the collapsed box would be wider. If the element held enough text to fill the space, the box might not appear to be collapsed at all. Absolutely positioned elements collapse as well, but the previous examples used images with inherent widths already so there were no ill effects of the shrink-wrap effect. But with our short title the collapse is clear, and clearly undesirable.

The shrink-wrap effect is easily remedied with a width property, but we need to compensate for the overlapping masthead by padding the top of the article under it, reserving some space for the masthead to occupy when the page first loads and the reader hasn't yet scrolled downward.

The padding needs to be slightly greater than the height of the masthead, pushing the article's title down the page. However, the masthead's height is dictated by the height of its content, which is just ordinary text, making the actual rendered height hard to predict. Even though we've specified a size for the text, users can still change the font size if they like. You should usually avoid setting fixed heights for any elements that contain text, but in this particular case it's unlikely that the text will need to wrap to multiple lines so we can probably risk it. Different content or a different design might lead us to a different layout strategy, but this will work well enough for demonstration.

We'll still accommodate varying font sizes by defining the height and padding in ems, a unit proportional to the size of the text. This way, if the font size changes, so will the height of the masthead and the padded space behind it. Listing 9-7 shows the style rules for the masthead and article, with the latest additions in bold.

Listing 9-7. Updating the style rules to create space for a fixed position masthead

```
#masthead {
  background-color: #819cae;
  border-bottom: 2px solid #98b8cd;
  color: #fff;
  padding: 10px 30px;
  position: fixed;
  width: 830px;
  height: 4.25em;
}

article {
  background-color: #e6f2f9;
  border: 2px solid #98b8cd;
  padding: 7.5em 30px 20px;
}
```

You can see the finished page in Figure 9-23. The article's top padding reserves some space for the masthead when the page first loads (top). When the viewer scrolls down to continue reading the article, the masthead stays in place while the content moves up and out of view, partially covered by the fixed masthead (bottom).

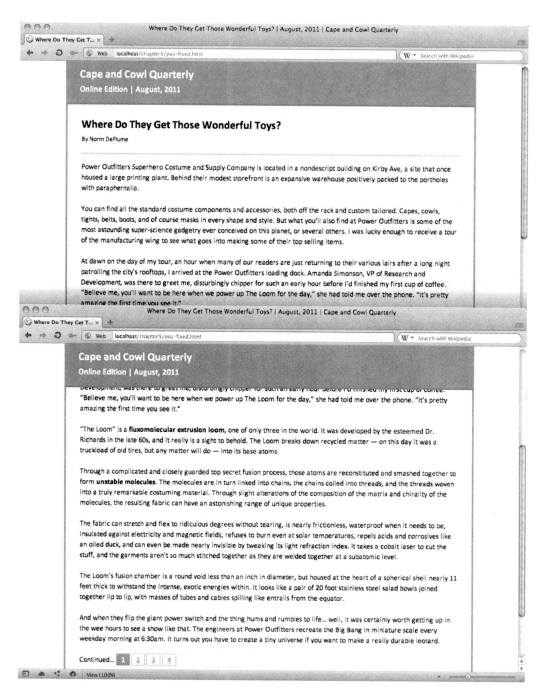

Figure 9-23. The masthead no longer covers the article's title when it's at the top, and it remains fixed in place when the reader scrolls down the page.

Internet Explorer didn't support position:fixed prior to version 7, though most other browsers have supported it for years. If you need fixed positioning to work in long-outdated versions of IE, you may have to resort to some special CSS trickery, or use JavaScript to reproduce the effect with position:absolute and dynamically update the offset as the window scrolls. You can find several solutions via the search engine of your choice; just search for something like "fixed positioning in IE6" and you'll be on your way.

Summary

This chapter showed you just a few techniques you can use to lay out your pages with CSS. When you get right down to it, page layout is a delicate art of arranging boxes, and you learned about the CSS box model to prepare you for that. Clever application of the float property can turn boxes into tidy columns, and sensible use of the position property can place those boxes anywhere on the page.

CSS is a rich language for describing the presentation of content, granting web designers powerful influence over color, spacing, typography, and decorative imagery. Alas, CSS is still a bit awkward when it comes to something as seemingly simple as arranging blocks of content into columns, or aligning boxes into orderly rows without sacrificing flexibility. Tables form rows and columns naturally, but tables are the wrong tool for describing page layout, so we make do with the tools we have.

CSS3 hopes to at long last address the shortcomings of page layout with CSS. The forthcoming Template Layout module (w3.org/TR/css3-layout) and Flexible Box Layout module (w3.org/TR/css3-flexbox) both hold great promise for the future, but they're still works in progress at the time of this writing near the end of 2011. Some browsers have implemented experimental support for a few aspects of these new layout modules, but other browsers don't support them in any way. Until the specifications are a bit closer to complete and the browser market has had a chance to get on board, web designers may be better off using time-tested layout techniques for now. And of course, all of this may have changed by the time you read these words.

Laying out web pages with CSS can be difficult and you can expect to make a lot of mistakes when you first dive in. Even the most seasoned professionals who have been at it for years still face tricky layouts that demand a lot of trial and error, and every new project brings new challenges. There are a lot more tips and techniques you'll pick up in time but we hope this chapter has at least given you a good head start.

In Chapter 10 you'll get to follow along as we design and build a simple website from the ground up, putting to use some of the techniques you've just seen, and showing off a few more while we're at it.

Chapter 10

Putting it All Together

You've learned a lot about modern, future-friendly markup in the last nine chapters, with a healthy dose of CSS along the way. Although HTML and CSS are rich and nuanced languages, the fundamentals are still quite simple, with just a few basic rules to follow. With a bit of practice and experience putting together websites, you'll become intimately familiar with these primary languages on which the Web is built until it all becomes second nature.

Of course, knowing the technical ins and outs of HTML and CSS is only part of a bigger picture. Assembling a well-formed, accessible, and flexible web page requires a bit of thought and planning. Consider the meaning of your content and choose the elements that best align with that meaning. Validate your markup to ensure that you've adhered to the specifications. Once you've built a solid foundation of valid, meaningful, structural HTML, you can move on to styling your document's presentation with CSS and adding behavioral enhancements with JavaScript.

In this chapter we'll cover the process of planning, designing, and constructing a simple website from start to finish, from concept to code. We'll walk you through the basic steps we followed to create the Power Outfitters website, offering an example of one workflow that tends to work well for many projects. You'll see how the site was put together from the ground up, exploring the combination of markup and style that makes the site a reality (or at least as real as a site for a fictional superhero supply company can be).

We'll build up a framework of semantically rich, accessible HTML and wrap it in layers of CSS to make it shine. We won't be able to cover every last detail of how this example website came together, however, and there are a few hidden gems in the code for you to discover for yourself. Then, later in the chapter, we'll at long last delve into some of the CSS3 we've been promising.

A Web Design Process

There is no universal, one-size-fits-all, written-in-stone procedure for designing and constructing a website, and the process we describe in this chapter is by no means the only approach you might take. With that said, it's important to establish *some* kind of process and to follow a logical sequence of steps to keep your work—and your thoughts—organized and on track. Developing a website without a plan of attack will only lead to frustration and chaos.

Every site you build and every project you undertake will be a little bit different, each with its own unique challenges, but all your web development ventures will share a few common guiding principles. With experience, you'll find a process that works best for you, and you'll also find ways to make your process adaptable enough to handle the curve balls every new project throws at you.

Generally speaking, most websites go through some form of the following stages:

- **Stage 1: Plan** – Before design and development can begin in earnest, you need to know what it is you're designing and developing. Formulating some sort of plan is crucial, especially when you're working as part of a team.

- **Stage 2: Design** – When you know what you're making, you can begin to think about how to make it. Layout, color, typography, imagery, sound, and even the style of writing all add up to a unique user experience.

- **Stage 3: Develop** – This is the actual construction and assembly of the site, the nitty-gritty code wrangling that transforms all that planning and preparation into a working reality.

- **Stage 4: Test** – Having executed the plan and built a beautiful, engaging, well-polished website with all the moving parts in all the right places, you should next try as hard as you can to break it. Find the flaws and fix them until you run out of things to fix.

At the end of these steps is a completed site, ready to deploy to a server and release to the World Wide Web. But before we skip to the end, we'll dig into each stage a little deeper.

Stage 1: Plan

Before you write a single line of code you should formulate a plan. The first stage of any project is a process of discovery and analysis so you can know what it is you're building and for whom you're building it. Defining goals early on will help you stay on target in every decision you make along the way, always moving toward a specific outcome. Deciding just what those goals will be and how you might achieve them demands some consideration, some research, and asking some important questions:

- What is the site meant to accomplish, and what sort of information should it impart to that end?

- Who will be using the site, what do they want to accomplish during their visit, and what information will they need to achieve their goals?

- Are there other websites that fulfill the same need, perform similar tasks, or appeal to the same audience as yours? If so, what do those sites do right? How could they be improved?

- Every site has constraints: time, budget, resources, equipment, technology, and so on. What constraints will you need to work within?

- Is your site dependent on any third parties—hosts, content providers, data APIs, and so on—that might impose limitations?

- How will you maintain the site after it's completed? What future additions, updates, or improvements should you plan for?

The answers to these and other questions form a set of goals and requirements to guide the entire project.

Information Architecture

With requirements in hand, you can turn your attention to mapping out the site's structure, beginning with the content. Determine what types of content you'll need to present in order to meet the site's goals, and then organize that content into logical categories. This kind of *information architecture* can be one of the more challenging steps in any design process, depending on the size and complexity of the website.

For our case study, we're imagining the Power Outfitters website as an e-commerce site with all the usual trappings: visitors can browse a catalog of products or search for specific items, then add those items to a virtual shopping cart to make their purchases. That sounds simple enough when it's boiled down to a single sentence, but it's actually a pretty complex workflow with a lot of variables to consider. Once an item has been added to the cart, how can a user remove it? When making a purchase, does she enter separate addresses for billing and shipping? Does she need to register an account on the website, and if so, what's that process? Once she has an account, what happens if she forgets her password? Every one of these questions sparks a new scenario that needs to be thought through and mapped out.

You can visualize a site's architecture as a flowchart with connections drawn between the pages to represent the path a user might take to reach them. Figure 10-1 is an example of such a site map, drawing out the relationships between different sections of a website. We've greatly simplified this example and a site as complex as Power Outfitters—if it existed—might have a much more sprawling map for a more complex architecture, with many more avenues and connections to draw between more tiers of information. Smaller and less complex sites might consist of just a few pages so their maps could be even simpler than our illustration.

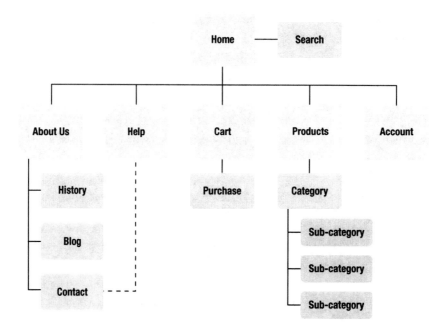

Figure 10-1. A minimal site map drawn as a flow chart

The real point of drawing a site map is to get you to think about organization and how to reach one page from another. Think about how your visitors will find their way to the content they need and how you can guide them along the shortest route.

Stage 2: Design

Everything to this point has been centered around discovery and planning, and the next stage is the point at which ideas begin to take tangible shape. Preparation is a huge part of the design process, but now it's time to put that plan into action and let the creative juices flow. As always, think about your users—what will they see, read, or hear, how will they interact, and how will the site respond to the users' needs and actions? Figuring that out is what designers do; design is making a plan for a sensory experience.

Explore your site map and identify the different types of pages your site will need and what components should appear on each page. Begin to think about hierarchy and what content is most important. You can express that hierarchy of importance as a *visual hierarchy*, with the most vital content drawing the most attention or taking up the most space, with less important, supporting content staying out of the way.

The *wireframe* is an invaluable tool for plotting the hierarchy and arrangement of elements on the page, and for gauging how blocks of content relate to each other. It's a rough, schematic blueprint of the web page, to act as a guide for the design and development steps that follow. Drafting wireframes is an extension of information architecture and usually falls under the domain of user experience (UX) design or interaction design.

Typically, at this stage in the process, wireframes should steer clear of the more visual aspects of design, and should lack any strong color, detailed typography, or complex imagery. Wireframes should be simple and clear, a skeletal framework that supports the layers to come, like chicken wire under papier-mâché.

Wireframes are a plan, not a product; they're a step on the way to a finished design. They're meant to be loose and non-committal, and many wireframing tools deliberately limit design options to force you to focus on hierarchy and utility instead of graphics and branding. Some wireframing software will even simulate hand-drawn sketches, complete with squiggly lines and scribbles, just to prevent you from getting bogged down in details too early in the process. Of course, you don't need to use any special software to put together wireframes; a pencil and paper can be just as constructive.

You can see some example wireframe diagrams in Figure 10-2, plotting a few different pages for the Power Outfitters website. We've kept things loose and free, and we aren't thinking yet about the final, polished presentation. We are, however, beginning to think about general layout and arrangement of elements on the page, but only insofar as establishing the visual hierarchy of where the most important content should fall.

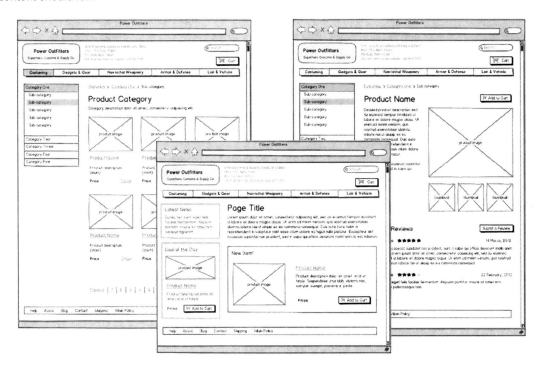

Figure 10-2. Wireframe diagrams of a few key pages on Power Outfitters

The page layout is still subject to change, and later we'll use color, texture, typography, and imagery to emphasize different blocks of content and lead the viewer's eye where it needs to go. The greatest benefit of drawing wireframes is that it helps you to understand your content and collect all the essential parts in one place before you begin visual design and development. The wireframing stage is also a good time to start thinking about the underlying HTML structure, considering which elements you'll eventually use to give the content a meaningful, versatile structure.

Visual Design

Visual or graphic design is the part most people think about when they hear the term "web design," but it's really only one aspect of the entire design process. With some sort of plan in place and an idea of just what it is you need to build, you can finally begin planning what the thing will *look* like. This is the stage when you'll think about color, texture, imagery, typography, iconography, and branding.

As with every other part of the process, there isn't any one definitive approach to the visual side of web design. You might start with sketches, color swatches, and scrapbooks of patterns and ornaments to grasp the general mood before focusing your efforts on the real thing. You might instead prefer to jump directly into designing the site with a blank canvas, trying out different styles and treatments to see what works and what doesn't. It's also a common practice to produce multiple design variations before finally choosing the one you like best (or the one your client or boss likes best). Or it may be more efficient to work through numerous iterations of a single design, gradually honing it to perfection.

Whatever approach you take, your finished design will be more enlightened because you took the time to understand your audience and your content. If you're only working on the HTML and CSS and someone else is defining the visual design—as is often the case in larger teams—the guidelines and wireframes you've worked so hard to put together will help the designer create a better product that aligns with the project goals and the site's architecture.

Any visual designer working on the Web should be familiar with the fundamentals of HTML and CSS, even if he or she isn't writing any code. For a web designer, knowing how web pages are made is like an architect understanding the structural properties of glass and steel, or an artist learning that oil paints and watercolors don't mix. HTML and CSS are the tools and materials of the Web medium.

Where Design Happens

Many web designers, especially those with a background in traditional printed graphic arts, prefer to design web pages with graphics software like Photoshop or Fireworks. They'll produce a polished *mockup* (also called a *composite*, or *comp* for short), a full-scale image of the completed site design, essentially a picture of a web page. Once the mockup has gone through all the reviews and revisions necessary and the complete design is settled and approved, only then can a developer begin to convert the mockup into HTML and CSS. This method works well for some, but it has some major drawbacks.

A static image of a web page can't demonstrate interactivity like opening dropdown menus or hovering a mouse pointer over a button, and certainly not complex actions like validating a form or dragging a box. It also can't reveal how a liquid layout moves and responds as the window changes size, and it doesn't illustrate how a design might degrade in less advanced browsers. Fonts render very differently in graphic design software and text can flow in different ways once the picture of a web page becomes an actual web page. Worst of all, some shapes and effects that are trivial to produce in Photoshop can be nearly impossible to achieve in markup and CSS. Focusing too much attention on a frozen mockup of a web page can lead to unrealistic expectations of what the end product will look like.

Rather than invest a lot of time into rendering a high-definition mockup, it's often more efficient to spend that design time constructing real HTML and CSS. You'll see exactly what the end user will see, and anything you design will be realistic and practical because you're using the tools of the very medium for which you're designing. Producing a prototype site and designing live in a web browser delivers a more accurate depiction of the final product. The prototype can even lead directly to the finished site because much of the code will be ready to use at the end of the design phase.

We designed the Power Outfitters website in HTML and CSS, using our sketches and wireframes as a blueprint and gradually arriving at the final design through experimentation and old-fashioned trial and error. We started with a plan and a general idea of what the end result should look like—we drew inspiration from classic comic books, and we knew it would have a blue and gold color scheme, with panels and a dot pattern—but the final design came together organically in the browser, right before our eyes. That's the process you'll see in this chapter.

Stage 3: Build

At last it's time to build the site, writing all the code that brings the content to life and makes the site a reality. For most commercial websites, plain HTML and CSS alone can't deliver all the functionality the site requires. Most websites of any complexity will be built on top of a server-side programming language like Python, Ruby, PHP, or ASP.NET. These languages perform the more complicated operations that make a site dynamic and interactive, such as handling forms, synchronizing data to and from a database, and assembling components from separate template files into a single HTML document to serve to the browser. This is also the stage when you'll integrate client-side behaviors with JavaScript.

If you're making a smaller, static site, and if you designed it in the browser, you may already have the bulk of the building stage completed when you reach the end of the design stage. If it's a larger, dynamic site, you can now work with your HTML prototype to add the programming logic and scripted behaviors, or work with other developers for implementation. Some complex dynamic sites can even begin the back-end work while the front-end design is still underway, just so long as everyone sticks to the plan.

For our Power Outfitters case study we've left out the entire back-end development process that such a site would obviously demand, if it really existed. For this book we're only focusing on building a static front-end prototype in HTML and CSS. The Power Outfitters site doesn't actually work, so unfortunately you'll have to purchase your capes, cowls, shrink rays, bionic eyes, and antigravity flight harnesses elsewhere.

Stage 4: Test

After you've done all the design and assembly and you have a beautifully styled and solidly constructed website at your fingertips, ready to release into the wild, now is the time to check it over and see just how well it's built. Go through all the links and navigation to make sure everything leads to the right place. Disable images and JavaScript and see if your site is still at least readable, if not fully enhanced. Fill in forms and test validation and data integrity. Be on the lookout for security vulnerabilities, especially if you're gathering any sensitive information from your users.

You can also conduct *user tests*, recruiting real people to try your site and give you feedback. Observe what they do and where they struggle in the course of completing a common task; it's amazing what you can learn from watching real users interact with your websites.

View the site in multiple browsers and devices—as many as you can get your hands on. Each browser may treat your CSS in slightly different ways. However, don't be misled into believing that a website should look exactly the same in every browser. Trying to achieve pixel-perfect, identical presentation across different browsers and operating systems is a recipe for distress. Some minor cross-browser differences won't bother anyone. After all, real users don't open two competing browsers side by side to compare where the pixels line up.

If you use some of the more advanced parts of HTML5 and CSS3, you're pretty well guaranteed to see some differences between browsers because they're at different levels of supporting these emerging standards. If you've practiced progressive enhancement and provided sensible fallbacks, your visitors may be none the wiser.

Instead of striving to achieve perfectly identical appearances in every browser, concentrate on offering a *consistent experience*. Is the site readable, functional, and does it look presentable? Are any elements the wrong size, completely misaligned, or in the wrong position? Some small variations are to be expected, but as long as those variations don't harm the design or make the site more difficult to use, they might not be worth worrying about.

Building Power Outfitters

Imagine you live in a world where superheroes are real, where daring defenders of right don colorful costumes and battle for truth and justice against equally colorful villains. In such a world it goes without saying that these masked peacekeepers would form a lucrative niche market for highly specialized clothing and accessories. After all, you probably can't buy a custom fitted cowl with matching utility belt at your local mall. This is a job for Power Outfitters Superhero Costume & Supply Co., a premier supplier of costuming, gadgets, and gear for the discerning costumed crime-fighter. And they need a website.

In the rest of this chapter we'll guide you step by step through the assembly of our fictional website for our fictional superhero supply company. We'll build the document from scratch using semantically rich, accessible HTML5, explaining our markup choices along the way. Then we'll apply a layer of presentation to that underlying structure with simple CSS, demonstrating a few more clever tricks you might find useful in your own work. We'll further enhance the site's presentation with some newer, more advanced properties and techniques from CSS3, showing you a few parts of this emerging standard that you can use on the Web today.

We're only focusing on building the home page in this chapter, and you'll just have to pretend this is part of a larger website. Even from this one page example you can see how the patterns we establish here could easily carry over to other pages, such as catalog listings, product details, and order forms.

Setting Up the Document

Unless you've skipped the previous nine chapters, you know by now that behind every web page is an HTML document (if you want to avoid more spoilers, go back and read Chapter 3). To begin construction on the Power Outfitters site we'll establish a base document with all the vital metadata we're going to need. Listing 10-1 is our starting point, just a bare skeleton of a document.

Listing 10-1. The blank document we'll be starting out with

```
<!DOCTYPE html>
<html lang="en-US" dir="ltr">
  <head>
    <meta charset="utf-8">
    <meta name="robots" content="index, follow">
    <meta name="keywords" content="capes, masks, tights, superhero, costumes, gadgets">
    <meta name="description" content="Power Outfitters manufactures and sells costumes,↩
      accessories, supplies, and equipment for the contemporary costumed crime-fighter">

    <title>Power Outfitters - Superhero Costume &amp; Supply Co.</title>
  </head>

  <body class="home">

  </body>
</html>
```

We've naturally included an HTML5 doctype, and we've declared the language (American English) and direction (left to right) on the root `html` element. The document's header also contains some additional metadata for search engine robots. We're concentrating on the home page in this example, so the keywords and description here apply to the entire website, and any interior pages would carry descriptions more relevant to that particular page. And of course we've given the page a descriptive and meaningful title in the required `title` element.

We've also taken the liberty of adding a `class` attribute to the `body` element, classifying this page as the home page, just in case we need to refer to that when we start writing the CSS. We could perhaps use an `id` attribute to serve the same purpose—distinguishing the home page from other pages—but because this is mostly intended as a hook for CSS rules, we'd rather avoid the higher specificity of an ID selector.

Speaking of CSS, we should go ahead and add links to our external style sheets: one with styles for regular screen display, and another for print. These style sheets are blank for the moment, but we'll be building them up soon enough. We'll keep all of our CSS files in a "css" folder on the server and we're using relative URLs to point to those files:

```
<link rel="stylesheet" type="text/css" media="screen,projection" href="css/screen.css">
<link rel="stylesheet" type="text/css" media="print" href="css/print.css">
```

We know we'll be using many of the new semantic and interactive elements introduced in HTML5, and we know we'll need to style them with CSS, and that raises the issue of element rendering in Internet Explorer. As we mentioned in Chapter 4, older versions of IE won't apply any styling to elements they don't recognize unless those elements are first injected into the document object model (DOM) with a bit of

JavaScript. We can use the HTML5 shiv script to do just that, but we really only need to send that script to IE and not to any other browsers.

> *We first mentioned the HTML5 shiv back in Chapter 4, and you can read more about its history—including why they called it a "shiv" when it should be a "shim"—in Paul Irish's blog post, "The Story of the HTML5 Shiv" (paulirish.com/2011/the-history-of-the-html5-shiv/). Download the script at http://code.google.com/p/html5shiv/*

Conditional Comments for Internet Explorer

Conditional comments are a proprietary browser feature—first introduced with Internet Explorer 5 for Windows in 1999—that allow developers to delineate blocks of HTML that will only be visible in certain browsers. They're not a standard feature and haven't been implemented by any other browser besides IE, but conditional comments are a relatively foolproof way to deliver content to IE while hiding it from other browsers (or to hide content from IE while showing it to all others).

A conditional comment looks something like this:

```
<!--[if IE]>
  Only Internet Explorer can see this text.
<![endif]-->
```

This special comment is *conditional* because it's structured as a logical argument, applying only if the browser meets the specified conditions. The argument above simply states, "if the user-agent is Internet Explorer, process the contents of this comment." All other browsers—even any non-IE browsers that might support conditional comments—will treat the entire thing as a normal HTML comment in and won't parse or render it.

You can target specific versions of IE by extending the condition with the version number: [if IE 7]. There are other logical operations as well, targeting versions less than, greater than, or equal to the stated version. The basic argument operators are:

- [if IE] – all versions of Internet Explorer for Windows
- [if IE X] – only version X (where X is a version number)
- [if lt IE X] – versions less than (but not equal to) X
- [if lte IE X] – versions less than or equal to X
- [if gt IE X] – versions greater than (but not equal to) X
- [if gte IE X] – versions greater than or equal to X

There are a few additional operators to produce more complex expressions, but these are the basics. Regardless, only Internet Explorer can interpret these comments; every other browser in the world ignores them entirely. You can learn more about conditional comments and some of the ways you can use them in Sitepoint's CSS reference (http://reference.sitepoint.com/css/conditionalcomments).

Listing 10-2 shows the conditional comment we've included in our header to load the HTML5 shiv script, and we've targeted it to versions less than IE 9. Newer versions of IE from 9 onward recognize these newer HTML elements natively and don't require the script to make them stylable.

Listing 10-2. Attaching a JavaScript file in a conditional comment that only Internet Explorer can interpret

```
<!--[if lt IE 9]>
<script src="js/html5shiv.js"></script>
<![endif]-->
```

Remember, the major caveat when using the HTML5 shiv is that it makes CSS rendering in older versions of IE entirely dependent on JavaScript, which some visitors may have disabled for any number of reasons: to protect their privacy, as a security precaution, to improve performance on a slow connection, or to block nefarious pop-up ads. Anyone using an outdated Internet Explorer with JavaScript disabled won't experience our site in all its glory, but we don't want to completely ignore these poor souls either. The very least we can do is offer them a word of explanation:

```
<!--[if lt IE 9]>
  <noscript>
    <p class="notice"><strong>Note:</strong> This website employs some features ↦
    that may not be fully supported by some versions of Internet Explorer. You ↦
    can improve your experience by enabling JavaScript.</p>
  </noscript>
<![endif]-->
```

We'll include this message in the body of the page and it will only be visible to people using versions of IE lower than 9, and—thanks to the `noscript` element—only if they have JavaScript disabled. If those users were a key demographic and a significant portion of our target audience, we might reconsider our approach and avoid styling unrecognized elements. But we're forging ahead and primarily targeting the current generation of browsers. We'll make a reasonable effort to ensure the content is still accessible and readable in some older, less capable browsers, but people using such browsers will have to be content with a diminished experience.

Assembling the Template

With our basic document established, we next need to think about the common elements that will appear on every page throughout the site. We know from our wireframes that the site will feature a branded masthead that in turn features the Power Outfitters logo, a block of store info (the address and business hours), a search box and a prominent link to the user's shopping cart, as well as the site's primary navigation. There's also a global footer with some supplemental navigation, the company slogan, and a copyright disclaimer. Between the masthead and the footer is a large area for the page's content, which will obviously vary from page to page; the masthead, navigation, and footer are the consistent elements that form the surrounding site template.

Marking Up the Masthead

The masthead is the branded header for the entire website, like a sign above a shop's front door. In the past we would have used a generic `div` element to gather these related components into a single block, but HTML5 gives us an element for just this purpose: header. Because it appears at the beginning of the document with the body element as its parent sectioning root, this header element acts as the header for the whole document.

We'll give the header element an ID because this element is unique; there will only ever be one masthead on a page. We could, of course, use a class attribute for styling purposes and avoid too many specificity problems, but using an id attribute reinforces the uniqueness of this header. A class is a classifier but an ID is an identifier; this element isn't just **a** masthead, it's **the** masthead.

We'll use an h1 element for the logo, even though the logo itself is an inline image (with appropriate alternative text, of course). An image by itself would lack the semantic weight of a heading, and this logo also acts as the top-level title for the entire document.

The store's street address, business hours, and phone number are each distinct pieces of content expressing a single idea, so it makes sense to mark up each piece as a separate paragraph. However, we also want to group them together as related statements. We might use a section element, but this content isn't really a section of a lengthier sequence of content, we simply want to keep it all together in a generic box. The old standby div element seems most appropriate here; it collects the content into a unit but doesn't imply any additional semantics.

We'll group the search form (using input type="search") and the shopping cart link together in another div because they serve similar utilitarian purposes. We're also adding an empty form element here with the ID "cart" so all of the "Add to Cart" buttons that will appear later can reference the same form. This form only needs to accept input from elsewhere on the page and pass it on to our shopping cart application; the form element itself doesn't hold any contents. It could really appear anywhere in the document, but we're putting it here in the masthead because it's as good a place as any.

The primary navigation calls for the nav element, once again with an id attribute singling this out as the unique element it is; it's the main navigation and there will be only one such element. The menu inside that nav element is simply an unordered list of links.

You can see the complete markup for our site's masthead in Listing 10-3.

Listing 10-3. The Power Outfitters masthead

```
<header id="masthead">
  <h1 id="logo">
    <img src="images/logo-big.png" width="265" height="145" ↵
      alt="Power Outfitters Superhero Costume &amp; Supply Co.">
  </h1>

  <div id="store-info">
    <p>616 Kirby Ave (between Romita and Ditko)</p>
    <p>Mon&ndash;Thu: <time datetime="08:00">8am</time>&ndash;↵
      <time datetime="22:00">10pm</time></p>
    <p>Fri&ndash;Sun: <time datetime="08:00">8am</time>&ndash;↵
      <time datetime="00:00">12am</time></p>
    <p>24-hour service and repair: call 555-1961</p>
  </div>
```

```
<div id="utilities">
  <form id="search" action="/search">
    <p>
      <label for="search-main">Search for products</label>
      <input type="search" name="search" id="search-main"↪
        placeholder="utility belts">
      <button type="submit">Search</button>
    </p>
  </form>

  <p class="cart"><a href="/cart">Your cart: <b>0 items</b></a></p>
  <form id="cart" method="post" action="/cart"></form>
</div>

<nav id="nav-main">
  <ul>
    <li><a href="/costuming">Costuming</a></li>
    <li><a href="/gear">Gadgets &amp; Gear</a></li>
    <li><a href="/weaponry">Non-lethal Weaponry</a></li>
    <li><a href="/defense">Armor &amp; Defense</a></li>
    <li><a href="/base">Lair &amp; Vehicle</a></li>
  </ul>
</nav>

</header>
```

Marking Up the Footer

We'll skip over the content area for the moment and get right to the site footer. As with the masthead, if we were still using HTML4 or XHTML, we would use a semantically neutral div element to surround the footer content, but now we can use HTML5's specialized footer element. And like the masthead, because it's not appearing within another sectioning root—such as an article or section—this footer element acts as the footer for the entire document. We'll once again assign an ID to set this footer apart from any other footer elements that might appear elsewhere.

The footer consists of another collection of navigation links (in an unordered list wrapped in a nav element), a paragraph for the Power Outfitters slogan, and another paragraph for the copyright statement. Listing 10-4 presents the complete markup for our website's global footer.

Listing 10-4. The Power Outfitters footer

```
<footer id="site-info">
  <nav id="nav-info">
    <ul>
      <li><a href="/help">Help</a></li>
      <li><a href="/about">About</a></li>
      <li><a href="/blog">Blog</a></li>
      <li><a href="/contact">Contact</a></li>
      <li><a href="/shipping">Shipping</a></li>
      <li><a href="/villains">Villain Policy</a></li>
    </ul>
```

```
  </nav>

  <p class="slogan">Proud purveyors of practical paraphernalia for the↵
    contemporary costumed crime-fighter</p>

  <p class="copyright">Copyright &copy; 2011&ndash;2012 Power Outfitters</p>
</footer>
```

A Space for Content

With our masthead and footer in good shape, we finally turn to the real meat of the page: a broad, blank canvas where the site's content will live. We know from our wireframes that we'll need a space for the primary page content and space for a sidebar full of supplemental content, but what's inside those blocks will change from page to page. We need general, multipurpose containers for these content sections, if only to group them together and provide a convenient wrapper for layout and styling.

When it comes to carving up chunks of a page like this, your first instinct might be to reach for the new section element. After all, they're sections of the document, aren't they? But the section element has specific semantics—it represents a distinct piece of a greater whole, a block of content that deserves its own title but doesn't quite stand on its own out of context (as an article element would). Don't use section only for styling or scripting purposes. If you just need a generic container, the trusty old div is the most fitting element:

```
<div class="main">
  ...
</div>
```

However, in the case of our sidebar, it's slightly more than a generic box; it's optional, supplemental content that relates to the main content of the page, but isn't necessarily part of it. HTML5 introduced the aside element for just such content. Even though a div could serve the same grouping and styling function here, wrapping our sidebar in an aside gives it that little bit of added meaning:

```
<aside class="extra">
  ...
</aside>
```

We've opted for classes instead of IDs on our content blocks because we expect to use them as style hooks when we lay out the page with CSS. We also know we'll need to fill these containers with a wide variety of content that may need different styling depending on their context; an h2 in the main body might need to be different from an h2 in the sidebar. A class selector is less specific than an ID selector in CSS, so classes are less likely to cause trouble when we need more specific selectors to override other style rules. An ID selector is powerful and can only be trumped by another ID. Relying too much on IDs for styling purposes can lead to "specificity wars," forever escalating the strength of your selectors with more specific IDs. If you like, you could certainly assign unique IDs to these content blocks but still rely on reusable classes for styling purposes.

We're wrapping our sections of content in their own containers and that should be enough to finish this template. However, we also know that we'll want to surround those two content blocks with a single container, partly for styling purposes but also to hold them together as the related content they are. Once again we'll use the old reliable div to generate a generic box and symbolically link our two content blocks. This time we'll give it an ID to identify the container because, let's face it, we might really need a more specific selector in our CSS at some point, so having that ID may still come in handy (we promise to use it wisely and sparingly).

Listing 10-5 shows our completed content area with the wrapper div and two inner blocks, a div and an aside. We've also added our noscript notice for IE users into the content area, rather than letting it run loose in the body.

Listing 10-5. The template's content area

```
<div id="content">
  <!--[if lt IE 9]>
    <noscript>
      <p class="notice"><strong>Note:</strong> This website employs some features ↪
      that may not be fully supported by some versions of Internet Explorer. You ↪
      can improve your experience by enabling JavaScript.</p>
    </noscript>
  <![endif]-->

  <div class="main">
    ...
  </div>

  <aside class="extra">
    ...
  </aside>
</div>
```

The Complete Template

After all this structural and semantic plotting, Listing 10-6 presents our completed site template, ready to fill in with useful content. You can download all of this book's source code at foundationhtml.com to study and pick apart at your leisure, or visit power-outfitters.com and view the page source in your browser.

Listing 10-6. The complete (albeit empty) Power Outfitters template

```
<!DOCTYPE html>
<html lang="en-US" dir="ltr" id="power-outfitters-com">
  <head>
    <meta charset="utf-8">
    <meta name="robots" content="index, follow">
    <meta name="keywords" content="capes, masks, tights, superhero, costumes, gadgets">
    <meta name="description" content="Power Outfitters manufactures and sells costumes,↪
      accessories, supplies, and equipment for the contemporary costumed crime-fighter">

    <link rel="stylesheet" type="text/css" media="screen,projection" href="css/screen.css">
    <link rel="stylesheet" type="text/css" media="print" href="css/print.css">

    <!--[if lt IE 9]>
    <script src="js/html5shiv.js"></script>
```

```
  <![endif]-->

  <title>Power Outfitters - Superhero Costume &amp; Supply Co.</title>
</head>

<body class="home">

  <header id="masthead">
    <h1 id="logo">
      <img src="images/logo-big.png" width="265" height="145" ↪
        alt="Power Outfitters Superhero Costume &amp; Supply Co.">
    </h1>

    <div id="store-info">
      <p>616 Kirby Ave (between Romita and Ditko)</p>
      <p>Mon&ndash;Thu: <time datetime="08:00">8am</time>&ndash;↪
        <time datetime="22:00">10pm</time></p>
      <p>Fri&ndash;Sun: <time datetime="08:00">8am</time>&ndash;↪
        <time datetime="00:00">12am</time></p>
      <p>24-hour service and repair: call 555-1961</p>
    </div>

    <div id="utilities">
      <form id="search" action="/search">
        <p>
          <label for="search-main">Search for products</label>
          <input type="search" name="search" id="search-main" ↪
            placeholder="utility belts">
          <button type="submit">Search</button>
        </p>
      </form>

      <p class="cart"><a href="/cart">Your cart: <b>0 items</b></a></p>
      <form id="cart" method="post" action="/cart"></form>
    </div>

    <nav id="nav-main">
      <ul>
        <li><a href="/costuming">Costuming</a></li>
        <li><a href="/gear">Gadgets &amp; Gear</a></li>
        <li><a href="/weaponry">Non-lethal Weaponry</a></li>
        <li><a href="/defense">Armor &amp; Defense</a></li>
        <li><a href="/base">Lair &amp; Vehicle</a></li>
      </ul>
    </nav>

  </header>

  <div id=content>
    <!--[if lt IE 9]>
      <noscript>
        <p class="notice"><strong>Note:</strong> This website employs some features ↪
```

```
            that may not be fully supported by some versions of Internet Explorer. You ↪
            can improve your experience by enabling JavaScript.</p>
        </noscript>
      <![endif]-->

      <section class="main">
        ...
      </section>

      <section class="extra">
        ...
      </section>
    </div>

    <footer id="site-info">
      <nav id="nav-info">
        <ul>
          <li><a href="/help">Help</a></li>
          <li><a href="/about">About</a></li>
          <li><a href="/blog">Blog</a></li>
          <li><a href="/contact">Contact</a></li>
          <li><a href="/shipping">Shipping</a></li>
          <li><a href="/villains">Villain Policy</a></li>
        </ul>
      </nav>

      <p class="slogan">Proud purveyors of practical paraphernalia for the ↪
        contemporary costumed crime-fighter</p>

      <p class="copyright">Copyright &copy; 2011&ndash;2012 Power Outfitters</p>
    </footer>

  </body>
</html>
```

Fleshing Out the Home Page

Before we dive into designing the Power Outfitters site with CSS, let's fill in some content so we'll have something more to work with. We're only working on the home page for now, but we can establish some patterns that might carry through to other pages on the site. The choices you make in marking up different types of content—which elements to use, in what order, and what classes and IDs to assign (if any)—are just as much part of the design process as your choices of colors and fonts. Think it through; consider how the content will be read and used, how that content might change and adapt to varying needs, and how you'll style it later.

Our home page begins simply enough with a title and short introduction—an h1 and some paragraphs. Nothing too fancy here, and you've already seen it a dozen times in this book. The one addition we're making here is a class for the page title:

```
<h1 class="page-title">Welcome, Heroes!</h1>

<p>Power Outfitters offers top of the line merchandise at rock-bottom
prices for the discerning costumed crime-fighter. From belts to boomerangs,
we're your one-stop shop for all your specialized gadgetry and costuming
needs.</p>

<p>Come browse our wide selection of capes, cowls, masks, boots, belts,
gloves, tights, unitards, and leotards in all the colors of the rainbow.
Our clothiers are on call 24 hours a day, always ready in a pinch to
replace a singed cloak or patch a ripped tunic, because we know crime
doesn't sleep and justice can never rest.</p>
```

The "page-title" class distinguishes a page title from any other headings that may appear on a page, including any other h1 elements that might occur inside other sectioning roots. It also gives us a convenient way to style page titles in CSS, and we can use this class with any level of heading to designate that heading as the title of the page, even if it's an h2, an h3, or even a caption or legend element if the need should arise. The "page-title" class disconnects the title's styling from whatever element it happens to appear on. This simple class is a tool we can use over and over again.

Markup Patterns

When you design a website, you're not only designing a collection of individual pages, you're designing an entire system of movable, modular, reusable components. As you're planning and constructing your templates, be on the lookout for patterns that you can repeat. Not graphic patterns like checkerboards or polka dots or paisley, but *markup patterns* that follow the same structure for the same kind of content wherever it occurs. This is called a *design pattern* in programming speak (again, not to be confused with graphic patterns). A design pattern solves a common problem so you can repeat that solution whenever the same problem comes up again, and the concept applies to markup as well. Identify common types of content and establish a flexible pattern that you can reuse each time that type of content appears.

Power Outfitters is an imaginary e-commerce site so it will need to display a lot of products (sadly, the products are also imaginary). We can establish a general pattern for how to mark up products, then follow that pattern throughout the site wherever and whenever we need to display a product. This consistency in our markup helps us maintain consistent styling and behavior throughout the site. Furthermore, in a complex dynamic site—which Power Outfitters would be if it were real—each product box would be programmatically generated from a common template and filled with dynamic content served from a database. Establishing this markup pattern now will save development time later because we won't have to ponder the same decisions over and over again.

On our website, a product will almost always be displayed with a name, an image, a short description, a price, a link to a product details page, and an "Add to Cart" button. We can vary the pattern as needed and those variations can form patterns themselves—a product without an image, a product with both a regular price and a sale price, a product without a cart button, and so on—but let's start with the basics.

The product image will be an img element, naturally, with a descriptive alt attribute. We can enhance it further with the figure element (introduced in Chapter 4) to semantically associate that image with the product name and description. After all, the picture is a figurative representation of a product. The title (a heading) and the description (a paragraph) act as the caption for the figure image so they're both wrapped in a nested `figcaption` element. Now the image illustrates the product, the text describes the image, and everybody wins.

You can see our product figure so far in Listing 10-7. Giving each piece a meaningful class not only offers us a set of style hooks for the CSS we'll add later, but also describes the function and purpose of each part. These classes will be even more valuable when we reuse the same markup pattern elsewhere.

Listing 10-7. A `figure` element for a product image, including a name and description in a `figcaption`

```
<figure>
  <img class="product-img" src="images/products/1-ar7111-bionic-eye.jpg" ↪
  alt="An electronic eye with green iris" width="300" height="225">
  <figcaption>
    <h3 class="name">AR7111 Bionic Eye</h3>
    <p class="description">See into the far reaches! Processes electromagnetic
    frequencies beyond ordinary human vision directly into your brain. Installed
    in a simple outpatient procedure.</p>
  </figcaption>
</figure>
```

There's more to add, but before we get too much further, we'll wrap our entire product in a container with the class "product." That container element may change in different situations; it could be a `section`, an `aside`, a list item, or even a table cell, but we'll use a plain `div` in this example.

Both the image and the product name should act as links to a page with more detail about that product. We can kill both of those birds with one stone by wrapping the entire `figure` in a single a element (making the description part of the link as well). This would have been impossible in HTML4 or XHTML, not least because the `figure` element didn't exist in those versions, but it was previously invalid for an inline a element to contain a block-level heading element. We would have been forced to link those two elements separately, leaving us with two links leading to the same destination (or else we'd need to find some other way to structure our content to avoid redundancy, such as nesting the image inside the heading). HTML5 has done away with the old "inline" and "block-level" content models, and now allows links to contain a much wider variety of content.

The price will appear outside the link, and we'll use a `b` element to make the text stand out but without adding the emphasis a `strong` or `em` element would imply; we want the price to be distinctive and noteworthy, but not necessarily more important than the content around it.

The "Add to Cart" button will be a `button` element with a product code as its value, and we'll associate it with the cart form that we built into the masthead (see, we told you it would be useful later). In HTML4 or XHTML, form-associated elements had to reside within their parent `form` element. We would have had to repeat a new `form` element for every cart button on the page, or else wrap the entire page in one big form. HTML5 and the new `form` attribute means any form-associated interactive element can relate directly to a `form` element elsewhere in the document. Clicking one of these buttons passes along its specific value to a single cart form for processing.

Listing 10-8 finally shows our finished product box, and we'll follow this same markup pattern wherever we need to display a product on the Power Outfitters site. This product box appears on the home page to promote a brand new product in the Power Outfitters catalog. We'll wrap that box in a section element because it forms a distinct part of the home page and it deserves its own title. We're using an h2 here, even though section begins a new sectioning root and we could justifiably use an h1. An h2 will preserve the overall hierarchy of the document and play nicer with current devices that haven't yet implemented HTML5's outlining algorithm.

Listing 10-8. The New Item box on the Power Outfitters home page

```
<section class="new-item">
  <h2>Brand New Item!</h2>

  <div class="product">
    <a class="url" href="/gear/exotics/AR7111-bionic-eye">
      <figure>
        <img class="product-img" src="images/products/l-ar7111-bionic-eye.jpg" ↩
          alt="An electronic eye with green iris" width="300" height="225">
        <figcaption>
          <h3 class="name">AR7111 Bionic Eye</h3>
          <p class="description">See into the far reaches! Processes electromagnetic
          frequencies beyond ordinary human vision directly into your brain. Installed
          in a simple outpatient procedure.</p>
        </figcaption>
      </figure>
    </a>
    <p><b class="price">$23,299</b> (each)</p>
    <p><button class="cart-add" type="submit" name="product" ↩
      value="AR7111-bionic-eye" form="cart">Add to Cart</button></p>
  </div>

</section>
```

A Modular Sidebar

The sidebar is contained in an aside element that indicates its contents are supplemental to the rest of the document, and it could even be removed without harming the meaning of the main content. Within that containing aside we can use whatever elements are appropriate for the content at hand, which will vary from page to page. We know the sidebar needs to be flexible and changeable because we've planned ahead for that. Each sidebar block needs to be a self-contained unit, a reusable module that we can easily add, remove, and rearrange to suit the needs of each page.

The Power Outfitters home page sidebar shows the latest news from the Power Outfitters blog, as well as a "Deal of the Day" promoting a special discount. We'll form distinct blocks for these two sidebar modules by containing each in a section element; they're sections of their parent aside element. Each section gets a "module" class as well as another class more descriptive of what that module does; remember that a single element can belong to any number of classes, with each class name separated by spaces in the class attribute.

You can see our home page sidebar in Listing 10-9. Note that we've reused the product markup pattern for the Deal of the Day box.

Listing 10-9. The sidebar on the Power Outfitters home page

```
<aside class="extra">

  <section class="module news">
    <h2>Latest News</h2>
    <p>Small things, big savings. All shrink rays are on sale,
    this week only! <a href="/blog/shrink-sale">Read all about it!</a></p>
  </section>

  <section class="module deal">
    <h2>Deal of the Day</h2>

    <div class="product">
      <a class="url" href="/gear/exotics/V900-shrink-ray">
      <figure>
        <img class="product-img" src="images/products/m-v900-shrink-ray.jpg" ↩
          alt="The V900 portable shrink ray is pistol shaped with control ↩
          dials on one side and a decorative fin on top" ↩
          width="260" height="155">
        <figcaption>
          <h3 class="name">V900 Portable Shrink Ray</h3>
          <p class="description">Shrink and unshrink inanimate objects
          with point-and-shoot simplicity!</p>
        </figcaption>
      </figure>
      </a>
      <p><s class="reg-price">$10,799</s> <em>marked down to
        <strong class="sale-price">$9,799</strong>!</em></p>
      <p><button class="cart-add" type="submit" name="product" ↩
        value="V900-shrink-ray" form="cart">Add to Cart</button></p>
    </div>
  </section>

</aside>
```

And with that, the Power Outfitters home page is completely marked up. The masthead, content area, and footer together form a base template that all pages to come will use as a common foundation. We've filled in some content for the home page, establishing markup patterns and reusable modules that will reappear throughout the site (or would reappear if we were going to build the rest of it).

We've only touched the home page but you can easily imagine a much larger and more complex website beyond this single page. Every other page template would follow a similar process of thinking through the content, choosing the most semantically appropriate elements, and planning for reusable patterns and modules.

Designing Power Outfitters with CSS

So far we've only shown you the markup for the Power Outfitters home page. We've been thinking ahead to how we'll eventually style this page, but we haven't yet written a single line of CSS. All our attention has been focused on building up the solid framework of meaningful, accessible HTML that will form the foundation of the website. After all that effort, our home page is lean and clean and ready to go, fully functional, readable, and accessible. But as you can see in Figure 10-3, it's not much to look at with only the browser's default styling. The next step is to enhance this sturdy HTML foundation with CSS, adding layers of presentation over our content to make the Power Outfitters site attractive, engaging, and unique.

Figure 10-3. The Power Outfitters home page with only the default browser styling

As you build your own websites, you may end up working on both the HTML and CSS simultaneously, styling each new element as you create it, building up the structure and style together. But it's good practice to separate content from presentation in your mind as well as in your code. When you think about HTML, think first about what the content means and how it works, not about how it looks. You may inevitably need to commit a few presentational markup transgressions—adding an extra span here and there, or giving an element a class just for easier selection in your style sheet—but try to keep presentational markup to a minimum.

In this section we'll describe how we styled the Power Outfitters home page with CSS. You'll see the design take shape bit by bit, from laying out the template to decorating the buttons. We won't cover every last detail of the design in this chapter, but we encourage you to download the example code from foundationhtml.com and tear it apart to your heart's content. Studying how other websites are built is one of the best ways to learn. The tips and techniques we'll demonstrate here are only a starting point.

Resetting Browser Defaults

Every web browser has its own built-in style sheet that establishes the default rendering for most elements. Those default styles are intended to make even an otherwise unstyled document at least readable if rather stark. Although most browsers' default style sheets are pretty similar and they'll display unstyled pages in much the same way—white background, black text, blue underlined links, and so on—there are often subtle differences between different browsers.

To compensate for these differences and to establish a more predictable baseline for our styling to come, we're starting off our style sheet with a *CSS reset*. It's a collection of rules that override browser defaults for most elements, giving us a consistent, cross-browser set of basic styles to add to. A reset strips a site down to the bare minimum and lets you restyle those elements to suit your needs, but without repeatedly overriding the browser defaults in every rule that changes them.

You can find a number of ready-made CSS resets online, often bundled with some broader CSS framework or library. Two of the most popular CSS resets come from the Yahoo! User Interface library (yuilibrary.com/yui/docs/cssreset/) and from the incomparable Eric Meyer (meyerweb.com/eric/tools/css/reset/, yes, Meyer again; he really knows his stuff). These resets tend to be quite thorough and override almost every single browser default, which can be something of a double-edged sword; you gain precision and control over how your pages render, but you'll have to re-declare your own values for every single browser default that was reset.

For our purposes we're happy to leave many of the default styles intact. Instead of opting for a plug-and-play reset we've defined our own, more minimal version. We're only resetting the basics, especially margins and padding so we can have better control over spacing between elements, and we'll let the browser keep its defaults for typography, list styles, and so on. We'll override those defaults if and when we need to later in our style sheet.

Listing 10-10 shows our simplified reset rules, which are the very first rules in our style sheet so later rules can easily modify these values. This reset includes a rule setting most of the new HTML5 elements to display as block-level because older browsers lack any default handling for those elements. Newer browsers don't require this added instruction, but it doesn't do them any harm.

Listing 10-10. Resetting browser default styles

```
header, hgroup, nav, section, article, aside, footer,
figure, figcaption, details, summary {
  display: block;
}

html, body, figure, dt, dd, li, form, fieldset, legend,
input, select, textarea, button {
  padding: 0;
  margin: 0;
}

p, ul, ol, dl, table, blockquote {
  padding: 0;
  margin: 0 0 1.5em;
}

input, button, textarea, select, optgroup, option {
  font-family: inherit;
  font-size: inherit;
}

fieldset {
  border: 0;
}
```

We've completely eliminated padding and margins from a number of elements that have default padding or margins, but for another set of elements we're declaring a standard 1.5em bottom margin (one and a half times the font size), with no margins on the top, left, or right sides. This ensures we still have some vertical spacing between paragraphs, lists, tables, and block quotations. Most browsers add default vertical spacing with margins both above and below these elements. By switching to a bottom margin only, we gain more control over where the tops of these elements will be, especially useful when elements need to align horizontally.

After cleaning the slate with a CSS reset we can start to build up more layers of presentation, working more or less from the top of the page to the bottom, and from the background to the foreground as elements nest and form layers over each other. The very first thing we'll work on is a backdrop for the entire page.

Multiple Background Images

Background images—using the background-image, background-position, and background-repeat properties we first covered in Chapter 5—have been part of CSS from the very beginning. Backgrounds are a cornerstone of a site's visual design and there are a million and one ways to use background images to great effect. However, designers were always limited to one image per element (though the image could tile and repeat infinitely within that element). Any visual effect that demanded more than one background required more elements to carry them, often leading to nested presentational divs or convoluted workarounds. CSS3 finally allows multiple background images in a single element, simply by adding multiple, comma-separated values to the same properties we already have:

```
.blurb {
  background-color: #e6f2f9;
  background-image: url(images/quote-left.png), url(images/quote-right.png);
  background-position: left top, right bottom;
  background-repeat: no-repeat;
}
```

There's no limit to the number of background images for a given element. The first value represents the top-most image, with subsequent values appearing on lower layers, and the last value declared appears on the bottom of the stack.

You can do the same with the shorthand `background` property, declaring each set of values separated by commas. However, even though an element can now carry more than one background image, it can still have only one solid background color; you can't layer multiple colors in a single element. If you include a solid fill color with a multiple `background` shorthand declaration, the color must appear with the last declared (bottom) background:

```
.blurb {
  background: url(images/quote-left.png) left top no-repeat, ↪
    #e6f2f9 url(images/quote-right.png) right bottom no-repeat;
}
```

Figure 10-4 shows the result: a single element with two background images in two different positions. Even with this basic example you can begin to imagine the possibilities, especially if you layer translucent PNG images over each other.

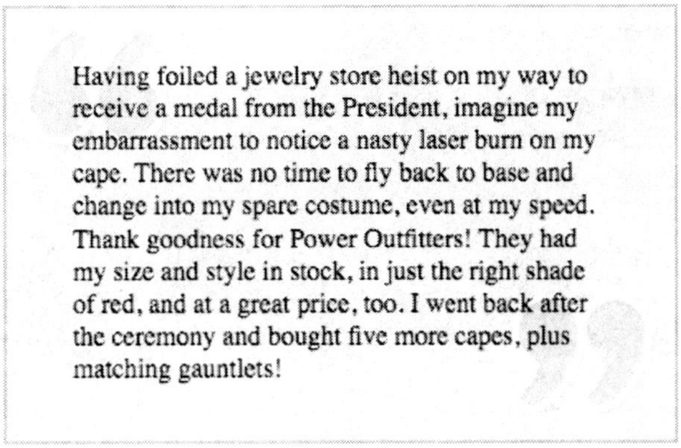

Having foiled a jewelry store heist on my way to receive a medal from the President, imagine my embarrassment to notice a nasty laser burn on my cape. There was no time to fly back to base and change into my spare costume, even at my speed. Thank goodness for Power Outfitters! They had my size and style in stock, in just the right shade of red, and at a great price, too. I went back after the ceremony and bought five more capes, plus matching gauntlets!

Figure 10-4. Two background images in the same element. This wasn't possible before CSS3.

For Power Outfitters, we're using multiple backgrounds to fill the browser window with two different patterns that repeat across the window, one positioned at the top and one at the bottom. We'll apply these backgrounds to the root `html` element rather than the body element; you'll see soon that we have other plans for the body element that don't make it a good candidate to carry this background.

We'll also add a value for the `background-scroll` property. By default, background images scroll in the window along with the content; as content moves up or down out of view, so does the background behind it. Declaring `background-scroll:fixed` (or including the `fixed` value in the shorthand `background` property) overrides the default scrolling behavior and allows the background to remain in the same position as content scrolls over it. This keeps our two background images affixed to the top and bottom edges of the window even as the foreground content moves and scrolls over them.

Although multiple backgrounds are well supported in all the latest browsers, older browsers from just a few years ago didn't support this feature of CSS3. When a browser encounters a style declaration it doesn't understand, it just ignores the declaration and moves on parsing the next one. When confronted with an unsupported value for the background property, older browsers won't apply any background to the element at all. We can accommodate those less capable browsers by first declaring a background the old-fashioned way, with only one image, then adding a second declaration with multiple images for newer browsers that understand it. You can see the style rule for the html element in Listing 10-11. The later, multi-image declaration overrides the previous one; it's the cascade in action.

Listing 10-11. Applying multiple, fixed, tiling background images to the html element

```
html {
  background: #fffae1 url(../images/bg-top.png) left top repeat-x fixed;
  background: url(../images/bg-top.png) left top repeat-x fixed, ↪
    #fffae1 url(../images/bg-bottom.png) left bottom repeat-x fixed;
}
```

Figure 10-5 shows the result, but you can't really appreciate the fixed scrolling effect in a printed screenshot. The lighter bottom image sticks to the bottom edge of the browser window even though the content overflows down and out of view. As the window scrolls vertically, more content comes into view from the bottom as content scrolls out of view at the top, but both the top and bottom background images stay right where they are, fixed to the edges of the viewport.

Figure 10-5. Our comic-inspired, dot-patterned background, accomplished with two images in two positions, filling the html element.

The Body Boundary

We've opted for a liquid layout for Power Outfitters rather than a fixed width, meaning the site will automatically adapt to the width of the visitor's window, however wide that may be. It won't be *completely* fluid, however; we'll include `min-width` and `max-width` values to impose some constraints on the overall page width. This necessitates some sort of containing element to bind the page within those constraints. By default, the `body` element fills the entire browser window so you could ordinarily apply a background color or image to the `body`. With a full-width `body` element, centering a page within that space requires some additional element—probably a `div`—serving no other purpose but to be a presentational container for the page, defining a box within the wider window.

But we planned ahead, and rather than using the `body` to carry a full-width background, we applied our background to the `html` element. The body element is now free to act as a narrower container, centered within the browser window by way of the `auto` value for both the left and right margins. We can add some padding to the `body` element to ensure there's always some space between the content and the window's edge, even in narrow windows.

While we're working on the `body` element we'll also define our base font styles for the document (16 pixel Calibri with a 1.4 proportional `line-height`) and add a global foreground color for text (#444, a dark gray, almost but not quite black). You can see our finished style rule for the `body` element in Listing 10-12. Without a specified width, the `body` element defaults to `width:auto`, allowing the browser to calculate the width automatically when it renders the page. If the window is wide enough, the `max-width` and automatic margins take effect to center the page. The page also won't become too squished in narrow windows thanks to the `min-width` property (very narrow windows will, alas, invoke a horizontal crawl bar, but that's better than making the content unreadable).

Listing 10-12. Applying some padding, margins, a minimum width, a maximum width, text color, and base font styles to the `body` element

```
body {
  margin: 0 auto;
  padding: 0 40px 20px;
  min-width: 640px;
  max-width: 1160px;
  font: 16px/1.4 Calibri, "Trebuchet MS", sans-serif;
  color: #444;
}
```

We'd show you a screen capture of the results so far, but there isn't much new to see right now because the body element is just an invisible box. You'll see how the body manifests soon enough when we begin styling other content. The width constraints we've applied to the `body` element make it act as a flexible, invisible fence to corral the page into the middle of the window, and without adding an extra, presentational `div`.

Styling the Masthead

The site's masthead features the Power Outfitter's logo, the store's (fictional) address and business hours, a search form, and a link to the customer's virtual shopping cart (flip back to Listing 10-5 to see the markup we're working with). There's also the site's primary navigation to deal with, and we'll get to that soon, but first we'll get the rest of the elements lined up where we want them to be.

The logo will appear on the left side of the masthead and the other elements—the store info, search form, and cart link—will appear on the right. That's easy enough to accomplish with the float property, and we'll assign widths to each block that will ensure the liquid layout can shrink and expand freely without the floats colliding. The logo gets a bit of extra width (50% of the parent element's width) so that even in narrow windows it will have enough room for the fixed-size image without clipping or overflowing. The image won't usually need that much room, but the extra width prevents the containing element from shrinking smaller than the image in narrow windows.

The store info and utilities blocks both float to the right, and including a clear:right declaration for these boxes ensures they will stack one above the other in a tidy column roughly one third the width of the page. We'll also give them a minimum width to prevent the blocks from being squeezed too tightly in narrow windows:

```
#logo {
  width: 50%;
  float: left;
}

#store-info {
  width: 32%;
  min-width: 260px;
  float: right;
  clear: right;
}

#utilities {
  width: 32%;
  min-width: 260px;
  float: right;
  clear: right;
}
```

Of course, we'll have to clear these floats to prevent the masthead from collapsing and other content from flowing upwards, around and between the columns. Any one of the clearing methods we covered in Chapter 9 might be useful here, but let's not overlook the simplest clearing method of all: an element that can clear the floats above it. Our masthead ends with a navigation bar that will span the width of the page, so we can use that element itself as a clearing element for the entire masthead:

```
#nav-main {
  clear: both;
}
```

At this point we only have a very rough layout with the logo on the left and the rest of the masthead content on the right. It's not exactly pretty just yet, as you can see in Figure 10-6, but it's progress. We'll need to give these blocks a little more individual attention to make them look better.

Figure 10-6. The masthead as it's styled so far, which isn't very far at all

The Store Info and Utilities

Any website for a brick-and-mortar business—like restaurants, mechanics, antique shops, beauty parlors, or the local comic book store—should prominently feature the business' address, hours of operation, and perhaps a phone number in a place where it's easy to find. If you want customers to come to your door they'll first need to know where your door is and when it's open. It's just common sense.

Power Outfitters' store information is a collection of paragraphs wrapped in a div element right there at the very top of the page. We want it to be easy to spot, but it shouldn't overtake its neighboring content; it shouldn't compete for attention with the logo, search form, and cart link. We'll give the store info some subtle presence by decorating the box it appears in, but not so much that it leaps off the screen. It just needs a little padding, a border, and some text styling.

Listing 10-13 shows our styling for the store info box. The negative top margin pulls the top of the box up beyond the top edge of the window to hide the box's top border, and the generous top padding pushes the text down into view. The combined effect is of a box that appears to hang from the top of the window like a shingle. Also note that we haven't added any left or right padding because it would be added to the box's declared width. Instead of trying to adjust the width to compensate for padding, we've added left and right margins to the paragraphs within the box to achieve the same spacing.

Listing 10-13. The CSS rules that style the store info box in the Power Outfitters masthead

```
#store-info {
  width: 32%;
  min-width: 260px;
  float: right;
  clear: right;
  padding: 38px 0 15px;
  margin: -20px 0 20px;
  border: 2px solid #0c2d8c;
  background: #102562;
```

```
  background: rgba(6,37,127,.75);
  font-size: .75em;
  color: #bec4d2;
}

#store-info p {
  margin: 0 20px;
}
```

The utilities block comprises a simple search form and a link to the visitor's shopping cart, grouped together in another div element. To get the search form and the cart button to line up horizontally, we can float each one within their container. We don't even need to clear these floats because the utilities box is already floating; floating elements automatically clear their floating descendants:

```
#site-search {
  width: 65%;
  float: left;
}

#utilities .cart {
  width: 30%;
  float: right;
}
```

Diving another level deeper, both the search field and search button will also float so they'll line up adjacent to each other on the same baseline. We'll float them both to the left with a small margin in between:

```
#search {
  width: 70%;
  float: left;
  margin-right: 8px;
}

#site-search button {
  width: 15%;
  float: left;
}
```

Image Replacement

Our search form includes a submit button with the text label "Search." It's a fine button, very simple, straightforward, with no frills. It gets the job done, but it's a little boring and a few tasteful frills could do it some good. We'd like to display a small magnifying glass icon—which has become well recognized as a symbol meaning "search"—instead of the plain text label. We could accomplish this with an input type="image", of course, but it's also possible to replace an element's text contents with an image while still preserving the original text in the markup.

Image replacement is a CSS technique (many different techniques, actually) whereby an element's contents are hidden and a background image appears in its place. It's a way to achieve visual effects only possible with images, but without sacrificing the semantics and accessibility of real text. A number of image replacement techniques have been around for years and they've long been trusty tools in the CSS designer's kit. You can find a helpful roundup of different image replacement methods at CSS Tricks (`css-tricks.com/examples/ImageReplacement/`).

The particular technique we'll use for our search button was first popularized by designer Mike Rundle way back in the mid-2000s and it's still one of the most common CSS tricks in the book. This method of image replacement uses the `text-indent` property with a negative value to push an element's contents aside and out of view, leaving the background image visible in its stead.

Listing 10-14 shows the updated style rule for our search button. We're adding a huge negative indentation to push the button's text far off to the left, well out of view on even the largest screens. We've assigned a width and height, and hidden the overflowing content to prevent possible crawl bars. You could use any unit of measure you like, but we're using ems in this example, and we're using 999 because it's the highest number with only three digits; an extra digit would be one more byte we don't really need. Any high number would work just as well, but 999 has a nice ring.

Listing 10-14. Using `text-indent` to replace a button's text with a background image

```
#site-search button {
  float: left;
  width: 15%;
  height: 26px;
  padding: 2px;
  border: 2px solid #fc0;
  text-indent: -999em;
  overflow: hidden;
  background: #fff4a5 url(../images/icon-search.png) 50% 50% no-repeat;
}

#site-search label {
  position: absolute;
  left: -999em;
}
```

We've also hidden the field's accompanying `label` element with a somewhat similar method, absolutely positioning the entire element far off to the left. The element is still there in the markup where screen readers can access it, but graphical browsers won't display anything at all.

> *Why not hide the search field label with* `display:none`*? The* `display:none` *declaration completely removes an element from the document flow, as if it didn't exist at all. Most screen reading software will honor a* `display:none` *declaration by not reading the text of the hidden element, assuming the author intended to remove the element entirely. Positioning an element outside the window allows its text to be read by screen readers, but still hides it out of view of graphical browsers that may not need the extra hint.*

With some additional styling added to the search field, giving it some color and a matching border, you can see our finished search form in Figure 10-7. This image replacement technique works well but isn't completely foolproof. It can prove troublesome in right-to-left languages in some browsers, and for any browsers that don't display images but still render CSS the button will simply appear blank, with neither text nor image. Some other approaches to image replacement work around this pesky "images off, CSS on" scenario, but for this particular button we've decided we can live with it. Know your users and test your sites thoroughly. You might choose a different approach for your particular situation.

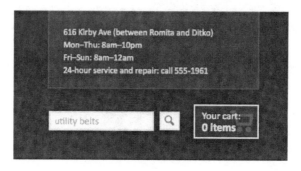

616 Kirby Ave (between Romita and Ditko)
Mon–Thu: 8am–10pm
Fri–Sun: 8am–12am
24-hour service and repair: call 555-1961

utility belts

Your cart:
0 Items

Figure 10-7. The finished search form. We've floated the shopping cart link to the right and styled it with a border, padding, and background.

Styling the Navigation

A navigation bar separates the masthead from the main content, forming the primary navigation for the entire site. It's a nav element that in turn contains an unordered list of links, each leading to a different category in our made-up product catalog. A list is an appropriate element here because that's what a menu is: a list of options from which to choose. But list items are usually displayed stacked one on top of the other, not lined up side by side. We can solve that easily by floating each list item to the left, and we'll also remove the default bullets from the list and zero out its margins:

```
#nav-main ul {
  list-style: none;
  margin: 0;
}

#nav-main li {
  float: left;
}
```

Because the list items are all floating, their containing elements will collapse, as you saw in Chapter 9. We'll prevent that by clearing those floating list items with generated content. That also means we can add a background and border to the nav element to form a bar that will stand out in our masthead. Without clearing the floated list elements, the bar would collapse to nothing and the list items would overflow their container. Also remember that the entire nav element itself is clearing the floating elements above it in the masthead. You can see the progress so far in Listing 10-15.

Listing 10-15. Floating the list items turns a vertical list into a horizontal row

```
#nav-main {
  clear: both;
  text-transform: uppercase;
```

```
    border: 2px solid #ff9e05;
    background-color: #fc0;
}

#nav-main:after {
    content: ".";
    display: block;
    clear: both;
    height: 0;
    visibility: hidden;
}

#nav-main ul {
    list-style: none;
    margin: 0;
}

#nav-main li {
    float: left;
    border-right: 2px solid #ff9e05;
}
```

We've also added text-transform:uppercase to display the text in all capitals, and a right border to each list item to match the border around the entire navigation bar. Figure 10-8 shows the current rendered state, but we're not quite done with it yet.

Figure 10-8. The navigation bar is horizontal now, but still needs more work

Without a width, floated elements collapse around their contents. These navigation links all line up, but they're bunched tightly together and nearly impossible to read. Links render as inline elements by default, so they take up no more space on the page than their contents. We could easily pad the list items to create some inner spacing between their edges and their contents, but the active, clickable links would be no bigger than the words themselves.

Small links can sometimes be a difficult target to hit with a mouse click (or finger tap on mobile devices). So why not pad the links and make a bigger clickable, tappable target? We've done just that in Listing 10-16. We've also removed the usual underline from the normal and visited link states, but the underline will appear when a user hovers over the link, focuses it, or activates it. We're declaring a background color twice: first as a fallback for older browsers that don't support RGBA color, then again for newer browsers that do support RGBA (this goes way back to Chapter 2).

Listing 10-16. Styling the main navigation links.

```
#nav-main a:link,
#nav-main a:visited {
  display: block;
  padding: .25em 10px;
  text-decoration: none;
}

#nav-main a:hover,
#nav-main a:focus,
#nav-main a:active {
  background: #f90;
  background: rgba(255,153,0,.3);
  text-decoration: underline;
}
```

Ordinarily, padding an inline element has little effect on how it behaves in a page layout, and other elements around them may not respect that padding, treating the element as if it weren't padded at all. Setting these navigation links to `display:block` makes them render as block-level elements, filling the space of their containing element—or to state it more accurately, it forces the outer elements to expand around the block-level elements within.

As you can see in Figure 10-9, the navigation links now take up a bit more space and offer much larger targets for clicking and tapping. The link's entire background, including the padded area, fills in with a solid color when the link becomes active.

Figure 10-9. The finished navigation bar separates the masthead from the content below (we'll be working on that content next).

"Fitts' Law" is an age-old axiom in interaction design, named for psychologist Paul Fitts who proposed it in 1954. To paraphrase roughly, Fitts' Law states that the time required to point to a target is a function of the distance to the target and the size of the target area. In other words, small, far-away targets are harder to hit than large, nearby targets. Bear that in mind whenever you're building navigation, buttons, forms, or other interactive elements. Give your users a large target area they can click with ease.

Laying Out the Content

Our dramatic dotted background makes a bold statement, but any text that overlays that eye-popping pattern will be almost unreadable. We need to wrap our entire content area in a box that will both define the space and provide a better backdrop for readable text. As it happens, we already have a wrapper element in place (almost as if we planned for it) so it's just a case of giving that box a solid background, along with some padding and a border:

```
#content {
  background: #fff;
  border: 2px solid #c9c5b4;
  padding: 25px 15px 5px;
}
```

But let's not stop there: we can use RGBA color to make the background *translucent*, solid enough to provide contrast for reading, but still allowing a very subtle hint of the pattern behind it show through. We can also add a tiling background image, itself a translucent PNG, adding another layer of texture. We can even use RGBA colors for the border, letting the colors and textures behind it come through slightly. We'll still include the opaque colors for both the background and border, just to offer a fallback for older browsers that don't support RGBA. Without that fallback background color, people using older browsers wouldn't be able to read our text. Listing 10-17 presents our revised rule for the content box.

Listing 10-17. Building up translucent layers with RGBA and PNG

```
#content {
  background: #fff url(../images/bg-texture.png);
  background: rgba(255,255,255,.9) url(../images/bg-texture.png);
  border: 2px solid #c9c5b4;
  border-color: rgba(150,150,150,.5);
  padding: 25px 15px 5px;
}
```

We don't need to repeat the entire shorthand `border` declaration, we only need to declare a new value for `border-color`, the only value we're changing. The original, opaque hex color can remain in place for less capable browsers.

Figure 10-10 shows an enlarged corner of the content box, showing off both the texture and the translucent effect. It's pretty faint, but it works nicely on the rendered page. Little details like this begin to add up to a unique design.

Figure 10-10. A close-up view of one corner of the content box shows the partially transparent background and subtle grain texture

There are two columns inside this outer content wrapper—or there will be as soon as we float their containing blocks in opposite directions. We'll need to give each column a width or else they'll "shrink-wrap" to the size of their contents, and we need to make sure the combined total widths don't exceed the width of the container to ensure the sidebar won't drop under the main column. Using percentages for the column widths allows them to contract and expand to fit the liquid layout.

We'll split the page roughly in thirds, with the main column taking up two thirds of the page, leaving the remaining third for the sidebar. Following basic mathematics, the main column should be around 66% of the page width and the sidebar should be about 33% (we're rounding these numbers off to whole percentages). The math is easy enough but these widths won't leave much of a gutter between columns, only 1%.

We need to add a touch more margin around each column but we have to keep the proportions liquid. Margins or padding declared in a fixed unit like pixels wouldn't adjust to the liquid page width, so we might see unfortunate float collisions in narrower windows. Using percentages for the margins will let the margins flex and adjust along with everything else, and we'll subtract the width of the margins from the width of the columns to keep things in order. Adding an extra 1% margin on either side of each column means subtracting 2% from each width, arriving at our final width values for the content columns, as you can see in Listing 10-18.

Listing 10-18. The main column floats to the left and occupies two thirds of the page while the sidebar floats to the right and occupies the remaining third

```
.main {
  float: left;
  width: 64%;
  margin: 0 1% 20px;
}

.extra {
  float: right;
  width: 31%;
  margin: 0 1%;
}
```

We'll need to clear these floating columns, of course, or else the content box around them will collapse and we'll lose that nice translucent background that makes our text readable. Once again the trusty generated content "easy clearing" method works like a charm. Now that we have columns in a box you can see our page layout really starting to take shape in Figure 10-11.

Figure 10-11. The layout begins to come together once we divide our content into two columns

Reusable Boxes

The sidebar's content will vary from page to page, displaying supplemental information, additional navigation, related products, or special promotions—in short, whatever extra, optional content is fitting for the particular page at hand. Instead of tackling every new piece of sidebar content one by one, we can plan ahead and establish some general, reusable styles for any sidebar modules we may need to create down the line.

We've already included the "module" class in our markup so now it's time to decide what a sidebar module looks like. It doesn't need to be too fancy, just some padding, a border, and a background color. A bottom margin separates modules when they stack up in the sidebar. Listing 10-19 presents the CSS rule for sidebar modules (actually any element in the "module" class, wherever it might occur).

Listing 10-19. A common style for modular boxes

```
.module {
  padding: 15px 20px 10px;
  margin: 0 0 20px;
  background: rgba(255,255,255,0.5);
  border: 2px solid #e1dcca;
  border-color: rgba(150,150,150,0.25);
}
```

Once again we're using an RGBA color—pure white at 50% opacity—so the box allows some of the background behind it to show through, but here we haven't bothered to include an opaque color for older browsers. We could certainly do that, but it's not really necessary in this case. The translucent background is an added enhancement for the browsers that support RGBA; other browsers can simply live without it. Web pages don't need to look exactly the same in every browser ever made. However, we do still want the module's edges to be visible so we'll include a solid fallback color for the border and more advanced browsers can display the RGBA border instead.

In addition to the generic module box we've also established product boxes as a markup pattern, and we can create some basic styles for those boxes wherever they may occur. We planned ahead when we were constructing our document so we have plenty of meaningful classes to use as style hooks, starting with the product image.

The img element is a *replaced element*, meaning it has no content and the element itself isn't rendered on the page, it's merely replaced by the source image file. Even so, some aspects of the img element's presentation are still susceptible to CSS; width and height, naturally, but also margins, padding, borders, and even backgrounds. We can create a frame effect around product images by padding the img element (selected by its "product-img" class) and adding an opaque white background:

```
.product .product-img {
  background-color: #fff;
  padding: 4px;
}
```

We'll add a thin white border as well, making the "frame" appear to be five pixels wide; 4px of padding plus 1px of border, merging seamlessly because they're the same color. When a user hovers her mouse over the link or gives it focus—remember, the product image is inside a link—we'll change the border color to offer some hint that the image is clickable.

You can see our final product image rules in Listing 10-20, including a rule for the image in hovered, focused, and active link states. We've declared display:block so the image will rest on its own line, and a bottom margin adds some space between the image and the text that follows it.

Listing 10-20. Creating a frame effect around product images

```
.product .product-img {
  background-color: #fff;
  padding: 4px;
  border: 1px solid #fff;
  display: block;
  margin: 0 auto 1em;
}

a:hover .product-img,
a:focus .product-img,
a:active .product-img {
  border-color: #fc0;
}
```

The `auto` value for the left and right margins will center the image in the box. Changing the border color when the link state changes makes a double border effect, as you see in Figure 10-12.

Deal of the Day

V900 Portable Shrink Ray

Shrink and unshrink inanimate objects with point-and-shoot simplicity!

Figure 10-12. The framed product image reveals a thin, colored border when a pointer hovers over it

The link wraps around the entire figure, including its title and description (in a `figcaption` element). That mass of underlined text isn't especially pleasing to the eye, so we'll override the underline and link color for these product URLs. However, the product name should still receive some text decoration when the link is hovered or focused, so we can restore those styles in another rule for the name alone, further overriding the previous override:

```
.product .url {
  text-decoration: none;
  color: inherit;
}

.product .url:hover .name,
.product .url:focus .name,
.product .url:active .name {
  text-decoration: underline;
  color: #1b46c3;
}
```

369

Designing with CSS often boils down to the artful application of overrides. You're providing your own style rules to override the browser's defaults, and often overriding your own previously declared style rules with more specific rules, or with equally specific rules and declarations further down in the cascade order. Understanding inheritance, specificity, and the cascade will help you keep track of which values are affecting a given element and which values are being overridden to arrive at the final presentation.

The New Item Box

The home page prominently showcases the latest addition to the Power Outfitters catalog of products. This is a big promotion of a hot-ticket item so it should really stand out and demand attention (but not in an obnoxious way). In the markup, this new item box is just another product box, though it has an extra wrapper and another heading to introduce it. We can give this product box a different layout and some extra decoration to make it look a little more special, but without changing the box's structure at all.

We want to place the product image on the left side of the box with the rest of the content on the right. Simply floating the image to the left is a good start, but it's not quite good enough. As you can see in Figure 10-13, the content would flow around the floated image, just as you'd expect. What we really want to do is keep the product name, description, price, and cart button in a neat column on the right with the image by itself in a column on the left. And we want to do this without changing the structural markup or adding any extra elements.

Figure 10-13. Floating an image works just as it should, but this isn't the layout we're after

The solution to this problem is a clever combination of padding and absolute positioning, just like we demonstrated in Chapter 9. We'll add some generous padding to the left side of the box, pushing the text to the right side to create the appearance of columns. Then we'll position the image into the padded space we've reserved for it.

Listing 10-21 shows the beginnings of our CSS. Declaring `position:relative` for the containing element establishes the positioning context for the product image and the `min-height` property ensures the box will be at least as tall as the image. The image is positioned out of the normal flow so without this `min-height` declaration the box would collapse to the height of the text, which might not always be as tall as the image.

Listing 10-21. Laying out the new item box

```css
.new-item .product {
  position: relative;
  padding: 25px 25px 10px 54%;
  min-height: 225px;
  border: 2px solid #00258e;
  background: rgba(255,255,255,.5) url(../images/new-burst.png) 108% 116% no-repeat;
}

.new-item .product-img {
  position: absolute;
  left: 25px;
  top: 25px;
}
```

We've padded the left half of the product box (slightly more than half, actually) with a percentage value, allowing the padding to adjust to the fluid width of the page as the box itself adjusts. However, bitmap images by their very nature are not fluid, so there's a chance this image will overlap the text if the padded space becomes too small for it, like you see in Figure 10-14.

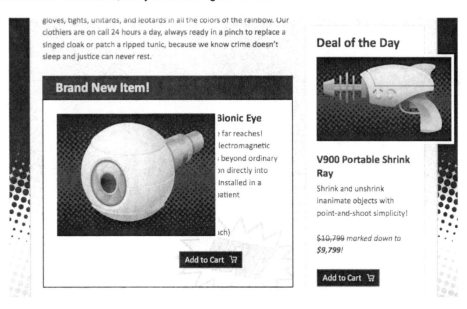

Figure 10-14. Images with a fixed width in a liquid layout can overflow their containers or overlap other content

This situation comes up all too often in liquid layouts: fixed-width content that overflows its liquid-width container. Luckily there's an elegant solution to this common problem.

Fluid Images

It's surprisingly easy to make a naturally fixed-width image behave like a liquid-width box. It takes one rule in a style sheet:

```
img { max-width: 100%; }
```

This simple CSS rule declares that all inline images (all instances of the img element) should never exceed the width of their containing elements. If the image is smaller than its container it will still display at its natural size, or whatever size it's been given in CSS or in a width attribute. But if the image is larger than its container, the browser will automatically scale the image down to fit. A max-width value in a style sheet will override an inline width attribute, but any widths assigned to an image elsewhere in the style sheet can still take precedence, especially if they're coupled with a more specific selector.

This rule so far only affects the *width* of the image, not its height. If you include an inline height attribute—as we have with our product images—that height value will remain in effect even when the width scales, changing the image's aspect ratio. This can lead to unsightly squishing like you see in Figure 10-15.

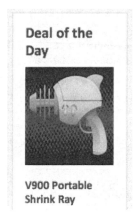

Figure 10-15. An image scales to fit the width of its container, but its height is unchanged. The result is a squeezed and distorted image, much taller than it should be.

There's a simple and elegant solution to the squishing problem as well:

```
img {
  max-width: 100%;
  height: auto;
}
```

With the addition of a height:auto declaration, whenever the image's width changes to fit its container, its height will adjust automatically to preserve the file's original aspect ratio, overriding the image's height attribute, if it has one.

What's more, this simple technique works for most other embedded media, not just images:

```
img,
video,
object,
embed {
  max-width: 100%;
  height: auto;
}
```

We'll add this rule to the CSS reset at the top of our style sheet so most embedded images and videos will fit their liquid containers automatically. The technique works well in current browsers but can prove problematic in older browsers, especially on Windows (which doesn't always resize images smoothly). You can learn more about fluid images—including some workarounds for older, less capable browsers—in Ethan Marcotte's aptly titled article, "Fluid Images" (alistapart.com/articles/fluid-images/).

Now we can get back to our new item image. Remember that it's positioned out of the ordinary flow of the document, and is positioned on the left side of its container. To fit into the space created by the box's padding, this image actually needs to be *less* than the full width of the box, so we'll adjust this image's maximum width accordingly. Instead of ensuring that it never exceeds 100% of its parent's width, we'll make sure it never exceeds 42% of its parent's width (42% because we still want to keep some space around the image, so it should be a little less than half of the container).

Listing 10-22 shows our final styling for the new item box and product image, and you can see the end result in Figure 10-16. The entire box will adjust to the width of the page because we've used percentage units for widths and padding where necessary. We haven't covered the styling for the title bar; you'll get to enjoy figuring that out on your own.

Listing 10-22. The complete style rules for the new item box on the Power Outfitters home page

```
.new-item .product {
  position: relative;
  padding: 25px 25px 10px 54%;
  min-height: 225px;
  border: 2px solid #00258e;
  background: rgba(255,255,255,.5) url(../images/new-burst.png) 108% 116% no-repeat;
}

.new-item .product-img {
  position: absolute;
  left: 25px;
  top: 25px;
  max-width: 42%;
}
```

Figure 10-16. The completed new item box

Styling the Footer

The site's footer is nothing too elaborate. It features some secondary navigation, the company slogan, and a copyright date—standard footer fare. We'll add a smaller version of the Power Outfitters logo but it's strictly decorative here so we can use a background image and avoid any additional markup. The entire footer will form a box with a border and background color, and we'll include some extra padding on the left side to make room for the logo:

```
#site-info {
  padding: 15px 30px 0 160px;
  border: 2px solid #ffc307;
  margin-top: 20px;
  background: #fc0 url(../images/logo-small.png) 20px 15px no-repeat;
  background-color: rgba(255,225,105,.8);
}
```

We've declared the background color twice: first in the shorthand background property with an opaque, hexadecimal color value for older browsers, then overriding that with a second background-color declaration providing a translucent, RGBA value for newer browsers.

The rest of the footer comes together quite simply, and you should be starting to get the hang of this by now. We'll remove the default bullets for the navigation list and declare each list item should appear on the same line with display:inline, overriding the default list item display. A modest right margin wedges some extra space between the inline list items. We'll include just a few more rules styling the slogan and copyright statement and we have ourselves a finished footer. Listing 10-23 shows the full set of CSS rules and you can see the result in Figure 10-17.

Listing 10-23. The CSS rules that style the Power Outfitters footer

```
#site-info {
  margin-top: 20px;
  border: 2px solid #ffc307;
  padding: 15px 30px 0 160px;
```

```
  background: #fc0 url(../images/logo-small.png) 20px 15px no-repeat;
  background-color: rgba(255,225,105,.8);
}

#site-info .slogan {
  font-style: italic;
  font-family: Cambria, Georgia, serif;
  margin: 0 0 .75em;
}

#site-info .copyright {
  font-size: .857em;
}

#nav-info ul {
  list-style: none;
  margin: 0 0 .75em;
}

#nav-info li {
  display: inline;
  margin-right: 10px;
}
```

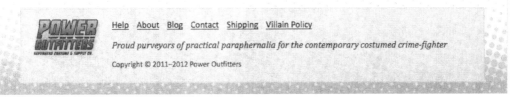

Figure 10-17. The Power Outfitters footer

And with that, we've reached the end of the document and we have ourselves a completed web page. Of course, we skipped over a few elements and only covered a handful of useful techniques, but we've assembled and styled a web page from top to bottom and from back to front. You can see the complete Power Outfitters home page in Figure 10-18.

Figure 10-18. The Power Outfitters home page

Not too shabby, if we do say so ourselves. And yet… it could still use a little something extra. This is a perfectly serviceable web page, but maybe we can add a few more details to enhance the visual experience.

Taking It Further

In this book we've shown you a lot of CSS properties and techniques you can use to design web pages, but it's just the tip of the proverbial iceberg. We've barely even touched on some of the new and exciting features of CSS3. In this next section we're going to take things a step further and demonstrate just a few parts of the emerging CSS3 standard.

Like HTML5, CSS3 is still a work in progress. It isn't a single specification; CSS3 consists of numerous standalone modules, each progressing separately and at a difference pace. Some parts of CSS3 are practically complete and already well supported by current browsers. Other parts are fairly well defined, but have only been implemented as experimental features in a few browsers, so they should be used with some care and caution. Some parts of the CSS3 specification are still in their early draft stages and have yet to be implemented by any browsers, making it impossible to use them on the Web right now, but they'll become available in the near future.

You can turn to the W3C website (w3.org/standards/techs/css) or to CSS3 Info (css3.info/modules/) to keep tabs on the current status of each module as they move through the standardization process. The Mozilla Developer Network has comprehensive, community-managed documentation for just about every CSS property you can imagine (https://developer.mozilla.org/en/CSS/CSS_Reference) to help you better understand how CSS works in both theory and in practice. Sites like Can I Use (caniuse.com) and CSS3 Click Chart (css3clickchart.com) offer at-a-glance guides so you can keep up with browser support.

Even in its unfinished and somewhat uncertain state, you can safely use many CSS3 features in your web projects right now, although often with some caveats to consider. Practice progressive enhancement and add CSS3 features wisely and responsibly, providing fallbacks for older browsers where sensible.

What you've already seen in this chapter is a working example of progressive enhancement in action. We're using tried-and-true CSS techniques to lay out and design Power Outfitters in a way that should work even in less capable browsers and devices, making the content functional and accessible to all (within reason). Now we'll add even more layers of enhanced presentation, improving the site in the latest and greatest browsers that can support these newer methods.

Vendor Prefixes

As the CSS specification continues to take shape, browser makers are busily trying to keep abreast of new developments and implementing not-yet-finished features of CSS3. The CSS language includes a built-in mechanism to allow such experimentation by rendering engines: the *vendor prefix*. Any experimental property, value, or selector in CSS that is only supported in one given rendering engine—meaning it's a proprietary, not-yet-standardized feature—should carry a coded prefix unique to that rendering engine.

In simpler language, experimental features are specially marked so only one rendering engine can understand them. Other browsers should ignore those unrecognized properties and continue parsing the style sheet as normal.

To offer one example, CSS3 introduces the ability to add a shadow effect behind (or within) an element with the new box-shadow property. For some time the exact syntax of a box-shadow value was still being decided, and browsers were figuring out how to render those shadows on screen. During this period of development and experimentation, browsers implemented preliminary support for box-shadow by adding a vendor-specific prefix to the property name:

- -moz-box-shadow for Mozilla Firefox (and other browsers that use Mozilla's rendering engine).

- `-webkit-box-shadow` for Apple Safari and Google Chrome (plus any other browsers using the Webkit rendering engine).

- `-ms-box-shadow` for Microsoft Internet Explorer.

- `-o-box-shadow` for Opera.

Each of these prefixed properties represents one browser's implementation of `box-shadow`; Webkit browsers should ignore Mozilla prefixed properties, and vice versa. Vendor prefixes allow both the browser vendors and web developers to safely experiment with in-progress specifications before they're widely available. You can use prefixed CSS3 features to target only browsers that support them with little concern about how they might impact other browsers.

Automatic CSS validators will usually indicate a warning when they encounter a vendor-specific prefix. That's just the validator doing what it's supposed to do and warning you about a non-standard or unrecognized property, selector, or value. If you know what you're doing you can disregard those warnings and bravely forge ahead into the frontiers of cutting-edge CSS.

Once the specification for an experimental feature is stable and the vendor has thoroughly tested and debugged their implementation, that browser should begin to support the property without the vendor-specific prefix. In due time, the browser should stop supporting the prefixed version in favor of the un-prefixed standard. Vendor prefixes aren't meant to last forever; they're intended for limited, short-term use, not permanent implementations.

Whenever you use a vendor-specific prefix in your CSS, always also include the un-prefixed standard version, even though some browsers may not yet support the feature without a prefix. Use vendor prefixes with the knowledge that they will soon disappear.

Furthermore, you can (and often should) also include the prefixes for *all* the major browsers, including those that haven't yet implemented the feature at all, even with a prefix. Covering all the bases can help to future-proof your websites for the next generation of browsers. Using only one vendor's prefix would unfairly exclude people using other browsers.

Throughout this section we'll be covering some properties and values that are only supported with vendor prefixes in some browsers, or that required a vendor prefix until recently. In each case we'll include the prefixes of all four major vendors as well the un-prefixed standardized version. It may seem redundant—because it is—but it's the responsible way to build websites.

Box Shadows

The `box-shadow` property renders a shadow around, behind, or even within almost any element's bounding box. An outer cast shadow can make the box appear to float above the page surface, or an inner shadow can make the box appear like a depression into the page surface or like a cutout window. A box shadow has no effect on the size or layout of the box itself, and shadows can overlap other content.

This property accepts a set of values describing different aspects of the shadow:

- offset-x and offset-y: These are two required length values that indicate the horizontal and vertical offset of the shadow. The first length indicates the horizontal offset on the x-axis and the second indicates the vertical offset on the y-axis. Negative offset values position the shadow to the left or top of the element, positive lengths offset the shadow down and to the right, and 0 indicates no offset at all.

- blur radius: A third, optional length value indicates the amount of blur to apply to the shadow. Higher values indicate more blur, and a blur radius of 0 (the default) indicates a shadow with no blur and a sharp outline.

- spread radius: A fourth, optional length indicates the overall size of the shadow, creating the illusion that the element is either closer to or further in front of the surface on which it casts its shadow. Higher values indicate larger shadows and lower values reduce the shadow's size, including negative values to make the shadow smaller than the element casting it. If not specified, or if specified as 0 (the default), the shadow will be the same size as the element.

- color: Specifies the color of the shadow using any valid color notation (keyword, hexadecimal, RGB, RGBA, HSL, or HSLA). This value isn't technically required, and Firefox, Opera, and IE will use the inherited color value for the default shadow if it isn't otherwise indicated. At the time we're writing this, Webkit browsers (Chrome and Safari) default to a transparent shadow, meaning they render no shadow at all if you don't specify the color.

- inset: When present, this optional keyword indicates that the shadow should appear inside the element rather than outside it. Inset shadows appear in front of any background color or images and behind any content. If inset isn't specified the shadow will appear outside, below, or behind the element.

The length values for offset-x, offset-y, blur radius, and spread radius must appear in that specific order; it's the only way a browser can determine what value applies to which aspect of the shadow. The blur radius and spread radius values are optional, but if you want to specify a spread radius you'll have to include the blur radius as well, even if it's 0, just to preserve the order of values.

Getting back to the Power Outfitters site, we'll add box shadows to several of our content blocks, including the store info box, the main navigation bar, the content wrapper, the footer, and product images. All of these shadows make the elements appear to lift off the page to add a hint of dimensionality to what would otherwise be a flat, two-dimensional design.

We've added box-shadow declarations to the footer rule in Listing 10-24, to show just one example. We're using an RGBA color (black at 25% opacity) so the shadow can seamlessly overlay whatever colors or patterns are behind it. When we've used translucent RGBA colors for backgrounds we typically provide an opaque value for older browsers, like we've done for this footer's background. That isn't necessary for box shadows; every browser that currently supports CSS3 box shadows also supports RGBA color.

Listing 10-24. Adding a box shadow to the site's footer

```
#site-info {
  padding: 15px 30px 0 160px;
  border: 2px solid #ffc307;
  margin-top: 20px;
  background: #fc0 url(../images/logo-small.png) 20px 15px no-repeat;
  background-color: rgba(255,225,105,.8);
```

```
  -moz-box-shadow: 0 2px 8px rgba(0,0,0,0.25);
  -ms-box-shadow: 0 2px 8px rgba(0,0,0,0.25);
  -o-box-shadow: 0 2px 8px rgba(0,0,0,0.25);
  -webkit-box-shadow: 0 2px 8px rgba(0,0,0,0.25);
  box-shadow: 0 2px 8px rgba(0,0,0,0.25);
}
```

You can see how repetitive it is to declare the same shadow values five times in one rule, each time with a different prefix, but it's the best way to make sure every browser that supports the property will display the shadows. That being said, box-shadow is a stable property and well supported in all the latest browsers. Current versions of Firefox, Safari, Chrome, Opera, and IE all support un-prefixed box shadows as a CSS3 standard. In fact, some browsers have already stopped supporting their prefixed box-shadow properties in their newer versions. If you're not concerned with displaying shadows in browsers a few years old, you can safely omit the prefixes and use box-shadow un-prefixed from now on.

Figure 10-19 shows the updated footer along with part of the content wrapper, both now sporting nicely blended drop shadows to separate them from the background and lift them off the page. A few years ago this kind of visual effect could have only been accomplished with images, but today we can do it with just a few lines of CSS.

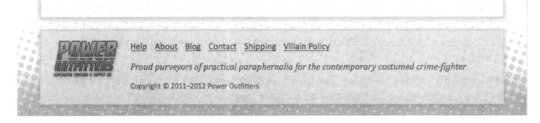

Figure 10-19. The site's footer, now with shadow

A single element can have any number of box shadows, with each set of values separated by commas. As with multiple background images, the last shadow declared will appear on the bottom of the stack with previous shadows layering on top of it. Listing 10-25 shows an example of a single element with three shadows, each a different color and different offset. Omitting values for blur radius and spread radius means the shadows default to no blur and no spread, so they're perfect shadow copies of the box that casts them. You can see the rendered effect of these stacked shadows in Figure 10-20.

Listing 10-25. Applying multiple, comma-separated box shadows to a single element

```
.shadow {
  background: #eee;
  color: #999;
  box-shadow: 5px 5px #ccc, 10px 10px #999, 15px 15px #666;
}
```

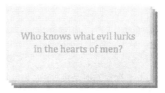

Figure 10-20. A stacked box effect created by three offset shadows

There's a lot more you can do with the box-shadow property, and we've shown a few more examples in Figure 10-21. With no offset or blur but increasing values for spread, multiple shadows produce a multiple border effect. With no offset but with a generous blur and spread, a light colored shadow over a dark background can make a box seem to glow from within. Inset shadows can easily produce a recessed or cutout effect. With a combination of light and dark colors, you can also use inset box shadows to simulate a beveled or embossed box—especially effective with rounded corners, which we'll cover later. The shape of the shadow follows the shape of the box, even when the corners are rounded off.

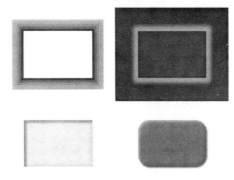

Figure 10-21. A few more effects you can achieve with box-shadow

Embedded Fonts

We first touched on typography in CSS back in Chapter 4. Browsers ordinarily draw text using digital fonts installed on the client computer, limiting a web designer's choices to the handful of common system fonts. For years web designers worked around this limitation and found clever ways to use non-standard typefaces on the Web. These ingenious hacks—from simple image replacement, to rendering text as an embedded Flash object, or even drawing text as an SVG image with JavaScript—opened up new avenues for creative expression through type. But they were still hacks and none were really the best solution.

Ideally there should be some means of installing a font on the user's computer that the browser could use to render text. CSS answered the call with the @font-face rule, specifying a font file on the Web that a browser can download and use temporarily. This special rule was first introduced in CSS2 way back in 1998, but it faced complications and browser makers couldn't agree on details of implementation. The @font-face rule was soon removed in the CSS 2.1 specification; hence the need for all those less-than-perfect hacks. Now @font-face is back in CSS3 and it's stronger than ever, fully supported by all the major browsers (though with a few idiosyncrasies, as you'll soon see).

The syntax is fairly simple: a specialized rule in a style sheet, prefixed with an @ symbol (and such special rules are called *at-rules*), defines a customized font name that can be used throughout the rest of the style sheet. That definition also includes a src property to specify a source font file residing on the web server, and it may include a few other properties describing the font. When the new custom font name appears in a CSS rule elsewhere in the style sheet, the browser will first seek any locally installed fonts by that name and, if it doesn't find one, will download the font file from the server to use for rendering the text.

Listing 10-26 shows a simple @font-face rule, specifying the family name "Lobster Two" and a source reference using the familiar url(...) data type to indicate the file's location on the server. Quotation marks around the family name are optional if the name is a single word, but multi-word names need to be enclosed in quotes. After the @font-face rule is a rule for h1 elements, with Lobster Two appearing as just another font in the list. If the embedded font can't be used for any reason—if the file is missing, if the browser can't support the file format, or if the browser doesn't support @font-face at all—the browser will use the next alternative typeface.

Listing 10-26. An @font-face rule defines an embedded web font

```
@font-face {
  font-family: "Lobster Two";
  src: url(fonts/LobsterTwo-Regular.woff);
}

h1 {
  font: normal 60px/1.1 "Lobster Two", "Monotype Corsiva", cursive;
  margin: 0;
}
```

According to these rules, browsers that support web fonts (and that support the WOFF format; more on font formats in a minute) will display h1 elements in Lobster Two at 60 pixels, shown in Figure 10-22. This is an open source typeface designed by Pablo Impallari and available for free from his website (impallari.com/lobster). Browsers that can't display the embedded font will instead display Monotype Corsiva, a fairly common system font, or else they'll fall back to a generic cursive typeface.

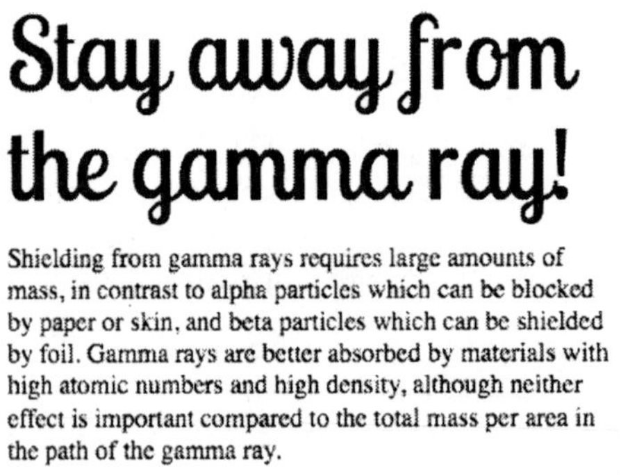

Stay away from the gamma ray!

Shielding from gamma rays requires large amounts of mass, in contrast to alpha particles which can be blocked by paper or skin, and beta particles which can be shielded by foil. Gamma rays are better absorbed by materials with high atomic numbers and high density, although neither effect is important compared to the total mass per area in the path of the gamma ray.

Figure 10-22. A heading displayed in Lobster Two, a font that isn't likely to be installed on the viewer's computer

Font Formats

Using web fonts seems easy enough so far, and the CSS itself really can be as simple as you've seen. But there's another side to this story that makes it a little more complicated. Like other electronic media, digital fonts come in a variety of file formats, and not all browsers support all of the same formats. The most common web font formats you'll encounter are:

- TrueType (TTF) – One of the oldest and thus most common font formats, TrueType is supported by Firefox, Safari, Chrome, and Opera, but not by Internet Explorer. TrueType fonts use the extension `.ttf`.

- OpenType (OTF) – An extended update of TrueType, OpenType fonts are also supported by Firefox, Safari, Chrome, Opera, but not by IE. They use the extension `.otf`.

- Scalable Vector Graphics (SVG) – Fonts in SVG format are intended for use in other SVG media, but some browsers can also use them to render ordinary text. Safari and Opera support SVG fonts, but not Firefox, IE, or Chrome. SVG fonts use the `.svg` extension.

- Embedded OpenType (EOT) – This is a compact variant on the OpenType format created by Microsoft especially for embedding web fonts, but the format was proprietary and never caught on with other browsers. Only Internet Explorer supports these fonts, which use the extension `.eot`.

- Web Open Font Format (WOFF) – A relative newcomer, the WOFF format supersedes TTF/OTF and is optimized for the Web. Current versions of Chrome, Firefox, IE, Opera, and Safari all support WOFF fonts. The file extension, as you might expect, is `.woff` (pronounced just like it's spelled, so it's also fun to say).

Note that the Web Open Font Format is the only web font format supported by every major desktop browser, though only in recent versions. Older browsers—and even some current mobile browsers at the time we write this—don't support WOFF fonts. To compensate for this and ensure your chosen fonts are seen by as many visitors as possible, you'll need to embed your web fonts in more than one format. That's no problem because the `src` property in an `@font-face` rule will accept multiple values, separated by commas:

```
@font-face {
  font-family: "Lobster Two";
  src: url(fonts/LobsterTwo-Regular.woff),
       url(fonts/LobsterTwo-Regular.ttf);
}
```

You can optionally include a `format()` value for each format after the `url()` value (the format must be enclosed in quotation marks):

```
@font-face {
  font-family: "Lobster Two";
  src: url(fonts/LobsterTwo-Regular.woff) format("woff"),
       url(fonts/LobsterTwo-Regular.ttf) format("truetype");
}
```

Browsers use the first supported format they encounter while parsing the style sheet; in this example, browsers that support both WOFF and TrueType will favor the WOFF file because it's declared first. The

Web Open Font Format is the emerging standard, gradually supplanting OTF and TTF, as well as Internet Explorer's proprietary EOT format. Internet Explorer didn't support WOFF before version 9 and has never supported OTF/TTF in any version, so you may also wish to include an EOT font for older versions of IE. Earlier versions of mobile Safari—the default browser on Apple iOS devices such as the iPhone and iPad—only supported SVG fonts, so you can optionally include SVG for older Apple gadgets.

> *Some quirks in older browsers and even in some current mobile browsers can cause web fonts to fail depending on how they're declared in CSS or how the web server delivers them. The syntax we've shown here—WOFF plus a TTF fallback—works most of the time for most of the latest browsers. If you like, you can be especially thorough and deliver custom fonts to the widest possible range of browsers and devices—those that support @font-face, of course—by using the so-called "Bulletproof @font-face Syntax" as described by Fontspring (fontspring.com/blog/the-new-bulletproof-font-face-syntax). And as always: test your web pages!*

We'll add a few more pieces of flair to the Power Outfitters site by using an embedded web font for headings. Komika Display by Apostrophic Labs (fontsquirrel.com/fonts/Komika-Display) has a bold, hand-lettered style that invokes the comic books that inspired our design. We wouldn't want to use such a stylized font for body text because it would be hard to read and just way over the top, but it's a smashing typeface for headlines. In Listing 10-27 we've added an @font-face rule defining our custom font, then applied that font to all of our heading elements.

Listing 10-27. Defining a new font for headings on Power Outfitters

```
@font-face {
  font-family: "Komika Display";
  src: url(fonts/Komika_display-webfont.woff) format("woff"),
       url(fonts/Komika_display-webfont.ttf) format("truetype");
}

h1, h2, h3, h4, h5, h6 {
  font-family: "Komika Display", Calibri, "Trebuchet MS", sans-serif;
  line-height: 1.2;
  text-transform: uppercase;
  color: #032587;
  margin: 0 0 .25em;
}

.page-title { font-size: 2.25em; }
h1 { font-size: 2em; }
h2 { font-size: 1.572em; }
h3 { font-size: 1.286em; }
h4 { font-size: 1.143em; }
h5, h6 { font-size: 1em; }
```

The same general styling applies to all headings, but we've declared their sizes separately so we don't need to repeat the declarations for font-family, line-height, color, and so on for every heading. We've also included a separate sizing rule for the .page-title class; we told you it would come in handy later. You can see the new font in place in Figure 10-23, with all the headings rendered in Komika Display and converted to uppercase with `text-transform:uppercase`.

Figure 10-23. Headings rendered in Komika Display

> The `text-transform` property takes a few different values: *lowercase*, *uppercase*, *capitalize*, *none*, or *inherit* (the default). This property changes the displayed case of the text but doesn't alter the text in the HTML source. Our headings are still capitalized normally in the document, with a mix of uppercase and lowercase letters, but the CSS transforms them to all uppercase on the screen.

Finding Fonts

As hard as it was to get the browsers to agree on a file format, *licensing* was the prime factor that slowed the adoption of web fonts. Digital font files are software, and the designers and foundries that make fonts invest a lot of time and effort into their creation. It's only natural that many of them want to protect that investment, and they won't necessarily be eager to give their fonts away. Most digital fonts you purchase will come with restrictive licenses that forbid their use as embedded web fonts. Some fonts can be downloaded at no cost but may come with other stipulations about their use, requiring attribution to the designer, for instance, or limiting their use to non-commercial websites.

Before you use any font in your CSS, be sure it's licensed for use on the Web and that you have the right to use it on your website. Otherwise you could be violating the font's license and breaking the law.

Although many digital fonts carry restrictive licenses, you can still find a wide variety of free, unrestricted fonts to use in your projects. Font Squirrel (fontsquirrel.com) maintains a catalog of hundreds of fonts in a broad range of styles, all completely free for commercial use. Google also provides hundreds of fonts for the Web (google.com/webfonts) and they will even host them on their own network, free of charge. Other hosted font services such as Fontdeck (fontdeck.com) and Typekit (typekit.com) will serve fonts for a modest fee, and they offer some licensed fonts you wouldn't otherwise be able to use for free.

Text Shadows

The text-shadow property adds one or more drop shadows behind an element's text. Such shadows can make the text appear to float above the page, casting a shadow as if it existed in three dimensions. This property is similar to the box-shadow property and takes a similar, but shorter, set of values:

- offset-x and offset-y: These are two required length values that indicate the horizontal and vertical offset of the shadow. The first length indicates the horizontal offset on the x-axis and the second indicates the vertical offset on the y-axis. Negative offset values position the shadow to the left or top of the text, positive lengths offset the shadow down and to the right, and 0 indicates no offset at all.

- blur radius: A third optional length value indicates the amount of blur to apply to the shadow. Higher values indicate more blur, and a blur radius of 0 (the default) indicates a shadow with no blur and a sharp outline.

- color: Specifies the color of the shadow using any valid color model (keyword, hexadecimal, RGB, RGBA, HSL, or HSLA). Most browsers will use the inherited foreground color value if this value is omitted, but it's usually best to specify a shadow color to ensure consistency.

Unlike box-shadow, the text-shadow property doesn't accept an inset value (sorry, no inner shadows on text) nor does it accept a spread radius value (the shadow is always the same size as the text that casts it). As with box-shadow, the text-shadow property can accept multiple, comma-separated values to stack shadows one on top of another.

The text-shadow property first appeared in CSS2 but was poorly defined and subsequently dropped from CSS 2.1. It has returned in CSS3, and is already well supported by most of the major browsers. Internet Explorer is the only straggler and didn't implement text-shadow until IE 10.

We've added a shadow to the .page-title class along with some extra decoration in Listing 10-28, and you can see the effect in Figure 10-24. The shadow is offset down and to the right as if the light source were above and to the left. There's no need for any vendor prefixes because every browser that supports text-shadow does so without any prefix, and they'll actually ignore a prefixed text-shadow property if you try. Those older or less capable browsers that don't support the property will just render the regular text with no shadow—a perfectly acceptable degradation.

Listing 10-28. Revising the .page-title class to add text-shadow and a bottom border

```
.page-title {
  font-size: 2.25em;
  margin-bottom: .35em;
  padding-bottom: .15em;
  border-bottom: 1px solid #0cf;
  text-shadow: 1px 2px 1px rgba(0,0,0,0.5);
}
```

WELCOME, HEROES!

Power Outfitters offers top of the line merchandise at rock-bottom prices for the
discerning costumed crime-fighter. From belts to boomerangs, we're your
one-stop shop for all your specialized gadgetry and costuming needs.

Figure 10-24. The redecorated page title, now with a drop shadow

As you've seen, it's easy to create simple, realistic drop shadows, but you're certainly not limited to simulating natural lighting. Clever application of the text-shadow property can also produce some really impressive graphic effects, like you see in Figure 10-25. With no offset and a generous blur, a light-colored shadow can appear as a luminescent glow against a dark background. Combined with RGBA colors, multiple text shadows can produce overlapping, translucent duplicates. You can stack multiple shadows and render a dramatic 3D effect by slightly adjusting the color and offset of each shadow in the stack.

Experiment with text-shadow and see what it can do. Just always remember that older browsers won't render these shadows, so make sure your text will still be readable even without them.

Figure 10-25. A few examples of text-shadow in action

Rounded Corners

HTML elements naturally form rectangular boxes when a browser renders them. It's an inescapable part of the medium's pixel-based nature. Applying a background or border to any HTML element reveals the rectangular, sharp-cornered box that surrounds its contents, and many early CSS designs tended to be boxy, sharp-cornered affairs. Rounding off those corners is one way to soften that inherent boxiness and make web pages feel smoother and more organic.

Unfortunately, earlier versions of CSS didn't make it easy. There was no means of rounding corners in CSS so designers found other ways to simulate the effect, usually with round-cornered background images positioned into the corners of an otherwise square-cornered box, often requiring multiple nested elements to carry those backgrounds (remember, multiple backgrounds also weren't possible until recently). Creating rounded boxes has become much simpler with CSS3 and the `border-radius` property.

The `border-radius` property defines the radius of an imaginary circle in the corner of an element (or two radii of an imaginary ellipse, but we'll get to that shortly). Instead of being drawn at a right angle, the box's corner follows the arc of this imaginary circle, like you see in Figure 10-26.

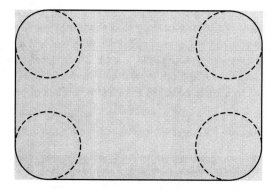

Figure 10-26. Visualizing the way browsers render rounded corners by tracing imaginary circles

Like other box properties—margins, padding, borders, and outlines—you can declare a `border-radius` in several ways to apply different effects to different corners. Most simply, the shorthand `border-radius` property with a single value applies equally to all four corners of the element:

`.pillow { border-radius: 10px; }`

The same shorthand `border-radius` property with two values applies the first radius to the top left and bottom right corners, and the second radius to the top right and bottom left corners:

`.pillow { border-radius: 10px 30px; }`

With three values, `border-radius` applies the first value to the top left corner, applies the second value to both the top right and bottom left corners, and the third to the bottom right corner:

`.pillow { border-radius: 10px 30px 12pt; }`

Lastly, `border-radius` with four values will round off each of the four corners clockwise in the order of top left, top right, bottom right, and bottom left:

```
.pillow { border-radius: 10px 30px 12pt 1.75em; }
```

You can also use full properties to specifically target individual corners:

```
.pillow {
  border-top-left-radius: 10px;
  border-top-right-radius: 30px;
  border-bottom-right-radius: 12pt;
  border-bottom-left-radius: 1.75em;
}
```

Of course, if you're rounding all four corners of a box, it's more efficient to use the shorthand property. These longhand properties are most useful to round only one corner, or to override rounding on one corner with a value of 0, returning the corner to its default 90-degree angle:

```
.balloon {
  border-radius: 30px;
  border-bottom-right-radius: 0;
}
```

A longhand radius property with only one value draws an evenly rounded corner, defining the single radius of a circle, like you see on the left in Figure 10-27. But a longhand radius property with *two* values indicates an ellipse with two radii, shown on the right. The first value is the horizontal radius and the second is the vertical radius:

```
.shoulder { border-top-right-radius: 10px 30px; }
```

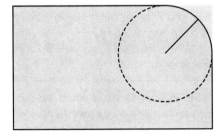 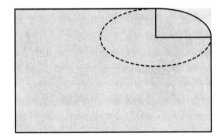

Circular rounded corner
(single radius)

Elliptical rounded corner
(two radii)

Figure 10-27. A diagram of circular versus elliptical rounded corners

You can specify a radius with any unit of measure—pixels, ems, points, and so on—or a percentage, but percentages do behave differently than fixed lengths. With a percentage radius, the browser calculates each half of the corner's curve as a percentage of the parallel side's length. In other words, a single percentage value will always draw an elliptical corner, especially noticeable if the box is rectangular rather than perfectly square. Listing 10-29 sets up two boxes with rounded corners, one a perfect square and the other an oblong rectangle.

Listing 10-29. Using percentages with `border-radius`

```
.square {
  width: 200px;
  height: 200px;
  border-radius: 20%;
}

.rectangle {
  width: 350px;
  height: 200px;
  border-radius: 20%;
}
```

You can see the results in Figure 10-28, with the square box on the left and the rectangular box on the right. Both of these boxes have the same single percentage value for `border-radius`, but the rectangular box has elliptical corners because it's wider than it is tall. This is important to know because, given a liquid-width box or an element containing text that can reflow and change height, percentages will rarely deliver consistent rounded corners.

Figure 10-28. Two boxes with `border-radius:20%`. The rectangular box has elliptical corners because percentage values are based on the lengths of each side.

> A corner's radius can't exceed the size of the box; the browser won't be able to draw such a mathematical impossibility. If the radius is too great the corners might be drawn with whatever maximum radius the box can accommodate, but some browsers may ignore the impossible radius and draw the box without rounded corners at all.

Although the browser draws the box with rounded corners, this is strictly a visual effect and the contents of the element can still overflow those corners. For example, you can turn a box into an oval with `border-radius:50%`, but any text inside the element will still flow as if it's in a box with 90-degree corners, like you see in Figure 10-29. Boxes with rounded corners often need some padding to keep the text within the border.

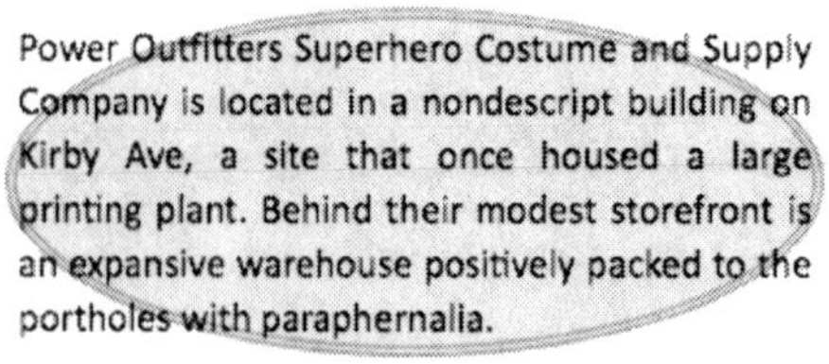

Power Outfitters Superhero Costume and Supply Company is located in a nondescript building on Kirby Ave, a site that once housed a large printing plant. Behind their modest storefront is an expansive warehouse positively packed to the portholes with paraphernalia.

Figure 10-29. Content inside an element styled with rounded corners still flows in the shape of a box

The current generation of web browsers all support border-radius quite well, and even without vendor prefixes in newer versions. Older versions of Firefox and Safari implemented border-radius with their vendor prefixes, but more importantly, they each initially implemented different naming conventions for the longhand radius properties that single out specific corners.

Older versions of Firefox used property names like -moz-border-radius-topleft because Mozilla implemented rounded corners before the properties were fully defined in the CSS specification. Webkit implemented the prefixed border radius with a different naming scheme, as in -webkit-top-left-border-radius. The Webkit naming convention eventually became the standard, but Firefox stuck with its own unconventional naming. For a time, web designers who wanted rounded corners in both Firefox and Safari had to declare them with completely different prefixed properties.

Thankfully both Safari and Firefox now support the un-prefixed, standardized properties, and have for a long time, so it's fairly safe to omit those vendor prefixes in your CSS. Opera, Internet Explorer, and Chrome jumped onto the rounded corner bandwagon a little later and mostly skipped the prefixing process; you'll only ever need to prefix border-radius properties if you're catering to older versions of Firefox and Safari. Any browsers that don't support border-radius will simply show the angled corners, which is usually a perfectly acceptable degradation if you've planned for it.

Our design for Power Outfitters is a bit boxy, and we're actually pretty happy with that. We've made those rectangular panels an integral part of the design, sharp corners and all. But there are still a few places where we can use border-radius to take some of the edge off (sorry, we couldn't resist).

We've already done some work on our "Add to Cart" buttons, styling them with a border, padding, a dark background color, an icon as a background image, and even a hint of text-shadow. It's a serviceable button already, but we can use border-radius to round off the corners, making it seem more touchable and, well, more buttony. A little box-shadow can add a dimensional effect as well. Listing 10-30 shows our updated cart button style rule and Figure 10-30 shows the rendered changes.

Listing 10-30. Adding rounded corners and a box shadow to the cart buttons

```
.cart-add {
  color: #fc0;
  cursor: pointer;
  padding: .25em 32px .25em 8px;
  background: #102662 url(../images/icon-cart-sm.png) 92% 50% no-repeat;
  text-shadow: -1px -1px 0 rgba(0,0,0,0.75);
  border: 2px solid #2446a8;
  border-radius: 10px;
  box-shadow: 0 1px 2px 0 rgba(0,0,0,0.35);
}
```

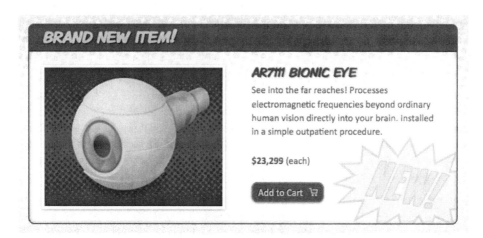

Figure 10-30. Rounded corners make our buttons and boxes squeezably soft

Color Gradients

A color gradient consists of two or more colors that seamlessly blend together, transitioning from one color to another over a given distance, usually filling the area of an element on the page. It's a common and popular visual effect, and web designers have achieved it for years with background images. CSS3 gives you the power to generate these gradient backgrounds right in the browser, without using an external image. A CSS gradient is essentially an image the browser generates when it renders the page.

Gradients in CSS come in two basic varieties: a *linear gradient* is a continuous transition from color to color along a straight line, whereas a *radial gradient* spreads out in every direction from a single point of origin. A CSS gradient is a background image, not a background color, so you'll define a gradient as a value of the `background-image` property. This also means you can layer gradients with other background images thanks to multiple background images in CSS3, and even layer multiple gradients in the same element.

A gradient value is a *function* that instructs the browser to render the image, consisting of a keyword and a set of parameters or arguments enclosed in parentheses. Color gradients in CSS are still in a somewhat experimental stage at the time we're writing this and most browsers that support them require a vendor prefix. Furthermore, some browsers have implemented slightly different ways of specifying gradients as the specification has been revised at different stages. The gradient notation we're showing here is the one defined in the W3C's CSS3 specification as it achieved *candidate recommendation* status, which means it's very nearly a finalized web standard and is less likely to change again. Browser vendors should follow the standardized notation for gradients going forward, but older browsers may require a different notation with their prefixes.

The simplest linear gradient only requires two arguments, defining the start color and the end color:

```
.zone {
  background-image: linear-gradient(black, white);
}
```

With only the two colors defined, the background will default to a vertical gradient with the starting color (the first one defined; black, in this case) at the top of the element and the end color at the bottom. The browser will smoothly transition from one color to the next, stretching the gradient to the height of the element, however tall it might be, and filling the element from side to side, however wide it might be.

You can specify the *gradient line*—the line along which the browser draws the gradient—as another argument, changing the gradient's start and end points. This can be one of the keywords to bottom (the default), to right, to left, or to top to indicate a side of the box, or to top right, to top left, to bottom right, and to bottom left to specify a line from one corner to the opposite corner:

```
.zone {
  background-image: linear-gradient(to top left, black, white);
}
```

You can also specify an angle for more precise control:

```
.zone {
  background-image: linear-gradient(65deg, black, white);
}
```

An angle of 0deg creates a vertical gradient from the bottom to the top, and a 90deg angle indicates a left to right horizontal gradient. Some browsers implemented an earlier draft of the CSS3 gradient spec that oriented the 0deg angle from left to right, rather than from bottom to top. Double-check your angles when you include prefixed linear gradients in your CSS; you may need to add or subtract an extra 90 degrees to get the correct angle in some browsers.

A linear gradient can include several colors, each separated by a comma, and the browser will distribute the colors evenly across the entire element:

```
.flame {
  background-image: linear-gradient(to right, red, orange, yellow);
}
```

You can also specify exactly where each color stops and the next one starts by including a length or percentage after each color, appropriately called a *color stop*:

```
.flame {
  background-image: linear-gradient(to right, red 30px, orange 80px, yellow 100%);
}
```

We'll apply a linear gradient to the Power Outfitters navigation bar to give it a slightly dimensional effect. We're including all the major vendor prefixes and following up with an un-prefixed, standardized declaration to future-proof our site. In browsers that support a property or value both prefixed and un-prefixed, the ordinary cascade is still in effect so the last declared value wins. It's usually best to include the un-prefixed version last in the rule, as we've done in Listing 10-31.

Listing 10-31. Adding a gradient background to the navigation bar

```
#nav-main {
  clear: both;
  text-transform: uppercase;
  text-shadow: 1px 1px 0 rgba(255,255,255,.75);
```

```
  border: 2px solid #ff9e05;
  box-shadow: 0 2px 8px rgba(0,0,0,.25);
  background-color: #fc0;
  background-image: -moz-linear-gradient(top, #ffed8e, #edb707);
  background-image: -webkit-linear-gradient(top, #ffed8e, #edb707);
  background-image: -o-linear-gradient(to bottom, #ffed8e, #edb707);
  background-image: linear-gradient(to bottom, #ffed8e, #edb707);
}
```

Note that the Mozilla and Webkit prefixed declarations differ slightly from the others. An earlier draft of the gradient specification used the *point of origin* to define a gradient line by keyword, rather than the *point of completion* the current standard uses. Older implementations still use that outdated notation, so we've included it for older versions of Firefox, Safari, and Chrome. Opera, however, currently supports both notations—albeit with a vendor prefix—and relies on the word "to" as the differentiating factor for keywords. Internet Explorer didn't support CSS gradients prior to version 10, which follows the latest standard notation and doesn't require a prefix.

> *Older versions of Safari and Chrome implemented an even more radically different gradient notation: background-image: -webkit-gradient(linear, 0 0, 0 100%, from(#ffed8e), to(#edb707)). Chrome prior to version 11 and Safari prior to version 5 required this verbose syntax, but current versions have adopted the simpler notation recommended by the W3C. If you need to support older Webkit browsers you can include this gradient notation along with the others, but we've left it out of our examples.*

Figure 10-31 shows the updated navigation bar. The gradient adds some natural shading, like a softly rounded bar lit from above. The hint of text shadow also creates a faint embossed effect, as if the text is stamped into the raised surface of the bar. It's subtle, but it's this kind of attention to detail that can help your site stand out from the rest.

Figure 10-31. A gradient background adds some dimension to the Power Outfitters navigation. We've enlarged this image so you can see the detail.

You can use RGBA or HSLA colors in gradients to play with transparency, transitioning from an opaque color to a transparent color, for example. This can be especially effective combined with a background image under the gradient, as we've done in Listing 10-32.

Listing 10-32. Using transparent RGBA color in a gradient with a second background image

```
.haiku {
  width: 400px;
  height: 150px;
  padding: 50px;
```

```
    border-radius: 50px;
    border: 10px solid #d2bdcb;
    box-shadow: inset 0 0 6px rgba(0,0,0,0.2), 2px 1px 2px rgba(0,0,0,0.5);
    background: #bba8b5 url(images/bg-pattern.png) center top repeat;
    background: linear-gradient(160deg, rgb(187,168,181) 30%, rgba(187,168,181,0) 70%),↪
                #bba8b5 url(images/bg-pattern.png) center top repeat;
}
```

Notice that we've declared the background property twice: first as a base for browsers that don't support gradients or multiple backgrounds, then a second declaration overrides it to add the gradient. Older browsers will still get the basic background, and those that don't display images will still have a solid color to fall back on. The latest browsers that support the more advanced features of CSS will display the enhanced version in its place, like you see in Figure 10-32.

Figure 10-32. A gradient lays over a tiling image and fades to transparent, allowing the pattern to emerge

> *We've omitted the vendor prefixes in most of these gradient examples, but you should certainly include them in any CSS intended for the live Web. Gradients are still experimental and only a few of the very latest browsers support them without prefixes. Furthermore, delivering gradients to only one browser—by including that vendor's prefix and leaving out the rest—is a disservice to your visitors. It may be repetitive to declare the same gradient five times in a CSS rule, but that's life in the fast lane.*

Once you're comfortable with linear gradients you can learn more about radial gradients from the Mozilla Developer Network (https://developer.mozilla.org/en-US/docs/CSS/Using_CSS_gradients) and from the W3C (http://dev.w3.org/csswg/css3-images/#gradients). We won't be covering radial gradients in much depth in this chapter, but we can at least give you a brief taste and some examples.

The simplest radial gradient is simple indeed, only requiring the start color and end color:

```
.orb {
    width: 350px;
    height: 200px;
    background-image: radial-gradient(cyan, indigo);
}
```

Unless otherwise specified, the gradient's center point will be the center point of the element. You can instead specify the position of a radial gradient's center point just as you would specify background-position:

```
.orb {
  width: 350px;
  height: 200px;
  background-image: radial-gradient(50px 50px, cyan, indigo);
}
```

The colors will spread in 360 degrees from the center point to fill the entire element, forming an ellipse to fit the element's dimensions. There are a number of other arguments to control the way the colors spread and the shape it forms. For example, the CSS rule in Listing 10-33 will produce the gradient image you see in Figure 10-33.

Listing 10-33. A radial gradient with four colors

```
.dusk {
  width: 400px;
  height: 200px;
  border: 6px outset gold;
  background-color: #006;
  background-image: radial-gradient(250px 50px, circle farthest-corner,↵
                    #ffe 10%, #fc0 20%, #f30 30%, #006 60%);
}
```

Figure 10-33. A simulated sunset generated with CSS. Take our word for it: the colors are breathtaking.

> A third type of gradient we haven't mentioned yet is the repeating gradient: a linear or radial gradient of a fixed length that can repeat as many times as necessary to fill the element. In a word: stripes. You can read about the repeating-linear-gradient and repeating-radial-gradient functions at the Mozilla Developer Network (https://developer.mozilla.org/docs/CSS/repeating-linear-gradient and https://developer.mozilla.org/docs/CSS/repeating-radial-gradient).

Media Queries

We first mentioned media queries in Chapter 3 where they appeared in a link element's media attribute. A media query is an extension of long-standing media types, allowing web developers to tailor style rules for specific media properties, such as a minimum window width, a maximum screen resolution, or even a device's orientation (portrait or landscape, for handheld smartphones and tablets). It's a logical expression that is either true or false, testing if the user-agent meets the conditions of the query.

In CSS, a media query is part of an @media rule—another one of those special *at-rules* like @font-face—comprising a media type, a logical operator, and the features the query is testing for, enclosed in parentheses. Targeted style rules are then nested inside that @media rule and a browser will only apply them if it meets the query's conditions. For example, this bit of CSS:

```
@media screen and (min-width: 1000px) {
   body { width: 960px; }
}
```

sets the width of the body element to 960 pixels, but only for screened media (desktop and laptop computers, as well as most smartphones and tablets) and only if the browser's viewport is at least 1000 pixels wide. Narrower windows, devices with small screens, or user-agents for other media types such as printers will simply ignore the nested body rule because they don't meet the query's conditions.

Logical operators in a media query use the keywords and, not, and only. The not operator negates the result of the query so the enclosed rules would apply whenever the user-agent does *not* meet the query conditions. The and operator is more common, applying the rules when the user-agent *does* meet the conditions. An only operator can effectively hide a style sheet from older browsers that don't support media queries, since only browsers that support the query will be able to interpret it.

You can also string together multiple conditions with operators to form one media query that resolves as true if all the conditions are met:

```
@media screen and (min-width: 640px) and (max-width: 980px) {
   ...
}
```

And you can include multiple queries in a single rule, separated by commas, roughly equivalent to an or operator:

```
@media screen and (min-width: 860px), print and (min-width: 8.5in) {
   ...
}
```

There are only a handful of media features you can use in a media query, though most of them also accept minimum or maximum values with a min- or max- prefix:

- width: the width of the viewport, that is, the browser window, expressed as a length in any unit (pixels, ems, inches, and so on).

- height: the height of the viewport.

- device-width: the width of the display device, that is, the entire screen width, not just the browser window.

- device-height: the height of the display device.

- aspect-ratio: the ratio of the viewport's width over its height, such as 4:3 or 16:9, written as 4/3 or 16/9 because the colon (:) already has a different meaning in CSS.

- `device-aspect-ratio`: the aspect ratio of the display device, not just the browser window.

- `color`: the number of bits per color component the device can render, such as 8 or 24 (for 8-bit or 24-bit displays).

- `color-index`: the number of entries in the color lookup table for the output device, such as 256 for an 8-bit display.

- `monochrome`: the number of bits per pixel on a monochrome (grayscale) device, or 0 if the device isn't monochrome.

- `resolution`: the pixel density of the output device, specified as dots per inch (dpi) or dots per centimeter (dpcm).

- `orientation`: the relative orientation of the output device, either `portrait` (taller than it is wide) or `landscape` (wider than it is tall). This feature does not accept min- or max- prefixes.

- `scan`: the scanning process for television devices (media type `tv`), either `progressive` or `interlace`. This feature does not accept min- or max- prefixes.

- `grid`: determines if the output device is a grid device (such as a teletype terminal or Braille reader) or bitmap device (such as a computer or television monitor). This feature's value is a binary integer: 1 if the device is grid-based or 0 if it isn't.

Of all these features, the ones you'll probably find most useful are those pertaining to viewport width and device width. With CSS media queries, you can easily alter the layout of your page depending on the available space.

Media queries are well supported by the current generation of web browsers. Firefox has supported them since version 3.5, Safari since version 3.2, Chrome since version 4, and Opera since version 9.5. Internet Explorer implemented media queries more recently, in version 9. Unfortunately there are still a lot of people around the world using IE 8, 7, or even 6, but those numbers are rapidly dwindling. People using outdated browsers won't benefit from your media queries so use them wisely and try to ensure graceful degradation.

> *CSS3 media queries are at the heart of a design trend dubbed* responsive web design. *This term, coined by designer Ethan Marcotte in 2010, is a useful label for the combined techniques of a liquid grid layout, fluid images, and media queries to tailor the page to the viewport. You can read up on responsive web design in Ethan's seminal article, "Responsive Web Design" (alistapart.com/articles/responsive-web-design/).*

The Power Outfitters website has a liquid width that can adapt and respond to the size of the viewport. However, as we mentioned in Chapter 9, this can present some problems in very narrow windows. We've addressed this for the most part by including `min-width` and `max-width` values in our CSS, setting the minimum and maximum widths of the page, and it can still move freely within those constraints. Even so, there's a problem with the main navigation bar when the window approaches the minimum width, as you can see in Figure 10-34. The navigation links wrap to a second line when the window is too narrow for all of them to fit side by side.

Figure 10-34. The navigation bar no longer fits on a single line in narrow windows

One solution might be to increase the page's min-width so it would stop shrinking before the navigation can wrap, but that's not really much of a solution and short-changes our liquid width layout. Instead, we can use a media query to shrink the navigation text when the window is too narrow; smaller text means more can fit in a limited space.

In Listing 10-34 we've added a media query reducing the navigation's font-size when the viewport is narrower than 880 pixels, a point just before the links begin to wrap. The text normally displays at the 16px base size inherited from the body, but now we're overriding that with font-size: 0.875em, dropping it down to 14 pixels (0.875 of 16 is 14). We've used ems instead of pixels to keep everything proportional to the original base size.

Listing 10-34. A media query to shrink our navigation bar in narrow windows

```
@media screen and (max-width: 880px) {
  #nav-main {
    font-size: 0.875em;
  }
}
```

While we're at it, we can also *increase* the size when the window is wide enough to accommodate larger text, making our navigation stand out even more for people who have room for it:

```
@media screen and (min-width: 960px) {
  #nav-main {
    font-size: 1.125em;
  }
}
```

As you can see in Figure 10-35, the navigation remains on one line no matter the size of the window. Older browsers that don't support media queries will still get the wrapping links in narrow windows, and users who increase the base font size may have to cope with wrapping links as well, but we've made sure the links remain readable and functional even if they do wrap. We also wouldn't want to reduce the text to an unreadable size. If our min-width was even narrower or our navigation was longer—if we added another category, or were translating into another language that might use longer words—we would probably find a different solution. Your content should lead your design; don't let design dictate your content.

Figure 10-35. The navigation resizes to fit the viewport

This is a rather simplistic demonstration of what media queries can do. The rising ubiquity of smartphones and tablets means more people are accessing the Web on small-screen devices every day. With media queries, fluid images, and a flexible layout, you can construct a website that responds and adapts to the viewport, shifting and rearranging elements to optimize the experience for the full spectrum of web-capable devices.

Figure 10-36 shows the website for dConstruct 2012, an annual technology and culture conference in Brighton, England (http://2012.dconstruct.org). The layout shifts and adjusts to different viewport sizes from mammoth, high-definition desktop monitors to pocket-sized smartphones. This is a shining example of responsive design using a flexible layout, fluid images, and CSS3 media queries.

Figure 10-36. The dConstruct 2012 website uses media queries to adapt the content to different viewport sizes

And Even Further…

We've just barely scratched the surface of CSS3 in this chapter, and we couldn't even go into depth on every last detail of what we did cover. This book is long enough as it is. But we hope we've given you enough of a taste to set you on your way so you can explore more of the latest innovations CSS is bringing to the table. Here are a few more topics you might like to look into:

- **Transitions** – Animate changes to CSS properties, such as fading a color or expanding a box (w3.org/TR/css3-transitions/)

- **Transforms** – Reshape, resize, rotate, and distort elements on the page (w3.org/TR/css3-2d-transforms/)

- **3D transforms** – Shift and distort elements in 3-dimensional space (w3.org/TR/css3-3d-transforms/)

- **Animation** – Create motion in timed sequences (w3.org/TR/css3-animations/)

- **Border images** – Use tiling images to draw decorative borders (w3.org/TR/css3-background/#the-border-image)

- **calc()** – A function to dynamically calculate the size and shape of objects on the page, used wherever a length value would appear, for example width:calc(100% - 40px) (w3.org/TR/css3-values/#calc)

- **Flexible box layout** – Position elements in flexible, expanding stacks (w3.org/TR/css3-flexbox/)

- **Grid layout** – Define a grid layout in columns and rows (w3.org/TR/css3-grid-layout/)

- **Conditional group rules** – Restrict CSS rules to browsers that support certain properties with @supports (a potential replacement for the vendor prefix system) or only to specific pages with @document (w3.org/TR/css3-conditional/)

Some of these specs are very "bleeding edge" and may have only been implemented in one or two browsers, or not yet implemented at all, so they're not all practical to use on the real Web right now. But that certainly shouldn't keep you from poking your head in to see how they work.

Summary

This has been one of the longest chapters in this book, but we hope it's also been one of the most enlightening. You've learned about just one approach to the web design process and seen it put into action, following the design and construction of our fictional site for Power Outfitters Superhero Costume & Supply Co. We didn't cover every last corner of the site, but we walked you through some of the more interesting parts in enough detail to give you a feel for how it all came together. All of the markup and CSS examples you've seen in this book are available at the Apress website (apress.com) or this book's companion site (foundationhtml.com) to download and dissect as you please.

HyperText Markup Language is the very foundation of the World Wide Web. It's the common root language without which this vast frontier of cross-referenced information at our fingertips wouldn't be possible. This language and the Web it weaves allows us to keep abreast of current affairs in our communities, delve into the histories of other cultures, stay in touch with distant friends and loved ones, watch robots on Mars, and giggle at adorable pictures of cats with poor grammar. HTML is a marvelous thing—powerful yet approachable.

Now that you've grasped the fundamentals of modern, semantic markup and CSS, you might be wondering, what's the next step? Keep learning, of course. This book has offered only a glimpse of what you can create with these core web languages. Go online and explore some of the many and varied resources available to you. Graduate to the next level and further hone your skills with CSS and JavaScript. If you're already a seasoned professional, don't be afraid to incorporate new HTML5 elements into your sites and apps. Charge boldly into the more advanced parts of HTML5 and its related technologies like geolocation, canvas, WebGL for 3D canvas graphics, offline storage, IndexedDB, and more—all those cool parts we didn't cover in these pages.

But above all, experiment. Open a text editor, grab your favorite browser, and just dive in. We've shown you that it doesn't require any expensive tools or arcane knowledge to create innovative websites. The Web was built by enthusiastic tinkerers. Now get out there and tinker.

Index

Q

R